Please return/renew this item by the last date shown.

To renew this item, call **0845 0020777** (automated)
or visit **www.librarieswest.org.uk**

Borrower number and PIN required.

Libraries**West**

OTHER BOOKS BY NIGEL HEY

The Star Wars Enigma
Solar System
How We Will Explore the Outer Planets
How Will We Feed the Hungry Billions?
The Mysterious Sun

WO*N*DERMENT

A love affair with adventure, travel, writing, philosophy, and family life

An autobiography by

Nigel S. Hey

Matador
9 Priory Business Park
Kibworth Beauchamp
Leicestershire LE8 0RX, UK
Tel: (+44) 116 279 2299
Fax: (+44) 116 279 2277
Email: books@troubador.co.uk
Web: www.troubador.co.uk/matador

ISBN 978 1780882 864

British Library Cataloguing in Publication Data.
A catalogue record for this book is available from the British Library.

Typeset in Bembo by Troubador Publishing Ltd
Printed and bound in the UK by TJ International, Padstow, Cornwall

Matador is an imprint of Troubador Publishing Ltd

MIX
Paper from
responsible sources
FSC® C013056
FSC
www.fsc.org

CONTENTS

INTRODUCTION

*There are only two or three human stories, and they go on repeating
themselves as fiercely as if they never happened before.*
− Willa Cather

Y ou are about to read the autobiography of a journalist, one who is driven
by curiosity and storytelling and who often assumes right of access to
people and places which many would consider none of his business. My
particular journey is also coloured by a fondness for adventure, from which my
magpie mind deposits its memories into an untidy nest of journals, articles, letters,
diary notes, and casual scribblings. This book is a selected blend of these,
emphasizing what I consider to be the most interesting and most significant events
of my life story. In reflection I suspect these experiences are no more than any
person would amass in so many years, had he or she the desire and determination
to record the milestone markers of life and the rewards of inquiry, observation
and reflection. All lives are rich, everyone does have a book inside, and each is
unique. This one is special for the sole reason that it is mine.

The word *wonderment* has been in use at least since the 16th century. The
Oxford English Dictionary defines it chiefly as a state of wonder or the expression
of wonder. I intend with this book to illustrate both definitions from personal
experience, and hope that the appreciation and enjoyment of both will be
enriched in the reader's mind.

The subtitle of the book was constructed with some care, but since words
have different meanings to different people, let me expand on what I mean to
convey with them. *Adventure* includes both physical activity and stimulating
thought. *Writing* in my case consists mostly but not wholly of nonfiction and
philosophy. *Travel* is tourism, business travel, and further explorations away from
my homes in the United States and Britain. *Philosophy* includes religion,
spirituality, metaphysics, and general thoughts on the state of humankind. *Family
life* is the sharing of experience with my immediate family, consisting at this
writing of exactly eight individuals on two continents. Chronic asthma was always

part of my life, but is admixed so much with the rest of the story that it hardly deserves special mention. Finally, though not included in the subtitle, amateur theatre played important parts in my life story, generally by accident rather than design.

For me as for most, life has been a matter of making a living; of being a spouse and parent; of failure and victory; pleasure and pain, births, marriages, breakups, deaths. The potential for success grew from my mother and father, mentors and friends, from people like Miriam and Sue, with whom I shared sweet experiences that I will not let be erased by memories of discord, and from the wisdom of my children. All of this was supported and enhanced by Dee, who joined me late in life for a journey that we knew would be difficult but which we were determined to enjoy in partnership with each other.

I have been fortunate to be enriched by human relationships and by my interest in virtually all things. I derived great pleasure from my love of language. Above all I have been blessed by finding beauty and godliness everywhere, from New Mexico to Yorkshire, London, Venice, Paris, China, Polynesia, and the Valley of the Kings, to the Milky Way that I saw so brilliantly one night between the cliffs of Embudo Canyon in New Mexico.

Nigel Hey, Los Ranchos, New Mexico, 2012

1. A JOURNEY BEGINS

Man's main task in life is to give birth to himself.
– Erich Fromm

The kid detached a lemon sherbet sweet from inside his pocket, picked off most of the lint, and stuck it in his mouth. He crunched down and the lemony crystals inside fizzed against his tongue. It was good, but it didn't really help. If he'd known the right swear words, he would have used them. He simply didn't want to leave northern England for an unpredictable life in a world of strangers.

It was late in the October of 1946 and it was raining, a usual sort of Manchester day. A man and a woman were walking up the wet and shiny metalled road to the railway station. They struggled with large leather suitcases while attempting to encourage the short, skinny boy who shuffled between them.

"Come along now," the woman urged the youngster. Dark curls threatened to escape from under her neat felt hat. Her glasses were round, with tortoiseshell frames, and behind them her teal-blue eyes betrayed a mild apprehension that she was trying hard to hide. Her husband, looking almost natty if damp under his trilby, muttered that there was plenty of time before the train left for Bristol. Then the woman smiled, remembering something, trying to be cheerful. "Any of your old pals working here at the station?" They stepped through the station entranceway into the huge whistling and steaming maw of the place with its background din of passengers, porters, and seers-off. "Policemen from the harbour?"

"Don't think so," he said stoically. "Far as I know, most of them stayed on."

The boy just listened, said nothing. He looked small beside his parents, and his feet dragged a little as he trudged toward the noise of the station. He tugged the nab of his cap down farther over his face. His new woollen pants were getting wet too, and a few glistening drops were getting ready to drip over his bare knees, taking the warmth out of those long gray socks.

He had just said goodbye to his two aunts and his uncle in Yorkshire. He would miss them, and the farm, the moors and the Pennine landscapes. He resented this transplantation to an unknown town 200 miles to the south. He was curious enough to see what was down there, but this removal was hardly like going to India or Africa or the Far East, and it was unknown territory far from friends and relatives.

Out in the larger world, the first nuclear bombs had devastated two Japanese cities; supercomputers were about to emerge from the monster machines at Los Alamos; India was on the verge of becoming independent; Palestine was beset with terrorism because the British were talking about forming a new Jewish state. He had heard the news on the radio, but such things didn't really interest him. John Cobb had just beaten his world land speed record – nearly 400 miles an hour in a three-ton car! Now that was worth remembering.

The boy was me, and I didn't know what I was in for. I was thinking of all the goodbyes I had made, maybe final ones, to Auntie Annis and Uncle Ted at Honey Pot farm, to Auntie Elsie at the house that teetered on the hill above the Wilsden main street, to Uncle Walter and Auntie Lucy and my two far-removed cousins Jimmie Power and Norman Binns.

Soon we were on the train, third class, our luggage making lumps in the netting that hung from the racks above our seats. A wide leather strap, like the old belt my dad used for working in the garden, was secured to a stud in the woodwork, holding the door window closed against the weather. My mother was nervously fingering the yellow sapphire, ringed with diamonds, that circled her finger. Dad had just bought it from a jeweller in Bradford. It might be a yellow diamond, the man in the jewellery shop had said. Like a gold sovereign, I thought glumly, just in case. I stared at the wide pictures framed in wood above the heavy upholstery: brown photographs of places you might want to visit by train now the war was over.

Someone blew a whistle. A last passenger was running to the train, a porter holding the door and urging him on. Then there came a two-tone, tenor-soprano "whooo-up" hoot from the big engine, a blast of steam, and the brakes were released. The train lurched forward and I looked out from the grimy window, watching the great black steel tracery of Victorian roofing slide overhead as we puffed out from its protection and into the open, where wind-blown tears of rain began to spatter across the windows.

We were on our way, making the right choice as it happened, though my mother would always struggle to admit the fact. None of us had the slightest inkling that Keynsham, a Somerset town near the West Country city of Bristol, would be only the first stop in a journey that would turn us into lifelong travelers.

In fact it was the start of many journeys, in time, place, and raw experience. Like any child I was born to be reborn – repeatedly, not only physically but in worldview as well. I was fortunate to have growing in my mind those aspects of personality which take on with pleasure the relentless new colourings of experience, observation, and meditation – all enlightened and enlivened by the gifts of curiosity. I would sire three fine children, survive two unsuccessful marriages, travel in many places, from Moscow to Polynesia, and because I was interested in all things would describe myself on legal documents simply as "writer" or "journalist." I would escape being blown up in a Greek tunnel and survive the experience of floating alone in the Pacific, out of sight of land and with no more than a scrap of plastic to help me stay afloat. I would hold a top-secret government clearance and become an overachieving member of a million-miles airline club. Though never what most would call a rich man, I would come to have residences on two continents, and when I celebrated my three score and ten years I would stare into my bathroom mirror and swear continuing allegiance to a life of curiosity.

❦❁❧

I feel I should apologize for the change of pace in the next few paragraphs. But what follows really is how everything started. It was the kickoff, the overture of my life story. The humorous stuff will come later but not just now.

The Initiating Incident happened when I was a small boy, on a cold winter night in Lancashire. In this, my first home, it was dark I had three blankets on my bed to ward off the invasive chill, with a thin quilt lying decoratively on top. My mother and dad had come upstairs and peeked in long ago, and Mum, thinking I was asleep, tiptoed in and turned off the electric fire. I had said nothing because I wanted to sleep. But I was awake, thinking. And I was cold. The town of Heysham sits on a promontory on the edge of the Irish Sea, and the winters can be bitter.

Twenty minutes passed. My parents would be sleeping by now, in the big bedroom on the other side of the house, and I was eight years old, too big to creep in with them for warmth. Raindrops rattled unevenly against my window,

3

driven by wind coming in from the west. I lay on my back, shielding it from the Atlantic assault that somehow penetrated the window and seemed to linger in my room like a small, invisible cloud.

Then I listened and realized it wasn't just rain at the window. There was a slithering sound against the glass, almost a squeak, or the scrape of the toothbrush-sized glass cutter my dad kept in his toolbox. Could it be a tree branch caught in the wind? But no, there were only shrubs down there, far too short to reach.

It was a lonely, plaintive sound. Curious, I gathered a blanket around my shoulders and walked to the window. I knew I shouldn't turn on the light because of the wartime blackout – the Germans could still bomb the shipyards across the bay – but the faint glow from the night-light would never be noticed and I could open the curtains and peer out unseen.

Moisture had condensed on the cool glass. I rubbed off the wet opalescent coating with my sleeve and looked through the wet window into the darkness below. Nothing. I looked left and right, but there was still nothing. Only the night, inky black, and the clatter of rain. I slipped back into bed and rubbed my feet against the sheets to warm them. The curtains were still open but that was all right. It would be light when I awoke.

Screee …eek. That apologetic little screech again. I turned to the window, thinking that perhaps the night-light would reveal something. The condensation was forming once more, and as I watched something was happening to it. A fine line was taking form on the glass, like the black graphite of pencil on paper, curving as if to sign a name.

Slowly the curve continued its path, into a quarter circle, then a semi-circle. I watched, captivated by the impossible, and an odd question crept into my mind. Was that subtle glass-cutter screech not a screech at all, but a whine, a whimper, a squeal?

The circle completed itself and turned into a fist-sized black spot as the glass fell outward. Within the continuing patter of rain I could just hear its gentle collision with the privet hedge. Then a thin seep of water welled through the opening, broadened, and became a vapour, not a teakettle vapour but a vapour with texture to it. I knew terror and my nape bristled in dread as it moved toward me, thickening, growing, the texture taking the form of a blood-specked face, the face slowly disintegrating until only a skull was there. The bony mandible moved and I heard a high, beseeching voice.

"*Ich bin tot! Helfen Sie mir!*"

The words were close enough to English that I could understand them: "I

4

am dead, help me!" But why in German?

I woke then, and the remembrance was so vivid that I looked up to make sure that the window was whole again. Finally I slept again, with a terrible question murmuring inside my head: *How can anyone help the dead?*

I woke again at sunrise, my shoulders heaving in an attempt to shake off an attack of asthma that may have been brought on by the night's cold. My mother and dad were already dressed and bustling about. It was a fairly familiar routine. I could hear them talking down there.

Mother: Aaron, do you think we should ring Milnethorpe?

I cringed at the thought, for Milnethorpe was code for Dr. Byrne, who lived there with the dreaded hypodermic needle that he used to give me adrenaline injections.

Father: Give him some water or tea first, then let's decide. Once Nigel starts moving around he might settle down – you never know.

Up in the bedroom I felt a sigh of relief. I was off the hook. For now.

These were scary enough times, and I didn't need nightmares. Asthma is a disorder in which the immune system goes mad when it encounters things that the body usually takes care of, like pollen or house dust, causing sinus and lung problems instead of doing what it is supposed to do, preventing them. You can control it with medications and common-sense care. And you can die from it. I was doing the final edit on this book when I read that the brave, truly remarkable foreign correspondent Anthony Shadid, of the *New York Times*, died from his asthmatic allergy to horses on Thursday, February 16, 2012, while walking the border of Syria and Turkey. It's estimated that, worldwide, 250,000 people succumb to the disease each year.[1]

The night visitor came back again and again, until the war was over. Of course I could never forget it, and – and this is odd – decades passed before I figured out why my visitor didn't speak English.

After I wrote these paragraphs about that childhood dream, I naturally stopped to think about them carefully because, well, because books should be enjoyable reading – fun – unless they are identified as horror stories from the get-go. As for autobiography – let it be known that this kid did not turn out to be a serial killer. In fact my life was and is crowded with totally enjoyable, un-grisly, even frolicsome adventures that enriched my brainbox with a treasury of ideas and thought.

Until that time my abstract notions of life and death were limited to the few

Sunday school classes I attended when my parents were trying different ways of healing their wheezy offspring. Sometimes I would look up at the great puffs of cumulus driving over the bakery and try to imagine angels and even people padding about up there, on the other side where I couldn't see them. What did it feel like? Was walking on clouds like walking on soft snow? Wouldn't you just fall through?

And yet, and yet ... when people ask me when I first started to get philosophical, my mind takes me back to some uncertain time in my English childhood, between dreams, when I wondered when all of this wonderful experience would stop, when the slow, soft whush-whush-whush of blood I could hear flowing in my neck would go silent and the thump of my heart stop forever. Then, I thought, there would be nothing. As far as I personally was concerned, everything would be eternal silence. The idea disturbed me, and dimly I hoped another answer would emerge. It was strangely fascinating, lying on my side in bed and listening, hearing the soft whisper of blood through my neck as life flowed through an entity that was not a magical eternal being at all, but a worldly creature that I called me.

What an awakening! I began to be bothered about my personal extinction, the last gasp, the oblivion, the nothingness. At the time I assumed I was an important part of *something*ness, only I didn't know what it was.

It was not long before I was wondering why I was here in the first place; why this little glob of consciousness was moving around, observing a sublimely wonder-full environment, in the simple-sounding but not-really-simple process of *being*. Why? I summoned the tiny bits of knowledge and wisdom that were available to my limited boyhood mind and thought this: I must appreciate this place where I am and be thankful for my ability to appreciate it; *I must be a good person; and when I die, I must be confident that I have left something helpful, however small, to humanity.*

And I must have adventures! I told myself. I must cherish and be grateful for this life, frolic in it, laugh in it, and I must come to love it with all the senses at my command. I will intimately know the delight of being with and of this natural cornucopia, and if I see a unicorn I will capture it even if I die impaled by its single magical horn!

Though I never found the unicorn, the adventures have been totally superb. Even the dangerous ones. Maybe especially the dangerous ones.

No real bogeymen would threaten my life, and so as I grew up I learned never to be scared by anybody. Insoluble *situations* intrigued me and yes, in a way they scared me. I knew they would defeat a part of me, and I knew that part would die off like a stalk on a wounded plant. A long while passed before I realized that those vanquished needs and desires would make room for new opportunities that, more likely than not, would prove more rewarding than those that I lost.

In their own way my parents were a daring couple, ready to explore new places and to make life decisions that would frighten most people in times when lifestyles were so much more confined by custom and geography. My father, Aaron Hey, emigrated from England to Canada when he was in his twenties, in 1930, to help start up a Yorkshire-owned woollen mill. He was followed soon afterwards by Margery Kershaw, daughter of a local greengrocer and my future mother. They were married in Huntingdon, Québec, a few miles from the U.S. border, on May 23, 1931.

In 1935, after the Canadian mill had begun operation, the young couple returned to the North of England, and by the time I came along were running their bakery and café in Heysham, Lancashire. Its larger sister town, Morecambe, was a two-pier Victorian resort from which Heysham was divided, invisibly, somewhere near a bus-stop we called Strawberry Gardens.

It was a vibrant place when my parents arrived, with donkey rides and Punch-and-Judy shows livening the windswept sands below Morecambe's two miles of gaily-gardened promenade. After World War II there would still be brave souls who on rare sunny days would trudge down to the beach and erect canvas windbreaks to protect themselves from the north wind before settling down into the gritty sand with their Thermoses of sweet milky tea. But the thin veneer of glamour that had stuck to Morecambe faded soon, despite plans for various revival efforts and the erection of "Frontierland," where I had the most frightening fairground experience of my life, bumping and lurching along a rickety model railway circuit high above the ground, without guard rails and from which there seemed no escape but a deathly drop. That venture, a rather awful attempt to emulate the atmosphere of a Western theme park, has now been abandoned. Somehow I think Morecambe's heart was broken when the Central Pier finally died, years after a near-fatal fire, in 1992.

Though Morecambe was my birthplace, I was without doubt part of a Yorkshire family. Both my parents were born and raised in Bingley, which lies in Airedale, on the eastern edge of the Pennine range between Bradford and Keighley. Highlands such as these require rivers to drain them, rivers mean water, water makes steam, and steam can drive factories. This is why the area is remembered for its textile manufacturing in the early days of the industrial revolution. But today's tourists sensibly avoid the factories' grim-looking remains and flock to Haworth, where they can visit the vicarage home of the Brontë family, ride the steam railway line, and brave the amazingly steep main street, buying postcards and sampling tea, scones, and fudge as they go.

My maternal grandmother Elizabeth was born in Wilsden to John and Maria Bartle in October, 1864, over the moors and a few miles away from Keighley and Haworth. She grew up to marry Fred Kershaw and together they ran a corner shop that sold fruit and vegetables in Bingley's Hill Street bottom-lands, near the Leeds and Liverpool canal, and bred wire-haired fox terriers.

My mother, born on July 6, 1908, enjoyed a happy childhood. She showed considerable talent as a pianist and artist, and dabbled in both until her eighties. As a child she enjoyed the friendship of her sister Doris, one year younger, and the care of her twin sisters Annis and Elsie, 16 years her senior.

In a snapshot memory that clings feebly to my mind, I can just remember my maternal grandmother Elizabeth looking out from her window at Honey Pot Farm. I must have been three or four at the time, and we were there to attend Annis's wedding to Ted Bower. Maybe for a fleeting moment my young mind was touched by thoughts of the loneliness of the old, peering from quiet cloisters into a vibrant world. Much later I remember seeing my paternal grandmother Clarissa at the Bradford Royal Infirmary in 1956, shaking with Parkinsonism. We had moved to the United States by then, and I was greatly touched by my father's deep grief in the knowledge that he would never see her again. She was the only grandparent I remember actually meeting, and on that occasion alone. My grandfathers were gone before I was born.

My father was born on June 6, 1907, to Harry Hey, an imposing, moustachioed textile-business entrepreneur, and Clarissa Binns, slim and handsome until the day she died. A very enthusiastic and accomplished Mason, Dad belonged to the Scottish and York Rites and the Shriners. He was initiated in 1932, in Canada; thirty years later he was the Grand Master for Utah; at his death he had a Masonic memorial service to celebrate the completion of his exemplary life. From all accounts, he was a much more outgoing, genially aggressive individual than the mild and quiet father I knew at home.

To my great regret I have only scraps of information about my parents' early life. I was eager enough to know about it, but, puzzlingly, they tended to get close-mouthed when I brought up the subject – unless I probed them on their experiences with motor vehicles. My father would rhapsodize happily about the vehicles he owned in his teens, while he was working at the mill. The first, acquired when he was 16, was an air-cooled Rover 8, an ungainly two-seater with horizontally opposed cylinders. It was an open car with a tonneau cover and engine; the front was louvered. Then he had a 600cc P&M Panther motorcycle and sidecar, made not far away by Phelan & Moore, in Cleckheaton. Next was a Dot, with a 350cc air-cooled Bradshaw engine. Next and last in this series of early vehicles was a classy TT Triumph motorcycle, with a single 500cc cylinder. My mother would sometimes ride pillion. "Oh yes, she would say, "I would tie my scarf over my hat, and off we'd go."

Every summer my mother would go on a group holiday by train to Morecambe, where she, Mary Brearley, and other friends would sneak cigarettes while their parents sipped tea in beach-side shelters facing away from the bitter wind. Mary was a lively lass, and as a youngster I was much impressed to learn that she had a boyfriend – who eventually became quite elderly in their lengthy relationship – whom she would meet in such exotic places as Nice and Istanbul. I was even more impressed when she brought us gift boxes of Turkish delight, delectable little cubes of jellied sugar flavoured with rose petals.

For shorter trips my mother and dad rode in 35-seater motor char-à-bancs (open vehicles so cold you had to take rugs with you) or, for a luxurious ride along the Morecambe promenade, an elegant six-seat horse-drawn landau. A nearby retreat was St. Ives, a 17th century country estate just up the steeply winding westbound hill road from Bingley to Harden and Wilsden, a favourite courting place for my mother and dad. Originally owned by the Ferrand family, this patch of sylvan wilderness, glorified in spring first with snowdrops and swathes of bluebells, then with primroses, and then with a commotion of boldly bright rhododendrons, was sold in the 1920s to the town of Bingley, where the family had lived for centuries.

I was born on June 23, 1936, on a Tuesday, a day that folklore misleadingly decreed that children entered the world "full of grace." It was a year of royal turmoil. The ailing, crusty King George V had died early that year, and his heir, King Edward VIII, not yet crowned, would abdicate in favour of Wallis Simpson on December 10, hardly a month after Franklin D. Roosevelt defeated Alf Landon in the U.S. Presidential election. So I can claim, stretching it a bit, to be "an Edwardian" as well as being a breech birth and not exactly full of grace at the time.

Soon the abdicated king's brother, a quiet man who stuttered and did not really want to become monarch, became King George VI. During the early 1940s he would do much to humanize the image of the royal family (his father was a notably gruff traditionalist) by visiting Britain's bomb-stricken city centers, often accompanied by his queen and their daughters Margaret Rose and Elizabeth, the future Queen Elizabeth II.

Times were bad all over Europe. The Spanish Civil War was just starting, with participation from Germany and Italy, and Picasso would soon paint his iconic "Guernica." Adolf Hitler's Nazism was in full spate and highly visible at the Olympic Games in Berlin that August, when I was just two months old. The world was apprehensive of Hitler, but did not yet know that Nazi expansionism, and the gathering Holocaust, would catapult Europe into World War II. Genocide was nothing new to the "civilized" world, but I doubt anything was ever so widespread and brutal as Hitler's coldly committed anti-Jewish, anti-Gipsy, anti-handicapped scourge.

I consider myself fortunate that my personal story started at Heysham, originally a small fishing village which lay on the south end of Morecambe Bay, sacrificed early to the nettle beer and donkey-ride whirl of country tourism, and eventually to the quieter but snootier hand of gentrification. It was a good place for a boy to spend his early years.

Away from the newer housing, atop a hill beside the sheltered crevice of the old harbour, stand the ruins of St. Patrick's chapel, which date perhaps to the 8th century. The charming 14th Century St. Peter's Church is huddled nearby, and to the southwest you look down on the seaweed-strewn reaches of Half Moon Bay.

St. Patrick's chapel sticks in my mind as an especially mystical, rather awesome place. Coffins are cut into the bare rock; fragments of seashells decorate the bits of mortar that remain encrusted in the walls. I could imagine Norsemen scrambling up the steep slopes from the sea, priests running for their lives,

Motoring. Mother and dad set off in 1930s-style crash helmets
on their 1922 500cc Triumph Ricardo.

Welcome aboard, mates! My mother was fond of dressing me in
different costumes so Dad could train his Kodak Brownie on me.

precious items being taken back to the longboats, the little chapel afire as invaders pillaged the town.

Not far from the church was a modest cluster of private enterprise – shops for buying sweets and souvenirs; tiny cafés where you could partake of afternoon tea; purveyors of nettle beer; and, a stone's throw from the clearing where brass bands played on the weekends, under the windows of the meeting rooms where my mother and dad used to play whist, two old men tending a wondrously huge pair of scales. The scales were like seesaws, painted green with highlights of red and gold. You'd give one of the men sixpence or a shilling and he'd guess your weight or give you twice your money back. Then you would sit on one end of the scales while his partner put brass weights on the other until your feet started to rise from the pavement. These two old pros were seldom wrong.

My mother and dad, refugees from the clanking textile industries of West Yorkshire, had started their little business not far away, on hilly land that was locally called Higher Heysham. Thanks to them I have a collection of black and white photos that show me there as a young boy in the early 1940s, in a baker's hat and apron, dressed as a sailor while holding a tortoise named Billy, who laid an egg.

It gives me pause to think of that boy's quiet, almost cloistered life, and what would happen in his future – the fall of Nazism at the close of World War II, the discovery and application of nuclear fission, guided missiles, the development of television, the invention of the jet engine, fast, long-distance passenger flights, satellite technology and live intercontinental broadcasting, moonwalks, and spaceflight to the far planets. Old-fashioned colonialism began to dissolve in the worldwide liberation of possessions formerly held by Britain, France, the Netherlands, Germany, and Portugal. Nelson Mandela led the successful struggle to end apartheid in South Africa, the fight against racialism ignited in the United States, flares of democracy began to flicker in the Middle East and North Africa, and Mao claimed China, after which his Cultural Revolution would with time give way to an amazingly successful experiment in applying capitalist trade strategies within the framework of a centrally controlled, single-party socialist republic. And then there was the wild explosion of electronic communication, from e-mail to the Web, e-zines, blogs, Twitter, and other new media. These would threaten the existence of newspapers and their partners in the Fourth Estate, which by then I had come to treasure as pillars of democracy.

On the international scene I was a stay-at-home civilian observer of the Cold War, Korea, Vietnam, the African genocides, Bosnia, Iraq, Afghanistan and many, many other terrible conflicts across the world. When I was in London in 1982, IRA bombs, first used against England in 1938, killed seven military musicians and, separately, two soldiers and seven horses on ceremonial duty. On September 11, 2001, I saw the Twin Towers of the World Trade Center crumble, live, on television, and I remember how my jaw fell open when I saw that tiny figure jump from one of the high floors, drifting to the ground like a scorched leaf from a bonfire. This coordinated commandeering of four airliners claimed the lives of 2,973 ordinary, decent people and 19 hijackers. Coordinated train bombs took 191 lives in Madrid in 2004. Then, on July 7, 2005, 56 were killed in four more London bombings, on three trains and a double-decker bus. The Spanish and British attacks pale by comparison with 9/11 but have a special importance because I was more familiar with the places where the atrocities occurred.

We learned hard lessons from the tsunami of militant, extreme Islamism that had been building particularly since the decolonization of British India and Palestine. Like everyone else I was shocked by the random killings caused by suicide bombers, and car bombs, and Improvised Explosive Devices. Some could understand the Islamists' distaste for certain Western ways – for example the materialism and extravagance of the industrialized nations, and the overly elastic definitions of morality. We can learn from dissent, but I was sickened by the killing and maiming of innocents, the use of fear as a tool for domination, by Islamists, Nazis, Bolsheviks, tribal despots, or anyone else. Doesn't the Koran say that mankind is a single nation, and that: "Be they Muslims, Jews, Christians, or Sabaeans, those who believe in God and the Last Day and who do well have their reward with their Lord. They have nothing to fear, and they will not sorrow."[2] If only we agreed on what is right! We might start out with "Thou shalt not kill"[3] or, again in the words of the Koran, "anyone who murders any person who had not committed murder or horrendous crimes, it shall be as if he murdered all the people."[4]

As a young man I had a simplistic one-word answer to such dilemmas – *compassion.* Apply the Golden Rule globally, I would say, for when it is ignored threat and fear stifle the human wish to be compassionate, and wake our defensive and combative inclinations. Later I learned that this is an easy thing to say and a wholly different matter to see it carried out.

Through the years I recognized genuine heroes, not so visible today, who fought for precious ideals and worked for the preservation and improvement of humanitarian goals. My first was Winston Churchill, the epic personage of World War II who could also assume the role of bricklayer (the garden wall he built at his Chartwell country home is ten feet high) while authoring 43 books including the masterful *History of the English-Speaking Peoples* (Cassell, 1956-58).

When I was a student, my hero was the Nobel Laureate, theologian, musician, and physician Albert Schweitzer, who was born in Alsace but elected to spend most of his life in the back woods of what is now the West African nation of Gabon. Here at age 30 he founded a hospital and wrote scholarly books, emerging to give lectures and, as a highly accomplished organist (and author of a Bach biography), to perform organ recitals. At the heart of this eminently remarkable man was the desire to uncover a universal ethical way of living that made sense to ordinary people.

Martin Luther King was another of my heroes because he was the bright symbol and inspiration of an anti-racial movement that would begin to eradicate the grim vestiges of slavery. I witnessed the strict segregation in 1940s Florida; one of my professional colleagues had been taught in a Mississippi journalism school that white adult females were to be referred to as "ladies," and black females as simply "women"; in Utah I learned that Mormon theology taught that black people were descendents of Cain, a dictum that held until 1978.

My most recent hero was Vaclav Havel, the gentle Czech poet and playwright who was imprisoned for his criticisms of the Cold War communist government, then after the collapse of the regime in 1989 was elected president twice in a year – first by the discredited, unseated parliament, and then by its democratic successors. His often-quoted favourite saying was both simple and stern: "Truth and love must prevail over lies and hate."

I remember looking forward, in my forties, to the year 2000, and thinking, my goodness, I wonder if I will live to see the 21st century! Surely not. Maybe I don't want to be around because by then I will be so decrepit … and so on. But I would publish my fourth and fifth books after the turn of the century and, most of the time, found it difficult to believe how old I was getting to be.

Of course, all this was a long way in the future for the boy hunting crabs with his dachshund Fritz in Half Moon Bay. Though I didn't know it yet, I had first to fly to America, go to college and, as they say, get a life.

2. COMING OF AGE

It is not death that a man should fear, but he should fear never beginning to live.
— Marcus Aurelius

Something strange was lying in my frying pan. It was brown, thick and flat and I didn't like the look of it. It vaguely resembled an old football that had been run over several times by a truck, only it was wet and possibly slimy as well.

I had just arrived back at the apartment I shared with four other university students. After a long day of classes I wasn't in the mood for a surprise.

Down the hall I found Les Sorensen in his room, hunched over a textbook, making notes. "Did you put that *thing* in my frying pan?" I demanded.

Les was an innocent-looking youth with blond hair about an inch shorter than mine. He looked up and answered with the affected insouciance of someone asking where I had put the communal ketchup bottle. "It's not a 'thing,'" he said, pausing for effect. "It's a heart."

I didn't immediately answer. I had seen hearts in the meat sections of supermarkets and this didn't look even vaguely like them. And then I remembered that Les was a medical student. "What kind of heart?" I asked, not looking forward to the answer.

"Well, human of course," he said, as though he thought I should have identified it as soon as I laid eyes on it. "Not very fresh, but I thought you might be interested."

I told him he could stuff it back in its bottle and went back to my room to think. I didn't mix with Les much after that.

***

I enrolled at the University of Utah in Salt Lake City in 1954, having failed to win places at Stanford, Midwestern and Syracuse. My parents, who kept our family home at Pleasant Grove, thirty-five miles south of Salt Lake City, had insisted that I should earn a degree at some college or university. This, they reasoned, would serve as another visa on my passport to what we hoped would be a rewarding life for English folk transplanted in America.

By that time I had already developed a sceptical turn of mind and should have been more enthusiastic about committing myself to four more student years. Unfortunately, I wasn't. To begin with, the very word *academic* suggested to me an over-appreciation of the past, an ossification of ideas. However, I did appreciate the importance of learning the basics of history, sociology, and politics. I knew that in my future life as a journalist I would have to know enough to explain the news in a context that made sense to my readers.

Though less than captivated by university life, I found several classes that were more interesting than I expected, including one on the Old Testament as literature and another on comparative religion. Our text for the latter course was *Introduction to the Philosophy of Religion* by Anthony Bertocci, a philosophy professor at Boston University. This was a wide-ranging, broad treatment, in which my favourite passage was: "The essence or core of religion is the personal belief that one's most important values are sponsored by, or in harmony with, the enduring structure of the universe, whether they are sponsored by society or not."[5] This idea would stick with me for the rest of my life, along with my special affection for the writings of thinkers like Walt Whitman and Ralph Waldo Emerson. I admired Bertocci because he had managed to discuss spirituality without scaring away readers by putting down religion (I reckoned spirituality to be mostly a matter of real-life personal experience and religion an over-dependence on much-revised scripture that came largely from folklore).

With time I learned of writers who were expert in the philosophy of religion and religious experience. William James's *The Varieties of Religious Experience* (1902) is reckoned to be a masterpiece in this subject area, and with a little research I was excited to find threads of agreement that ran back to Meister Eickhart, a fourteenth century German, to Johannes Scotus Eriugena, a ninth century Irishman, and eventually to Plato himself.

❧

I had made two reliable high school friends, which says something about how coolly non-Mormon "gentiles" were received those days in the small town of Pleasant Grove. Andy Hall lived in a log cabin with his siblings and invalid mother in the farmlands on the outskirts of town. He was unpretentious and unusually bright, and I thought he was the smartest kid I ever met. Bob Fenton was a chubby, gregarious, and relatively rough-edged friend whom I met through Andy. The three of us enrolled at the university immediately after leaving high school and shared a basement apartment in Salt Lake City, suffering at times from visits to a dusty cabinet stocked with a sickening variety of crème de banane, crème de menthe, and, most noxious of all, crème de violette. We enjoyed each others' company thoroughly, but after our freshman year Andy and Bob disappeared into the Air Force and sadly I never heard from them or any of my other high school classmates again. From then on, Pleasant Grove was a closed chapter except for weekends with my parents.

In Salt Lake I took up with folk-music types and intellectuals like folk singer/composer Bruce "Utah" Phillips and my enduring friend Norman Ritchie, then a budding archaeologist. I played bridge at the campus Protestant center until I couldn't stand it any more, and ruined my left knee forever when, absurdly, I fell backwards off the center's front porch while practicing fencing for a production of *Romeo and Juliet*. (I was fortunate: one of my fellow thespians had to go to the emergency room to have an abdominal sword wound stitched up.) I recovered in time to take a small part in *Witness for the Prosecution*, in which Basil Rathbone would play the lead role. I had followed Basil's career in the early Sherlock Holmes films, and was surprised to learn that this stereotype Englishman was a native South African with a residence on Central Park West and a passion for baseball. Another member of the cast was Arthur Maud, a musician from a few miles from my parents' hometown who like me sang in university and community choirs. To our mutual amazement, we met again in 2011, when I was a choir member for an anthem, *Veni, Creator Spiritus*, which Arthur wrote and directed for St. John's Church in Bethnal Green, London.

I was active enough in my early university days, but worried about my shortage of "social capital." My skills as a raconteur, a flirt, or even a conversationalist had not benefited from growing up in a rather reserved household, living with an asthmatic lack of breath, and being largely excluded from friendships in my teenage years. In retrospect, my college years should have included classes in debate and studies of Dale Carnegie's *How to Win Friends and Influence People*. I hate to admit it, but in this department my highest cards consisted of my English background and accent, having published a few pieces of writing. and having traveled the world a bit. And, in the Hey household, modesty was a virtue. There was more depth in me than one might have thought, but it tended to stay secluded, even reclusive, except for when I sensed it was the right time for intimate one-on-one talking, lubricated perhaps with a bottle of good wine. For quite a while I lacked the courage or patience to attract anyone into a productive tête-a- tête. This, I am glad to report, would change.

Gradually my circle of friends expanded into a motley bunch that included Dennis Spain, the jack-Mormon, British-born son of a war bride, who was to cross my path again in England, when he worked for a competitor of the newspaper I was working with at the time, and folk musicians Jim and Rosalie Sorrels. Norris Peery (later the promoter of a hydrogen-helium fusion scheme) and Bob Parker (who claimed to be a descendant of Butch Cassidy) were among other friends. Others were Kim Braithwaite (Russian/Georgian translator), Maureen Derrick (onetime congressional staffer), Guy Spiesman (I attended his mother's funeral), Judith Levine (widowed early in life), Howard Glasgow (changed his first name to Lukman when he joined the Baha'i faith), and Bruce Miller, whom I knew through the university newspaper, the *Daily Utah Chronicle*.

I also made friends with Joe Buckle, sociable, red-haired, legally blind habitué of the university's Protestant center, a remarkable little man who was a tournament-calibre bridge player. I remember a time we went golfing, during which, as we approached each hole, he would ask me to tap the flag into the cup gently so that he could aim at the sound. He beat me fairly that day. For some reason, not necessarily this one, I never played golf again.

Some who occasionally stopped in at the Protestant center were Moslem. They were part of the family of the Iranian shah, Mohammad Reza Pahlavi; in fact the youth I talked with most was *called* Reza Pahlavi. In the brief time that I dated his sister I was rewarded with the thrill of driving her magnificent new, sky-blue Buick convertible.

Though I lost touch with him the moment we left university life, Bruce Phillips was the friend who impressed me most. He was then a good-looking, tallish, skinny, outwardly austere type who had a particular liking for the Seegers and the left-wing lore of American work/protest songs. I didn't know much about left-wing politics but I thought that my relatively sophisticated new friend might be even smarter than Andy.

We were drinking coffee in the Student Union "Huddle" after classes one day when I brought out my old bugaboo and asked Bruce what he thought happens to us (i.e. our personalities) when we die. His answer was immediate and it was confident. Well, what do you think *thought* is? he asked. I said why, there are neurons and dendrites and all that stuff, sparking out spasms that we call thought, and then I passed the ball back to Bruce. He persisted. Do you think it's all electrochemical activity, or does something else, something special, exist independently of the body? I caved in. It is something special, I said lamely and shut up, for I couldn't see how mere biology could account for whatever it was that constitutes the marvellous mind. I thought the exchange was over, but then Bruce pounced. Remember what Einstein said? That energy cannot be destroyed? If he's right, and your body dies, doesn't it follow that the energy of mind somehow continues? I was too soon defeated, ready to believe that Bruce had successfully defended the existence of soul, even an afterlife soul that had the characteristics of its living predecessor mind.

Journal, 1957 – The ability to accept death without expecting some kind of paradise is a treasure atop a high mountain bounded by sheer cliffs. Every once in a while I try to climb those cliffs, only to lose my footing before I get anywhere near the goal. It is a Sisyphean challenge. Someday perhaps I will fall for the last time and wake up with my head in a social whirl. And that scares me, too.

Somewhere in the Student Union mix of discussion, snacks, and coffee binges – we liked to think of it as Utah's imitation of Hemingway's Montparnasse bar – my ideas concerning death turned an important corner. I decided death was not a problem; death simply *was*. The *fear* of death, the bleak scariness of it, was to blame for driving humanity toward a state of avoidance and escapism – most often through mass entertainment, booze, sex, drugs, gambling, or the money-controlled demilife of the business workaholic.

At the time the most accessible remedy for this puzzle seemed to lie in Oriental philosophy, which teaches the unity of the individual with all other individuals and all things. I found great wisdom in the Buddha's teaching, faithfully perpetuated by his modern followers, from the Dalai Lama to Deepak Chopra, that: "The secret of health for both mind and body is not to mourn for the past, not to worry about the future, or not to anticipate troubles, but to live in the present moment wisely and earnestly."

I would not realize how much Buddhism and Taoism had influenced me until late middle age, when I became more aware of the spiritual experience that had accompanied my life. Buddha was the greatest luminary, but Plato and Plotinus were there, too. So were Maimonedes, St. Thomas Aquinas, and many other great theological thinkers from 500 B.C. through the middle ages to the present day. I was no scholar in such things, but I knew that these thinkers were right when they reasoned that *all* people are linked with an all-inclusive divine quality that might be called the presence of God. From this point it was easy to believe that the highest and most precious state of each human existence occurs when we recognize this divine connection. It is then that we touch and blend with the divine.

While I didn't know much about Oriental thought, it will be obvious that what I did know, I liked. However, I was still stuck with the idea that the world was headed on the wrong course and that somebody ought to fix it. Holding on to the self-centered old notion that I had been "put" on Earth for some purpose, I thought I might still somehow contribute to the business of easing society onto a better path. Another bit of conditioning told me I should do this through writing. I still had to figure out how this might be accomplished. I had yet to learn that the direction of the world as planet and ecosphere had not gone wrong. It was humankind that was misguided, often ignorant, and understandably confused about its role in the scheme of things. There is nothing basically wrong with the planet. It's just having a helluva hard time coping with everything that those billions of naked apes – us – are doing to it, and it will not be able to cope with these cascading insults forever. The ecologist Joseph Malthus warned against planetary population overload *three hundred years ago*, in 1798. "The power of population is indefinitely greater than the power in the earth to produce subsistence for man," he wrote, and has been derided for his views ever since.[6] The mathematician Joseph Fourier detailed the greenhouse effect and global warming in 1824, and a vocal minority still refuses to accept this proposal despite a wealth of modern scientific support.

Can humans and the planet coexist? I wondered. I tried hard to find ways of shouting confidently "Yes!" but consistently failed unless I weaseled out and said "Well, yes, I suppose for the next (insert a number) years we'll be able to get along just fine." Even then I would have to limit myself to the relatively rich and well-armed world.

I lugged only a few books with me on my post-university travels. These survived for decades as ragged, dust-stained volumes on my library shelves. One was Bertocci's; another was *The Path of the Buddha*, edited by Kenneth Morgan of Colgate University. Though it stuck to its Buddhist theme, it channeled me a little farther into the wider universe of Oriental mysticism, to Lao-tse in particular. Not long after I left college I found myself in the strange position of advising an unhappy older woman (she must have been thirty) with the backing of Taoist thought. To my great surprise, it seemed to help.

This early and, I must admit, superficial exposure to philosophy left a lasting impression. After my college years I had a greater respect for all forms of life. A greater feeling of partnership with the non-human world took form as I learned about the close and generally helpful relationship that we share with all other living things. I was aware of the unavoidable tiny deaths I caused by the simple act of washing, and began to avoid stepping on (most) insects. When two large centipedes showed up in the house, I carefully removed them to my woodpile. I was both saddened and alarmed when the local population of wasps and bees crashed in the early years of the century. I was fascinated by the aerial skill of hoverflies, the beauty of fallen leaves that had transformed into delicate skeletal designs, seeing brilliant autumn leaves against a backdrop of smoky clouds, and the silent work of humble earthworms, turning and processing the soil to enrich it for next year's garden.

Caring for life extended to plants, too. Some might think of plants as being mere solar-powered extrusions of water and organic material, but not me. When I was in a particularly good mood, and especially if no one was looking, I might step to the plants on the windowsill and breathe on them – not a sharp purse-lipped plosive puff but an appreciative close-up sigh from the bottom of my lungs, *haaa-a-a*. I knew it was silly, and you are allowed a polite reader's chuckle. But I gave in to the silliness and imagined the geraniums invigorated by that gentle gift of carbon dioxide. I reflected that very likely the geraniums reciprocated with an unthinking, microscopic *quid-pro-quo* gift of oxygen. Call it madness, but I could afford the whim, I enjoyed the eccentric moment, and it harmed no one.

⚜

In the summer of 1957 I took the long train ride to New York City, mostly because I wanted to be near my ballet-student girlfriend, who was staying the summer with her parents, and took a job with an export company in midtown

Manhattan. One afternoon I had a bright idea and took a bus to Broadway and 43rd street. First for curiosity's sake I walked over to the Metropolitan Opera and from the lobby heard the wonderful voice of the great Swedish tenor Jussi Björling, singing an aria in a matinée performance of La Bohème. Then I crossed the street to a huge building, crowned with French-style windows and parapets, with great green-painted doors on its giant garages, an archaic revolving pedestrian door, and little lit-up globes that bore the sacred name *Times*.

By now some readers will feel strongly inclined to call me a fraud, because everyone knows that the Met is uptown, at Lincoln Center, and the *New York Times* is lodged in a handsome skyscraper home on 8th Avenue. But remember, this was 1957.

I gave my name to the security guard at the reception counter and before long a neatly turned-down young man appeared from the elevator bank and introduced himself. I gave him a résumé that showed a few years of mostly part-time experience and he looked vaguely impressed. He took a few folded sheets of typewritten paper from his inside pocket and studied them briefly. "Tell you what," he said, "we have this job as a copy boy. It's only forty-five dollars a week, but it's a start." When I hesitated, trying to take this all in, he smiled. "Think it over and call me tomorrow." He gave me a card, we shook hands, and he disappeared back to the golden elevators.

I called the man at the *Times* the next day and told him with some reluctance that I had decided I had better return to college: after all I had only one year to go. Also, I thought to myself, it was miserable living in a hot and sweaty, non-air-conditioned room in August. The air was dirty and I had to wash my shirts thoroughly every day. Some of the pedestrians were vaguely threatening, *and there were so many of them!*

In later years I wondered whether it had been smart to turn down that job, for I very definitely wanted to be a journalist, and perhaps even a menial job with the *Times* could have put me on the path to journalistic greatness. In the days when there was greater faith in the decency of social institutions, the long gray columns of newspaper type made me think of the grave columns of a courthouse, a state capitol, or some other imposing architecture, suggesting truth and trustworthiness. I believed with all my heart in the role of the press as the Fourth Estate, which had the responsibility of informing a free democratic electorate fairly and truthfully so that the people could express their common desires and common wisdom to their Washington representatives.

It was a good time for journalism, a time before anyone could even imagine the delivery of current information by something that would be called the Internet. We had no idea that competition and corporate fear would cause journalism to shatter its own ethical rules and, as advertising income dived, caused the loss of many once-great newspapers and the dislocation of many fine writers. In fact the Internet would cause a jarring if not intentionally hostile revolution in a world that was quite unable to predict how this unorganized new way of communicating would change the ways of humankind.

My courting activities in Manhattan included one chaste night sharing a bed with my ballerina friend's portly father and going on a family trip to Long Island, where I met hundreds of pregnant horseshoe crabs, face-to-face, and had the opportunity to actually "catch the brass ring" as originally intended, by spearing a ring proffered by a mechanical arm while I rode a carousel horse. Meeting the crabs was the most enjoyable of these events. Our love-making was limited to hopefully romantic walks along Riverside Park and furtive fumbling on the carpeted floor behind the putative in-laws' living-room couch.

It was not long before the aspiring ballerina left me for someone she met in Indiana. I didn't mind her keeping the ring (yes, we were engaged), but was indignant to learn later that her mother gave my stamp collection, put together with care over a period of many years, to someone I like to imagine was a snotty-nosed kid somewhere up the street on Riverside Drive. I growled to myself that he probably glued them in an expensive new album with rubber cement.

⚜

In my senior year at university, beginning in December 1957, I took a temporary job as overnight editor at the Salt Lake City bureau of United Press International (UPI), which was then a full-fledged wire service in close competition with Associated Press. Our office was on the sixth floor of the *Salt Lake Tribune* building, midway up the huge pulsating *Tribune* sign. This forest of neon proved to be an irresistible magnet for night-flying arthropods that often strayed from their mark, bumbled through the open windows, and transferred their attention to me.

Bugs notwithstanding, this was a great job, and challenging, highlighted by an interview with the eminent physicist Edward Teller, accidentally starting a fire by knocking out my pipe in one of the *Tribune's* wastepaper bins during election night, telling a woman for the first time (while checking out a news story) that her son had apparently died from a spider bite, and being called on the carpet for sending coded Teletype messages to a Michigan colleague when business slowed to a near-stop in the wee hours. The main drawback was that this was a 9 to 5 job – 9 p.m. to 5 a.m. – and I had to spend the night alone in an empty office. I didn't get much pleasure from dragging in at dawn, finding the remains of a party scattered around the house and being too whacked out to do anything about the nubile young thing who on occasion I would find asleep in my pull-out double bed.

It would be wrong to stop recounting my UPI days without explaining how I produced stories about games played in the regional baseball league. The routine always struck me as odd, or even bizarre, and this is how it went. The league had provided itself with a set of connected Teletype machines, upon which commentators, sitting up with the scorekeepers, would provide play-by-play accounts of games that were in progress around the circuit. Our bureau had been provided with one of these Teletypes, and these were evening games – so you can guess the rest. As the 9 to 5 bureau chief I was privileged to write up two or three baseball games every night the league was in action. I kept copies of these by-lined articles for years, and can report that fortunately none of the collection indicated that the writer was in Salt Lake, Billings, Boise, and Evanston, all at the same time.

In case you haven't caught on to this yet, my parents had been faithful to their old-fashioned ways and did not give me a helpful introduction to the differences, either the obvious or the subtle, between man and woman, and for reasons that I have yet to explain my teenaged years were no more instructive. My adventure with the ballerina made up somewhat for this lack of important knowledge, after spending an adolescence afflicted by the unhelpful impression that the female sex was somehow superior to the male if not necessarily on top. At least partly for these reasons (to which I should include my UPI work schedule) I had come late to the dating game, and unlike my colleagues of both sexes could seldom be said to be on the make.

A fair student at a fair university, I ended up with a 3.15 average on a scale of 4.0. I would have liked to have done better, but classwork bored me. My test results were unambiguously lacklustre because, I told myself, my mind simply had trouble remembering information I wouldn't need at some indeterminate future time.

P-38 pose. This World War II fighter was parked in front of the University of Utah journalism building, part of old Fort Douglas and itself a wartime relic.

Sometime in the spring of 1958 I drove to Fort Douglas, a short distance up the hill from the university's journalism building, itself an old barracks, and volunteered for the Army. The Korean War had been over for five years, but things were looking ugly in Vietnam, where the French colonists had been defeated in 1954 at the Battle of Dien Bien Phu. Warlords in Vietnam and its neighbouring countries were at odds and American soldiers were already over there as non-combatant "military advisors."

I was pretty sure what would result from my generous offer to join the Army, but young men were still being drafted and I didn't want to have to sit around waiting for the government to call me in for my physical. As expected I was branded 4-F, unfit for combat because of my record of asthma.

❧

My parents offered to put me through graduate school. I was grateful for that, but why? I asked — after all, I wasn't planning to be a brain surgeon. My major subject had been journalism, the art and craft of preparing news and opinion for the general public. Since leaving high school I had worked on the university's student newspaper, the *Daily Utah Chronicle*, written for its literary magazine *PEN*, then moved downtown to write copy for radio station KUTA and UPI. I believed that if anyone had enough basic talent the best way of learning the ropes was to get into the business and practice it. I had already started doing just that.

While working on sensible nine-to-five day jobs in the years immediately following my graduation, I produced a number of essays, articles, and short stories on the human situation, mostly inspired by an abundance of sophomoric epiphanies. Happily, these ended at about the time I began serious work on a better-thought-out thesis on science and society. On close inspection later in life I found most of my early writings to be embarrassingly self-important, others verging on the loony, some relatively level-minded, and all quite immature. As you might expect, they rambled on about the origins and meaning of religion, railed against the escapism of people who watched TV instead of exercising their gray matter, protested the warping of human minds by advertising, and anything else that happened to be bothering me at the time.

After reading about my life in the Fifties you might think I wasted a fair amount of my college years, but not so. By the time I received my diploma, I had learned that, in addition to becoming rich and famous, being adored by the most beautiful women in the world, getting laid, and the rest of the Top Ten Aspirations of All Men Aged Under Twenty-One, there were certain more serious desires on my list, of which four life goals were particularly prominent:

To create and celebrate a good life centered around a stable family environment. I would find a decent job and marry wisely, while being a good son, husband and father, enthusiastic to raise children who would become honourable and commendable adults.

To excel in the art and craft of writing. This was a predictable goal, though at the time I had no idea how I would achieve it. Most likely I would be a journalist or, if I wanted to earn more money, a public relations practitioner. I much preferred the idea of being a newspaper or magazine journalist.

To discover a spiritual path that I could truly believe in. I thought this was a

26

highly personal affair by its very nature: in other words a goal to be found privately through study and reflection. Partly as a result of my nightmare experiences I also wanted to confront and calm the fear of death, which I had decided was a major cause of Western discontent, and write about it if I could.

To cultivate good health and defy the physical drawbacks of having a genetically mismanaged respiratory system. Without showing myself to have this slight disability, I would participate in a normal social life and compete in the job market with those who were physically more able.

I was determined to achieve Goal No. 1 (building a family life) in tandem with Goal No. 2 (moving up the ladder toward success in journalism). Goal No. 3 (the spiritual quest) was an exciting and intriguing work in progress and should also support No.1. Finally, Goal No. 4 (healthy habits and keeping my asthma invisible and in check) was a habitual routine, though the condition was subject to unexpected and hard-to-disguise flare-ups.

I expected this list of goals to be more an evolution than a solid plan, and naturally it did not include the unplanned happenings that would result from three of my more risky characteristics – adventurousness, a strong sense of curiosity, and an over-romantic nature. More about these later; simply be warned that I will defend to the end my belief that the most important word in the creative world is "Why?"

Practically speaking, the important thing was that, in the right-now world, I was ready for a career, the first task in supporting Goal No. 1. Journalism was a license to be non-specialist, accurate but superficial in the presentation of information, a dabbler in just about anything and ready to write about it. If I did well, I would prosper at least enough to support a wife and family.

That said, I performed as a hack for most of my short time at UPI, where I had to produce a large amount of reports on varied subjects, borrowed almost exclusively from articles that were to appear in the next morning's newspaper, so that at that time I was not much of a journalist at all. In fact I had no need to demonstrate expertise in any particular field other than an ability to construct messages in correct and understandable English – editing and writing alone, with practically no reporting.

I had already caught on to the fact that, because I would need to write about *everything* from crime to fashion, I would live off inexpertness while playing the usual start-up role of a general-assignment newspaper reporter who packaged information for the non-specialist public. My greatest claim to uprightness, as with any good journalist of that day, lay in the Fourth Estate concept, which required that every practitioner had to adhere to the values of being understandable, true, and balanced: in other words, virtuous to a fault. I thought I could manage that, at least on the written page. The question was, could I be the same in private life, or would those virtuous life goals I had composed so carefully simply dissolve? By now I knew pretty well who I was. But who would I become?

3. A LANCASHIRE LAD

Beauty is a pledge of the possible conformity between the soul and nature, and consequently a ground of faith in the supremacy of the good.
— George Santayana, *The Sense of Beauty*, 1896.

My earliest remembered experiences are of being wheeled around in a grand, buggy-style pram by one of the bakery helpers, in a far corner of Morecambe called the Battery. I'm not sure why it was called the "Battery," but later, when I started school, my friends and I came up with the silly notion that a string of cannon must have been emplaced there at some unknown time, to repel foreigners intent on stealing away with our most precious treasure, Morecambe's world-class fish and chips.

My childhood was blessed with happy times. There were sunny days when I was put out in front of the shop, in a pushchair I think, where I could scrutinize the comings and goings of our customers, study the then-vacant lot across the road, and admire the passing parade of holiday house-trailers. Our home, bakery, and café were housed in a whitewashed two-storey building. A big greenhouse abutted a back garden that included a pear tree from which I once fell like a bungee jumper, ignominiously suspended by my trouser braces. I loved the big laburnum tree at the front of the house, with its bright hanging skeins of yellow bloom, and for some unknowable childish reason derived curious pleasure in peering down the mysterious drain-hole a few feet from its trunk.

This all happened years before we learned the meaning of the term "central heating." We heated the house with a variety of "fires" – not necessarily by the glowing embers and bursts of flame that were the campfires of our ancestors, but more often by a variety of then-modern technical appliances. These often were fitted into manmade fireplaces – one per room –- warming our house with electrical coils or tidy arrays of minute gas jets. Most of the electrical ones had cleverly constructed inserts of celluloid, painted to resemble coal, which flickered enticingly as, out of sight and behind them, a piece of metal revolved in front of a light bulb, patterning the light that enlivened our imitation fire.

These modern ideas were fine, but what we all relished was a good coal fire. Coal at its best is a handsome mineral, glassy black, a cache of creature comfort bequeathed by the trees and forest life of millennia past. For our part, the wartime stuff was often gray with slate, yielding morning hauls of dust and clinker, robbed of its ungenerous warmth and as cold as a corpse.

Coalmen delivered our ration through dinner-plate-sized, iron-capped holes that opened from the pavement into our cellar, from which my father would at special times emerge with buckets of precious fuel. With care and time a real coal fire would emerge from a carefully built flaming cage of kindling sticks and transform into a miniature Hades. The fire would emerge at first reluctantly, then rather slowly gain a sort of mineralogical courage, often with help from my parents, who would dangerously put a broadsheet of paper against the fire-screen to increase the draft and draw the fire. Then the coal would erupt into a satisfying bonfire of flame, flaring merrily in a blackened theatre not quite the size of an orange box. We would turn off the lights and my parents would huddle contentedly on the sofa while I sat cross-legged and revelled in this Lilliputian spectacle. Eventually the flames would subside into a chaotic glowing city of red and orange shapes and I could imagine complicated neighbourhoods within them, moving inexplicably, changing their shades of red, brightening the room with occasional sparks that were yellow, almost white.

Wish You Were Here. The family spent holidays in Morecambe for a century or more. This post-card of the "promenade," hardly an advertisement for sunbathers, was sent by my Auntie Elsie to her father in 1908.

"Look Mum, Dad, see the blue bit. Look, there's a speck of green!" I would cry. Too soon the suburbs of my glowing city would darken and Dad would poke it back to life for a while. Within a short time all started to turn gray, and the cities began sullenly to click and tick, surrendering slowly into a smallness of ash and cinder. This meant bedtime, and we would stand and stretch and Mother would fill the rubber hot water bottles before we climbed the stairs to our cold and waiting beds. Sometimes Dad would stay behind and bank up the dying fire with more coal, often shovel-loads of "slack" grains that lasted longer because they were too fine to admit enough air to ignite an active blaze. Somewhere inside the mount of slack there was glowing ash, and smoke seeped through it, up past the firebrick and into the crooked maze of chimneys that ended in the neat row of chimneypots that crenellated our roof.

Certain other early memories stuck with me through the years. With a guilty pride I remember throwing an egg accurately at my great-grandmother Binns, a widowed, black-clad "mother-in-eighty"; going to my Auntie Annis's wedding to Ted Bower at St. Matthew's Church in Wilsden in 1939; and getting a Mother Goose book from Auntie Elsie for Christmas in 1940. The sanctuary of my childhood now houses a chain convenience store, and next door there's a Lloyds chain pharmacy, where Swaites the Chemists, a family-owned business, used to be.

When war broke out in 1939, my father was too old for military service but compensated by taking a second job as a police constable, attached to the London, Midland, and Scottish (LMS) Railway at Heysham Harbour. He was also a proud member of the St. John Ambulance Brigade, a charity-supported volunteer first-aid organization that offered first-rate paramedical training and came complete with smart uniforms and a fleet of ambulances. This was and is a remarkable institution, rooted in medieval times through the Order of St. John.

My first encounters with high technology were parades of tracked Bren-gun carriers whose drivers enjoyed converting run-over cats into something that looked vaguely like hamburger meat, and anti-aircraft guns, and the "wireless" that brought us war news, via the BBC Home Service, in the measured baritone of broadcaster Alvar Liddell. Liddell accented the second syllables of both his names, causing me to imagine that he must be an Algerian named Al-Var LaDelle. I loved to listen to those broadcasts, on a wireless with a yellowed tuning dial printed with exotic radio-station names like Hilversum and Luxembourg. These began with the stately, portentous words, "Here is the news, and this is Alvar Lidell reading it," and went on to give the latest communiqués from various places in

Europe and North Africa. I held radio programming in great esteem even at this early age, particularly the BBC commentaries, and my love for it remained for the rest of my life. Despite the hysterical monologues of radio politico-entertainers, despite competition from television and the attractive cacophony of so-called social media, my affection for radio strengthened through the years.

Radio also gave me an early introduction to a version of spoken English that I could call "standard," and helped to increase my vocabulary. I fell in love early with the word "communiqué." I thought it was a grand word. The same went for the word "ejaculate," meaning to throw out an exclamatory phrase during conversation, and to the silent amusement of my elders I used it in my childhood writings as often as I could.

Dad was an avid radio listener too – he had built his own primitive receiver in the 1920s. He also read the *Daily Express*, the Conservative Party newspaper, and as part of his conservatism harboured a strong dislike for P. G. Wodehouse, after having read over-hyped, suppositional accounts of the author's wartime collaboration with Nazi propagandists. When he heard of something happening that he really, *really* disliked, he would sometimes say, "People who do things like that should be lined up against the wall and shot." I was disturbed by this and never figured out whether he was serious or speaking in jest.

❧

I began school at Miss Smith's kindergarten at the age of 5. I was unconvinced by my parents' enthusiasm for my academic career, but I had a plan. On registration day I watched my mother closely as she prepared to take the bus for the short ride to Miss Smith's establishment. First she walked the short distance to the bus shelter. Then as soon as the bus hove into view I loosed our dachshund Fritz, who shot off toward her, barking for dear life. I suppose I hoped he would delay her and she would miss her appointment. It was a futile attempt to delay the inescapable At Miss Smith's I had my first lessons in French, learned arithmetic by pretending to shop with empty bottles and tins, took early classes in spelling and geography, and, importantly, opened war-gift packages of chocolates and other goodies sent to the school by well-wishers in the United States and Canada.

During these years asthma took me briefly to a Christian Science church, to a chiropractic practitioner (an Italian who sang "O Antonio" as he kneaded my back), and it brought me herbal medicines (for example garden snails stewed

32

with sugar and garlic) – and the Milnethorpe doctor who would give me adrenalin injections once I was coaxed or plucked screaming from under the dining room table. Antibiotics and modern anti-asthmatic medicines had yet to reach the pharmacists' shelves.

The first thing I wanted in my first eight or ten years, other than sustenance and protection, was air. I wanted to breathe, except that at the time I was so young that I didn't know what good, adequate, sufficient lung function was, since I had never experienced it, and I had no idea that asthma was an "issue." When as an infant I cried, it was not because of this but for one of the usual reasons – for food or for comfort, or to have my nappy changed.

I remember periods of desperate illness when, in those days before the general availability of antibiotics, I was bedridden with the simultaneous onset of bronchitis and asthma. I was never taken to hospital; it was as though there were never enough time for that. But I remember my mother, almost panicked, carrying me to the open window and holding me there so that I could breathe the freshest air possible. I remember wheezing by an open fire, and being held over a chamber pot by my father because it was difficult for me to climb the stairs to the bathroom. I remember a white enamel pail of water beside my bed, or beside my chair because it seemed easier to breathe sitting upright. My mother would pound me on the back and call out, as I leaned over, "cough it up, cough it up, Nigel!" And I would, in little plops into the pail, until it seemed the water was coated with pale frothy algae. It was a revolting procedure, but it seemed to help. I survived quite aware of what would happen if eventually the infection and the allergy made it impossible for me to breathe. Reflection and self-analysis were important to me from the time I was a small boy.

My parents were genuinely good, well-meaning, kind people, but they were too busy to be intellectuals and had little time to read. My grandfather had a huge mahogany bookcase full of interesting books; they had obviously been read but, I wondered, by whom? There were no dinner-table discussions of Darwin or the Huxleys, no Dickens or Montaigne at the fireside, not even any Bible stories. My parents did not talk to me about religion, philosophy, politics, or any other thought-stimulating subjects. Above all, they encouraged and cared for me in all respects, mutely teaching me the value of empathy, sowing seeds for everything that would prove to be "good" about my adult life.

While I was ill in bed a ten-volume bound set of *Arthur Mee's Children's Encyclopædia* introduced me to the wonders of the world and served as a magnificent substitute for the schoolwork I missed. Thanks to these wonderful volumes my general knowledge blossomed, and I was doubtless the only boy in the school who knew about Michelangelo's Pietà and what the statue looked like. Nonetheless, I did poorly on my rigidly structured 11-plus school exam, which would have "streamed" me into more vocational than academic education and likely converted me into a school-leaver at 16. Thanks to my parents I would be saved from this fate.

My boyhood reading also included *Boy's Own*, a rather upper-class and sometimes jingoistic magazine, until its publication was suspended with the imposition of wartime rationing in the early 1940s, and John Buchan's thrillers. Though confined to my imagination, these brought me the first tastes of high adventure, and my real-life exploits never would approach those of those early 20th century fictional heroes. Fortunately I escaped the lure of climbing sheer rock faces without a safety rope, relying only on fingers and toes and my judgement of the firmness of a piece of rock. I may have briefly enjoyed casting myself in such roles but wisely dismissed them as personal goals. Many of my "real" adventures were merged with the more individualistic quality that I called wonderment. This could arise from subtleties such as driving the dirt roads of the Navajo reservation, savouring the awe of scanning my eyes through the Milky Way, hearing the tinkle of sand running down the side of a dune, or seeing the rare early-morning beauty of a rainbow in the western sky. Ultimately all explorations of one's environment and oneself are personal. I imagine one man's adventures can sometimes be another man's yawn, though to me it would be a sad thing to reject the pleasure of hearing the stories.

Boy's Own appealed to me greatly. It was full of the masculine derring-do stories that appealed to most boys of my age, including tales of heroic exploits by servicemen in the Army, Navy, and Air Force. At various times Robert Baden Powell, the founder of the Boy Scout movement, Jules Verne, and Arthur Conan Doyle had contributed to the magazine, which was a far cry from the treasured comic sections that were brought home by my dad, coloured inserts salvaged from American newspapers abandoned at Heysham Harbour. Arthur Mee notwithstanding, I am sure I was one of the few kids in England who at that time had heard of *Bringing up Father* ("Jiggs and Maggie"), and *The Katzenjammer Kids*, cartoon favourites that are long gone even in the States. ✈

⁊⧉⧈

I think of myself as having "grown up" on Heysham Road, although I was by no means a grownup when I left. It was there that I fancied I had a girlfriend in Ann Holroyd, and two more in the sisters Heather and Ann, who lived across the road. My best friend was a lad called Ernie Greenhalgh, who lived at the top of Longlands Crescent, across the road from a shrubby corner where another child, Caroline, introduced me to the instructive game of playing doctor, pants down, using of all things a crab-apple for a stethoscope.

I was eight years old at the time, and Caroline a year older, hardly mature enough for a love tryst yet curious enough to harbour a good deal of interest about the difference between boys and girls, details of which were being left strictly to my personal discoveries. Caroline was plump and strong-willed, and her round face, which I noticed had become slightly pinker as we approached the shrubbery, was clustered with freckles. My pulse also must have quickened a little as it dawned on me that this would be my first sexual encounter, even though I had yet to learn that term and its meaning. First she instructed me to move the crab-apple to the pale cleft between her legs, and introduced it proudly as her pussy, something very special and not to be explored until she was an old lady. Babies came from in there, she said, introducing a fact that I ingested with a great deal of scepticism. Then she moved my hand, and the crab-apple, under her shirt and to her nipples, which had yet no breasts for them to perch upon. "Nipples like yours," she said. "But I will grow boobies soon, underneath them. Mummy told me it would be soon." She favoured me with a wide, toothy grin. "I can't wait."

The brief gynaecological exam was over. She plucked another crab-apple from the tree and nudged up against me. "Now tell me about your things." The moment of truth!

I could only summon a stifled "Well, er –" before she moved her crab-apple between the opening of my shirt. "Don't worry, we're just playing doctors." She unsnapped my belt, deftly unbuttoned my pants, and, assuming a clinical air, peered down and poked at the flaccid finger of undeveloped manhood that lay there. "What do you call your thing anyway?"

I felt a slight tinge of resentment at that. I was sure, though defensively so, that this was more than a mere "thing."

"It's my doings," I said defensively.

"Your *doings*?"

From that moment the doctor's appointment came rather rapidly to a close. We straightened our undergarments, said goodbye, and I wandered home. For reasons unknown, but probably linked to some puritanical admonishment from past generations, my penis was always in those days called a doings, dropping the "g" as if were a technical word and, I suspect, to ward off questioning by the less educated. Later, after I acquired a sexual lexicon, I wondered if my family possibly were the only people in the world who used it. But the time I first used the word outside the family is indelibly imprinted in my mind.

It was a year or so before the Caroline incident. I was lying in my bed one afternoon when my mother came in to get ready to meet some friends. She was in a hurry and had not yet dressed herself below the waist. I was taken aback by what I saw (or rather did not see) there, which I fancied may have resulted from some horrific accident. "Mummy," I asked, "why haven't you got a doings?"

She wasn't fazed. "Because ladies don't have them," she said, and flounced out. This was the only morsel of sex education ever imparted to me by my parents.

You're probably wondering why I was so poorly informed about sex at the age of seven or eight. *What*? You're thinking, You didn't *know*? Well no, I simply didn't, with semi-puritanical parents, a lack of siblings to observe and, in those days, no equivalent of the bike-shed activities that help to enlighten today's young Brits in such matters.

An abundance of personal adventures happened in my still-earlier Heysham days. I seem to remember (perhaps prompted by a photograph) taking my first steps on that strip of lawn outside the bay window at the south side of the house. With more clarity I recall my short journey along a narrow stone windowsill, several feet over the ground-floor bay window, quite unafraid, to rescue my teddy bear. This was a futile attempt because the teddy bear had come to rest on the roof of the bay window, and there was no possible way of retrieving it. I was not particularly concerned when I realized this; instead I was flattered by the commotion of people running into the house and shouting "Mr. Hey, Mrs. Hey, your little boy is trapped on the upstairs window ledge!" It had been a most gratifying experience. In fact I suspect it may be responsible for the first notes from the Lorelei of adventure that would sing to me regularly in later life.

I also remember the time I took a small alarm clock apart in the spare room, being scolded for the deed, and then, encouraged, moving on to a wrist watch. I suspect that many children with such proclivities eventually become science writers, or even lettered scientists.

There are so many old memories. I recall accidentally poisoning two guinea pigs that made the mistake of gnawing on a silvered ball I had put in their cage opposite the big cistern in the greenhouse; marvelling at the wartime food-aid boxes of dried bananas (they made wonderful firelighters), and the big metal cans of Chinese pickled eggs; smuggling Robin cigarettes from the café to American servicemen who stopped to rest in the then-vacant lot across the road; seeing Jewish European refugees swigging brown sauce from the tables when they thought no one was looking; having scary dreams about savage cats; eating and enjoying sweetened potato tarts; watching my mother make Christmas cake/pudding with carrots and apple rings that had been dried on the wash-line; going blackberrying; playing host to the Italian refugee girl Gloria Poleidri; picnicking on mysterious tidal flats where the tide could strand us from civilization and life itself; hunting crabs with our dog Fritz on Half Moon Bay; trying to figure out the secrets of the mind-reading performances at the Heysham Head resort; watching Flash Gordon serials at the Odeon cinema; goggling at the colourful night-time "illuminations" that gave a gay Christmassy touch to the summer tourist season; fishing with my dad (once or twice) from the stone jetty; a billboard that advertised, side by side, the still-popular "Gone With the Wind" and a warning against V-1 buzz-bombs that didn't have the range to reach us; seeing the steam lorry puffing by, sprinkling sparkling ash on Heysham Road, then marvelling at the vehicle with a great bellows on top for its supply of coal-gas fuel; Dad returning home with a canvas bag of tiny dabs that fluttered about the sink like miniature plaice; Mum preparing a rabbit for dinner the day my aunt Doris died from a brain tumour; going with Mother to take lunch to my dad on duty in his policeman's uniform and tin hat near the field full of ack-ack guns; the huge naval gun (never used) pointing out from Heysham Head; sneaking sweets from the café shop with cousin Michael; having a Polish Air Force man join us for Christmas dinner; a high, grim wall of sandbags shielding the once-dignified library, behind the stubs of metal railings that had been harvested for ships and guns; and that dreadful first visit to the dentist, when I had to be subdued, crying, with laughing gas.

These were something less than adventures, but they added richness, in terms that were happy, sad, and neutral, to the tapestry of my childhood years, Remember that these were the old times, when at elementary school we wrote on wood-framed slates, pens had nibs that we dipped blue-fingered into ceramic wells inserted in the corners of our desks, and one used absorbent paper to keep from blotting one's copybook.

One bright afternoon my mother took me to have tea with a remarkable lady who lived not far away, down the hill from the bakery and on the way to Heysham Village. I know little about her except that her name was Miss Dalgleish. She lived in an old railway coach, handsomely appointed inside and surrounded with the most beautiful flower garden I had ever imagined. Miss Dalgleish was a period-piece ex-colonial from the India that was still, at that time, united with Pakistan/Bangladesh/Burma/Ceylon as part of the British Empire. She was old, tiny, and gracefully beautiful, with white hair worn neatly "up" and a dainty black band fastened around her neck. She had also apparently lived in the Far East, for in her rosewood cabinet she kept a genuine Tibetan prayer wheel, a tiny shrine that could be made to rotate on a hand-held spindle. She explained that it contained, inside, a miniature scroll inscribed with a special prayer, and that to use it properly one had to rotate it on the spindle – a finely made centrifugal chain was attached to help it along – while speaking certain magical words. "Say it with me," she would say, and then she would recite, slowly and reverently, "*Om mani padme hum, om mani padme hum.*" I had no idea what the words meant, but I was only six or seven years old and believed they were very, very special. Later I learned that these Sanskrit words are a mantra that was probably inscribed inside the prayer wheel, remindful of the Buddhist belief in compassion.

I loved Miss Dalgleish, and from that time on I suspected there must be something special about Oriental spirituality too. True, it was odd that this immaculate old lady lived in a railway carriage, and I wondered how it had come to be there, and if it had been brought from India, or Tibet, complete with its cargo of carved camphor chests, anti-macassared armchairs, and prayer wheels. It was strange and exciting too, which made me love Miss Dalgleish all the more.

In later years it occurred to me that, no matter what kind of residence she occupied, Miss Dalgleish must have been part of the upper class, or a fragment of an upper class that had declined rapidly from being a super-rich monolith at the turn of the century, much of it becoming, with the accelerated downward push of World War I, an almost-contrite collection of people who talked about better days while drinking Scotch and port in decaying country houses and castles that looked out over shrunken acreages. I can't remember my family ever talking about class, though they defended the royal family and I admit we once went to a public event at the Roxburghshire estate of the Duke of Buccleuch, who fared much better than most of the peerage and became the largest private landholder in the United Kingdom. In real life we existed in a sliver of society that one might call the entrepreneurial class or the *petit bourgeoisie.*

In those days, boys and girls were required to behave in ways that were considered to be "proper." They were expected to be polite and helpful to older people and to treat women with special deference. While eating, you ate with knife and fork simultaneously, knife in the right hand, fork with tines down in the left; never put your elbows on the table, and stayed seated until excused. When you met someone, you were expected to say "How do you do?" and shake hands gravely without waiting for an answer. For no particular reason except that they were patently unsuitable for real boys, these rituals infused me with a peculiar, resentful sense of dread. I would descend into a psychological purgatory when my parents invited someone to tea and we all had to sit in straight-backed chairs in a circle around a table full of biscuits and cakes that waited interminably for the arrival of the teapot. For what seemed like hours I had to pretend I was listening and that I had no interest at all in those tempting goodies. For Miss Dalgleish, however, I had all the time in the world.

⚬⚭⚬

It was still wartime when my mother and dad sold their business to a couple who wanted to convert it into a fish and chip emporium. Our new home was at 68 Middleton Road, at the corner of Brooklands Drive, a "real house" away from the commercial centers, away from the café and bakery, and closer to Dad's place of work at Heysham Harbour.

Here I was fascinated to see Italian men from the Middleton prisoners-of-war camp walk by the bottom of our front garden, apparently unescorted, in special boiler-suit uniforms with big round patches like brown moons on the back. They always seemed cheerful and friendly, even happy, smiling and waving as they went on their way. Italian prisoners at some of the camps would sculpt statues or create huge floral arrangements, and place them beside the main-line railway tracks as a heart-warming and effective public relations exercise.

Across the road from No. 68 was a jumble of boulders and twisted trees, covered with undergrowth, still there, to my delight, in 2008. Above, and separated from it by a covering of near-impenetrable bracken ferns, was a hedged field. If you wandered over the field and farther from Middleton Road, you might get to the cliffs overlooking Half Moon Bay, and the rock-pools and the crab-running sands, but I seldom ventured that far. I didn't need to because the little universe of rocks and wild shrubs and bracken was my tiny Eden. There were mysterious caves in those rocks. At least I pretended they were caves and not the haphazard result of some quarryman's dynamite. And there were tunnels in the thick grass and ferns, formed by rushing rabbits and frothy-tongued foxes, just large enough for a small boy to explore. Here was born my interest in natural history.

We were a closer family in Middleton Road. The house included a cramped attic room that made a fine hidey-hole for an asthmatic kid who – because physical exertion could worsen a bout of asthma – had a lot of time on his hands and was perforce inclined to introspection and bookishness. Here I set up my tiny Corona portable, cultivated my stamp collection, and catalogued a minuscule library. One Christmas my dad made me a model aerodrome with an electric light inside, and another time made a foot-propelled scooter that I would ride to school at a furious pace. My parents made our house a home by talking lightly together and sharing household activities that would range from rolling out pastry dough to simply setting the table and sitting down to a meal together.

Physically, school was a pretty bleak place (it still was, when I saw it in 2008) and we would write our class-work on slate boards. A science master, Mr. Glass, threw a piece of chalk at me after I unexpectedly gave him the right answer to the question, "What material lies under most of England?" "Chalk, Mr. Glass," I chirped. I was caned, once.

Primary school was an on-again, off-again affair dictated by the state of my health – though I remember good days, like trading postage stamps in the schoolyard, attending cricket matches and brass-band concerts, and the time the bus-driver, with a grin, complimented me on my whistling expertise. The scooter, the whistling, and a great many other things sprang from my parents' efforts to improve the condition of my breathing apparatus.

Thoughts of mortality returned when I thought of being in the position of the unfortunate goat which met its end when a stray German bomb fell in the field across the road from No. 68. There had been several bombings before, when we lived at the bakery. When the sirens began we would huddle under a heavy table until the all-clear sounded. But these incidents were almost surely haphazard – the German pilots would simply jettison any leftover munitions to save fuel as they started their return trip from bombing the shipyards across Morecambe Bay at Barrow-in-Furness.

Yes, bombs were falling, but things were far, far worse in the big cities. Life was with me and in me. It was good, and I had tunnels in the summer bracken to explore, and the tide pools on Half Moon Bay. Somewhere, Dylan Thomas was writing, in his "Poem in October":

> *These were the woods the river and sea*
>> *Where a boy*
>> *In the listening*
> *Summertime of the dead whispered the truth of his joy*
> *To the trees and the stones and the fish in the tide.*
>> *And the mystery*
>> *Sang alive*
> *Still in the water and singing birds.*

And yet I did not grow up to be a wimp. Thanks to my parents my early years saw me developing into a firmly independent soul. This was partly because my mother and dad were so busy running their business (Mother always felt a little guilt for this), so that I had to spend time by myself or in the care of one of the bakery/café helpers. I never actually had a nanny, but do remember being trundled about in my pram or pushchair by a succession of young women – Peggy, Maud, Alice – between the Battery and our own little neighbourhood at Strawberry Gardens.

⚜

With his heart-throb baritone voice, Dad was popular in amateur theatre and light opera in the 1930s and 1940s. I remember him coming home one night from a performance of *Rose Marie*, and telling us about a character who staggers on stage after being caught in a blizzard on the Yukon Trail. The way Dad told it, the actor muffed his lines and said he was caught in the gizzard on a hook and nail. I've fractured some lines on stage, but nothing like this.

On the one night he invited me back-stage, I appeared before my first audience after I took it in my mind to inspect the set after the curtain had gone *up* at the beginning of the third act of *Rose Marie*. This little experience turned out to be one of the unplanned germinative events that change the pattern of one's existence. Modest though it was at the time, it would eventually bring significant changes to my life.

⚜

In the summers we usually spent holidays in Yorkshire at Wilsden and Honey Pot Farm. The journey featured a huge black locomotive with a moustachioed driver and muscular men who shovelled coal into the fiery red firebox. This wondrous and magical contrivance, followed by a train of caterpillar carriages, took us over the Pennines with stops at places with names like Giggleswick, Carnforth, and Hellifield. *Where did they get those funny names?* I wondered. I loved the smell of coal smoke from the engines, and didn't mind when a stray particle of ash found its way into my eye: it was an indispensable part of the adventure.

A steam train service carried Wilsdeners to and from town until 1955, thanks to the Great Northern Railway Queensbury line, but during our summer trips from Morecambe it was easier to take a faster train to Bingley and continue the few extra miles in the dark by taxi, reflective cat's eyes glistening magically in the middle of the curly road up the hill, showing which was the right (or more properly left) side of the road and which was not. We would generally stop in first at Auntie Elsie's, at 62 Lane Side, where gas lighting fizzed and grumbled through evenings of tea, cakes, and gossip.

The Queensbury line continued to carry freight for a while after passenger service was discontinued, but was closed completely in 1965 during the wholesale slaughter of small British stations consigned to an extermination list that also included a special station opposite Morecambe's gloriously art-deco and still extant Midland Hotel. Subsequently my second cousin Jimmy Power bought the dressed-stone Wilsden station buildings, which sat a few hundred yards from a great 300-yard stone viaduct that featured 16 arches, 125 feet over Hewenden Beck and its wooded valley.

Auntie Annis was a big, jolly, bustling woman with a wart on her cheek, married to a wiry, olive-skinned farmer, Ted Bower. I loved to sit in their front room, the place smelling of farm; the steady-ticking grandfather clock in the corner; coals glowing in the ancient cast-iron fireplace/oven; the mantel, plate-racks and picture rails crowded with knick-knacks, mementoes and crockery; a greyhound (or two) sometimes lounging on the couch. Giant pigs grubbed their days in the great wallow outside the front door. Cows pushed their noses on little levers to fill their water bowls. Cats were everywhere, and there was always a friendly black and white border collie around.

At Honey Pot during wartime, a revolution occurred when modern Alfa Laval machines were brought in to milk the cows, but the hay was still harvested by hand and placed in stooks until it could be brought to the farm by wagon.

There it would be baled by a machine that was linked by a long drive belt to a steam-powered traction engine. Like any small boy, I was fascinated by the engine, which gave off important puffs of steam and sported a firebox glowing red with coals. The threshing machine itself was identical to, if not the same as, the one that destroyed my aunt Cis's arm when she was a child. I was never told exactly how this happened, but imagined that somehow she had been struck by the flailing mechanism that beat the grain out of the straw, or that, maybe worse still, she had been caught in the great belt that connected the traction engine to the thrashing machine.

Ted was talented with a sly, wry sense of humour. He had gypsy friends in his younger days and would work when he felt like it, a disposition for which my mother never forgave him, for like my father she and her siblings had been brought up to believe that hard work was both necessary and virtuous, something that one would never dare (or wish) to shirk. But when not sitting in his rocker with a cigarette, staring into the fire, or studying the nasturtiums climbing around the front window, Ted much preferred to stroll around the farm talking to the animals or, better yet, to walk down to the Ling Bob pub for a pint or two and a bit of gossip and horse-betting with his pals.

You had to like Ted because of his humour and his easy-going way, but he was a slightly shady character who did some black market deals with his livestock during the war. "He's a rascal, that Ted," my mother would say, curling her lip in disapproval.

Ted was quite unlike his sister Emma, an austere, chain-smoking old lady much admired around the village, who had an educated air and a fondness for antiques and tournament tennis. Aunt Em's environment was crowded with old carved furniture, useless but curious ornaments, and family photographs. The pictures on the wall were dingy, and when I moved them aside to peek behind I found only pale rectangular squares, where the wallpaper had been shielded from the sticky pall of Aunt Em's cigarette smoke.

Auntie Annis' twin sister Elsie was similarly different from her closest sibling. She was a stringy old spinster until she mysteriously married a Mr. Yewdall in her late middle age. Though she had a reputation for selfishness I reserved a special fondness for her. Reason: she would treat me to fine desserts when I visited and never failed to present me with a big bag of cake, chocolates and sweets for the road when we said our goodbyes. After Elsie moved to Lane Side, where her front door faced the track to Honey Pot Farm, Annis could keep an eye on her from the farmhouse kitchen window a hundred yards up the hill.

It was at Honey Pot that I became intrigued by the West Yorkshire dialect, and perhaps this fuelled my love of language itself. There was a special way of speaking the local language, and to master it meant you were a member of the West Yorkshire brotherhood, for style of speech is one of the old-fashioned strangenesses that cement friendships among a region, a county, or even a smaller patch of land (think of Cockney, said to belong to those born within earshot of the bells of Bow Church in East London).

Yorkshire old-timers would sometimes slip into the old-fashioned familiar forms of personal pronouns – "Art thou going out tonight?" which came out "Atta goin' aht t'neet?" and "Hast thou made the tea?" became "'Asta mate tea?" It was all great fun and after a while I prided myself on what I naïvely considered my ability to speak fluent Yorkshire. "'Ow ter doin', lad?" Uncle Ted would ask, "How art thou doing?" And if it had been a hard day I would nod my head and answer solemnly, "Ah'm fair sluftered," (made profoundly sluggish by the experience); or, if the day had been *really* miserable, I'd pronounce myself "ready fer 't knacker's yard," the dismal factory where dead farm animals were converted into glue and pet food. Later I learned that "sluftered" is a derivation of the word "slaughtered."

The food was unwaveringly good at Honey Pot. Wartime rationing had little effect, since this was a working farm with plenty of meat and vegetables on hand. Late in the evenings, when the farm work was done – very late indeed when British Double Time advanced wartime hours by 120 minutes – we would have Supper, which meant a thick slab of bread slathered with genuine beef dripping, taken cold from the pan and sparkling with salt. It was heavenly.

The only thing I didn't like about Honey Pot in those days was the long damp walk down the garden flagstones to the privy, with its pair of ice-cold stone seats, when I had a call of nature that I could not postpone. When it was raining, and/or when nature called in the night, the misery was quadrupled.

For no particular reason I started to write modest little compositions, using scored journal paper while seated in Heysham at the big oak dining table that we used as a shelter during air raid warnings. It started with a poem, "To a Celandine," doubtless inspired by Wordsworth's "Daffodils" or some other romantic verse that caught my fancy. "Dandy the Nigger" and "Jumbo the

Elephant" followed on November 16 1943, "nigger" then being shorthand for a dark-skinned person, derived from *negro*, the Spanish word for black.

In later years I would joke that my mother had twisted my mind forever by firing my interest in writing. She was certainly responsible for it, and that early encouragement served me well. When I was a kid, she drew beautiful illustrations for a version of "Mr. Prickles the Hedgehog," and we tried unsuccessfully to sell it to Jonathan Cape. Finally, on October 16, 1946, it was read on the BBC "Young Artists" program, earning me two guineas, equivalent to about $10 at the time, and rebroadcast by another Children's Hour production, "Your Own Ideas," on April 16, 1947.

At least part of my writing activity has to be credited to a carriage clock that my mother and dad brought back from an auction in 1943 — I thought (mistakenly, as it turned out) that it was intended for me as consolation for that ghastly visit to the dentist, and in gratitude I wrote them "Jumbo the Elephant."

In the late spring of 1945 we took a trip to Windermere on a Magnet bus, a vehicle with a conductor who had a ticket machine hanging from his shoulder, equipped with a fare stamp that he created with something that reminded me of a telephone dial. I had a special affection for those little single-decker buses, painted in cream and burgundy with a rakish chrome-rimmed curve of colour sweeping down from the front door like a fat comet.

We left the coach at Bowness, the central meeting-point for holidaymakers who were spending a day or a weekend at Windermere, which must be one of the most beautiful lakes in the world and whose admirers included William Wordsworth, Beatrix Potter, John Keats, and so many others. Clutching our picnic lunches and woolly jumpers, we boarded the Victorian-era *Tern* for a cruise trip around the lake via Ambleside and Lakeside and back again. As we eased back alongside the Bowness jetty, sirens were sounding. Nazi Germany had surrendered and the Führer was dead. It was VE Day, May 8, 1945, and a couple of hundred miles south of us a million people were deliriously celebrating in Trafalgar Square and down through the Mall to Buckingham Palace. Victory in Europe!

4. THE TRAVELLING LIFE

A large volume of adventures may be grasped within this little span of life, by him who interests his heart in everything.
— Laurence Sterne

Now and then, maybe once a year, I reminisce about certain private adventures long ago at the Keynsham lime kiln, back in the warm summer of 1947. Workmen had once used the structure to produce quicklime by roasting chunks of limestone over a hot coal fire. But its brick walls had been salvaged for new buildings and nature had transformed much of what remained into a pond, invested by time with a rich population of happily coexistent life, with the ruined remnants of the kiln mirrored in its surface. Few aquariums could have taught me more about natural history.

Sitting cross-legged in the thick grass beside the pond, I would reach into a metal tobacco box and extract a small earthworm. This I tied, without need for a hook, to a piece of string. Then, stretched full-length on my belly, I would clear a space in the pond weed with my free hand and carefully lower the captive into the depths. If I was rewarded with a gentle tug at the string, and this was a gratifyingly frequent event, I would carefully pull my prize to the surface.

My catches always consisted of newts, the most handsome of amphibians. I would take each struggling creature gently in my hand, pull the bait harmlessly from its insides, and put my catch in a glass jar before I took it home to get acquainted before returning it to its watery home. It seemed there were two kinds of newts in that pond. What I called smooth newts were like sleek aquatic lizards, whereas great crested newts were delightful little orange-bellied dragons ornamented with a wavy yellow and brown fin along their backs and tails.

The pond was edged with algae and with pond weed that filigreed the surface with minute floating leaves. In the center there was often a mysterious pink cloud. The cloud could expand and shrink, and had the ability to move quite quickly from one side of the pond to the other. Someone told me that the clouds were giant schools of tiny *daphnia*, which were crustaceans and thus

46

distantly related to crabs. I caught some with a muslin net and studied the flea-like creatures through the microscope my mother and dad had bought me for Christmas. How did they know so precisely when to move right and left, and up and down, in company with thousands of companions? How could any of these tiny creatures know *anything*?

Why should I think of my encounters with creatures like newts and water fleas with such happy reflection? For one thing new opportunities for such experiences are rare. Look for the kiln today and you will find only a tracery of roads and housing. And there is constant competition from other ways in which a youngster might spend his time. I suppose a lot of little boys, and girls, enjoyed such pursuits in the days before television and video games.

Possibly my memories were strengthened by a gift that arrived from my Auntie Elsie at about that time. It was an anthology named *Nature in Britain* (Collins, 1946), edited by W. J. Turner, and it was the only early book that I would keep, year after year, until I was well past retirement. This short volume was full of information and illustrations, yet easy and fun to read, the plants and animals described with knowledge, admiration, and a certain tenderness – I have never seen such appreciative words applied to insects! It was my introduction to truly fine science writing, and to science itself. Reading this book, and spending the year in Keynsham after my explorations of the old quarry in Heysham, heightened my interest in science – more correctly, in *natural history* – while hinting at a budding philosophy that sought an amicable reunion of human personality with the more cosmic realities of Earth's ecosphere. I knew a little bit about Wordsworth in those days, and enjoyed his poetry. If I had read Thoreau, it might have changed my life completely.

⬩⬩⬩

We were in Keynsham because my dad had arranged a transfer to nearby Bristol shortly after the war ended, not long before the LMS and all the other great railway companies were nationalized. We moved into a nice house on Chandag Road, where I continued my mouse-rearing hobby with unwarranted enthusiasm. The mouse population totalled 66 at its peak, at which time my father decided sensibly that enough was enough and took most of them away to a pet shop.

My great friend in Keynsham was Robert Hember. We decided to build a tree house and I nearly lost a finger when a sheet of corrugated iron slipped from where it was intended to serve as our roof. Robert and I fished for perch, tench, and roach on the wonderful, wide and transparently weedy Somersetshire River Avon. We rode a rubber raft down its tributary River Chew, so lovely that it would someday be celebrated with its own Web page. And I seldom missed listening to the radio series *Dick Barton, Special Agent*, which seemed especially tailored for lads of my age. At our one Guy Fawkes' Night together, Robert and I built a huge effigy of the infamous would-be bomber of the Houses of Parliament, spiked him with fireworks, and when it was dark we delightedly set him alight in the company of our school friends.

On sunny weekends my parents and I would go by car on trips to fabled places like Stonehenge, Salisbury Cathedral, Glastonbury Abbey, the Cheddar Gorge, Bath Abbey, Brunel's Clifton Suspension Bridge. At Wells we visited the cathedral and bishops' palace, the latter with a crystalline flooded moat – more pond life! – and swans that rang a bell to order a meal.

For a kid it was special to live in a place named for St. Keyne, who had turned the local snakes into stone, and you could still see them in tight petrified coils, not just in museums, but cemented into garden walls as well. I knew they were really the petrified remains of the large sea snails called ammonites, but it was more fun to think of young St. Keyne zapping those serpents.

Asthma continued to bother me during the Keynsham months, which meant it would be a short stay. At the time I was still using Potter's Asthma Cure – fun, because I had to breathe heady fumes from a fizzling mixture of stramonium and potassium nitrate as an alternative to ephedrine tablets and the dreaded stab of injected adrenaline. Sometimes such preparations included cannabis and lobelia, but I don't know whether mine did, only that medicinal use of *datura stramonium* was eventually banned by the U.S. Food and Drug Administration. In fact while its profusion of large white trumpet flowers makes a beautiful sight, and while it does reduce asthmatic spasms by calming smooth muscle, it is a dangerous alkaloid containing scopolamine and atropine, carrying a number of names including Loco Weed, Jimson Weed, Stink Weed, Devil's Trumpet, Mad Hatter, and Crazy Tea.

I soon was carrying a perfume-bottle contrivance consisting of a glass reservoir with a large rubber bulb attached, for dispensing a spray of Rybar – a mixture, I think, of adrenaline and ephedrine, or maybe isoprenaline – into my mouth and lungs. This was the first of a line of steadily less dangerous, so-called "inhaled short acting B_2 agonists," followed by Medihaler, the much-improved medication albuterol (US), aka salbutamol (UK), and longer-acting drugs.

It was probably in Keynsham that I first saw the holocaust photographs and films that were taken at the Nazi prison camps at the time of their liberation. I was appalled by the nightmarish pictures of incredibly thin, hollow-eyed people clutching the wire fences in their striped prison gear, the gas chambers, the stacks of shoes and clothing taken from those who were to die. I was also extremely confused. Germans are civilized people, like us, I thought. They laugh, cry, fall in love, have kids, attend church. They wear the same kind of clothes, go to school, go shopping, see movies, drive cars. How could this happen? And how was it that in such a cultured place a little man with a silly moustache could rant and scream like a madman from the podium of a sardine-packed hall, after which everyone would shout "*Heil Hitler*"? I couldn't understand it, just as I couldn't understand how an advanced, spiritually inclined country like Japan could indulge in torture and death marches.

In a family given to dinner-table conversation I might have asked, "Dad, how come these people do those terrible things?" I didn't. I would learn elsewhere that the social depression that emerged from Germany's defeat in World War I, and the economic depression that accompanied it, exerted a terrible toll on the public psyche, and for some twisted, crazy reason the Jews were blamed. I know this is a simplistic explanation, but it will have to remain, with my apologies, for the moment. Suffice it to say that the question, and those terrible pictures, were never erased from my mind.

The Soviets were supposed to be our allies in those days, and the cruelties of the Stalin regime – on Russian people as well as foreign enemies – were soft-pedaled. No one heard of the terrible 1939 massacre, by the NKVD, of more than 20,000 Polish officers and intelligentsia in the Katyn Forest. No one heard of the arrests and killing of ordinary Russians whose allegiance to Stalin had been questioned. Acts of retribution against Germany, which mounted (and lost) the terrible siege of Leningrad, were particularly barbarous. More people lost their lives in the Leningrad siege than died in Allied uniforms during all of World War II.

It's extremely important that young people learn about totalitarian regimes like Nazism and Soviet communism, and the smaller ones that proliferate around the world; and not merely so we can puff ourselves up and crow about how fortunate we are, or how virtuous. Regimes like this have no time for opposing views, no time for critical thinking, no space in which people could, peacefully express their anger at social injustice and, when required, work for political change. Totalitarian regimes depend on the suffocation of these and a great many other human rights, otherwise they would be weakened and most likely overthrown.

These points came out in stark relief during a visit to Moscow when I had a chance to talk about Mikhail Gorbachev and the fall of the Soviet empire with the physicist Dmitry Mikheyev, who had spent some Cold War time in a gulag prison camp. Dmitry's opinion was that the Soviet general secretary made a grave tactical mistake by encouraging *perestroika* and *glasnost* – restructuring and openness – in the mid-1980s. These allowed the revival of debating societies, the support of which had landed Mikheyev with six years' imprisonment during an earlier Soviet regime. But the new debating societies didn't work as Gorbachev expected. "They didn't suggest ideas to strengthen the Communist Party control of the country, to make their rule more efficient – the things that Gorbachev was dreaming about," Dmitry said. "They began to dismantle the whole Soviet ideology."[7] The rest of course is history.

But then the new Russia failed rather spectacularly to transform itself into a society that valued the human rights typical of western nations. Harsh methods of managing government, social values, and human rights – coarse old ideas – have a staying power that can outlive an overthrown autocratic regime, when the names and faces of the government have changed and even when new constitutions have been framed. Young people should learn this too, but that is another story and I am straying too far from my intended script.

Though we had survived the war safe in England, the need to travel stayed with us, the rationale yet again that "Nigel needs to live in a healthier place." That place, now, would be the United States. Again I was reluctant to move. I was happy in Keynsham. America would be all concrete and cars and the Yanks were a noisy, swanky, boastful lot who would laugh at my short pants and the way I talked.

I was quite wrong to think that America would prove anything less than a happy experience. We were all wrong. My mother and father, who had married in Canada but still harboured some misgiving for this giant leap back to North America, tried to keep their doubts from each other. They were leaving friends and close relatives behind, and everything we had was packed in a few suitcases. We had to go. My parents felt they had little choice.

At first the idea was to forge a new home in Gainesville, Florida, where Great-Aunt Alice had settled with her American husband James Cullen, who owned a carpet-cleaning establishment. I think she once worked for him; at any rate, she always called him "Mr. Cullen." She was the only person of that generation that I feel I really knew; sadly she proved to be an alcoholic and ended up in a sanatorium.

With identification tags hanging from our necks like luggage labels, we took off from Heathrow in an American Overseas Airlines Lockheed Constellation, powered by four piston engines and described aptly in Wikipedia as "distinguished by a distinctive triple-tail design and graceful, dolphin-shaped fuselage." We topped up the fuel tanks at Shannon, Ireland, where I tasted my first white bread and was not overly impressed. I played board games on the floor with other kids most of the way to Goose Bay Air Force Base, Labrador. This was an exciting stop for a boy because flight suits hung in display cases so realistically you wondered if someone had been accidentally left inside.

We arrived at LaGuardia airport on December 12, 1947 and took a taxi to Manhattan via the Triboro Bridge, which was the most impressive piece of iron architecture I had ever seen in my short life. In other words I was well and truly gobsmacked and thought I might like America after all. At Pennsylvania Station we caught a southbound train (my first non-steamer) with pull-down beds and curtains and a plump porter to make sure we were comfortable and our curtains were drawn for the night. Our porter was the second black person I had seen close up, and I imagined that perhaps he was related to Louis Armstrong. But no matter, we were bound for Gainesville, the sleek Diesel locomotive blaring its Klaxon horn, the porter murmuring an approving "u-*hum!*" when I lit up my Potter's Asthma Cure cigarettes.

The next morning we sped through wild and jungly country, sounding the mighty Klaxon at every crossing. The Okefenokee Swamp! The very name was enough to send a happy thrill down my spine. Then we were in Florida and we were reminded that, though I thought it was warm enough for me, it was a cold start to the winter for Floridians. People at the railway stations were huddled around giant pot-bellied stoves, and there was a great concern for the orange crop and the need for smudge-pots, which I learned were huge oil lamps, designed to produce voluminous amounts of smog, to keep frost from the delicate trees.

Finally we were in Gainesville. To my amazement the big train slid down the tracks and lurched to a stop in the middle of town. This struck me as a vaguely rude thing to do. They'd never do such a thing in England, where they had real stations and real platforms! Since there was no platform, the porter brought a midget stairway to help us down to the road. He gave me a huge toothy grin as he helped me down, but I don't think he would really like my Potter's Asthma Cure.

My father soon found an office job at the University of Florida, as a key-punch specialist at the eve of the computer age, and for fun played the lead in a local production of J. B. Priestley's new play *An Inspector Calls*. And my mother bought me my first pair of long trousers.

Florida proved intriguing, with its plantations of mysterious tung oil trees, slash-pine forests, fields of wild Spanish bayonet, amazingly beautiful butterflies with oval wings, roads deep with pale powdery sand, forests and waterways flashing with tropical fish, and a society in which Cypress Avenue separated the white and African-American communities. To my astonishment, blacks drank from different water fountains from whites, used different public toilets, and sat at the back of the bus. Down from the carpet-cleaning factory there was an evangelical Negro church, and to hear their music wafting down the street to our house was a marvellous and beautiful thing. The racial situation was extremely strange to me. And I suppose I was strange to everyone else, with my funny accent, wearing short woollen pants for my first week of subtropical heat.

We moved into a clapboard house on Penn Street, in a subdivision served by a network of deep and dusty sand roads. There I became acquainted with new concepts of family living – a breezeway walled with unfamiliar mosquito screening, and an icebox that accommodated a huge block of ice that had to be brought from the icehouse next to the Coca-Cola plant. We never needed to artificially cool our food in the North of England; we used a meat safe on the back step, windowed with metal netting rather like the stuff on our Florida breezeway. In Florida they even drank a beverage that was at least as exotic as dandelion and burdock. It was something I had never heard of before, iced tea!

No more did I have recourse to Alvar Liddell, Tommy Handley (ITMA, "It's That Man Again"), and "Dick Barton, Special Agent" on the radio. Instead, I had Edward R. Murrow, "Amos 'n' Andy," Judy Canova the Ozark Nightingale, and the Grand Ole Opry. I liked them too, but missed ITMA and successors that incorporated a peculiar brand of British humour that never made it to the States.

I made two good friends in Gainesville – Rebel Bellamy, a noted biologist's son, and Norbert Morales, who was special because he had a Red Ryder BB gun, named for the 1940s cowboy star, and distinguished himself by shooting me in the back with it, fortunately from some distance. After that I sold enough packaged seeds and first-aid ointment that I could win a Red Ryder for myself.

Rebel's prize possession was a Radio Flyer, a four-wheeled pull-wagon that was to me an exotic and marvellous invention, especially with its bright red paint and its swept-back logo lettering. So one day I asked if I could join him and a couple of friends to help with its speed trials. "Sure," he said. "So what shall I do?" I asked. "You can be the moda," he replied.

Moda? What on earth could he mean? I could be the mother? Surely not. This was the first time in America that I had trouble speaking the language. Rebel wanted me to be the *motor* – I was expected to push the thing. You see, in my world Ts didn't sound like Ds when they came in the middle of a word, though we too ignored Rs when they came at the end of a word. I'm pleased to say that soon we unearthed a large gopher tortoise that was fully able to pull the Radio Flyer without complaint.

When I entered Gainesville Junior High School in January 1948, my name proved unfamiliar and I was called either Frenchie, because I knew some French, or by my middle name, Stewart. I undertook the first of numerous future amateur theatrical roles by taking the part of a carrot, I think, in a sort of morality play about nutrition. And my parents were delighted when they were visited by a school representative who gushed over the results of my "IQ" test. This small victory probably was mostly due to my vocabulary, but it helped me overcome the internal humiliation of my abysmal test performances in England. Maybe America would be all right after all.

In retrospect, Gainesville was a continuous series of adventures that, together, represented my introduction to the United States. You may disagree, but let me give you my opinion about the truth of adventure. If not overly hurtful, it is something exciting or intriguing that you do, or which happens to you, for the very first time. It is a wondrous happening that can raise the hairs on the back of

Gone West 1948. Our 1938 Buick straight-eight, shown in the background, got us
safely to Utah and Pleasant Grove. The photo was taken at Aspen Grove, a popular
picnic ground in the nearby mountains.

your head, or simply cause you to realize what's happening in such a way that
you quietly say "wow" to yourself, shake your head, and wonder why you have
been so fortunate as to witness it or, better, be in on the act. When the same
thing happens a second time this may be exciting too, but never quite so
exciting. The sharpness and poignancy will be muted, and may be totally unfelt.

If today I told the adventure of my first airplane flight to a crowd of people
at a dinner party, it would likely fall rather flat because so many have had exactly
the same experience or (heavens!) even more magnificent ones to relate. So
please don't groan when I admit that I once said "Wow! I remember my first
banana!" I was 11 years old at the time and the only bananas I had seen
previously were dried – brown, sticky tiles that were not remotely appetizing.

But the first *real* banana truly was an adventure. This magnificent, seductively curved fruit with its cool, smooth yellow skin was one of my first American delights. The banana had been hard and green a few days earlier, but now it yielded to a tentative finger prod, and when you summoned the cruelty to disrupt that first gift of beauty you would break its dark neck and like a nascent lover pull down the soft coverings until its naked sweetness was revealed and ready, draped in a skirt of delicate white ribbons that brushed the hand like a rain of flower petals. The smell — like no other, but promising sweetness, alluring, by some magical vegetal pheromone that invaded my senses like the exotic perfume that it was — made its secret way through forests of cilia, labyrinths of neural networks, to the place in my brain that says *yes* to desire. Though it took no act of daring, this to me was genuine adventure. I was hooked on bananas.

My health did not improve in Florida, possibly because of an allergy to mildew spores, and so the late summer of 1949 found us driving west in a massive straight-eight 1938 Buick, towing our belongings first in a one-wheel trailer, which soon collapsed, and then by its replacement, a two-wheeler built like a tank. We now were moving to Utah at the invitation of Mormon relatives, via Tallahassee, Mobile, Baton Rouge, Amarillo, Albuquerque, and Flagstaff. Finally we reached our relatives' residence in Springville, a farming community proud of its dedication to "education, religious faith, patriotism, and volunteer service."

We were deep in Mormon country, close to Utah Lake, which was connected to the Great Salt Lake, the remains of an ancient sea, by what was soon named the Jordan River by Mormon pioneers. It was not long before I learned that the local citizenry considered us to be "gentiles." We were living in a culture as strange to me and as oddly fascinating as the openly colour-segregated American South.

While all high-school boys expected that, in this day of military conscription, they would have to spend at least two years in the armed services, Mormon boys spent an extra two years as missionaries, spreading the Mormon Word far and wide, dressed always in suits and ties whether in the cities or the desert heat of Indian reservations. Girls were expected most of all to become mothers, bringing purgatorial souls into a world where they could be prepared for everlasting life in the Celestial Kingdom. We miserable gentiles, if we were good but not good enough, won the Terrestrial Kingdom; those who were bad but not too bad went to the less desirable Telestial Kingdom. Neither of these venues involves hellfire and torment. But truly bad people, sons of Perdition, were "doomed to suffer the wrath of God, with the devil and his angels in eternity."[8] I was intrigued to hear that the Mormon Latter-Day Saints (LDS) elders taught that, according to the *Pearl of Great Price*, God lives in a solar system called Kolob,[9] yet to be found. The *Pearl of Great Price*, revised periodically, is a collection of documents originally put together by the church founder, Joseph Smith, who said he translated its *Book of Abraham* from papyrus scrolls.

All of this was wild and wonderful to my newly adolescent mind, as were the extra front doors featured in some of the houses built in the days of officially sanctioned polygamy. Supposedly polygamy was long gone, traded for the glory of statehood, but about 40,000 fundamentalist, polygamous Mormons were still populating a few isolated western towns at the dawn of the 21st century, disowned by their orthodox brethren.

Many years later, on a Sunday morning, there came a knock on the door. I opened it and there were two attractive young women, one Anglo, one African-American. They introduced themselves as Mormon missionaries. How times had changed! And Mormonism was on the march. The church began to advertise its Christianity widely; in 2011 two of the three Republican frontrunners for the presidential primary election were LDS stalwarts; the Internet was well-stocked with LDS information as well as Mormon genealogical and dating services.

My dad first took a job moving pianos in Provo; then he and my mother again decided to become bakers, this time in the town of Orem, where I attended Lincoln Junior High School for a couple of years. During the day, when she was not baking, my mother managed the household and gave piano lessons. They worked unbelievably, backbreakingly hard, but the bakery failed for the simple reason that its owners were not Mormons. My dad's donuts quickly became famous enough that a big company wanted to buy the recipe, but we were still not welcome. The *coup de grace* was delivered after local church leaders made a huge order for an upcoming banquet. My parents worked like slaves on this project, alone, from before dawn until night. Then the church elders coolly cancelled the order and my parents conceded defeat.

My dad believed that part of his job was to be the optimist of the family. "America is the land of opportunity," he would pronounce during our early immigrant years. "It's the land of milk and honey." In his eyes I could see hope mixed with a faint trace of scepticism, and sometimes with irony. But the hope was always there, and it would be rewarded. Already my wheezing bouts were beginning to subside.

By the time I graduated from high school we had all become U.S. citizens, having studied basic American history and the Constitution and answered the right questions before a judge in Provo. Filling in the forms imposed a brief puzzlement on the courthouse staff. My father's full name was Aaron Hey. American bureaucracy seemed baffled by the fact that he had just the two names. Thus to the government my dad was Aaron NMN Hey, the NMN standing for "No Middle Name." My mother used this opportunity to take her maiden name, Kershaw, as an official middle name. I was home free. Unlike my parents and, as far as I can tell, *all* my ancestors, I already had one.

After closing the bakery, Dad went to work at the nearby steel plant and we had a new home in Pleasant Grove (PeeGee for short), another small all-Mormon town with a big high school. It lay on the western flank of majestic Mount Timpanogos and had a movie house, post office, mandatory state-run liquor store, and a library that was then housed in the old town jail. This was a small cube-shaped structure built with blocks of unusual bubbly soft-rock limestone, the same ancient hot-spring tufa that was used to build our barn. (Things have changed. PeeGee now has a magnificent library and arts center.)

Ours was a gingerbread house built on several acres, much of which was devoted to a big apple orchard, an old barn, and a set of large and sturdy chicken coops. My mother and dad transformed a patch of open land at the back of the house into an English-style garden, making the desert bloom, as they say, like a rose. A picket fence ran across the front, and four huge evergreen trees darkened the area between the fence and the house. The original house was a small adobe room, but successive owners had added walls of soft rock and clapboard over a large cellar. It came with a wood-burning stove and, on the front porch, an icebox. It was not long before my father bought a second-hand coal-fired furnace. He installed the whole thing himself, singlehanded, including forced-air ductwork, propping up the floor and sawing a large opening in it to lower the cast-iron furnace into the cellar.

When winter came and we needed a warm house, Dad raised a door-sized trapdoor, descended a flight of rough wooden stairs, and shovelled coal into the maw of the furnace, diligently, for re-lighting the thing was a difficult job that wrenched one's nerves to the breaking point. Finally he bought a self-stoking device with a big hopper and a screw conveyor, another marvel to be assembled by a veteran of days when people had not the luxury to call in specialist workmen.

This, our first American home, and a large adjacent acreage, are now occupied by a modern subdivision.

My favourite memory of my mother is a glimpse of her and my father in the beautiful garden behind the Pleasant Grove house. Utah was such a dry place that I was sceptical that an "English" garden could ever survive. But survive it did, and it was gorgeous, with wonderful flowers and a bright green, weed-less lawn. In that garden was epitomized the great vision, determination, and strength of character that my mother possessed. (Another, selfish, fond memory was sitting with her when I was young and sick, as she illustrated my first story with superb original drawings.)

My mother told me that I could be anything that I set my mind to, and I believed her. That spark of self-confidence and self-belief stayed with me throughout my life, and served me well. Like my father, she was good at many things – certainly she was a patient and wise parent – but she truly excelled in things artistic. It is wonderful that she was able to derive great pleasure from the piano and the paintbrush until late in life, and a shame that she was too self-effacing to take these talents further, and they did not achieve the recognition that they deserved. When I was a child she encouraged me to write, write, write, a skill I could practice even if I were not in good physical health. The greatest lesson I learned from my mother: Believe in yourself!

My favourite memory of my father is watching him conducting the choir at the Community Presbyterian Church a few miles north of our house, in American Fork, Utah, while my mother patiently played the piano. This was something in which he took a particular delight, and pleasure such as this was particularly precious. Besides, he was a fine singer, and I loved to see him stand up and sing "The Lord is My Light," Malotte's "Lord's Prayer," and other great old church solos.

I was stumped when someone asked me "where we worshipped." At home, I supposed, or on trips to the woodlands and mountains; the closest we had to a family church was Wesleyan Methodist, in the old pre-war days. In Pleasant Grove, the best formal answer I could give was the American Fork Community Presbyterian church. Someone else asked when I had my first Communion and I said never. Same with baptism. I remembered seeing a child being immersed in a transparent glass tank of water behind the altar of a church, and prayers being said, but I don't remember the specifics. I was just glad I wasn't him. Still I think of our family as being a spiritual one – we just didn't *talk* about religious things;

it was as though they were too special to be talked about, and better left to the quietness of personal meditation.

Perhaps I was destined to have a ragged relationship with churchgoing. I always fidgeted through the services, and distrusted religion because for all its piety it had caused a great deal of suffering in the world. Yet religion alone defined evil. These days it is sometimes difficult to determine which events deserve the term, and anyway it seems an indelible part of human nature. Good and evil were given to us in the indefinable Adam-and-Eve age when apes began to think of past and future events and to devise (or remember) scenarios for them. Wasn't evil a natural, God-given part of our species?

Through religion we have clues to that mystery. We are taught that evil is bad nevertheless and that our challenge is to keep it at bay. Inside my agnostic self I regret the decline of the churches. Religion is useful; Sunday schools are useful. With their decline it has fallen almost wholly to harried parents and teachers to explain what is acceptable and what is not. But unlike the churches these interpreters have no agreed-upon texts to guide them. In a parallel universe perhaps philosophy could help. The brains are there, but few dogma-free explainers have the luxuries of pulpit and congregation for the exploration of right and wrong. We are left with the ministrations of motivated, liberal clerics to their shrinking congregations.

Such things were not discussed in my life at home. On winter evenings I enjoyed playing cards or board games with my mother and dad and friends. We listened to the radio, which had good plays and variety shows (having converted from Tommy Handley in England to Judy Canova in the States). We did not get a television set until I was in high school, which meant we had more time outside together, to explore things that would help satisfy my unflagging curiosity. Now and then my dad and I would go fishing at the Deer Creek reservoir at the top of Provo Canyon, though these were rather fruitless excursions to a lifeless desert shoreline perfumed by the sweet putrescent scent of discarded fish. We caught a few pathetic perch and that was about it.

The most fun was taking the "irrigation turn." I knew nothing about irrigation when we first came to Utah – none of us did – but the house came with "water rights," which is to say that we had access to a communal source of water for our garden and crops. Our turn could come any time of the day or month, but when we were notified we were ready for action. Even if it was two o'clock in the morning, my dad and I would be out there with rubber boots, shovels and flashlights, opening and closing the sluices, redirecting the little subsidiary water channels, now and then stanching a runaway flow of water with a clod of muddy sod.

Less fun was helping to care for the flock of Leghorn chickens, which would turn cannibal if one of their number were injured or prolapsed, no matter how well fed they were with scratch and milk solids. There were usually several hundred chickens in the coop, and sometimes I would help with candling the eggs before we put them in cases and hauled them off to the co-op in American Fork. I raised a hundred "broiler" chicks as a high school project, and learned rather unwillingly, while holding a chicken by the legs with one hand, to perform the deathly deed of an axe murderer.

Life in Utah was difficult and trying at first, but my dad's remarkable character enabled him to climb out of it and be an "American success story." For me at that time, his best story about his own boyhood was the time his parents gave him a crystal radio set, and with this, poking around on the tiny chunk of germanium with a fragile wire that he called a cat's whisker, he heard some of the early broadcast radio programs.

When I say my father was a genuinely good man, I mean he was possessed of great kindness, with wisdom and spirituality that he practiced at all times. He was a man of his word, of great character, and he lived up to his high principles. As a spare-time activity he was especially good at carpentry and joinery. In fact he was good at a great many things – parenting, baking, gardening, bookkeeping, even keeping chickens – but his care and patience was manifest in the love that he expressed while working with wood. He let me help by holding his workpieces steady while he sawed them, or perhaps sanding or rubbing the wood before it was varnished. Sadly, joinery was an art that I never mastered.

Dad's move to US Steel's Geneva Works was extremely fortuitous. In this more sophisticated environment his industriousness, dedication to work, and quiet braininess were recognized and appreciated. At home, after dinner, he would sometimes take a can of Prince Albert tobacco and a ledger from the living-room cupboard, then fill his pipe and, with an enjoyment that I did not then understand, go to work on the family accounts in the wondrously meticulous copperplate writing that he must have learned when a young accountant in the Yorkshire woollen mills. Over the age of 40 now, and without even an eighth grade education, he would become a full-fledged industrial engineer for what was then one of the nation's industrial giants. Mild-mannered, kind and scrupulously honest, with the solid encouragement of my indomitable, unstoppable mother, he managed to achieve a minor miracle. True our bakery failed. But nevertheless Dad quickly worked his way up to the position of industrial engineer – an efficiency expert. My mother and I were intensely proud of him, and remained so. His success, born of hard work and dedication, would allow him to retire at the age of 60 after he soldiered his way toward the American Dream.

In the summer of 1955 I worked as a "test provider" at the steel works, measuring the thickness of coil steel for exactly one week and for that short time was a member of the United Steelworkers of America. An x-ray taken as part of my physical exam supposedly showed one of my vertebrae was a fraction of a millimetre out of line with the others, and this meant I was out of a job. I had no back pain then, and never had any in the future, even after soaring through the air on a toboggan and crashing on a sheet of ice; even after an accident that transformed my borrowed motorcycle into a metallic omelette.

One day in 1952 I heard a news report that another nuclear test was to be held in the South Pacific – Britain's first – and this set me to thinking of the enormity of this unnatural explosion, and the general lack of knowledge about such explosions and their effects upon people and the natural scheme of things. I wondered if the nothingness that I had earlier associated with my own death could be visited upon everyone, even to all life. My young mind reeled to think of what might result from the use by humans, such fallible creatures, of forces so great and poorly understood.

Why on earth did they have to take this risk? The world was somehow *wrong*, I thought. Somebody ought to fix it.

Ironically, with time, fate would take me into the midst of America's nuclear weapon design and production enterprise, though I would never lose my inner uneasiness about this most perilous of human inventions.

5. PRINTER'S DEVIL

*That learning which thou gettest by thy own observation and experience, is far
beyond that which thou gettest by precept; as the knowledge of a traveler
exceeds that which is got by reading.*
— Thomas à Kempis

I t must have been the summer of 1952 that Abe Gibson walked through the
mat of fallen pine needles to our side door and found my mother cooking at
the wood stove. He came straight to the point: Did she think Nigel would
like to have a part-time job in his printing shop?

I was listening from a short distance away and my heart must have skipped a
beat. This wasn't just a printing shop, I thought. It was a bona fide publishing
house, producer of the *Pleasant Grove Review.*

We didn't know Abe Gibson, so this was a wonderful surprise. Perhaps Guy
Hillman, who supervised school publications, had told him about me. My
mother was delighted with the idea too, and it turned out to be a red-letter day
for all of us. Until that day I mowed lawns, helped pick fruit, and trimmed
vegetables at the local packing plant, all the usual twenty-five-cents-an-hour
teenager jobs. Now I would be a newspaperman!

Abe was a small-town printer of the old school. "No relation to Hoot
Gibson," he said merrily when we met, not realizing that I wouldn't know the
name of the old-time Western movie actor. Remember when his movie "The
Utah Kid" came out in 1944? I didn't know that, either.

Abe was a gruff old Westerner who spent his work days wearing the printer's
regulation green eyeshade and an ink-stained apron cinched around his waist
with twine. His establishment produced an assortment of products that ranged
from the weekly *Review* to hand-set wedding invitations to invoices for the local
cannery. The last-named was quite a production. First Abe printed six numbered
copies of the invoices, so that he ended up with six stacks of them, each in a
different colour but with the same numbers. It became part of my job to put
together the invoices in new sets of six different-coloured pages each. You may

say this was a humble task, but all the same it tested my brain and fingers mightily, not to mention my patience. Why? First, the pages were very thin so that the carbon-paper image would register all the way through; second, each page in the set had to bear the same number; third, each colour in the set had to be in the correct sequence – white, then pink, then yellow, and so on. It was a horrendously frustrating job, especially when a couple of flimsy pages stuck together and a wrong-numbered page sneaked into the succeeding sets. When I finally jogged those uncooperative onionskin pages into a neat block – an ordeal in itself because the paper was so thin – and brushed on the strange-smelling pink emulsion that would dry and glue them all neatly together into a tear-off pad, I had the feeling that I had accomplished something significant. I'm sure no one at the cannery had that impression, but it had been noteworthy to *me*. It was also a great discipline for my young brain, and for that I appreciated it.

Abe hired me as printer's devil just a couple of weeks before my fifteenth birthday. No other job could have suited me better in the entire State of Utah, yet today that printer's shop would be a museum piece. It was a dark old building, going on a hundred years old. It smelled of printers' ink, and had a rickety reception desk at the front, a giant hand-fed press and foundry at the back, a large and scary modern guillotine for cutting thicknesses of paper at the front, and a number of "stones," heavy metal-topped worktables sitting on an ancient planking floor that glittered with particles of printer's metal. We had an old Linotype that kept breaking down, three presses including the 60-year-old flatbed, and scores of cases of type for hand-setting invitations and advertisements.

I was absolutely fascinated by Abe's printing skill. He would mount the little wooden platform beside the big newspaper press and slide the big, thin broadsheets one by one into the broad teeth of a row of metal grippers. These held each sheet in place over the paper-padded cylinder as the form, inked with each pass, rumbled underneath, pressing its images into the paper. The huge, heavy press was like a noisy, dangerous beast, and once Abe turned on the ancient heavy-duty switch it rumbled into life with masterful power, obedient only to his left hand on the lever that stuck up from beside his little platform. Every once in a while he would stop to run a scraper along the ink distributor to even out the sticky stuff so we'd get an even image, or open up a new can, but mostly he was feeding the pages, two hands slipping large, flimsy, unwieldy rectangles of paper into those grippers just right, so that the paper would never end up with an off-center image or, God forbid, get stuck in the works.

Linotype Machine. This marvel of the mid-1800s was at the center of all the magic I found at Abe's print shop. It could produce two-inch lines of type as a solid metal unit. Photo: Grey Roots Museum & Archives

After Abe had done a full run printing those two pages we'd put a new form on the bed, lock it into place, and print the *other* side of the sheets. That was our weekly ritual, along with collating the pages into the complete newspapers, then bundling them so that they could be thrown on our subscribers' lawns the next day. Thank God we had such a small circulation. But the press – the press was the mechanical patriarch of that little shop, and its servant was the old, clanking, intriguingly engineered Linotype. Abe was neither young nor handsome nor particularly agile, but when he sat at that machine he became an artist, and – here I am not exaggerating – his fingers would glide over the keyboard with the grace of a concert pianist.

I was never invited to run the big press and secretly was relieved not to be involved in its operation, and it was unthinkable that I would ever be trusted to sit at the console of the Linotype. My greatest challenge was a small, early version of the Chandler & Price platen press, built in the first years of the 20th century. This was a frightening contrivance too, despite it small size. A small chase with its load of delicate, slanted type for a hand-set wedding invitation would be locked onto a vertical bed just above and behind a set of soft rubber ink rollers. I'd paste some black ink onto the circular "palette" that faced me, make sure I had a supply of the right kind of paper on the little shelf at my waist, and, perspiring slightly, hope for the best.

My job was to place the sheets of paper or card onto a padded rectangular platen that would lean forward and come into contact with the type, then return so that I could remove the printed item, place it on my little shelf, and start again. The problem was that all these components – rollers, ink disc, chase and platen – were moving at the same time, at different speeds and directions. In the tiny interval of time available each cycle restarted, I had to remove the printed card and place a blank one in its place. There was a sort of clutch/brake next to the big flywheel at my left hand to start and stop this 1200-pound monster, but it did not ease the fear that somehow my coordination would fail and my right hand would get mangled in the machine.

On less taxing days I would read copy (for example replacing the word "sumptuous" that was used with such delight by our society correspondent), proof-read, or write local articles. But once a week I would load the rusty foundry with silvery scraps of lead-tin-antimony alloy, light the gas, and melt the metal down. Acting on Abe's instructions, I would jab a stick of rolled-up newsprint into the melt, and when the paper scorched, the metal was ready to pour. Some of it I decanted into moulds with a long-handled ladle, producing raised "type-high" mirror-image casts of advertisements for the local movie house, for grocery stores, or for liquor distributors. After the casts were sawed and routed to the correct shape, they were taken to the worktable and positioned among the thousands of Linotype slugs that made up the rest of the newspaper. The rest of the melt I poured into moulds that converted them into long ingots called "pigs" that had loop handles to hold them from chains as they slowly collapsed into the mouth of the Linotype's ever-hungry crucible.

While the big press awed me, the Linotype absolutely fascinated me with its intricate design. Before 1886 every page of every book was set by hand – that is, each letter, space, and punctuation mark was plucked from a box (called a job case) of metal letters, each about an inch high with the letter in mirror-image relief as in a rubber stamp, placed individually in a tray-like hand-held "stick," then locked into a frame that would be put in a press for the printing operation. Hans Morgenthaler, a German-born American inventor, changed all this when he invented his amazing mechanical monster the Linotype.

This machine manufactured entire lines of type mechanically, after assembling individual letter moulds (keys) into rows of words. Each of Abe's keyboard strokes would liberate a brass key from a big magazine, forming words, then separating them to create a justified line, then casting them into solid lines of type. After each line was cast, an elevator arm would grab the row of keys and take it to the top of the magazine, from whence its parts would be dropped magically back among its companion *a*s, *b*s, and *c*s, ready for re-use.

We would make up eight or twelve full-sized pages for the local newspaper each week, locked two together for printing side-by-side. It took the two of us, straining and praying that none of the pieces of type would fall out, to carry the form to the press. After locking it in place, Abe would turn on the bulky, dust-rimed electric motor, step up to his little platform as though he were about to drive it away like a steam train, release the clutch, and feed in the big sheets one by one until 800 were printed. We repeated the process for each pair of pages until the run was completed. Then his wife Geneva and their children, and sometimes their children, would arrive and we would all join in, collating, folding and bundling the newspapers for delivery the next morning. Alas, the *Review* is now merely a demographic edition of the Provo *Daily Herald*. It ceased publication as an independent newspaper in about 1997; all that remains is the microfilm record stored at Brigham Young University.

Looking back on it, this tale sounds like something from the Victorian era. Not many years later I joined United Press International, where I could convert news articles into punched paper tape like that used for the Telex messages of the time. When fed into a specially equipped Linotype, the tape made the machine work at dizzying speed all by itself, as if controlled by an invisible operator like a player piano. Alas, there was soon no more need for Abe's wondrous talent. It was not long before the technology of "cold type" or phototypesetting was producing computer-generated images that would be transformed into curved plates, instead of the old flat forms, for high-speed offset printing. With time I would be lucky enough to be an early participant as these new ideas came to reality.

In later life I would think of the Pleasant Grove and Orem years as times of difficulty. Yet Abe Gibson, a gruff old guy with a heart of gold, and a good Mormon to boot, gave me my start. He and his friend Neff Smart, who owned the Orem print shop and newspaper, helped me believe firmly in my talent for words and journalism, and made a real newspaperman out of me.

My days on the *Review* coincided with the rise of an electronic revolution that would transform the world of media and threaten to drive newspapers out of existence. We were approaching a new cascade in the never-ending battle between reality and humanity's special gift, the virtual world. Though for all I know this may have started with the cave painters in Lascaux, the greatest, most giddying force was yet to come – the Internet. But first came television.

In the early days TV was a wonderful novelty, with outstanding talent imported by the giant networks from their radio days. It bred a new generation of personalities and exciting new formats. But when the great networks lost their punch, and as cable and satellite channels proliferated, audience ratings became even more important, and it seemed the quality of TV commentary and entertainment fell as a result. By the end of the old century I would lose interest in all but a few of the thousands of programs that were available each week. In England I mostly listened or watched the music and commentary stations available through the BBC. In the States my news and commentary appetite shifted toward the Public Broadcasting System (PBS) because I was bored by the limitations and bias of other networks.

I can't let that statement go without mentioning the beneficial side of radio and TV. Certain information, and here I think of in-depth reportage of history, archaeology, anthropology, politics, art, and human ecology – in particular those subjects sometimes lumped together as belonging to "the humanities" – reveal much about global human nature while moderating general perceptions of civilization and the planet. Often before it has chance to reach our classrooms it is eased into our minds by way of television and radio, particularly by public-funded broadcasters such as the BBC and America's PBS and National Public Radio (NPR). Increased public knowledge of humanities and science has to be a good thing, for along with more direct right-now news messages it reminds us of the shared qualities and in most cases the shared interests of humanity.

My worldview had begun to change during those years at the *Pleasant Grove Review*. I had real work now, and real responsibilities. And I was beginning to think beyond myself. Maybe it started when I first heard the murmur of my neck veins; maybe with my apprehension at Britain's imminent test of its first atomic bomb in 1952. Or the impression, early on in my life, that death was always a heartbeat away. I think these thoughts and experiences were important early contributors to the idealism that flowered in my university years and the decade that followed.

I attended Pleasant Grove High School from 1950 to 1954, the year I began filling out income tax forms. I worked on the school yearbook that year under Mr. Hillman (Miss Fenton taught English, Mr. Johnson science, and Mr. Miner typing), so it was not surprising that we embryonic journalists were interested in the clamour caused by Joe McCarthy's House Un-American Activities Committee, far away in Washington. As a result of McCarthy's zeal, many, many people were brought before the Senate on flimsy evidence and pilloried with the allegation – or suggestion – that they were communists or socialists. The hint that they might be contacted by McCarthy's minions was enough to cause them to lose their jobs, even their careers. We teenagers, at least most of us, thought the whole affair was a sad and bad thing, and we wanted it to go away. Fortunately, with help from the Fourth Estate, it was on its way out. But the bad taste stuck with me, and in 2001, when President George W. Bush signed into law the "Uniting and Strengthening America by Providing Appropriate Tools Required to Intercept and Obstruct Terrorism Act of 2001," the "Patriot Act," I feared that history might be about to repeat itself, more insidiously perhaps, now that the government had access to all manner of new technology for domestic espionage.

My teenaged years, stunted socially by the outsider status of being a non-Mormon, saw an increase in my writing interests, which were destined with time to broaden into many aspects of mass communication. They had developed quickly after early successes with Walt Disney Comics and BBC in England. Thanks to an introduction from Abe Gibson, Neff Smart (later a University of Utah lecturer) took an interest in me, so that I was earning pin money writing children's columns for three Utah weekly newspapers, the *Orem-Geneva Times, Pleasant Grove Review*, and *American Fork Citizen*. My short story "Cave of Fantasy" came out in the March 1953 issue of the high-school-level magazine *Literary Cavalcade*, published by Scholastic Publishing Company of Pittsburgh. I wrote for the Provo *Daily Herald* as sports stringer for a while in 1954.

Though my social life was a disaster, I had grown in my mid-teens into a young man who – though I may be mistaken – looked like a reasonably acceptable Anglo-Saxon male. My drivers' license said I was 5 feet 10 inches tall, weighed 155 pounds, had light brown hair, and was possessed of blue eyes, though I never was quite sure whether it would be more correct to call them blue or grey. No distinguishing marks. Quite ordinary, really. When I looked in the mirror I saw a moderately good-looking chap, albeit with rather small eyes the appearance of which benefited, I thought, from the use of eye-glasses. But when I opened my mouth to speak it became obvious that I came from Some Other Place, and word quickly got around that, unlike so many other blue-eyed European immigrants to Utah, I was not a convert to the Church of Latter-Day Saints.

The rules soon became clear. I could lust after but never date my female classmates; the only schoolmate who showed any interest in me was a local farmer's homosexual son, whose tentative advances I discouraged without causing ill feeling. There was some overt harassment from the boys; my applications to become a Boy Scout were ignored even though I was allowed to attend the Tuesday night Mutual Improvement Association meetings that combined religious services and scout (and "Seagull Girls") meetings. In the Pleasant Grove of the early 1950s, it was assumed that proper social life would be composed of Mormon-organized events and little else. Still, I was selected to attend the American Legion Utah Boy's State in 1953, won essay competitions, sang in the senior-class musical, graduated as eighth-best student in the senior class, and was elected (don't laugh) the boy with the best complexion. But I never made it into high school society.

There were of course plenty of girls at Pleasant Grove High School. While the boys strutted their stuff in tight jeans, the girls paraded their young cleavages, affecting modest pride. The hormone level spread through the school like a fine mist, and one couple surprised the rest of the student-body by getting married in the middle of our senior year. I suffered from no lack of hormones, but there was that ideological wall between us, so you might even say that at times I *suffered* from the presence of hormones. Once, when I tried to breach the invisible wall, I was rewarded undeservedly with a pair of deep scratches to my left arm, and a visual clip of this uninvited event stayed in my memory for decades. True, in my high school years I did manage a couple of chaste dates with a Protestant girl from the next town. But otherwise I was left to my own devices, including but not restricted to ruminations on why the then-current fashion in breast management had produced brassieres that raised young bosoms to their most protruding, cleavage-enhancing, cone-like shapes. Thank goodness that fashion disappeared with bobby socks.

Playing the pariah role naturally made life difficult. I remember being cornered by three or four boys in the gym. "You know what," one of them said, "you're an asshole. Do you know what an asshole is?" I knew what they meant, and I knew that it made no sense. I also knew that I had to respond. "Of course,"

I said. "It's a hole that an ass goes through. Probably someplace he sleeps." This surprised them. They laughed uncertainly and jostled me, but then they backed off, sniggering to themselves.

Another time I was provoked by a boy outside Smith's grocery store. He said insulting things and spat a couple of cherry pits into my face. This time I lost my reserve. I punched him a couple of times to cool him down. This worked, but it also started an asthmatic attack and I staggered home wheezing while he nursed his bruises. A third fight was more private, with a boy I thought was a friend, in the orchard behind our house. The boy began with a teasing session, then started pushing and punching until I didn't like it any more. Some inner voice told me what to do. I grabbed his arm, bent down, and then to my surprise he was flying over me, landing with a thump on his back. This had been an unplanned gift from the gods, and I never figured out quite how it happened. The kids were nicer to me after that. I guess they heard about the judo inspiration.

Now and then the high school kids gave me unpleasant nicknames. The most bizarre was "dog-breath," given me by a girl who could hear my asthmatic breathing behind her in Miss Fenton's English class. Another was "Nicotine," which resulted, I think, from my admission that yes, I had once tried a taste of wine. Neither nickname stuck, and I privately thought they were rather strange, even comical. Imagine, these Mormons thought wine contained nicotine!

I kept up my spirits without much effort, and took a Board of Education test to see what kind of career I should set in my sights. The result: key-punch operator, by some odd chance part of my dad's first American job, at the University of Florida. Later, when key-punch operators were an extinct technological species, I could admit that this result ranked with my 11-plus test – which hinted strongly of an inability to cope with college life – as a low point in my academic life. At age sixteen, the main thing was that I knew I could prove them wrong. The IQ experts in Florida had the right idea, I told myself, and this test meant nothing. I simply typed a lot, and the test showed I had good manual dexterity.

Besides these there were adventures, and inventions that may never have seen the light of day if, instead of exploring my small world alone, I had been regularly involved in social activities. I am embarrassed to admit that my inventions included the idea of turning a small electrical generator with pressure from the gas main. When I was a young teenager, I found a 12-gauge shotgun shell someone had dropped probably while hunting pheasants. It fascinated me and I thought, "Wow, I could set this off!" I determined I would do just that. But I would, I thought, do it safely and just detonate the cap. I gingerly removed the shot and loose powder. Then I centered the "empty" shell on top of my upended Red Ryder BB gun and pulled the trigger. The result scared the daylights out of me, almost literally. There was a tremendous *BLAM*, the BB gun went flying, and I hit the ground as though I were on the front lines somewhere and not in the orchard behind my dad's chicken coops.

On some days I would go exploring with our dog Martha in the marshes, ponds, and drainage streams that characterized the eastern precincts of Utah Lake. While Martha went ratting I would fish with hook or line or simply with a spear consisting of a knife strapped to a stout pole. There were trout in the streams, and bluegill and a few trout in the ponds. The place was flat, mysterious, unpopulated and strangely dangerous. Once we came on a place where the turfy roof of an underground stream had caved in, complete with the corpse of a horse that had died of hunger after blundering into the watery trap. Another time we found a horse that was attached to a wire fence by its foot, blood spurting from a vein like wine from a skin, and me absolutely helpless to do anything about it.

One of the great adventures of my early life happened in the summer of 1953, when I was between my junior and senior high school years. I could hardly believe my ears when I heard we were going to visit England on vacation, on the great Cunard ships the original *Queen Mary* and *Queen Elizabeth.*

Those two transatlantic voyages were magical from the moment the *Queen Mary* eased away from the dock on Manhattan's west side and sailed majestically down the Hudson, the Statue of Liberty and Ellis Island gliding by on her starboard side. As we made our way into the Atlantic I learned the secret, unmarked doors that led to the first class deck, and explored this forbidden realm carefully, delighted with that special young person's delight that I could have discovered them without being discovered myself. Sometimes I would go to the bow at night and look down into the sea as the steel of the great ship cut into the water, and marvel at how the water hissed in the night, sending giant Vs of white foam into the ocean, and how tiny the great ship was in a sea so huge that it would take us five days to cross.

What else do I remember from this first ocean crossing? Being deeply touched at hearing the ship's pianist playing "Jesu, Joy of Man's Desiring" alone, one Sunday morning an hour or two before the religious service. Seeing Alfred Hitchcock coming down one of the first class stairways and nonchalantly waddling off down the deck. Listening to passengers betting on the number of miles we would make the next day. Finding the row of Sherlock Holmes books in the library. So many memories must have been recorded and cherished by so many people over the years in those two ships alone. Today the *Queen Mary* is a hotel, restaurant, and entertainment center in Long Beach. The remains of the burned and capsized *Queen Elizabeth* lie with mountains of other forgotten debris in Hong Kong harbour.

I learned early to be independent, confident, and motivated without curbing my curious instincts and without being self-destructively ambitious. These qualities I credit to my parents' encouragement and good example, to my childhood need to occupy myself while my parents busied themselves in the bakery, and later to the realities of living in a social environment where I was different from the others and not easily incorporated into social life. Though this may sound unlikely or ironic, it was partly for the same reasons that I began to care more about other people and the state and future of the world in general. Nobody really scared me. I considered most people outside my immediate family, who were special, as equals, and continued to do so throughout my life while practicing a certain circumspection (too often a quiet spectator at dinner parties) and choosing my trusted friends carefully. If someone tried to intimidate me, I generally ignored them or did what I needed to do by going around them. People who were less fortunate than I were considered equals, and people who were more successful than I were also equals. I could easily accept the fact that other individuals were smarter than me – in their own way – but also knew that I had strong points, too. At 17, when I interviewed the eminent physicist Edward Teller for the UPI news service, I had no qualms at all. Many years later, when I traveled with world-class physicists to tell Sandia National Laboratories' story to the media, I considered us to be colleagues even though I had earned only a lowly bachelor's degree in a patently non-scientific subject, journalism, at a little-known university. My self-belief must have been infectious, for my more intensely educated (and much better paid) colleagues seemed to believe it too, and in general we had great times while working hard together on our business trips to New York, Washington, Chicago, San Francisco, and London.

By their own example my parents also taught me to work hard, and to use my resources wisely. In retrospect I think we all benefited from the hard days of the 1940s (in England) and 1950s (in the U.S.). When I was a kid, "austerity" was an important, slogan-like word all over England, where rationing lingered until 1952. It was important to live an austere life because, despite our determination to keep our chins up, the realities of post-war life required a somewhat severe, even ascetic, overlay to one's worldview and the conduct of one's life. Some of that stuck with me always. I worked hard for my pay, enjoying the process, and, though I suspected this was a sort of luxury, seldom finished a job without being sure that I could be proud of the work.

In later life, like my dad I was determined to present my colleagues and staff with good examples. It was my rather mild way of exercising the power of personality rather than hands-on management. When the quality (or quantity) of their work began to fail, I would let them know, gently, that they would not move up the company ladder if they did not achieve the standard of quality that I demanded of myself.

My determination won success first at the *Review*, where I was a happy camper earning 40 cents an hour, saving my shekels to buy my first photographic light meter: such things were separate hand-held instruments in those days. I was soon ready to leave home, though a little less enthusiastic to begin college. In some ways, college life would not prove as satisfying as that of a printer's devil; on the other hand the experience of getting to know a diverse set of bright young people changed my life. And my life was going to go on changing: I would make sure of that.

In August 1958, I removed myself from the limited, inward-looking Utah scene and launched myself with a vengeance. I accepted a job offer from the *Bermuda Mid-Ocean News*.

6. MID-OCEAN MEMOIRS

*Twenty years from now you will be more disappointed by the things that you
didn't do than by the ones you did do. So throw off the bowlines. Sail away from
the safe harbour. Catch the trade winds in your sails. Explore. Dream. Discover.*
  – Mark Twain

After my cloistered years in Utah, a combination of blind audacity and plain good luck landed me in Bermuda. Just before my graduation from college I had sent personal résumés to dozens of U.S. newspapers – and, on a whim, to the two Bermuda dailies listed in the *Europa Year Book*. There were exactly three positive replies – one from a newspaper in Frankfort (Indiana) and one from each of the two in Bermuda. There was a pleasing irony in all this. I had spent half my life in Britain and the other half in the States and Bermuda is as mid-Atlantic a scattering of dry land as you can find.

And so, on a sunny day in September 1958, I presented myself at Pier 95, on the western end of 56th street in New York, and jubilantly boarded Furness-Withy's *Queen of Bermuda*. I was jubilant because this was a scheduled passenger sailing, something special, for my taste for this kind of travel had been whetted forever in the summer of 1956 by the family trip to England on the *Queen Elizabeth* and *Queen Mary*.

The *Queen of Bermuda* was built across the bay from Morecambe, at Barrow-in-Furness, and fitted as a first-class luxury liner. She was launched in 1933, and six years later was requisitioned for military service, serving as an armed cruiser until she was refitted for the tourist trade in the late 1940s. She had a long life for an ocean liner, but ended up at a Scottish scrap yard in 1966. I made friends with some of the crewmen and sometimes, when she was tied up at the quayside near the Royal Bermuda Yacht Club, we would get together for drinks at the Kenwood Club or the more homelike sailors' club, nearby on Reid Street.

We approached the islands from the north on a fine, sunny morning. It seemed to take ages to transit the ship channel, which runs between reefs from St. George's Island to Spanish Point before turning south and hooking around to

Hamilton Harbour. Then a street came into view, running right next to the docks, and soon I could make out the signs – Trimingham's, Butterfield's Bank, Gosling's, Gibbons, Bank of Bermuda. From the deck, after so many years in America, the English cars looked small, but one stuck out from the rest. It was a bright yellow Singer sports car, and to my delight it was waiting for me when I came out of the customs shed. The attractive, youngish driver was my new editor, Liz Pengelly. I remember her appraising look as we drove away along Front Street, with the top down and people staring. "You'll find things quite different here," she said, grinning at the understatement as we drove off to Gracie Crichton's boarding house, Rose Cottage.

Gracie stood no more than five feet tall. She was the benign despot of an old house that had a tall avocado tree in the back and, hidden below the building, a huge cistern that stored rainwater from the whitewashed roof catchment and provided a home to numerous mosquito-hungry guppies whose population was regularly topped up by the vector control man.

Though no one dared ask Gracie how long she lived in Bermuda, she was undeniably Scottish to the bone. She kept a sharp eye on her half-dozen lodgers' dining habits, and if anyone failed finish their breakfast porridge they would likely get it the next morning, sliced and fried. She terrorized the youngsters but had a soft heart for Johnnie, a fiercely curmudgeonly, skinny and frail old man who worked for the planning office. Johnnie was an unrepentant drinker, had an amazing capacity for flatulence, and after his morning bathroom concert would stalk belligerently into the dining room, glaring malevolently at his fellow boarders before taking his chair. The one exception to his general misanthropy was Gracie, who I imagined knew a sad and terrible secret about Johnnie, enough to pardon him for any unseemliness or lack of manners.

Gracie was a stickler for tradition, observing New Year's Eve – which by Scots tradition she called Hogmanay – as strictly as if she were home in Kirkintilloch. If I came home before midnight on the last night of the year she would appear from the garden shadows and bar my way, for my hair was blond and by Gracie's law only a tall dark stranger could be admitted to the house, preferably carrying a lump of coal and a slice of black bread. This duty generally fell to Jim Murray, a genial Scots air-conditioning specialist who met the physical requirements and relished the ritual.

Bermuda life was a drastic change from Utah's dry, mile-high environment and its conservative population. If I had been older and more cautious I might have decided that plonking myself down on this remote spot, with unknown medical resources, would pose too great a health risk to take the chance. But I had begun daily doses of the corticosteroid drug prednisone in the States, and with its help I was able to explore the offshore marine life close up, seeing analogues of my own cellular makeup among the corals, the sponges, and in fact the whole rich community of life that teemed around me, each particle doing its part in that other greater organism the reef.

These experiences inspired me to give the title *The Bionic Reef* to one of my later writings. They also gave me an early sensitivity for the meaning of globalization, which could be viewed as a man-made, socioeconomic reef analogue. Beyond this there was the image of Gaia, the Greek goddess of Earth, whom in 1979 James Lovelock would introduce to modern minds with the reminder that ours is a thoroughly interconnected, living planet.

Life was fabulous, and I made it my business to explore every nook and cranny of Bermuda's 21 square miles – and some of its close-in waters as well. I would leave Rose Cottage early and buzz to work on my sky-blue Mobylette, its saddlebags crammed with snorkelling equipment, work four hours, then spend four hours in the water, then return to help put the newspaper to bed. Soon I was tanned and fit, and I must have looked pretty good on the beach. My love life could have been magnificent, but my upbringing and teen years had not prepared me well for a flirtatious life and instead I fell in love with the reefs and the sea. I was the biophilic boy peering into the Somerset pond-life that fascinated my boyhood, all over again. In and around the reef off Elbow Beach, if I were lucky, I would come across a sea hare, a marvellous winged mollusc, flying lazily through the water; a watchful, spine-tailed ray; a cat-eyed octopus, settling carefully into its lair at my approach; or a foraging row of squid, strung like pegs on an invisible clothesline, the largest at one end, the smallest at the other. I spear-fished for spiny lobster and grouper, dived for all manner of shellfish, and became accustomed to the company of curious barracuda. My skin became honey-dark and my hair white with the sun and salt.

I was in my prime. My ribs still stuck out a bit, slightly flared as a reminder of my childhood asthma. The knot in the middle of my right collarbone was a memento of a crash in northern Italy, when I had declined the surgeons' offer to pin my green-stick fracture, and the same incident had denied me the ability to point straight with my left hand. (Since my friend Helen had a collarbone shaped like mine, we developed a silly Romanesque salute, and to our delight

Bermuda 1958-59 The standard Bermuda male's formal dress, as modeled by the author. My faithful Mobylette moped, considerably less elegant, is in the background.

people would stare when, on meeting, we pressed our palms briefly to each other's right clavicle.)

In those days the sea off Elbow Beach was so perfectly clear that, after a 50-yard snorkel-assisted swim at low tide, I could stand ankle deep on the reef, squat with my mask in the crystalline water, and feel a moment of vertigo before letting myself fall weightless into that wondrous world. Another favourite spot was on the grounds of Admiralty House, near Spanish Point. I came across it quite by accident, while riding my Mobylette across a stretch of crabgrass toward the north-shore coastline.

While walking across this flat and featureless landscape one morning I was surprised to find myself confronted by an open, unmarked hole in the ground. It looked dark down there, but I could see light and, excitingly, and old stairway. I grabbed my bag of tricks – snorkel, flashlight, string bag, mask, flippers, pole-spear – and ventured downward into a passageway. I paused to let my eyes adjust to the dim light and realized with a shiver of alarm that I was at the edge of a gaping hole that stretched almost all the way across the passage. The edge was thin and frail looking, and the sea was boiling underneath. I manoeuvred carefully around it and continued gingerly onward, still moving downward, and found myself at the water's edge. Here the sea was calm, and I was standing at a place where, when Britannia ruled the waves, boats could easily have landed passengers from ships anchored off the north shore or from the Royal Navy dockyard across the channel at Ireland Island. I slipped into the water, which was deep and clear, and started to paddle about. Almost immediately I saw the largest spiny lobster I had ever seen, anywhere. I tightened the power band on my spear and dived.

The lobster saw me coming but had no place to hide and simply catapulted himself away, clouding the water. I went up for more air and paddled about again, searching. There he was again. This time my spear point glanced off his carapace, so that he made a series of rasping sounds, *erk-erk-erk*, and made off again. Attempt No. 3 was successful. I struck him amidships, the spear tip flared out into a t-shape, and there was no way he could get away. But fight he did, like a fish, making those strange sounds until I got back to the tunnel entrance, just in time to have the prize catch photographed by our general manager, Harry Austin.

People ask me if I ever use SCUBA equipment, and the answer is always no. I have tried it, and I dislike the heavy weight and bulkiness that comes with the gear, as well as the meticulous care that is required to make sure it is working safely. By contrast, after you become familiar with "free" diving you can imagine that you are porpoise-like, able to fly through the water, streamlined and quiet. Jacques Cousteau's fantasy – and in Bermuda I visited his boat *Calypso*, a converted British minesweeper – was that someday someone would learn how to graft gills to his body. I can relate to that.

The *Mid-Ocean News* was housed in a cavernous building in the back streets of Hamilton. On the dimly lighted ground floor were the presses, the Linotypes, and the casting machinery familiar from my Pleasant Grove Days. We had a mixed workforce of Afro-Bermudians and whites (including a few local people of Portuguese descent), who seemed to get along marvellously, sharing tasks and joking together. Oddly to me, Bermuda had separate sports leagues and separate local militias, and dark-skinned people were expected to sit upstairs at the cinema. But as a reporter I covered the news of all the communities equally, and once had the distinction of being presented with a free beer as the first pink person to attend a Bermuda Football Club match. The only personally sour note in all this was the time I was quietly cautioned for being too friendly with a female member of the newspaper production crew. I hadn't so much as touched her on the shoulder, but apparently someone thought I was getting close to crossing some invisible line.

The reporters and editors, including our radio operator Percy Ball, worked in an office with windows that overlooked the production floor. This large area, the size of the furniture store next door, was dominated by two Linotypes and a big broadsheet press. These Linotypes could operate with instructions from Teletype-style punched tape produced from our local news reports by Percy's wife Betty, using a machine fitted with the familiar QWERTY keyboard layout. One of the Linotypes was run by a good-looking and talkative, husky Portuguese, Corky Gonsalves, and the other by Charlie Mason, an emaciated, middle-aged Englishman with a strange sense of humour. One day when I was proofreading I noticed that Charlie had named a famous Boston team as the Red Cox. I politely told him of the error, and he promised to change it. When I checked the new proof, it read "Boston Red Sex." Finally he capitulated and got it right.

I spent one year at the *Mid-Ocean News*, editing the entire paper once a week, including the time that a great solar storm sent our Teletypes berserk and forced the heroic Percy to transcribe scraps of international news from staticky live radio broadcasts.

That July an ancient ketch, the *Havruen*, came into harbour and her master, Group Captain T. H. Carr, asked if I would like to join his crew for their continued voyage westward and around the world. How my life would have changed if I had accepted the offer!

I wrote about just about everything. In March 1959 I produced a long feature article on the discovery of Bermuda by a Virginia-bound ship, the *Sea Venture*, that had been cast on the rocks in a storm 350 years before. I drank vodka with visiting Soviet seamen, and passed over another chance for a glamorous job in colonial journalism, working for a newspaper in Hong Kong. I served as "foreign correspondent" for Thomson Newspapers in the U.K., filing just one significant dispatch, on plans for the "first piece of legislation against racial discrimination since the abolition of slavery in 1834." This paragraph was included in a story published in the London *Sunday Times* of January 21, 1961:

The aim is to change the [democratic] balance in this small self-governing colony of 45,000 people where Negroes — nearly two-thirds of the population — are considered manual labourers, the Portuguese are thought of as farmers and fishermen, and the Bermudian whites are seen as "natural leaders of business and government."

The franchise was then extended only to land-owners aged 21 or more. In 1963, universal suffrage was granted for all Bermudians aged 25 or more. The voting age was restored to 21 in 1966, and then stabilized at 18 in 1990.

In a short time I was becoming a member of the Bermuda community. I played the clarinet, and sang, in the St. Matthew Passion at the Bermuda Cathedral. Then a man from Kitson and Company tried to sell me a house. Life could scarcely have been better. But I wanted to return to England despite this surprisingly successful introduction to island life, for I was only 22, young and curious, and I was eager to see what if anything my native land could offer.

⚅

My bags were almost packed when I decided to orchestrate one final Bermudian adventure. It was a perfect night. I had £150 in my wallet, most of it for a freighter trip to London, and I was at Elbow Beach with Zelda, a lissom Canadian blonde who, as far as I was concerned, was the most attractive young woman in Hamilton. At my suggestion she had hopped on her scooter and followed me out on the south shore road, then along the unpaved "Tribe Road No. 3b," which followed the big hotel/resort property line, making straight for the beach. We had sandwiches and wine, and made a kind of nest in the big mattressy clusters of sea-grape that cluttered the higher part of the beach.

We pulled off our outer clothing and stuffed it into our saddlebags, and then we were running off toward the sea. The moon was so bright that it made shadows of our forms as we ran through the dry sand into the surf and threw ourselves laughing into the warm water. We lay there for a while, drunken with the moment as we let the water wash our more sober thoughts away. We lay on our backs looking at the moon and the bright stars. We held each other in our arms and wiped the sand from our cheeks. We lay on our sides and admired each other, touching gently. The water evaporated on our skins, making us cold, and we put our arms around each other's waists as we trudged back to the sea-grape nest.

The nest was not there. The wine and sandwiches were gone, the panniers of our Mobylettes were empty. Our clothes had disappeared along with everything else, including my travel money.

Somewhere, the sexual revolution was winding up and soon would be in full swing. Obviously this would not be my *grand entrée*. Damn! And things were going so well.

Miserably we tramped to the nearest beach cottage to phone the police, since we would need to make insurance claims. I walked up the thin sandy carpet of crabgrass and knocked on the door. It took a while for anyone to answer, but when the door opened I had yet another shock. Standing in the doorway was Corky Gonsalves, the Linotype operator! I knew what he would be up to, entertaining young ladies who had come in from the States for a few days of fun. I was embarrassed, and afterwards I realized that he probably was, too. I got quickly to the point and phoned the police station in Hamilton. Shortly a police car arrived, followed by a motor scooter. The fates still had me in their malicious sights.

I knew the policemen, and knew they would sympathize with a distressed couple who wanted to spend a pleasant private evening on the beach. I paled, however, when I recognized the man with the scooter. It was Zelda's cousin Mark, looking rather grim.

Somehow we avoided any embarrassing questions – any insinuation of questionable conduct would have to be based on imagination anyway. I signed the police-report papers, we mounted our Mobylettes, and that was it. In a couple of days I would fly to England on one of Guest Airways' Comet airliners, and I would never see the lovely Zelda again.

7. THE BOY WHO ASKED IF I WAS GOD

*It is eternity now. I am in the midst of it. It is about me in the sunshine. I am
in it, as the butterfly in the light-laden air. Nothing has to come; it is now. Now
is eternity; now is the immortal life.*
— Richard Jefferies[10]

The market town of Ashford, in Kent, was the last settlement of any consequence that pre-freeway travelers would encounter on their way from London to England's south coast. At first sight it not the most welcoming place in the world. When I approached it by road from the north I was challenged by the ruin of a World War I British tank, apparently built to confuse the Germans by making it look the same upside down as it does right-side-up. If I approached Ashford from the south the first substantial building to come into view was an old Victorian workhouse. In most cases it was best to take the bypass road and come out the other side of town, looping around the Bachelors factory, where peas were processed.

Unfortunately, that was not an option. Though I would have loved to settle near my Uncle Tom and Auntie Betty, with whom I had stayed in the sylvan gentility of Surrey, fate determined otherwise. In short, Ashford was the only place I could find a job. To be fair, I am sure the town pulled up its socks and became a more pleasant place when its railway station became one of the few English portals for cross-channel trains to Paris and Brussels, at speeds seldom imagined in my Kentish days. At the moment I am sharing my remembrances of a time when one could — and I did — travel to London on one of Britain's last-surviving steam-engine rail services.

I seem to have blotted out the details of how I actually got the reporting job on the weekly *Kentish Express*, on the high street fifty yards or so down from the tank. When I first arrived the weather was wet and wearying and I felt universes away from the pink beaches of Bermuda. For a short time, however, fate actually smiled on me. The editor wasn't ready for me to start for a couple of weeks yet, so I decided to ready myself for my new venture by taking a morale-boosting holiday in Belgium, continuing on to Paris.

Preparation for the trip required a somewhat unusual strategy. Since my wallet was stolen shortly before I left Bermuda, I was short on cash. So I bought a motor scooter, joined the International Youth Hostel Association, and headed for the Dover docks. The scooter had wheels not much bigger than bagels and would have made a Lambretta look like a Rolls Royce. The machine was touted "the center of attraction wherever it goes," but somehow I knew no one would ever want to steal it.

In Paris I parked the Piatti near a youth hostel, registered, and started a walking tour that would take in Montparnasse, the Île de la Cité and Notre Dame, and the Left Bank, my gait modified somewhat by posterior bruises from the mistaken detour that I undertook on tiny wheels across several miles of cobbled Belgian roads. The weather was good, the food delicious, the wine helped anaesthetize my derrière, and I saw everything I planned to see. It was different in the hostel, which featured three-tiered metal beds, an ancient washroom with "á la turque" kangaroo toilets and dodgy plumbing, bangs in the night, and other travelers muttering *Plastique! Plastique!* as they tried to sleep. Why the bangs and *plastiques*? The Algerian fight for independence from France was in full spate, complete with guerrilla attacks on Paris. It would end only when independence was granted in 1962. Plastic explosives – those deplorable Semtex *plastiques* – were a favourite weapon of urban warfare.

I then put-putted my way to Brussels (my delectable introduction to *moules marinières*), turning south to Bruges, a delightful old city with canals, picturesque bridges, and a handsome couple of new female friends from Milan, one of whom revealed that her father was choirmaster at the La Scala opera.

On my way to the port city of Ostend, from whence I would ship for Dover, the Piatti stopped dead. It refused to respond to an exhausting series of attempts to kick-start its engine and assumed a donkey-like air of disinterested immobility. I had just started to unscrew the sparking plug when I heard the sound of a much larger engine stop behind me and the tread of large boots. I was sure I was in even bigger trouble now.

But no, the man in the sunglasses and sharp uniform was an officially designated good Samaritan for the regional Automobile Association, then called the TW. He had seen my license plate and guessed correctly that I wouldn't speak Flemish, so he gave me a "no problem, it'll be all right" gesture, kneeled in his beautiful uniform, and proceeded to tinker. I looked at the flat fields and wondered how long it would take. And then he stood and gestured at the kick starter. I gave it a pump and it started like a dream. The TW man was a genius. He put away his tools, saluted, gave me a little bow, and roared off.

A few miles farther on, exactly the same thing happened, with a different TW man. And then again. The whole thing could have inspired a Monty Python sketch, only it was a decade too early. Finally I decided the machine would stop every time its coil became hot. It was a pleasant enough day, so I took off my crash helmet, gritted my teeth, and walked the Piatti to Ostend, where I caught a ferry back to Dover. I parked the scooter at a garage, in the hope that it would be adopted by someone else, with luck an obsessive-compulsive mechanic with a penchant for masochism, and looked for the bus stop.

After my return to Ashford I found lodging in the neighbouring village of Great Chart and started nine months of Dickensian misery in the chilly cloisters of the *Kentish Express* (Igglesden and Company) for the wage of £12 a week, which each Friday was proffered in cash sealed in a small brown envelope (the minimum wage was then about £8 for a 44-hour week). The misery extended to the bathroom, where in backhanded deference to the memory of wartime austerity the management had provided our loos with Jeyes toilet paper. This was provided in boxes of individual sheets of fiendishly non-absorbent, semitransparent paper, remindful of the paper we called "greaseproof" in England. Some marketing wag at Jeyes had labelled their product "the acme of toilet refinement." My opinion was somewhat different, and I wondered, very briefly, about the toilet refinement of other Jeyes products if indeed this was the acme and not the nadir.

Doubtless this dismal portrait changed vastly after the KM Group bought the *Express* in 1971, but in my days the newsroom was a lean-to building where a partitioned shelf of desk spaces, which reminded me of the nesting boxes we provided for our chickens back in Utah, kept the junior members apart at an elbow-to-elbow distance. At the most sheltered end an elderly gentleman who reminded me of the character actor Edmund Gwenn represented the Guild of Journalists and performed the duties of copy editor; at the other end a very thin, thoughtful man sat and wrote about sports. Miss Leech, the chief reporter, sat in tweeds and woolly jumpers under an antique clock on the other side of the room, radiating nascent irritability. I sat in the middle of the nesting boxes, where I performed such brain-deadening tasks as rewriting canned film reviews, waiting for Wednesday.

Wednesday was the day when my job became transformed and I took charge of a company vehicle (with heater) to scour the small outlying villages for news. Cruising over the narrow, curving country lanes while seated behind the wheel of that Austin A40 van, I felt like a genuine reporter, possibly even of the investigative variety, one week writing about mink farming near Lenham; another week about the Pluckley churchyard ghost, for which the vicar was planning a special service to put her to rest. I always had lunch at the Chequers pub in Smarden, around the corner from a house where the actor George Sanders used to visit his mother, which in turn was across from a meticulously restored, timbered Cloth Hall built in 1430.

The Chequers faced down a short bend in the road that led to Bethersden and Biddenden. Around that bend, out of sight from the pub, was an ancient timbered house with a thatched roof. In front was a well-kept garden, with a brook that sparkled at its foot, not far from the road. It was for sale, the price seemed reasonable, and I coveted it. This was the kind of house I would like to move into someday with a young bride, and begin the life I had dreamed of, with a roast on the dining room table every Sunday and with children laughing all around. But at £12 a week? I would have to wait.

The villages were lovely, still-rustic pockets of old England. They are the kind that romantics like me lust for. We let ourselves pretend that these represent the "real" England when so many are in truth gentrified townships whose closest claim to fame now is the occasional provision of locations for TV period dramas. While I would sip my beer at the Chequers under a fringe of fragrant hop vines and have my lunch in a small family dining room, it is now a full-fledged, high-end bed-and-breakfast establishment.

The closeness of these villages made it a shade more pleasing to work in Ashford – this and the proximity of Canterbury, where high fluted cathedral columns, spreading into fan vaulting at their tops, never failed to remind me of great forest trees, and to wonder whether they had been intended as an invitation to followers of the animistic old religions. Similar Gothic architectural features were used for London's 19th century Museum of Natural History, where the front entrance is designed to look as though one were entering the Cathedral of Science.

This period of my life was brightened by the peculiar delight of sharing, with my colleague Tony Moss, a dusty, unheated upstairs apartment in a barn attached to a converted oast house (built for hops storage) once occupied by the writer George Orwell. Tony and I shared our fresh water with surly Orwellian pigs on the ground floor; we warmed water (for tea or, optimistically, for a bath) on a tiny paraffin heater. One morning I woke with a white diagonal stripe across the thickness of blankets that covered my chest – it was a miniscule drift of snow. Despite the warped windows, the pigs, and the lack of heating, I enjoyed life at the farm better than spending hours of typing with my feet pressed to the two-inch hot water pipe that was the newsroom's sole source of heating.

I nearly died that year, during an April trip to continental Europe, riding high in my leather jacket and white skid-lid astride Jimmy Hey's 250cc Zundapp. I spent my first night at a hostel in the delightful town of Chalon-sur-Saône. Then on to a hostel at Milan where prostitutes at the curb outside waited for johns to pick them up. Then, fatefully, I turned southwest toward the Savona coast, where, coming around a corner on the curve of a hill, I encountered a large dump truck.

I saw the word "Fiat" on the radiator, then everything went away. In a split second I flew over the handlebars and hit the radiator with my right shoulder and helmeted head, while the bike continued under the truck chassis.

Once I regained consciousness at the Finale Ligure hospital, Sister Agostina, who had trouble pronouncing my real name, told me, "Ah Stefano, when you arrived we did not know whether to take you upstairs or downstairs." When I asked the investigating *caribinieri* officer what happened to my bike, he replied, "*Ah signore, è como una omeletta*," like an omelette. In fact when I finally saw the Zundapp it looked as though it had been mechanically baled, ready for melting down. By law I would have to ship it back to England.

I was very lucky to get away with relatively minor shoulder, hand/arm injuries, and slight concussion. Unfortunately I smashed the middle joint of my left index finger, and the visiting doctor ("*il Professore*") insisted on trying to re-set it without anaesthetic, compassionately murmuring to the nurse "Close the blinds" before he went to work. For the rest of my life I had to point with a slightly bent finger. I would never play the guitar again, but then to tell the truth I wasn't much good at it anyway.

At the precise time of the accident, a local policeman had a vision that someone was in trouble, then knelt and prayed for the life of whoever it was. The poor man became so obsessed by his vision that he had to be suspended on paid leave. He would stand outside my open hospital window, calling "Stefano,

Stefano!" while begging the reluctant nuns to let him come to my bedside. Though his behaviour seemed irrational, I did have a miraculous escape. And in Italy, where it seems more miracles are born than anywhere else.

June 13, 1960 letter to my mother and dad – In racking my brains for reasons for the crash, I decided (at least it was a good excuse, suggested by the caribinieri) that I lost consciousness due to a liver ailment, and that is why I ended up on the wrong side of the strada. The people at the hospital decided my liver was badly inflamed – I had a fever, a pain in my stomach – and they nearly took my appendix out!! As soon as that mistaken idea was satisfactorily put to rest I had a two-day reaction to the penicillin shot that covered me with a horrible rash and itch, even under the casts. Thankfully, the fever kept me "dozing" for most of the time, but I was that way for about five days and it left me weakened. Now I'm strong as a horse, I tell myself, and feel perfectly normal except for these blessed casts. I believe I'll have 'em off in a few days, and maybe after a couple of days of physiotherapy they'll throw me out.

June 18, 1960 letter to my mother and dad – Yesterday my chest cast, a useless thing anyway, was cut off, so that I was able to spend time exposing my chest and ample paunch to the sun on the pebbly beach. Steak and red wine at mealtimes! It is a pretty sweet life – una vita dolce – though I must wear my left arm cast for six more days and the right one for "qualche giorni" – several days. I am getting the feeling that Suora Agostina and her monastic friends want to prolong their hospitality as long as possible, so that they will continue to get insurance payments.

Last night I visited a church built in early Christian times. It is really intriguing. A well-educated, English-speaking young Benedictine priest, Frate Rodolfo, showed me around He wears the traditional brown habit, with a long gown and hood, and sandals. Like the rest of his order, he has an untrimmed beard. So now I know what it's like to walk in an abbey – (should I say monastery?) – garden between avenues of unripe grapes, at dusk, when the rondinelli (swallows) swoop across the sky. Fr. Rodolfo took me up a flight of ancient steps and to a high point from where we saw fishing boats out on the sea, each with a light shining to attract the sardines. By then it was nearly nine o'clock, and time to return to the hospital. Only a foolish person would moan about being stranded here with a wrecked scooter.

Because I was so blond, the hospital staff insisted that I was German (*"Haben Sie schmerz diese morgen, mein Herr?"*), and despite my protests the young assistants would search the town to find German tourists who would talk to me. One was an unusually attractive girl, tall and slim, whom the staff insisted on calling *la giraffa*. Over a period of two weeks I did get to talk with another English-speaker, an American patient called Jan, and got leave from the hospital to go with her to Florence. Once there, she checked for mail at the American Express office and, to our horror, learned that her brother had died of burns after a military plane crash. Instead of realizing my long-held dream of visiting the Uffizi gallery, I immediately took her to the Milan airport, then returned to Finale Ligure. Soon I was released from the hospital, six weeks after the accident, and made my way back to Ashford, where I was accepted back into the newsroom by an unwelcoming Miss Leech.

By far the most important experience of this year was meeting Miriam, a skinny, effervescent nurse I encountered while hospitalized with asthma at Willesborough Hospital, and who was destined to be my future wife. Otherwise the most fortuitous event happened just after my editor-in-chief, who had a large, cosy office of his own and suspected without reason that I was homophobic, advised me to find another job.

One morning less than a week afterwards, Miss Leech answered the phone and shouted out to the hutches in her commanding baritone, "Hey?" (meaning me).

"Yes Miss Leech?" I piped.

"Telephone, Hey."

To my delight it was Liz Pengelly. She invited me to come back to Bermuda for the princely wage of £35 a week – almost three times what I had been earning in Kent, and with no tax – to start a weekly tabloid supplement for the *Mid-Ocean News*. I accepted without a second thought.

And then I was back in Bermuda, by airliner this time, and at my new employer's expense.

◦⊰⊱◦

Miriam was full of love and bonhomie, yet pursued by invisible and ill-defined demons. We all called her Mim. She was tallish, neither lissom nor fashion-model slim, nor particularly graceful in her movements, yet was slim and angular, with a keenly sculptured face and mischievous eyes, with a recurrent dancing gaiety even as she did the often trivial and distasteful duties of a state registered nurse.

I first noticed her with interest one evening when she was pushing a chrome-plated trolley down the wide center of the high-ceilinged Harvey ward, serving bedtime tea and biscuits with a diminutive, pleasantly plump colleague. Mim said they were like Mutt and Jeff. The ritual always occurred after the visitors had straggled off home, after seeing some of the dozen male patients who waiting, in neatly spaced beds, between high sash windows, under the high ceilings of what used to be a workhouse infirmary. If you have ever watched the old British comedy film *Carry on Nurse*, you know exactly what the men's medical ward was like. Even the other patients reminded me of cast members in this side-splitter from 1959.

Mim was the second daughter of Claud and Marguerite Lamb. Her elder sister Joan had married a Lithuanian geologist who had a good job with Shell, and had moved away with him, first from England to the Netherlands, then to Brunei and Australia. Soon they would have four vigorous children, three girls and a boy.

Claud was a retired customs officer and "receiver of wreck" who had a part-time job in which he personally collected small insurance premiums, typically for seven shillings and sixpence per knock on the client door. Marguerite ("Rita") took care of the household and was a talented amateur artist. (While I have no evidence that Claud ever exercised his duties in this arena, receivers of wreck are officials who work out what happens to "found" objects and materials that are cast ashore from wrecked vessels: how they are shared among the finder and the owner, and sometimes among museums and archaeologists.)

◎✖◎

I proposed marriage to Miriam soon after starting my second incarnation in Bermuda. She accepted; I sent her a ticket. The banns were published in the *Royal Gazette* on September 7, 1960; and we were married at St. John's, Pembroke Parish Church, on October 13. Coincidentally, my second cousin Jimmy Power was in Hamilton at the time, conducting a Geraldo band at the Bermudiana hotel, and I recruited him as best man. Fewer than a dozen spectators were there to see Mim say "I do" in the lovely wedding dress and veil she had brought from England. But that didn't keep us from enjoying a few hours of post-ceremonial merriment with our friends and colleagues.

89

After the ceremony I put Mim on the back of my shiny new green and white scooter and we zoomed up the hill to our flat, her white dress flying in the wind. Soon a lively party was under way, full of fun and friendly people.

Our first home was the charming guest house at Juniperhill, a beautifully manicured property just up the hill from the church, with lizards hiding behind the picture frames and a view of Hamilton from the front window. I was having a great time as creator/editor of a weekly news magazine and, one day a week, editor of the daily newspaper. At the same time I was corresponding for the Thomson Newspaper group, which then included the London *Sunday Times, The Scotsman* and the *Western Mail*.

I wrote my first science-related articles for the *Mid-Ocean News* in 1960 and 1961, including one on a Soviet Mars probe, a series on mental health, and three or four articles about snorkelling. I also wrote about finding a rack of small cannon in shallow water near St. Catherine's Fort. The day after the article appeared there was a raft over the site, and salvagers were pulling the cannon out of the water.

Popping the Cork. Mim and I look on approvingly as Jimmy Power pops the first cork at our wedding reception. My landlady Gracie Crichton is just visible at the far right.

In the days when it was still legal, I liked to spear-fish from the shore at Achilles Bay, on the northwest shore of foot-shaped St. George's Island. I had caught some good fish there, and a few lobsters, and was forever eager to repeat these successes. One time I was out there with a couple of friends when I realized that we were being circled by a flotilla of barracuda. The others thrashed for shore, but I'd been around a few barracuda by then and knew these were just a gang of curious juveniles.

And *then* I got into a dangerous situation. I was paddling on the surface, looking down, when a grouper that would have fed us for three or four nights came out from under a reef. I positioned the power band on my spear, pulled it back against my thumb as hard as I could, and dived. The fish swam in a leisurely way to a sheltered place under the reef. I chased him a bit but since I was down 15 or so feet and because my air supply was confined to my lungs I resurfaced and took another look while catching my breath through the snorkel. Yes, he was still there, so down I went again, flippers to the sky. Again the grouper spotted me and found a resting spot under another small reef, a little farther from shore.

I was excited by the chase, and the adrenaline was running fast, but then something happened that quite probably saved my life. I was seized with an extremely scary idea. What if I was successful in spearing my jumbo-sized quarry? The rubber band could catch around my wrist and unless he was very badly injured the grouper could pull me out to sea. And I was steadily diving to depths farther from the surface. I gave up the chase and as a consolation prize collected a claw-less slipper lobster on the way back.

This was not the most dramatic near-death experience I ever had in Bermuda, but believe me, it was the closest to becoming reality.

You can see that snorkelling had again become a surprisingly important part of my life, and even more enjoyable when Mim joined in. This might seem a strange hobby for an asthmatic, but there was no problem with pollens or mildew or cigarette smoke out on the reef, I could carry a pocket inhaler in my shorts, and if I felt winded or tired all I need do was float until I recovered, breathing through the snorkel. My only worry was that the strap on my mask might break in deep water, for despite all the hours I spent in the water I never became a skilful swimmer. I imagine I can blame the ease of using snorkelling equipment for that.

Many Bermuda memories stay bright in my memory – chasing and catching that elusive octopus on the North Shore and miraculously concocting the recipe for a meal that tasted as sweet and tender as lobster or shrimp. Diving for shellfish and barbecuing them on that small island we found after a precipitous walk through the brush on the north side of Harrington Sound. Finding a hideout for delicious gray snappers through the hatch of that shallow wreck off Sandys Parish. Spearing my last barracuda, shamefully, for he was a laid-back old loner that I had already met, off Church Bay in Southampton Parish.

Snorkelling stayed in my blood even after I left Bermuda, though I had to give up catching my own fish suppers. As time went by I would snorkel in Tahiti and the Balearic Islands, in Hawaii and Florida, Santa Barbara and Argos. At Santorini I found myself suspended in absolutely clear water above a giant basin of unbelievably clean white and gray gravel. Not a shred of seaweed was to be seen, not even a rock or a broken bottle. The only sign of life other than me was a lone langouste lobster, scrabbling for a morsel of nourishment on the floor of that unearthly setting.

⚬⚬⚬

April 1961 – Spring in Bermuda! This evening you can see every conceivable type of human expression, right here in Hamilton, while the moon hangs overhead and tree-frogs whistle plaintively from the hibiscus. Situated firmly on the opposite social plane from the Gibbonses, Triminghams and Tuckers in the Legislature is one of Bermuda's most notorious and most-loved citizens. He is nicknamed "Weatherbird" – I don't know his real name, but I do know that though he may not have a five-shilling note to his name, he is one of the best-known men in Hamilton. Weatherbird, his tattered beret askew and a bloom of grey whiskers on his mahogany face, is the sort of person to whom one takes a liking for no particular reason – unless it's because he is so unashamedly human. You can see him strolling along the docks with his two dogs trotting at his heels, or simply sat in a doorway smoking, a benign and somehow paternal expression on his face as he watches the people walk by. It is well known in Bermuda that, when Weatherbird is taken in for loitering or drunkenness, his dogs will return to the prison every seventh day to see if their master will be released. In the past, people say, he made a point of being arrested every Christmas so he'll be sure of a good bed and dinner for the season.

April 5, 1961 – My New York friends René and Mort have come to visit! The pair had decided to think of me as a sort of bearded beachcomber king (the better to embellish the stories they would tell their city friends), and I was no man to shatter their illusions. I showed them my "secret" swimming spots, ferreted out native craftsmen from whom they could buy those rare souvenirs not imported from Hong Kong or Japan, and generally showed them around the island. It was fun playing Caliban.

We dived for mussels and clams, some of which we roasted on an open fire; some of which we saved for stew. To complete the illusion, I went to work with my spear-fishing gear. The spear (I neglected to tell them I bought it in New York) brought me enough fish for a kedgeree (seasoned flaked fish cooked with boiled egg and rice) on Thursday; bonito steaks on Friday; and stewed octopus on Saturday. The octopus, which I originally found in embrace with my speared bonito, was a pleasant surprise to the palate, tender and with a flavour not unlike Bermuda lobster. It was first beaten (tenderized), then cut into small pieces and stewed with Portuguese Nabo wine and spices.

René and Mort left me feeling more alive than before, even more appreciative of my island home. After all, I hopped on a scooter, not a sardine-tin subway train, to get to work. My recreation might be watching the antics of small anole lizards on my living room, rather than watching an old film on television. And, best of all, I could swim in the clean clear sea a couple of hundred yards away without having to fight my way out to the Long Island beaches or immersing myself in a chlorinated swimming pool. Still, once the visitors were gone, the kitchen seemed to have lost some of its glory, the spear had been put in the corner, and beefsteaks, rather than glassy-eyed fish, lay on the refrigerator shelves.

Then, unexpectedly, Jan turned up, looking for the man who had been kind to her in Italy. She hadn't written, didn't know I was married, and came unannounced. Fortunately I was able to pass her over to my friend and newspaper colleague Lew James.

❦

Ordinary Bermuda life – just being there – was delightful in this first year with Miriam. Even more importantly, and most unexpectedly, it invested me with a taste of personal spirituality that I had not known before, probably partly because of my association with the sea, partly because I was having increasingly serious encounters with asthma. But access to the experience would remain with me when I was well and when I was away from Bermuda. Life goal No. 3, to discover a spiritual path that I could truly believe in, was dawning in earnest.

The hillside near our flat was bearded gray with the woody skeletons of native junipers, an entire woodland killed by an infestation of sap-sucking scale insects that had hitchhiked to Bermuda from the United States. A few of these beautiful trees, of a species which existed nowhere else on earth, still graced the archipelago's landscapes. They were still dying off, though I'd heard that the experts were optimistic that some individuals would prove resistant to the blight. Perhaps a tiny few of the millions that once made up the juniper population might survive, enough to repopulate the islands.

◦◦◦

A strange and not quite rational connection made its way to my mind one afternoon as I walked along one of the Juniperhill footpaths, looking up at the silent gray wall of trees around me. I'll tell you about it. But first I must tell you a story. I had adopted the Swiss psychiatrist Carl Jung as one of my heroes during my university days. I suspect that if he were alive he would approve of the story.

You may remember that during my college years I convinced myself that my mind was being invaded by fleeting, spiritually empty thought, entertainments and distractions that crowded out the mind-stuff that I had decided was far more important. I changed my ways a little as a result, and continued in my belief that it is important that we try to understand what makes humans tick, including our thoughtful selves. I never lost my desire to understand the secret workings of humankind. And I always believed the people should help each other to manage the huge challenge of coping with the strange, wonderful, and sometimes dangerous things that happen between our individual and collective ears.

Daniel M. Ogilvie of Rutgers University warned that too often "We become like trees that are unaware of their roots and the nutrients that sustain them."[11] In my opinion the ability to recognize these "roots and nutrients" is at the heart of the rare, *good* part of the brainpower that separates humankind from other creatures. You may or may not completely agree with me, but when I use the word *good* I think of qualities like *compassionate, kind, generous, considerate, humanistic, humanitarian, and benevolent.*

94

Such thoughts were already implanted in my mind – the "dark intracranial recesses" – well before I started off on my Juniperhill walk, and yet they were far from my thoughts. It was a pleasant day and I was relaxed. I looked quietly at the trees, the blue sky with its lazily floating cumulus, and the town below. Then quite unexpectedly something interposed itself in the front of my mind, a clearcut, pure and inexplicable *awareness*. Since this occurrence was and is unlike anything else, it is impossible to describe satisfactorily. All I can say is that it amounted to an amazing sharpness of perception – we might call it insight – in which all creation came into full view as a naturally tranquil one-ness, blending notions of life and death as part of a serene continuum. And I knew without question that I was part of it.

I realized that this insight was a very thin thread of awareness, and afraid that if the thread broke I would not notice it, and that I would never return to this state of mind that I knew was precious. I was not ready to leave ordinary life, ordinary thought, and ordinary experience. These thoughts made me lightheaded, yet at the same time I felt joy and thankfulness in my expectation that the link with another reality would not be cut away by time and circumstance.

In other words I knew, without an ounce of doubt, that I was connected intimately with nature and with the cosmos. This flash of realization, and conviction, had struck me unaware. It overwhelmed me for a minute or less, and then dissolved. A year earlier, in the deep Arcadian forest near Haslemere, drunken in the sweetly primitive scent of humus and peat, I had felt something inside me brush against the shutters of the same light, but they had not yet opened to me.

I can't remember how the moment in the junipers happened, only that it *did* happen. My ego liberated itself and hid away somewhere in the ether. When I was a kid, or simply more naïve, I might have considered it as something especially for me; but no, I had learned that many others had written of such things. Still, to experience it personally was thoroughly liberating and empowering. I had escaped from time. It seemed I had experienced the release of self that the Taoists and the Zen masters had talked about, without even trying. I wondered if I could bring back that experience at will, and later learned that yes, I could.

I was unsettled to think that, one of these times, I might not return from one of these strangely magnificent detours from the ordinary world. On the other hand, I had come to know, briefly and subtly, a kind of wholeness with everything that was, and for that short time this had washed away everything, including the discord, which existed in myself. In some subtle way it transformed me, so that when Deepak Chopra said that "healing is the memory of wholeness that goes beyond the ambiguity," it had a new and special meaning.

On those infrequent occasions that I am of a mind to pray, it is generally to give thanks for these short bursts of cosmic connectivity, which I imagine some religionists consider to be communion with the Holy Spirit.

The boy must have spied me as I walked home from my morning swim off the North Shore rocks. He couldn't have been more than six or seven. Seeing a deeply tanned, bare-chested man with sun-whitened hair and uncombed beard, he followed me, confronted me, and asked calmly and quite seriously, "Are you God?"

I weighed the question in bewilderment and wondered what the proper answer would be. Others may have dealt deftly with the situation, but for me it was a surreal moment, extraordinary and rather unsettling. This side of Juniperhill was wide and bare with the curvature of a skull, and the native crabgrass stretched over the chalky soil like strands of an old man's hair. There were no houses nearby, and no grownups with the boy. I had not seen him until he appeared in my field of view and spoke those three words. There were suddenly just the two of us in the world, with me standing next to a child who was looking up into my eyes and waiting. Who was this boy?

I thought of sitting the boy down and explaining, "No, I'm not God, but you see I'm part of God and so are you." I was confused because, thanks to those brief moments of intuition, I knew that, *somewhere* within themselves, all people are outside of space-time, transcendental and boundless; for there is no place that God is not. But I merely patted him on the shoulder and assured him I was not God, and walked up the hill back to the guesthouse, wondering if I had taken the coward's way out.

Would God be carrying a face mask and flippers?

I am afraid that by now some of you will worry that perhaps you are reading the words of someone who is a roaring nutter, or at least slightly off his rails. Not so. The day after the Juniperhill episode, and an hour or so after the boy asked if I was God, I looked like any other journalist in the newspaper office, writing articles and marking copy in my shirt and jeans, and possibly with a tidy haircut as well. What I just told you is dead true, but the story is hard to describe in any detail, and that is why I have mostly kept it to myself.

❦

Acute, life-threatening allergy to mildew spores, and the threat that I would lose my U.S. citizenship for living too long (then three years) on British soil, finally made me realize that I would have to leave this wonderful place. Despite the asthma I had become an expert snorkeler and apart from my lungs I was in good physical condition. What irony! But I became so ill at one time that I overdosed on an inhaled medicine and started to lapse in and out of consciousness. Mim called an ambulance and the next thing I knew (I slept through the part when the ambulance got mired in the cesspool), I was in an operating room at King Edward VII Hospital, under a big bright round lamp, like a synthetic sun, with white-garbed people looking at me while cortisone oozed into my vein from a drip.

Not very long afterwards, I was sitting on the sand at Elbow Beach, talking with three friends. Jill, an American woman working at the U.S. consulate, had just told the story of the Bishop of Bermuda's visit to Noel Coward, just after he had moved into a house in Southampton Parish. Coward had been working in his kitchen, wearing nothing but an apron, when the bishop rang his front-door bell. Like any decent householder, the famous writer and performer hurried to respond.

"Good afternoon, Mr. Coward," said his visitor. "I am the Church of England bishop of Bermuda, and I thought I would drop by to welcome you to the islands."

"Just a moment," said Coward, "Let me put on my dressing gown. Won't be a moment."

With that the famous man pattered off down the hall, exposing his unadorned derrière to the visiting cleric. Jill told us that, when Coward returned, there was nothing left of the strait-laced bishop but the disappearing image of a car retreating quickly down Lighthouse Hill.

We all laughed, and I turned to Jill. "Sounds like you have a great job, being posted to Bermuda. Some people would give their eye teeth for it."

She smiled, then sobered. "Not always. Last week I had to go to this guy's house and ask for his passport back."

97

"Maybe a criminal hiding out," I ventured. "Had dual nationality, perhaps."

She tossed her head. "He'd just been on his native soil for more than three years. We don't allow that for naturalized citizens."

I checked my mental calendar and went cold. The shock was real. I had two weeks left, after one year in the British colony of Bermuda, one in England, and (almost) one more in Bermuda.

The three-year law is long gone, but in those days it was even more compelling than the vagaries of chronic asthma, and it was evident that Miriam and I would have to leave.

I didn't feel quite ready to return to the States. Young people should invest their time in gathering new experiences – I believed that then, and happily I would live to see my children living their lives in accordance with this way of thinking. Still, I was in a spot, but I thought I knew a way out. Since I could spend *eight* years in a variety of places without having my passport yanked, so long as I didn't set foot on British territory, I might be able to satisfy my humanitarian urges by getting a job with the United Nations in Geneva. A good idea, but it didn't work, at least partly because the U.N. quota for American and British staffers was brimming over. I checked, but Radio Suisse didn't need me for its English-language service based in Bern. Back at the Palais des Nations in Geneva things looked brighter at the bureau maintained by my old company, UPI. It happened that the bureau chief, Nicholas Daniloff, was to be transferred to Moscow the next day and since no replacement had arrived perhaps I could take his place. What a stroke of luck! Maybe this would be one of those serendipitous coincidences they talked about!

Nick asked me to translate a French-language news story from Agence France Presse as a test of my linguistic capability. This was successful, so I went to bed with high expectations. But Nick's boss in London, Paul Allerup, had been at work. Miraculously Nick's replacement arrived in time to keep the bureau going. (Later, after he had moved to *U.S. News and World Report*, Nick was arrested in Moscow and held for 13 days by the KGB.)

Nick did not know the true extent of my acquaintance with the French language. When I sat down for coffee with my elderly landlady at her bed-and-breakfast *pension*, I decided I should attempt some friendly conversation. The lady was clad in black, so I thought I would start by asking if she were widowed. "*Pardonnez-moi, madame, mais dites-moi, est-ce que vous êtes une vierge?*" I asked solicitously. And then I must have gone pale. In a flash of horror I remembered that, in French, a widow is *une veuve*. I had asked the poor woman if she was a virgin.

After that there was nothing for it but to retrace my steps. Reluctantly Mim and I packed our bags, and I gave our Portuguese gardener a barracuda I had speared but which had annoyed us anyway, by swinging its head out of the refrigerator door every time I opened it. Then we returned to Utah. My mother and dad were overjoyed to see us at their door in Pleasant Grove, and we were glad to find safe harbour. But Salt Lake City wasn't quite ready for the peregrine's return.

8. RETURN TO THE WEST

You are free and that is why you are lost.
— Franz Kafka

No one wanted me in Salt Lake City. The *Salt Lake Tribune* didn't want me, the *Deseret News* didn't want me, the television and radio stations were getting their news from UPI and Associated Press, who didn't want me either. One day in desperation I drove off in my car and applied for a job at the U.S. Army's Tooele Ordnance Depot, in the desert 35 barren miles west of town. Like the huge Dugway Proving Ground, 40 miles away, it was involved in chemical and biological weaponry. A few years later, in 1968, Dugway would become infamous for the accidental deaths of thousands of grazing sheep, caused by the inadvertent escape into the atmosphere of biological weapon agents.

Fortunately, Tooele didn't want me, either. The government would take its time.

Mim and I lived off my parents for three months at their new home in Pleasant Grove, in the foothills of Timpanogos, which appropriately means Rock Canyon Mountain in the Ute language. I had the bright idea of shaving off my beard. The next day I was hired by Weltech College, a privately owned electronics trade school whose president, Dale Smith, had been worrying that I might be a Castro supporter.

I'll say one thing about Weltech. It was a great ego-booster, my first executive position, with a grand desk in the school's spanking new, two-story red-brick building. My job was to set up and run the school's promotional campaigns, concentrating on the use of direct mail to find high school seniors who might want to join the ranks of California's booming defence industries.

Was I worth my money? Apparently yes, for my efforts were fruitful to an extent that surprised us all. And, amazingly, *all* our graduates were finding jobs, which was fortunate because in the headiness of an early success we were offering money-back guarantees to those who did not. Then, trapped in the euphoria of success, my colleagues over-expanded the business and it began to fail. Miraculously I came out ahead.

My bank account fattened during my thirty months at Weltech. More importantly, the job introduced me to public relations and specialized marketing, and gave me the opportunity to write and direct my first documentary film, a 20-minute feature about jobs that the aerospace industries needed to fill.

The siren song of adventure filled my head when I heard that Edmund Hillary was visiting Utah, and in fact was touring the wilderness of the Uinta Mountains, east of Salt Lake City. The fame of this New Zealand mountaineer, born of a Yorkshire family, became part of history when on May 29, 1953, he and his Sherpa companion Tenzing Norgay were confirmed as the first climbers to reach the summit of Mount Everest. I was captivated by the idea of meeting Hillary and interviewing him for a freelance magazine article. Should be great fun, I thought.

Soon Mim and I were packing the old Chevrolet with supplies – too few, as it turned out – for a magical quest to mountainous forest lands where one peak, measuring more than 12,000 feet in elevation, is named after the Swiss geologist Louis Agassiz, one of the great heroes of natural history.

The Uintas cover a huge amount of breathtakingly magnificent territory, branching off in an east-west direction from the main Rocky Mountain range and containing more than 500 lakes. One of these, Rainbow Lake, was our destination, for we had news that Hillary, his family, and his forest-service guides would be making camp there.

Inexpert at map-reading and solar navigation, exhausted, and pursued by huge and hungry mosquitoes, we did not find the camp until late afternoon. We met the great man, who was in a genial mood. We had to confess that we possessed not a single blanket, let alone sleeping bags. The interview was forgotten; survival was the priority in country where the temperature plummets at sunset. We managed a brief exchange of information, but Hillary had grasped the situation immediately. "Why don't you sleep in our food tent?" he suggested amiably. "We have a few extra blankets."

Next morning, carrying a few notes and half a roll of photographs, we stumbled back onto the trail (the right one, we were assured) after sharing beans, eggs, and conversation with our tall, craggy-faced host. We promptly got lost again. The mountains were becoming ever more fascinating to me, which was an odd thing because I was already enthralled by their beauty, and then I stopped in my tracks. Something in my addled brain had clicked.

"I need to lie down," I told Mim. "Need to get some of my energy back."

"Oh, it won't be far now," she said with feigned brightness, "let's keep going for a quarter mile or so."

Fifty yards farther along the trail I stopped again. "Gotta lie down," I said, looking longingly at the peaty earth. "Just give me five minutes."

But Mim's nursing training had come back to her, and she kept me going. She knew I was exhausted, no other people were in evidence, and she couldn't carry me out. As for me, I didn't know how much longer I could last. Fortunately I was too tired to think about it.

About quarter of a mile from my first relapse, we saw the glint of metal through the trees. Then a whole car, then a whole parking lot, and then we caught a lift to where we had left our car. Survival! This time I let Mim drive.

I never did write that freelance article.

A couple of months later Mim and I made time to work on a social survey of an old silver and lead mining community that lay directly east of Salt Lake, now 40 minutes by road on the other side of the pine-clad mountains of Wasatch National Forest. There was a story, so strange that at first I suspected it was *not* an apocryphal tale, that the original town was built with bricks sent by mail in individual packages because this was cheaper than hiring wagon freight. The tale may have been borrowed from a similar, well-documented story. Not very far away, during the 1910s, it *was* decided to build a bank using the bricks-by-mail scheme in the town of Vernal, Utah. More than 40 tons of brick were delivered over a 420-mile route by the post office.[12] Shortly afterwards, the federal government declared that "it is not the intent of the United States Postal Services that buildings be shipped through the mail."

For a couple of weeks Mim and I worked our way between huge potholes, the rickety, rusting hulks of mine buildings to either side of us, talking to the remaining residents. What would they think if their town were to be redeveloped for tourism? They would stare at us as though we were visitors from Mars. They didn't know. They just wanted to have decent jobs and get off welfare.

Not too many years later the developers moved in, and Park City was poised to become a ski resort, with an international reputation that landed it a spot as a venue for some of the 2002 Winter Olympic Games. By the turn of the 21st century the chamber of commerce would say "Park City has the appearance of a picturesque, nineteenth-century mining town, and it is a modern alpine resort." In other words it was absolutely nothing like the rotting ghost town that Miriam and I canvassed when Beatlemania was about to bloom, in 1962.

Most of my old university friends had drifted away by now. But one day there came a knock at the door and I opened it to Howard Glasgow, the potter who during my absence had changed his first name to Lukman. It seems this happened when he joined the Bahá'í Faith, a religion that spun out of Islam in 19th century Persia. He didn't talk about it much, but from what he did say it occurred to me that, if one felt the need for a religion, this might not be a bad one to investigate. I introduced Lukman to Miriam, and then he excused himself to go back to his car, returning with a large, heavy cardboard box. In it was a ceramic mural composed of many carefully packed, irregular pieces of glazed, fired clay – stars, a moon, planets, feet, hands. We watched dumfounded as without asking he removed my pictures from their hanging-places and fixed his masterpiece in their place. That very large ceramic foot, he explained, symbolized Jesus, who walked everywhere with his message. Howard/Lukman had apparently not given up all of his Christian grounding.

Soon after our arrival in Utah, Mim and I had begun periodic visits to St. Christopher's Mission, founded in 1943 by Father H. Baxter Liebler, an Episcopal priest from Connecticut. It is located in Bluff, an aptly named Mormon outpost at the foot of huge sandstone cliffs at the extreme south-eastern corner of Utah on the north-eastern edge of the huge Navajo reservation. Here was a virtually treeless, grass-less land that might terrify a city-dweller. But to the curious man it was a paradise. It was an adventure to negotiate the rickety swinging suspension footbridge, one plank wide, to explore the cliff-dwellings that sat in shallow caves overlooking Montezuma Creek and finding tiny old corncobs in their sandy corners. It was exciting to know that Navajo Indians lived all around us – and to be waved away from the private healing "sings" used by shamans to cure illnesses, then invited afterwards to share mutton stew and deep-fried flatbread by these friendly, deeply tanned desert people.

Above all it was a joy to go walkabout with Father Liebler in his beaten-up but marvellously rugged Jeep camper on the difficult 150-mile trail to Navajo Mountain, where we made miniature campfires from twigs gathered from the desert and cooked eggs that we had carried frozen in a butane-powered refrigerator.

Making the rounds. Navajo elder visits St. Christopher's Mission, 1964.

How Father Liebler navigated that huge area west and north of Kayenta mystified me. He seemed to be able to follow trails over bare rocks, finding his way unerringly to his flock's octagonal, log-built *hogan* homes to hand out gifts from his trove of supplies – canned foods, powdered milk, toys for the kids. On Sundays he would say Mass on a folding table we carried with us, his figure clad in a plain black cassock, illuminated in the light admitted by the smoke-hole of a borrowed hogan, the greying Navajo-style ponytail bobbing jauntily over his neck.

I remember seeing the head of a stone axe on the ground outside the door of one of the hogans – an oval-shaped rock tapered at both ends and grooved around the waist for leather strapping – as if it had been dropped there a few minutes before. But how long *had* it been there? The idea sprang to my mind that I might take it home with me, for Navajo people consider it correct to take things that belong to other people provided their owners have no longer any use for them. But I didn't even mention seeing it because of Navajo superstitions about the dead. When someone dies, a malevolent ghost, a *chindi*, hangs around, and people do everything they can to avoid it. Perhaps the axe had been hexed by *chindi*.

St. Christopher's Mission became a National Historic Site in 2003.

By the time we started visiting Bluff much of the romanticism that had infused my early thinking about Indians had worn away, and good riddance. I was never a hippie, though I had a slight leaning that way. Now that proclivity was gone. As Stewart Brand, creator of the *Whole Earth Catalog,* said, hippiedom was "a notion that civilization is going downhill, that bad people and bad institutions and bad ideas are shaking all that is right and good out of the world and this must be resisted even though it's a losing battle. It's a wonderfully coherent way to think and live. It just happens to be wrong. But that's part of the fun of being a romantic: you get to defy reality." [13]

My curiosity about the Navajo and Pueblo Indian traditions, which have many similarities with aboriginal ways in other parts of the Americas and the world, arose because I could see there was something remarkable about this land and the people who inhabited it. On one of my peregrinations with Father Liebler, while talking with a Navajo man who would walk miles for a bucket for water each day, he confided that he once had a good job with the Santa Fe Railway. Why did he leave? He smiled gently. Because he missed his homeland, he said. What could be more natural? And yet he had left all the comforts of modern life behind, to rejoin a culture that, in this remote spot, was little more than Neolithic. I was coming face to face with something I had never known before. Being curious, I wanted to know what it was.

I learned that, in their Night Way ceremony, the Navajo people rejoice that, "In the house made of dawn ... I walk, with beauty all around me, I walk." And that a favourite blessing that Navajos offer to their friends is the simple, "May you walk in beauty." This seemed to be at the heart of the worldview shared by the people who inhabit this inhospitable desert terrain. The fact that it should hold so much power in a place of such isolation made it all the more attractive. I consider myself unusually fortunate that I was able to experience the all-embracing beauty of a wide, vastly open, magical land that I too came to see as a beautiful place.

At Bluff I gained my first inkling of the special knowledge that is absorbed from their earliest years by the desert Indians, and which epitomizes their very strong affinity with the natural environment. I wondered why this quality seemed to exist in so *many* Indian cultures, which are spread all over the Americas and communicate in many different languages. What was the essential element of that cultural bridge? The word that first comes to my mind is gentleness, but that is incorrect. Rather, there is a quiet and humble confidence of one's place in the cosmic scheme of things and the desire to preserve it. Once arrived at this point, it seems, one feels no special need to acquire an overabundance of the necessities of life – food, water, clothing, shelter – just a sufficiency, no more. "The story resembles the Old Testament in that its origins reach deep into the inscrutable loam of a primeval past," wrote Paul Zolbrod in his book about the Navajo creation story. "The central theme is the attainment of *hozho*, a fairly untranslatable term which can only be approximated in English by combining words like *beauty, balance*, and *harmony*."[14] The idea of *hozho* carries the essence of Buddhism and the Tao.

Today, almost all Indians have TV, radio, and the Internet, and are fully aware of the comforts of mainstream American life. So it is not surprising that so many are lured by the abstractions of the white man's media and drift away from their homelands to find the artefacts of the rich. Many are successful. But others are soon overtaken by the spectres of loneliness and defeat. The town of Gallup, New Mexico, is sadly famous for its cases of Navajo depression, violence, drunkenness and suicide. Some Indians learn to compromise, like my Cochiti Pueblo friend, a certified public accountant who would drive fifty miles to and from work in Albuquerque, every day, and my Acoma Pueblo friend Myron, who bought a home in town but quite soon returned to a government-built house even farther away than the home of the man from Cochiti. He telephoned me one night. "Come see me, Nigel," he said. "It is so beautiful out here. I can sit on my front step and see the Milky Way."

Indians have their own versions of how the world began, and how humans came to be – versions that sometimes vary within a single tribe. And there are superstitions galore. I heard of a spooky event when a coyote (they say) jumped up on the roof of a hogan and blew ghost dust down the smoke hole and one of the family died and the rest got sick. *Chindi*, ghost sickness. Even the Navajo Police were called. As a result the hogan had to be "killed," its side broken in and the place abandoned. Coyote is a trickster, but more than that, he's a pretty bad *hombre* out on the Big Rez.

All the Indians fascinated and awed me, and they forever retained that position in my mind. One evening, after a few drinks at the National Press Club bar in Washington, I rather carelessly told a political columnist friend that, as role models, "the Indians are America's most precious natural resource," because I saw the growing urgency for all people to moderate their materialism and embrace the natural scheme of things.

These people were nothing like the "redskins" in the Western films I had seen first as a child in Morecambe. Later I learned that, in the Nightway ceremonial, the singer reminds his people:

In the house made of dawn,
in the house made of sunset light
in the house made of rain cloud
with beauty before me, I walk,
with beauty before me, I walk,
with beauty all around me, I walk.[15]

"With beauty all around me, I walk." How I loved that stanza! The thought was so empty of pride and full of warm thanksgiving that it inspired me. It was very much in tune with my Juniperhill awakening, but it would be years before I realized this.

Six months or so before Weltech went ignominiously out of business, I answered an ad in *Editor & Publisher*, and a plain-speaking, white-haired man named Ed Lewis, a Welshman by name, physique and inclination if not by birth, flew up from Albuquerque to make our acquaintance.

I reported for work at Ed's Newspaper Printing Corporation the first week of April, 1965. Mim and I drove into Albuquerque on the pre-Interstate, supposedly romantic Route 66, marvelling that a few snowflakes were falling as we drove down Nine Mile Hill to our new home. We had a U-Haul trailer in tow behind the '65 Chevy (Mim timorously at the wheel) while I trailed behind in our Austin-Healey 3000.

At this newspaper there was no Linotype, only a row of paper-tape-driven, typewriter-like Frieden machines that produced the "cold type" of the time. They created printouts that supposedly looked like conventional hot type, but which had ugly, oversized punctuation marks and had to be cut up, pasted into the correct format on light tables, made into photographic negatives with a big Brown camera, transferred onto zinc sheets, and printed by the offset method. Frieden-type technology was then in the early stages of being replaced by computer typesetting.

I learned that, since my hiring, the editor of the smallest member of this little chain of weeklies, the *Valencia County News*, had resigned and started her own paper in the same circulation area, taking most advertisers with her. Some of the business owners had felt bound to follow her because advertising service was about the only way she could pay off the debts she had run up with them. My first New Mexico job would be to rescue the *Valencia County News*.

The Los Lunas paper was like its brethren in Albuquerque a weekly "shopper" (i.e. a giveaway publication), and only just paying its way. I felt the ex-editor of the rival sheet competed in an underhanded way – including rumour-mongering and smear tactics – but we managed to prevail and my competitor disappeared from the scene 10 months later, a trail of creditors behind her.

New Mexico was like Utah in that it offered a sunny combination of high desert and mountain, in that part of America known casually as the Mountain West, where rain was scarce and day-night temperatures could differ by as much as 30 degrees Fahrenheit. Otherwise it was quite different. The Mormon population was small and the Hispanic population was large. Indians mixed easily with the supermarket crowds, the older people sometimes wearing traditional dress. Whereas Salt Lake City has to its west the huge dead sea from which it takes its name, mile-high Albuquerque has the Rio Grande running through its young metropolis. One midsummer day I managed to walk across the river, emerging on the other side with dry feet and muddy shoes for evidence.

Los Lunas was an instructive introduction to the state. Nearly everyone in town spoke with a distinctive New Mexico Spanish accent, which with some regret I realized would die away with their owners and as central New Mexico was flooded with English-speakers drawn in by the big government labs and industries, by retirees seeking the sun, by out-of-state educators who cared nothing for the local lingo. Across the street from us, Simon Neustadt's big supermarket towered over Mili Castillo's tiny grocery. There was a locally owned electrical appliance shop nearby, and a big hardware store, Huning's. All of these, including Neustadt's, were in the path of the march of one-stop-shopping superstores, and would not survive for long.

Twenty-two miles south of Albuquerque, Los Lunas was founded in 1808 by its namesake, Antonio José Luna, who raised sheep and sold them to rich Californians so successfully that he hired enough workers to form a town. Mim and I loved the Hispanic flavour of the place, and learned from it. Few Anglos lived there in those days, and some had Arabic-tinged names (Salazar, Alvarez,

Alcalde, etc.) that advertised their ancient origins in this onetime Spanish colony. Los Lunas was then a close-knit town; in a couple of decades it would become a bedroom community of Albuquerque. The local political chieftain, based a few miles south in the old railroad town of Belen, was Filo Sedillo. A colourful character, Filo liked to preside at traditional outdoor feasts (*matanzas*), and I imagined him quite capable of using a liberal amount of good-ol'-boy pressure to win votes.

My Los Lunas education ranged from pulling porcupine spines from a feral dog's nose with pliers to dealing with a red-faced local service station entrepreneur who, after I published something mildly unfavourable about his school-board opinions, threatened to withdraw his advertising. I published a photo of a fugitive who had been captured by the sheriff while hitchhiking, dressed in his dead wife's clothing, and felt badly about it afterwards because he was obviously deranged. In addition to school board meetings, I covered county court trials, fatal accidents, everything I could lay my hands on. At one time, to my delight, I helped with the local rodeo, publicizing the event from a pickup truck equipped with a loudspeaker, and introducing some of the events from the announcers' booth. The English accent must have sounded strange to local cowboy ears.

By the time we arrived in Los Lunas, a couple of subdivisions had sprung up between there and the city, at Bosque Farms and El Cerro, but some truly large housing development corporations had their eyes on much, much bigger things. A large tract of land was sliced into lots east of the town of Belen, and a truly gargantuan plan had already begun at Rio Rancho, just northwest of Albuquerque, on the other side of the river. They already had a country club, looking rather grandiose in a little housing estate that was surrounded by scrubby desert. With time, it would become the fastest-growing city in the United States.

⊙≋

At one time, Ed Lewis and I made an unsuccessful attempt to launch a Laguna Pueblo edition of the *Valencia County News*. It was a strange experience, sitting in a tribal council meeting and listening mutely as the conservative elders defeated the young bloods in their own Keres language, nipping our proposal neatly in the bud. The period also included my "discovering" an unmarked rectangular kiva (Pueblo ceremonial room) to the west of Albuquerque, being nearly run down by a bull while photographing a rodeo, playing host to an Englishman who was riding a Vespa from Québec to Panama (never heard from him again), and driving the Austin-Healey we had brought down from Utah through the blinding dust-storms that would descend on the narrow route to our Albuquerque printing establishment across the tracks from what was then Fred Harvey's Alvarado Hotel. It was at our pitched-roof adobe Los Lunas house that we saw Winston Churchill's funeral, live, on the first TV I ever bought, while I was trying to patch the floor-to-ceiling adobe crack through the living room wall that allowed us to see visitors approaching. In April 1965, Mark Acuff was hired as editor of the *Valencia County News*, nominally under my direction, with the assistance of his wife Mary Beth.

In 1966 our landlord decided to sell the house with the dirt roof and we moved to a new home on Guadalupe Trail, not far away in Los Ranchos, a semi-rural incorporated village adjoining Albuquerque's North Valley. That fall our editor-in-chief quit and I inherited the responsibility, meaning that I had to generate, single-handedly, the editorial content of both papers with no help except for that of part-time neighbourhood correspondents.

In the following two years the public impact of the *Albuquerque News* increased, though its material prosperity was a source of disappointment. I knew the *News* was being read by a large percentage of the people in its distribution area, and that it was respected by some of the city's top people. Aside from this there was no indicator of success. Advertising was on a plateau, and had been for 12 months or more.

Aside from a gratifying stream of praiseful letters from happy readers, a bonus of producing the *News* was winning two New Mexico Press Association awards, one for weekly newspaper editorial writing and another for news feature photography. I used the position to meet a lot of interesting people – a local druid, for example, and the wealthy Wilhelmina "Willy" Coe, whose "Seven Heavens" holistic vegetarian enterprise I wrote up in the February 3, 1966, issue. More than 20 years later, after Willy's death, I was called to testify in a court action that questioned her soundness of mind when she left much of her considerable estate to local charities. I gave them my honest, amateur opinion that she had some unconventional ideas, but was nevertheless completely sane. One of the lawyers asked for my autograph.

My metaphysical inclinations received a jolt of reinforcement when I went to hear Alan Watts speak at the University of New Mexico. Watts, the English son of an Anglican clergyman, railed against the myth of skin — the absurd, unthought presumption that skin separates us from the universe — and I applauded it in my heart. Soon I had all of Watts's writings on my bookshelf, and they are there still.

Watts notwithstanding, I had decided by the late 1960s that among my many interests the most joyous things in life were writing and making love. Later the most joyous would become writing, which leaned increasingly toward philosophical matters, though I am an amateur intellectual at best. For many of my friends, conversation and good food were the most joyous things, that is, most capable of producing delight. I enjoyed these too, but they never made the No. 1 and No. 2 spots in my list of earthly delights. Sometimes I wonder what sort of a man I would have become if I had given them greater priority.

Making love and nonfiction writing are similar in that they are both about sharing, which I define as a good thing. But of course there are differences. Making love depends upon the participation of a receptive partner; otherwise one way or the other it falls flat. But writing is famously an occupation that requires some seclusion.

⊙❈❨

The Korean War was long gone by now. Martin Luther King was a hero in the U.S. and Nelson Mandela was heading the anti-apartheid movement in South Africa. But John F. Kennedy had been assassinated; the Cold War was heating up, and things were turning very ugly in Vietnam. Hippies were crowding into New Mexico, some in flower-painted school buses and Volkswagen campers. They squatted in out-of-the-way hideouts from Tijeras to Taos, and I visited some of them, trying to figure out who they were and what they believed. This was mostly disappointing. The flower children I met were vaguely interested in Zen and free love, and some pretended, unsuccessfully, to emulate Indian ways. Many were rich kids trying to escape parental values. In a few years most would drift away, via San Francisco and then home perhaps, leaving rusting cars and broken-down shelters in their wake. Some live in New Mexico still, getting greyer, making a slim living, caring about ecology and "green" causes, and being spiritual.

The hippies did intrigue me, however, and I suppose that in a mild way they helped strengthen my penchant for thinking philosophically. From the beginning I thought it an amazing excess of mass narcissism to believe that humans were created in God's image, if indeed God existed. I thought it was even more

111

excessive, even mad, to claim that, by joining one church or another, one would earn the right to speak personally with God or Jesus.

So what were humans about? How and why had they developed into a creature so powerful it could destroy not only its own kind, but most of the animal kingdom as well? Humanity was apparently unique because its membership could speak, muse upon the future, and conceive rules of conduct that they could then extol for the good of individuals and their tribes. They could mull over the meaning of life, find ways of rationalizing an answer, and arrive at ways of dealing with that answer. And they could investigate the ways of nature and cosmos; invent ways of healing the sick; and make wondrous machines. Our predecessors rightly believed these to be wonderful things, for they had made it possible for physically weak humans to survive in difficult circumstances and physically hostile environments.

I also thought that too large a chasm yawned between the desires and capabilities that nature had provided to humankind and the material resources she provided on this small planet. Perhaps Rachel Carson (*Silent Spring*, 1962) influenced me a little at this time; certainly I had been impressed, among others, by the writings of Malthus, Aldous Huxley, and George Orwell. Their influence may have gone overboard, for there were times that I wondered seriously whether *homo sapiens sapiens* was in fact Nature's Great Mistake – a malign organism that was fated to slay the planet with the finality that tiny bark beetles will destroy a forest of drought-weakened New Mexico piñon pines. I considered that humans, with their intelligence and their tools, are able to halt their destruction of the planet. But *will* they, I asked, in view of the consumptive greed of a population that is increasing at juggernaut speed? I wasn't sure. In fact I was profoundly sceptical that anything could be done to slow our species' destruction of the things upon which we depend totally for our existence.

Is it wrong to suggest that our kind has broken free from the benevolent ecological bond, running helplessly and hopelessly amok, irreversibly bound to destroy the planet upon which we depend? I believed my fear was justifiable, though I know many would find the idea heretical or even blasphemous in some radically anthropocentric way. I am not inclined to recant this opinion. I remember one time asking a scientist his thoughts about the earth's animal life, and the apparently unstoppable extinction of species. What will we do about the animals? I asked. "We will eat them," he said immediately and in a very matter of fact way, with no indication that this was even a bad joke. It was not funny. In fact it may turn out to be an appallingly prophetic idea, and I urgently hope otherwise.

Thinking of such things, I would fall into a mild, middle-distance depression, thinking that only a pandemic, an asteroid strike, an enormous volcanic eruption, or nuclear war could reduce the population enough to make the survivors think seriously about the requirements for continued survival. Some manic dreamers spend millions on ideas for the future colonization of Mars, so that the last few humans could go there and propagate our kind in shielded houses, *in vitro* as it were. I tossed off such ideas as ill-conceived and unworkable. Fortunately I had also read Teilhard de Chardin, whom many people dismiss as a teller of legless dreams, and then became caught up with the idea that *homo sapiens sapiens* – "the man who knows he knows" – had been on a learning curve for centuries, and that human *thought*, and thence our behaviour as well, was steadily evolving into something better, wiser, more respectful of nature's inescapable way, and less inclined to conflict. I could perceive some truth in this embroidered extension of Teilhard's philosophy, though faintly and not without scepticism. I had trouble imagining that the species could ever escape from the global, choking tsunami of toxic materials, plastic bottles, excrement, and hunger-starved bodies that already were accumulating from the consumerism that nearly all of us call civilization. On the other hand, we might consider that humankind is perhaps only halfway through its term of existence. If that is the case, there may be time to realize Teilhard's dream of blending the totality of human consciousness with the cosmos, at what he called the Omega Point.

The idea never lost its allure. In 1955, an eminent geneticist, the Nobel prizewinner H. J. Muller, noted that, though the path to these goals is laden with difficulties, the "seed of self-awareness and self-transfiguration" in human beings gives them "the means whereby life is conducted onward and outward, to forms in ever better harmony within themselves, with one another, and with outer nature, endowed with ever keener sentience, deeper wisdom, and further reaching powers."[16]

Imagine my delight when Martin A. Nowak, an expert on evolution and game theory and professor of biology and mathematics at Harvard University, said something similar in a book he wrote with my science-writer friend Roger Highfield. For many decades it had been accepted that mutation and natural selection alone lay at the heart of evolutionary processes. Now, in 2011, Nowak was arguing convincingly that there is additionally a third necessity for evolution, especially important to the human species. This, he said, was *cooperation*, "the constructive side of evolution" and its "master architect."[xvii] Very soon thereafter, the eminent evolutionary biologist Edward O. Wilson endorsed this "eusocial" cooperation theory in his book *The Social Conquest of Earth* (Liveright, 2012).

Life at the Albuquerque *News* – there were three editions, Valencia County, Heights, and Valley – gave me time to get to know Albuquerque and its environs, to get to know personalities like Pete Domenici, who would later become New Mexico's senior senator, and of course to think and occasionally work on my own books and essays. My first child would be born during those eighteen months, introducing me at last to fatherhood. And I would start to take acting parts in local theatrical events. I was not an actor. I had the requisite ego and could speak the language well, provided I had a script, no more. It would have been a better use of time to spend more time with the family, read some good books, and, maybe, write.

My first child would be a gift from God, but in retrospect I cannot say the same about theatre. Here the blessings proved to be mixed.

9. THE GREEK MADNESS

Only those who will risk going too far can possibly find out how far one can go.
— T. S. Eliot

People I meet at parties quite often get the idea that I have fallen into a hallucinatory state when I tell them I once worked as a civil engineer. Their doubt deepens when I explain that I acted in this capacity while driving a tunnel into the side of a mountain in the wilds of western Greece. I have twinges of disbelief myself when I think about it.

Though this will seem unlikely to those familiar with my life as a dedicated journalist, legal documents show that, in June 1966, I abruptly declared a leave of absence from Newspaper Printing Corporation and moved out of our rented Albuquerque house, to do just that. This was just one of the twists in my life that resulted from my on-again, off-again affair with local theatre.

The Greek escapade started when I recruited Don "Sparky" Buddecke as spear-carrier for the Old Town Studio theatre, where I was playing the title role in Shakespeare's *Richard II*. It happened that Mim was pregnant with Brian, and we both liked the idea that the newcomer could be born in England, which was more or less on the way to Greece. It also happened because I was prone to the lust for adventure, and to seizures of compulsion so captivating that whatever it was *had to happen*, before I considered whether disaster would result. Throughout my life this propensity has bedevilled my relationships with scores of friends and lovers, but there it is – once the impulse strikes, it sticks like superglue. Darwin wrote of the "delusion of free will," but for me its expression was tantamount to necessity.

This time the compulsion proved to be stupendously worth carrying out, and dangerous to boot.

Sparky was not a natural actor. He was a mining engineer, short of stature, with a great head of wiry, strawberry blond hair. Good natured and humorous to a fault, he had agreed to enunciate four words from the Bard's immortal text, which he unfailingly forgot. "My lord, I come!" Or something like that.

One evening when I went to pick up Sparky for rehearsal he had just taken a long-distance telephone call, and his face was flushed. "I've been offered a job in the mountains of Greece!" he announced. Apparently the U.S. Agency for International Development had financed construction of the largest earth-fill dam in Europe, the King Paul Dam. But it leaked, causing beautiful but worrisome waterfalls to spring from the walls of the valley downstream. This meant that tunnels would have to be driven into the canyon just below the dam, so that crews could inject waterproofing cement into the leaking strata and prevent the erosion that was even now beginning. Sparky was being invited to drive one of these tunnels, or drifts.

"Great!" I said. "That sounds like wonderful fun. When do we leave?"

Now this of course was a flip spur-of-the-moment comment. I had a job, Miriam was well along in her first pregnancy, and we had established residency just up the road from the Buddeckes' in an old house that was served by an old silting-up well with a pump that at times delivered not water but a light muddy slurry, like potter's slip.

Flip comment or not, the idea grew on me fast. The job editing the *News* no longer presented the stimulus of a new challenge, adventure called, and, wouldn't it be nice for the newcomer to be born in England. Soon Sparky was telling me yes, he could use someone in Greece to work with the local government, keep a log, and so on. Since I was not gifted with the prescience to know that this could be an unwise choice, it sounded perfectly plausible to me. Next day I told Ed Lewis that I intended to take a "leave of absence" from my regular job. He may not have liked the idea, but he understood my need.

In an excited flurry Mim and I put our belongings in cardboard boxes and left them in the Buddeckes' garage, and then we were off. We decamped at the Folkestone house of Mim's mother and father, and then – they probably thought I was stark, raving mad – I continued blithely onward and alone to Greece, fragmentary images from *Zorba the Greek* tapping at my brainbox.

I arrived in Athens in a cheerful mood, checked in at a hotel near the botanical garden at the top of Constitution Square, and called our employer's local manager, Fred Stewart.

Though he was hospitable enough to buy me a cup of coffee, there was a strange lack of enthusiasm in my new boss's greeting. I suggested I fly up to Agrinion, the market town nearest the dam site, but he advised me that flights were fully booked for 30 days or more. I could, however, catch a ride by car with Leo Broderick, who was driving up in the morning.

Stewart's coolness left me feeling very unsettled. I left his office and immediately encountered a well-dressed man who engaged me in conversation, expressed his lifelong devotion to Britain and the States, and invited me to have a drink with him. Already confused by Stewart's manner, I agreed and before I knew it was whisked into a restaurant in a nearby alley. To put it briefly, we sat at the bar, drinks arrived, then the man disappeared and was replaced by a nubile young woman. The woman was definitely attractive, but her friendliness was applied with an assumed ardour that made alarm bells ring. I made an excuse and made for the door, chased by a waiter who demanded an exorbitant payment for the drinks. I ignored him, and when I entered my swanky hotel he disappeared from the picture.

Leo didn't help either. He was cordial but quiet and I suspected he was also being secretive. Something was happening that affected me, but I wasn't being let in on it. I was also tense because I was afraid he would ask me questions that would reveal my ignorance of civil engineering and mining. The joy of adventure was waning, just a little.

The next day's drive took us northwest, in Leo's dusty green Chevrolet sedan, across the Corinth Canal by bridge, then along the northern edge of the Peloponnesian Peninsula to Rion/Antirrion, then northward to Agrinion and

Two and Only. This is the only formal photograph of my parents together that I possess. It must have been taken around the time I was in Greece.

117

the south-western edge of the Pindus mountains. It was spectacular but arduous; eight hours elapsed before we saw the sprinkling of lights that was the construction camp, spread below as we shot around a corner in the dirt road that snaked through the mountains to Kremasta. Peasants waved angrily and shouted warnings as the big car roared onward: *Arga! Arga!* Slow! Slow!

As we descended from the mountains an hour and a half later we could see the lake behind the dam, shining pallidly under a half moon. Leo drove past a number of warehouses and a single, rickety-looking restaurant before parking in front of a small complex of modern stone-faced single-story buildings. When he knocked on the door, I finally experienced a feeling of relieved anticipation. At last, after this long and confusing trip to one of the most isolated spots in Europe, I would be able to get the straight story from my friend.

Shortly the door opened and there was Sparky, my friend. But something was amiss. His eyes widened with surprise and I thought, "Hello, what's this?"

We shook hands but he didn't waste time with pleasantries. "Didn't you get my note in Athens?"

"No. What did it say?"

"It said, 'Go home immediately.'"

Leo left for some unknown destination, leaving Sparky to explain out the mystery in his own way. I never saw Leo again.

Apparently there had been a falling-out between the management in Athens and the home office in Los Angeles. It was a miracle that Sparky still had a job, but this was tenuous – a friend of the local manager had been hired to do his work while a man called Alex Diamantis, from the Dodecanese Islands, had been hired to do mine. Cronyism strikes in the Greek wilderness!

Sparky didn't see how he could justify keeping me on the staff, hence the note that never arrived. But he did need *mining* help, and since I was already there well, maybe I could manage a crew of local miners.

It sounded risky – I'd never done anything remotely like this except for a few days of half-hearted scrabbling at a tiny uranium mining claim, back in Utah. But what an adventure! When I agreed Sparky took out a small spiral-bound notebook and on a single page gave me the short-short course – the tunnel was to be so wide, so high, and the gradient one half of one percent. The normal placement of powder was in this particular pattern for that size tunnel, with a row of lifter holes at the bottom, equipped with caps that were delayed to detonate a moment after the other charges blew. Then the crew would muck out the debris, chuck it over the side of the canyon, and we'd do it all over again. He wrote all this down, with a diagram of where the drill holes were to go, tore off the page, and gave it to me. That was my education as a civil engineer.

The next morning I got to see the canyon, the great dam with the huge new lake spreading beyond it, and the hydroelectric plant, which at that time was still being outfitted with generators. It was an awesome and beautiful sight.

The practicalities were not so pleasant. Our equipment fleet consisted of one 1963 Jeep pickup with no spare parts, oil or grease, a cracked frame, bad tires, no horn, a broken fuel gauge and a passenger door that was held shut with a clothes hanger. Its fuel tank was replenished by some means unknown to me, for the nearest service station was in Agrinion, a dozen miles over rough, unpaved mountain roads. The vehicle was unlicensed, which meant we could not drive it off the construction site. For that we had to call a taxi, for Leo and the Chevrolet were gone, never to return.

Sparky had been refused the use of surveying equipment, but the future tunnel entrance had been designated, with unknown accuracy, by a yellow stake driven in the loose dirt and rock on the steep hillside on the opposite side of the canyon from the road. It was not accessible by motor vehicle. A Greek crew had nabbed the contract to build the portal that was closer to the access road. So we usually parked at the foot of the dam and walked across the dam face – tons of coarsely broken rock – to the growing hole that we grandly called the portal site.

Little preliminary work seemed to have been done with the government, so that a week elapsed before we could legally employ workers. Arrangements for licensing explosives and explosives handlers, still called powder monkeys, were confused and delayed. A new Land Rover had supposedly been ordered for us but was lost in a customs compound – we didn't know the fine points of bribery and suspected the vehicle had been appropriated by revolutionaries in Athens. For weeks we were working without electrical power.

At one time we were supplied with an instrument that could have been a deadly way of checking the wiring to the dynamite charges. We had been supplied with half-ton mine cars and large carbide lamps, which produced a source of light from acetylene gas that was generated when chunks of calcium carbide inside the thing were exposed to drops of water dripping from built-in reservoirs. It was a long time before we got water injection equipment for the drilling operations, with the result that the drillers inhaled a lot of dust but did their best by tying kerchiefs around their faces. The best we could do was to assign one of the workers to spray water on the rock as the rest of them banged away with jackhammers.

Miraculously, the project got under way. At first there was just that yellow-painted wooden stake to mark the tunnel site. Then our men got together with pick and shovel; then we started to blast the overburden of sand, gravel and rock; then we were tunnelling through conglomerate into the leaky mountainside. We put in rails for a mine car. These were to be used with a mucking machine that we had been expecting for a long time. This machine was like a small mechanical hippo, a ton of heavy steel with a bucket at the front designed to pick up each load of muck blasted from the rock.

The three crates that contained the disassembled machine had been trucked to Kremasta from the ship at Piraeus, and unloaded on the road that crossed the dam. Eight or nine men with ropes manoeuvred it down the gravel of the dam face, tugging and shouting, hoping to hell that the giant mucker would not slide past its mark – we knew we'd never get it back up.

And then there it was, sitting on our newly laid tracks. And it was indeed a monster, operated by high-pressure air. While it was being used there was a constant background noise of hissing and sucking; but when the machinery was engaged there came a great roar, like a prehistoric animal seizing its prey – *aa-aargh-aa* – each time it lunged forward to bite a load of muck before tossing it, accurately, we hoped, overhead and into a mine car coupled to its rear.

At about this time Sparky called an old mining friend – we'll call him Jeb – to put the operation on a three-shift, 24-hour schedule. He was a big, red-faced man with a foul mouth and an unpredictable temper that was aggravated by serious rear-guard attacks from his haemorrhoids. We built a storage shed, diverted water from a spring into a cistern that fed a water supply for the jackhammers, brought in an electric generator – and our most experienced miner, Aristide Rizos, put up a shrine to Santa Barbara, the patron saint of miners. The grizzled Aristide would take me into the drift and show me what happened when he jabbed a metal-spiked wooden stake – a scaling hook – into the dripping tunnel ceiling. It made a hollow, "chok" sound instead of the hard clink that one would expect to hear from solid rock. "Bad," said Aristide, using Greek words that were becoming distressingly familiar, "*polí kakós*. Very bad, Mr. Hey." I didn't know what to do, except to jam more borer-holed Bulgarian boards between the new supports that were beginning to line the tunnel.

One afternoon after quitting the day shift, I went to Papadopoulos' café, the only business left in Kremasta, and sat there drinking retsina while chickens and various other farm animals scavenged among the tables. Then I saw a slim, official-looking figure striding down the gravel path. A policeman in full regalia! I hadn't seen one since my last trip to Agrinion.

The policeman approached, smiled, shook my hand, and introduced himself. He seemed pleasant enough, slim and affable with a beaky nose, his uniform neatly pressed. I shooed the chickens away and offered him a drink. He ordered a *limonada*, which seemed to bode trouble, and then we got down to business.

His English was not very good, but he got the message across. "I just want to let you know, sir, that if there is an accident at the mine, or if someone is killed, your company will not be held responsible." He paused for effect. Then, "Your company is not responsible. You are."

He paused again and my stomach went hollow. Personally responsible, I thought, *personally responsible!*

The policeman gave me a regretful smile and, no doubt because he considered himself a helpful individual, restated the message in mime, crossing his wrists to symbolize the handcuffs and adding a grave, affirmative shake of the head – a 45-degree tilt, not up-and-down as in the West, accompanied with a closing of the eyes which gave the impression that this information would sadly remain valid for the rest of my days. "I thought you should know this, sir." And then rather quickly he was gone, his lemonade untouched.

Next morning Aristide, my wiry little driller, pointed to a gigantic block of conglomerate in the tunnel ceiling, traced out the thin seams of clay in it. Again he said gravely "*polí kakós,*" with a fatalistic look on his wizened 42-year-old face. He knew I could understand these words. I could see all nine workers crushed under the merciless weight of that great boulder like victims of a steam hammer. I could see the heron-like chief of police, the handcuffs and everything. Even Miriam was in my daymare, struggling her way to my mountain cell to show me our newborn babe through the bars.

We asked Sparky's genial friend, the boss-man who got us into all of this, what to do. What if the tunnel *did* collapse? With a smile, in his unflappable way, he said "Oh, we'd just have to arrange, very quickly, for a reassignment of the Kremasta tunnel crew." I was not comforted.

The moment of truth came on the night of July 9, 1966, when the bull cornered the matador. Later I would reflect that perhaps our lives were saved by Jeb's haemorrhoids.

Schumacher, Stewart's studious-seeming, irritating, nit-picking, indecisive geological engineer friend, had been grating on our nerves ever since we arrived. Then his college buddy arrived unexpectedly from Athens and the two were on their best behaviour, sporting khakis with knife-edge creases, trading stories, and generally engaging in a revolting, nonstop session of reciprocal ego-feeding.

The disaster began about 3 p.m. on the second day, when Schumacher on his boss-friend's orders brought Jeb and me blank copies of an employment contract to fill out. While we were considering its implications he strode back to Papadopoulos' café to order a banquet complete with retsina and ouzo, with the addition of American beer to make it into a classy event. Sparky, Jeb, and I convened an impromptu meeting to discuss the contract, couldn't decide what to do, and after a few drinks we joined the party. It was a decent enough event, and Papadopoulos had even locked up his animals for the night so they wouldn't disturb the proceedings. But Jeb was decidedly uncomfortable, and we could imagine his haemorrhoids were driving him close to the edge. Not quite knowing what was about to result from the three-way battle between Jeb, his haemorrhoids, and the Schumacher-Stewart mutual admiration duo, we left early and hit the sack.

The next day, Jeb rashly told Papadopoulos to roast a lamb for a party *that* night. Clearly he did not want to be outdone by Schumacher. So we invited our friends Ruth, Maria, George, Fred and Alex.

After work we had sweet Vermouth at Maria's beautifully decorated cottage, and then went on to Papadopoulos' establishment. Mrs. Papadopoulos had thoughtfully put jars of wild-flowers on the tables. Our lamb was served in delicious hunks flavoured with mountain herbs; the salad was studded with luscious Kalamata olives and topped with feta cheese. We drank the white unresinated *aretsina* wine from Patras before moving to the ouzo. Kiki, a caretaker from the glory days of the dam's construction, joined us and then the Greek mining executive.

We started to do the traditional Greek dance – first Papadopoulos, who was as drunk as any of his patrons, and his waiter. Then Ruth did it with Papadopoulos. Then I smashed a bottle at their feet and Papadopoulos broke off to improvise a dance with Jeb, who was now too drunk to reciprocate.

The air was like champagne; it seemed that we were in a villa overlooking the Mediterranean, not the Acheloös dam. In the moonlight we could see the surrounding hills and the debris of the construction camp, the flash of water behind the dam. Jeb was violently sick over the edge of the veranda. Yet Ruth was attracted by his bovine roughness and bravado. They left for the walk to her cottage, and then Sparky and Tiki and Alex and I drove off, eager to collapse into our own beds. Sparky and I fell into slumber reading from our one source of English-language literature – left-behind volumes of Edward Gibbon's *Rise and Fall of the Roman Empire*. Merciful sleep!

CRASH! The two of us leaped out of our beds, shocked awake by an uproar in one of the other dormitory rooms. I snapped on the lights. It was 1:30 a.m. We went to investigate. Jeb, roaring like a bear with rage, had overturned Schumacher's bed and spilled him on the floor, and now Schumacher was gingerly trying to regain his feet. Sparky told me to keep out of it and I retreated to our room. Sparky, five foot seven or less, had inserted himself between two men of over six feet, essentially telling them to behave. Dressed in his flowered pyjamas, Stewart was watching quietly from the shadows behind the doorway.

"The sonofabitch lied to me," Jeb shouted at Sparky, then to Schumacher, "You sonofabitch, you lied to me. You had the Jeep keys. I've been walking around for three hours. An American isn't expected to walk. You're as useless as tits on a goddam boar hog. I'm a miner. I gotta make goddam footage. I'm not gonna walk any more. You sonafabitch, I gotta drive a tunnel." To Sparky: "I've gotta kill the sonafabitch. Nobody's gonna hurt me. The sonfabitch lied to me. You don't expect an American to lie to you."

Schumacher and Stewart carefully disappeared while Jeb was blabbering his explanations to Sparky. Ten minutes later, or less, the two friends were riding away into the pitch-black night, taking the gentle Alex with them as chauffeur for the long trip to Athens. Schumacher's pristine suede shoes were left in his closet, along with a dozen boxes of tissues and a bottle of antiseptic.

Alex showed up two days later with news that he had instructions to phone the boss in Athens at 5 p.m. After work we relaxed on our cots and awaited his return from the settlement's one telephone, which resided in the OTE "office," a tiny lean-to shack festooned with a chaos of different-coloured wires. When we heard Alex's footsteps in the hall we looked up from our books and shouted with fake bravado, "Everything all right?"

But Alex was grim-faced. "All is not all right. I call Mr. Stewart and he says 'Why do you call? I want to talk to Mr. Sparky.' He sounded very angry."

It took about 90 minutes to make the connection again. The telephone people were maddeningly incompetent, but there was nothing we could do about it. While he was waiting, Jeb and I walked down to the cafe and ordered beers. About 7 p.m. Sparky arrived, red-faced, with Alex. "Well," he pronounced, "we're tramped. All of us."

We were stunned. We thought it possible that Jeb might be fired, with justification, but for all of us to be dismissed in one fell swoop was unbelievable. We also were concerned for the men, to whom we had become much attached. There were 11 Greek workers now in addition to Alex, all of them fine men with families.

Damn!

After eating we went down to meet the crew in their quarters. We gave them the full story and announced their laying-off. Jeb gave his boots and his lighter to his favourites. The men showered us with eulogies and we toasted each other with beer and ouzo.

There is a silver lining, they say, to every cloud. At least now there was no chance that I would have to spend the rest of my life rotting in a Greek country jail, waiting for Miriam to save enough money to bring our baby to peer at me through the bars.

Many more adventures, albeit less dramatic, happened in this short stay in Greece. Do I really want to leave out the memory of cool country mornings waiting for the farmer's boy to bring us *yaourti* and fresh goats' milk for our breakfast, meeting the crone who was tending her huge cooking-cauldron over an open fire, encountering the mule-back wedding party high on the mountain where I thought no one lived, the bizarre excursion to the local whorehouse, the deathly ride to the bottom of the Greek tunnel, lying back flat on something that resembled a bobsled on rails as the rock rushed by my face? Not at all. Again I must apologize, for the plain reason that I have space for the text of one book alone.

Greece was an amazing and sometimes dangerous experience, whetting my taste for new adventure, though things might have been worse if I had stayed for another nine months, when a *coup d'état* installed a military junta. Or my adventures with the language, which presented a challenge that I enjoyed immensely. These days if I were to see the urgent capitalized word *ARGA,*   ! I am sure that I would perceive that it warned of danger, without having first to translate it knowingly into English. The process happens visually. With time the shape of the word is enough to perceive the idea.

In the thousands of words that make up my daily journal of this experience in Greece, the word "asthma" doesn't show up once. That's a mystery to me. Maybe it's an unspoken tribute to the helpful therapeutics of self-generated adrenaline.

The year after we left, the Greek royalty was overturned, and then King Paul Dam was renamed Kremasta Dam. I hope it will not dispirit you when I disclose that we had nothing to do with this historic turn of events or, for that matter, with the wreck of the tanker *Torrey Canyon*, which that year loosed the first major oil spill in an era that would be marked with disasters of this kind.

While planning my way back to England I succumbed to yet another flash of compulsion, arranging brief stopovers in Rome and Madrid. In Rome, I simply started walking, to the Coliseum, then to the *Daily American* office, where I met and chatted with its young English managing editor, Leslie Childe. I drank Carlsberg beer at the Foreign Press Club, and ended up at the station, booking my Comet 4 airliner ticket for Madrid.

I was better organized in the Spanish capital, where I found a centrally located hotel and booked a tour of the city's flamenco clubs – I would never turn up my nose at bus tours again – and spent my free time the next day enjoying the wonderful paintings at El Prado museum. I was acquainted with Velázquez, Raphael, Rubens, and Bosch. But this was my first up-close experience with El Greco and Goya. El Greco dropped my jaw with his brilliantly individualistic use of colour and his elongated figures. Goya was even more amazing, producing conventional, formal court paintings at the outset, then transitioning into disturbingly black paintings after producing his provocative *majas* and a number of realistic, emotionally evocative mezzotints.

The next day I was back in England, and Albuquerque was still crouching a very long way back in my mind, almost forgotten. As the plane's wheels touched down at Heathrow I felt a satisfying calmness, having experienced so much and survived to come back to Miriam and that palatial if slightly musty room, overlooking the well-trimmed lawn and rose garden at her parents' house on the Kentish coast. I hired a car and zoomed down the A20 highway, scattering traffic cones in my path, waving at a pair of girls in short shorts who were hitch-hiking outside my father-in-law's house, and deftly removing the top of his gatepost as I turned into the driveway.

10. FATHERHOOD

Childbirth is more admirable than conquest, more amazing than self-defence,
and as courageous as either one.
– Gloria Steinem

Soon Miriam was settled in a pleasant room at Hythe Nursing Home, west of town and up the hill from the Royal Military Canal, which, with a set of bulky fez-shaped Martello Towers arranged along the East Kent coast, were built at the dawn of the 19th century to help repel a Napoleonic attack that never happened. We settled our minds to await the appearance of our first child. But, though the future Brian was energetic enough, he seemed reluctant to make up his mind and greet the outside world.

"Why don't you take Miriam for a ride on the canal?" suggested the matron. "That might help. You know, the motion of the boat, the change of environment, all that."

So we went down the hill and rented a boat and Mim sat serenely in the front watching the ducks while I heaved rather ineffectively at the oars. Nothing happened, not even on that desperately steep climb back to the nursing home. The same the next day. And the next.

Soon I was afraid for Miriam and our unborn child, and to pass the time I found myself rather desperately driving around the nearby villages, visiting the little medieval churches and uttering more prayers than any sane agnostic would admit. One night, while I was watching a barn dance at Lympne Castle, vainly trying to get my mind off the subject of childbirth, I climbed the stairs to the 13th century battlements to enjoy a few minutes away from the crowd.

It was a fine warm night, and a full moon was casting a streak of silver over the English Channel, giving enough light that I could see the ruined Roman wall on the hillside below. It struck me that maybe the gift of this delightful moonscape was an omen, and perhaps it was. The next morning, September 21, Miriam's doctor was zooming through Sandgate to the hospital so that he could assist with Brian's arrival. I was miles away, since these were the days before fathers were welcomed to such events. Like my own, and my future grandson's, it was a difficult birth. Poor little thing, Brian Douglas was less than a week only when I took him to a photographer so he could have his wrinkled countenance recorded for his passport on our return to New Mexico.

Within the month it was time for us to make our way to the Underground station for the one-hour ride from Kings Cross to Heathrow. I kept looking at my son, turning to Miriam, squeezing her shoulder, and looking at him again. And when I held the tiny body of my child, and looked into his innocent and unknowing face, I was filled with a chorus of feelings. I would care for this little son for as long as I could care for him, without impinging upon the joy of his mother in sharing this divine responsibility, and I would cherish every opportunity to give him the best of what I knew was in the world and the cosmos. With the uplift of these thoughts came the realization that I would not, could not, care for him forever; and indeed he and we would at some time want him to revel in his independence and take wing. Where would his wings take him? Where would the world *let* them take him? I foresaw the dangers of his future and knew I could do nothing about them, and was afraid for him and for the world. I still am.

⊛

And then we were back in Albuquerque. Memories of Greece, Rome, and Madrid were consigned to the back shelves of my mind, and I was a family man. A couple of years earlier I would have quailed at the idea, but now I loved it. I thought of family dinners, festive foods magically arriving on our plates, the wine glasses automatically refilling with the best vintages, jolly good conversation – and the well-behaved children, not to mention the faithful Old Dog Tray at our feet. We all wanted to experience this Edwardian fantasy, as did the kids when they came along, maybe especially the kids. We knew it would take work, and patience, but we believed we could make it happen.

Rather conceitedly, I assumed my old job would be waiting for me, and very fortunately Ed Lewis went along with the idea. It seemed I had been away for a lifetime.

We rented a picture-postcard adobe cottage (even its roof was made of dirt, which was effective enough in this dry climate), just north of Albuquerque in Alameda. I helped Mim furnish the place, joined her in gathering wild asparagus

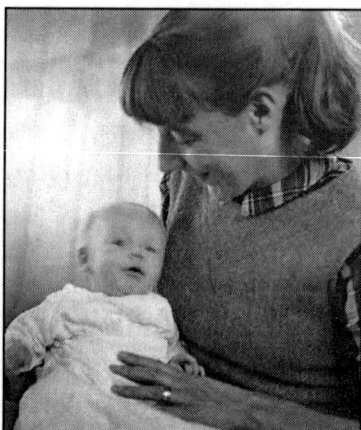

New Mexico Babe. Brian gets a briefing from Mim at his first New Mexico
residence, north of Albuquerque in Alameda.

along the *acequia* irrigation ditch, generally helped around the house, and bought
a reasonably acceptable household dog. I say reasonably because Mac proved to
be unusually neurotic and so frightened of storms that he would stick his head
up the fireplace chimney at the sound of the first thunderclap. At other times
Mac's favourite place was the kitchen, partly because it was the repository of
food, but also because he had friends living there. One afternoon he was lying in
his usual place under the kitchen table when to my astonishment I saw two mice
run out from a corner and vault nonchalantly over his paws before continuing
on their way. One Thanksgiving he pulled the turkey off the kitchen counter and
devoured both drumsticks before we discovered the deed. And then, on a
thundery day when he couldn't hide in the house, he disappeared forever. In
time he was replaced by an adorable German shepherd cross puppy whom we
rescued from the pound and gave a Yorkshire name, Lass.

I had returned to Albuquerque with new enthusiasm for revamping the
News format and image. I gained a degree of success in this endeavour, but the
business community was not ready to include us in the advertising budgets that
it allocated almost entirely to products of the Albuquerque Publishing Company.
Also, with a reportorial staff consisting of myself plus one person working two
days a week, I did not have the resources to increase the flow of editorial ideas
that would continue to improve our news content. Our newspaper was ahead of
its time, the first locally-produced tabloid, and it did not flourish. By the late

1990s there would be a large number of successful tabloid weeklies in the city, catering to the business-oriented, the hip, the artsy, the retired, and so on – some of them printed perhaps by the same press as the then-defunct *News*.

My stint as an Albuquerque journalist was a life-changer in that it introduced me to local theatre, through my weekly column, "The Chaff Barrel." Theatre then introduced me to Sandia National Laboratories and, separately, to the woman whom fate had cast as my future wife.

One particular column offered a tongue-in-cheek account of my few experiences in theatre, most of which had been tinged with disaster. These included my unintentional childhood début as a pint-sized walk-on in *Rose Marie*, and the embarrassing night in the high-school operetta *In Old Vienna* when, while playing the role of a subtle and light-fingered gypsy, I dropped a fellow actor's heirloom gold watch through my sash, not twice but three times consecutively, from whence it fell noisily onto the stage. I also mentioned my walk-on college parts in *Witness for the Prosecution* and *Romeo and Juliet* and how I temporarily crippled myself in an inexplicable fencing accident, and further mishaps in a play whose name I fortunately cannot now remember.

At that time my life was full enough and rewarding enough that there was no need – no excuse – to branch out into theatre. But the column had intrigued Crawford McCallum, a Sandia National Laboratories astrophysicist who had recently started an enterprise that he called Old Town Theatre. Mistakenly inspired, he picked up the phone and invited me to audition for a part in one of his productions, Shakespeare's *Richard II*. My ego, and my passion for the language, would not let me refuse.

I was nervous at the reading, having previously played little more than the parts of a carrot, a juror, a pageboy, and Gigo the Gypsy King, and my voice shook as a result. I suspect Crawford was taken by the Gielgud-like quaver that anxiety had brought to my vocal cords, and that's why he offered me the title role, Shakespeare's second-longest, not realizing that I had a memory like a sieve.

Crawford realized the folly of his choice in the opening scene of an early performance of Richard II when, in the part of the Duke of Norfolk, he had a huge argument with Harry Bolingbroke (Phil Mead), precipitating a duel. Everything was going well, with insults satisfactorily flying back and forth, when the dialogue suddenly halted and the stage went deathly silent. I was naturally taken aback although of course I could not show it. I mean, who was the fathead who dropped his lines? To fill the lengthening silence I glared back and forth in my most kingly way and roared, "Well?" No response. This is really getting bad, I thought, and stood up from my throne. "What sayest thou?" I bellowed.

The play resumed, and at the end of the scene I stormed into the wings, determined to scalp whoever had precipitated the screw-up. As you might have guessed by now, it was I. I had missed my cue completely. Offstage, the impersonators of Norfolk and Bolingbroke would gladly have finished *me* off. Which illustrates that when you're doing a live performance, there is no way you can edit out the blunders. Fortunately the play had already been reviewed, by a writer who was impressed not so much by the performance as my diction.

More plays followed. One performance attracted an audience of exactly seven people, all friends and colleagues. I can testify that it is extremely difficult to deliver lines when one's advertising manager is sprawled across a front seat a few yards away, fast asleep. Fellow actors recall gleefully how terrifying it was to look on as my Capulet, having lost his lines, faked them for endless minutes, roaring away in north-country-dialect iambic pentameter until one of my fellow actors, Louise Laval as Lady Capulet, rescued me with authentic words from the Bard of Avon. "Well, I had to do something!" Louise told me later. "You might have gone on all night. And besides, Juliet was beginning to weep real tears."

Later I played Joey the boxer in Harold Pinter's *The Homecoming*, and Lois Fleck played the female lead, Ruth, wife of the hapless homecomer Teddy. Bruce Hawkinson directed and John Gardner played Lenny. I was at first irritated by the play's rather ambiguous storyline, but then got intrigued by the language and dark interplay between the characters. It features a dysfunctional set of individuals dominated by the vile ex-butcher Max, played with venomous relish by my friend Bill Carstens. The script required that every night of the run, after deciding that Lois/Ruth was "just up my street" I would climb on top of her on the sofa. We were supposed to be snogging away in plain view of Max and Teddy when, winding up a barrage of nasty-but-clever misanthropic innuendo, Max leers at Ruth and says, "we're talking about a woman of quality. We're talking about a woman of feeling." This was our cue to slip off the couch and onto the floor, causing the audience to fall about in paroxysms of laughter. Problem was that, in a most unprofessional way, I enjoyed the role and part of me, I won't say which, was reluctant to take the cue until it was too late to catch the laughs. Later I wondered how many of the audience heard Lois whisper desperately, Nigel, get *off* me! If Bill had the presence of mind to whack me on the derrière as he ended Max's speech, which would have been in character, we might have scored the desired effect more often.

My favourite parts were Algernon in Wilde's *The Importance of Being Earnest*, young Charles Marlowe in Goldsmith's *She Stoops to Conquer*, and the customer in Pinter's one-acter *Last to Go*. They all had one great thing in common. They gave me more opportunity to make my audience laugh than any of my other roles.

Onstage I relished using my talent for good diction; offstage I stifled it. Shakespeare gave me the opportunity, in the States, to speak the language I love with the clarity which, after years of listening to standard BBC speech, I thought it deserved. In everyday life I developed a habit of relatively poor diction because speaking "proper English" made me into a freakish novelty and would stop conversations not because of *what* I said but *how* I said it. Consider the time when I asked a young woman if a certain unmarked place on the curb was a bus-stop. She simply stared, so I repeated, "Is this where I should wait for the bus?" She shook her head slightly. "You're putting that on," she said coldly, and walked away. Years passed before I realized that she may have made an honest if mistaken comment, thinking I wanted to pick her up for a seductive flirt on the bus.

Another time, when I had difficulty getting along with one of Sandia's administrators and could not understand why, one of my colleagues suggested that perhaps it was because of my accent. This was hard to believe, but my informant was an unusually perceptive and trustworthy man, so perhaps it was true. Other friends thought my accent was to my advantage. But I never did learn to "speak American" very well.

Which reminds me. While I'm on the subject I must apologize for the confusion that you may experience, here and there, by my use of wording that is peculiarly British or peculiarly North American (the spelling is Microsoft Word's "Canadian English"). I have spent a good part of my life proving Shaw's observation that "England and America are two countries separated by a common language." Linguistic confusers tend to creep in when I am least expecting them, especially when I'm telling what is intended to be a good story, and in a natural if idiosyncratic sort of way I simply use the first words that come into my head. Lexicographic rules are ignored and I am shown nakedly in my true form, as a linguistic hybrid. In other words, the fact that I am a binational sort of bloke complicates communication, so that the two vocabularies get intermixed and what you end up with is a mid-ocean version of the Queen's English.

Just before Christmas 1966, when John Gardner, Bill Carstens and I were rehearsing *The Homecoming*, Bill suggested I apply for a job in his technical writing department at Sandia National Laboratories. Sandia was and is a very large federal government R&D outfit on the southeast corner of town. It had the awesome responsibility of designing and overseeing the manufacture of *all* of America's nuclear weapons except for the nuclear explosive itself – the so-called "physics package" cared for by Los Alamos and Lawrence Livermore national labs. (Only after the Cold War would Sandia's nuclear weapons expenditure drop to less than half its total budget, as investments in the outwardly strange bedfellows of homeland security and civilian energy programs turned the balance.)

At first I brushed off the idea with a made-up false assumption: "What, *me* work at the bomb factory?" But with some misgivings I followed through on Bill's suggestion and one afternoon, after a couple of hours' discussion, slunk away from an embarrassingly disappointing session with his technical writing supervisors. They wanted me to write technical manuals. Perhaps I was wrong and perhaps unfair, but I got the idea that this would consign me to writing verbiage such as "when securing the bolt, exert 18.5 foot-pounds of torque in a counter-clockwise direction" and similar mind-numbing tasks. Convinced that I had neither the required rigidity of mind nor the taste for binary choices that this would require, I had to tell them as politely as possible that I wasn't a good match for the job they described.

After that episode I went back to my desk feeling that I had been right from the first – I'd always be a newspaperman. But then I was offered a second interview. Sandia's public relations manager, Jim Mitchell, a shrewd, well-read Oklahoman, sized me up and showed me a list of twenty or twenty-five subjects that I might write about. I looked them over, and my ambivalence for the idea of working at the "bomb factory" dissolved. The people at Sandia were doing things that no one had ever done before. They were learning the secrets of electronic materials, making small and highly original mechanical devices, learning how interconnected crystals unzip in the process of corrosion. This was about learning the way nature worked, and using that knowledge to make new or better gadgets. (They didn't even make bombs, though they designed large numbers of non-radioactive bomb parts and tested them mercilessly to make sure they worked right.)

I was hooked. "When do we start?" Jim didn't hesitate. "How about Monday?"

It was a huge jump. Never before had there been such a challenge to my writing talents. I had done rather poorly in science in school, felt a vague distrust for technology, and like the hippies who were moving into New Mexico suspected that humankind was suffering from technical over sophistication. Still, I had convinced myself years before that there was little if anything I could not do if I really tried. This being the case, how could I possibly refuse the Sandia challenge!

Jim offered me a salary considerably higher than my newspaper wages, a 40-hour week, and what by comparison were fabulous benefits. More than that, I would have access to the insides of a huge research and development lab, able to search out and write about any of the unclassified work that was going on behind the tall barbed-wire fences.

Beyond Sandia and his immediate family, Jim Mitchell had two big interests – following the stock market and doing public relations work for Maxie Anderson, a local entrepreneur and balloonist who had lost an eye after being struck by a sharp-ended American football. Jim had a Bachelor of Arts Degree in English and a Master of Science Degree in Journalism from Oklahoma State University, and had lived in Albuquerque since 1961, when he started his 31-year Sandia career. He grew up in the Dust Bowl of Oklahoma during the Depression, was tough and also one of the smartest and nicest men I knew at the time.

This was the big time, for Sandia was a 6,500-plus-strong research and development organization run for what was then the Atomic Energy Commission by the world-famous Bell Labs and Western Electric. Soon I had navigated through the lengthy application procedure, with its requirement for a top-secret DOE "Q" clearance.

I joined Sandia with two ready-made PR winners already on Jim Mitchell's drawing board, one being miniaturized, marvellously friction-free mechanical devices (rolamite) and the other an unusual electro-optical ceramics for solid-state displays, Cerampic. These made major national science news (a full page in the *Wall Street Journal* and a half-page in the *New York Times* amounted to a career success), and endeared me to Sandia's administration. (A year later the *Journal*'s Jerry Bishop wrote a semi-retraction in which he said rolamite appeared to be the *second* best way of doing almost anything, but we won't go into that. And the Cerampic was eclipsed by the liquid-crystal display.)

I discovered something about myself while learning and writing about these esoterica. Not only was my mind curious in an inquiring way, it was also strange, in that it was capable of rather quickly making a mental, semi-visual model of what was being explained to me. The model might present a fuzzy picture, but it was a mental foothold, and I could build on that because one learns from intuition and mistakes. This talent, or peculiarity, served me well in decades of science writing.

While rolamite and Cerampic were good stories, I had missed the biggest of all, the laminar air flow clean room, which used "HEPA" filters to create a moving layer of ultra-clean air from the top to the bottom of a room that was cleaned before being recirculated. Masked workers were now able to assemble tiny, unsoiled electronic devices within an amazingly clean environment, pharmaceuticals could be packaged with little danger of contamination, and even surgeons were able to do their lifesaving work in ultra-safe quarters. A delightful, self-effacing engineer, Willis Whitfield, won the patent for this invention in 1963, four years before I signed on.

I genuinely *liked* working with the people I met at Sandia. I enjoy the company of intelligent, creative, and level-headed people, and Sandia had thousands of them, in administration and particularly in the technical departments, with their cadres of top scientists and engineers. These people were delving into the wonders of science and engineering with an enthusiasm that I greatly appreciated, and I followed their work with vicarious delight.

A year after my arrival, armed with material I had written as handouts, I was explaining Sandia's story to people at *Business Week, Scientific American, Popular Science*, and elsewhere, and soon they were writing about it too.

That's why, when people ask me how I got into science writing, I have to say it started with Shakespeare.

◉❈◉

I had written a few articles about space technology as a journalist in England and Bermuda, and still have yellowed clippings of my articles on manned space flight, starting with the failed Mercury Atlas flight of July 29, 1960, which was tracked from Kindley Air Force Base, Bermuda (closed in 1995). But my professional interest in science and technology writing didn't get serious until I joined Jim Mitchell at Sandia in March 1967.

During my first half-decade at Sandia, in the midst of the Cold War, I moved within a very different world, secretive and coddled by the federal government, where in those heady days there seemed no limitation to the amount of money available to do jobs which the lab decided were vital to the nuclear deterrent that would keep Soviet missiles from American shores. These also proved to be maturing years in which I became more familiar with the communication arts and the wide variety of media technique. Sandia may have been cloistered and spendthrift to some, but it also did excellent science and engineering. Fortunately, much of the basic science was unclassified, meaning I could tell the world about it and win applause for the lab. And so I travelled to Los Angeles, San Francisco, Washington and New York, developing and managing Sandia's national media relations program. I directed short B-roll film clips, placed articles with a number of significant national media, and appeared on one of the three 30-minute science programs I helped produce on Sandia's behalf for KCET, the public television affiliate in Los Angeles.

Traveling solo as a one-man ambassador for a genuinely superb laboratory was a valuable and at times daunting experience, requiring me to acquire a working knowledge of subjects ranging from laser science to mechanical engineering. There are horror stories about public relations practitioners who are forced to lie for the company, or to magnify trivial accomplishments. This never happened to me at Sandia, nor was it ever suggested.

Sandia brought its interesting special experiences, like the telephone call with the serious-sounding chap who wanted to see our collection of alien remains and fragments from crashed saucers – because he wanted to see if those spaceships were like the one he rode when he was a kid in Utah. For the first time I also came up against the mistaken notion that there is an intractable incompatibility between science and religion. I thought this was rubbish because, when I looked at it through a religious lens, I could see that science reveals myriad wonders of creation that we cannot see with our naked eyes. I came to know that this was irrelevant to the ardent religionists; that their moral indignation came from differing ideas of the planet's age and the point at which fertilized human eggs become actual human beings. They were in a frantic race for final, indisputable answers, unlike scientists, who focus on theory, experimentation, and refinement of the theory. I fancied a tenuous link between religionism and superstition. And, to me, superstition is the darker child of the mother of discovery, wonder.

In April 1967 Mim, Brian, and I had moved into our first "owned" house, on Aspen Avenue, near Albuquerque's Old Town. It was a big step – a house of our own with two bathrooms and plenty of room to grow into a real family. I suppose it could have been our dream house, far from England yet large enough to host the Pickwickian imaginings of my college years. Mim helped Brian through his weaning and into his teething; I repaired the long garden fence and helped, awkwardly at first, in caring for our child. I dressed the house up a bit and put new tiles in the kitchen, but something in the family atmosphere was out of kilter, and would quench the dream.

The house was a roomy three-bedroom gingerbread concrete-block affair, with hardwood floors that we liked more than the cement floor pads that had come into vogue. There was a square hole with a grille over it in the middle of the living room, and under this, just barely visible, a large gas heater that provided warmth for the entire house. A previous owner had converted the garage into a den with fireplace, and then added a bedroom suite with a large sliding patio door. After I did a bit of exterior painting and tiled the kitchen it seemed perfect except for occasional invasions of the main sewer pipe by thirsty cottonwood roots. We settled down to have babies.

Our neighbours spoke Spanish at home, which suited us fine since they also spoke English, and I particularly enjoyed the company of Ernesto Mares, a jovial machinist who lived across the road and worked, like me, at Sandia. I still treasure the brass belt buckle he made for me.

I also took acting roles in *Oliver!*, *The Importance of Being Earnest, She Stoops to Conquer*, and two Shakespearean medleys. And I wrote, wrote, wrote. I wrote too much. In 1965-66 I wrote a novel, *Safari for Three Spies*, that I promptly destroyed, and churned away at a nonfiction book about science and society. Three articles came out in the short-lived magazine *Interplay*, on the would-be New Mexico revolutionary Reies Lopez Tijerina (1968), on the Indians of the Southwest (1969), and finally "Skylab: The Next Space Spectacular," a preview of the Space Shuttle program (January 1971). My article "Remote Instrumentation" came out in *Industrial Research* in June 1970. I wrote "Sandia Bonus" for *WE* magazine. The popular science books came soon afterward, along with a column for an electronics trade journal and a self-produced newsletter, *Euroscience Intelligence Report*.

I can rationalize that part of the reason for my writing addiction arose from my desire to avoid Miriam's tempestuousness. I can argue that Miriam was overly possessive of Brian, which she may have been. But in later years I would realize that I did not give Brian the fathering he needed in his boyhood, but instead spent more time in non-domestic activities than was good for the family life I wanted so much.

Jocelyn arrived in the scorching heat of an exceptionally dry summer, on August 18, 1968. My mother, who flew down from Salt Lake City for the event, recalled waking at about 5 that morning to find Miriam walking about "like a princess, about ten feet tall." I could imagine Mim doing just that, and it made me glad.

Soon we sallied forth to Presbyterian Hospital, where Miriam was whisked into a pre-labour room where she could take whiffs of anaesthetic if and as she was inclined. And then I was dismissed by the hospital staff, for unfortunately this was some years before the idea of the father being present at the birth was accepted and encouraged. I wanted to be with her, though I would have been empathetically scared. But I was at my Sandia desk when I got a call from the hospital: "Mr. Hey, you have a daughter, and she and her mother are in fine health."

I first saw Jocelyn through the observation window of a huge room full of tiny newborns with dark hair that included Jocelyn, a future blonde. Fortunately they were all labelled with a surname and the designation "boy" or "girl."

I loved my new little daughter, cherished and dandled her, shared with Miriam the happy chores of feeding her baby food and (less happily) changing her nappies. It was a warm time for parents and children. We bought bunk beds for the two children, and it was a delight to tuck them both in and read stories and say prayers. They were happy little children, and a joy for both of us.

We flew to England to show off the little ones in 1969, when we saw the first manned lunar landing, live on TV, at Miriam's parents' house. I published two hastily compiled popular science books that year – on elementary solar physics and the world food problem (respectively!) – and completed a third on interplanetary spaceflight and the outer planets. They were written for young readers, and nothing to boast about, the first two having been derived largely from photocopies, clippings, and other material furnished by a local book packager, Norman Carlisle.

Though my early books were not very good, I made it a point always to insert at least one editorial comment on the importance of the human gift of wonder. Wonder is at the base of all science that is not directly aimed at the production or perfection of a certain material, tool, or medicine – for example in astronomy and planetary exploration, which were the focus of three of my first four books. Kids love thinking about the heavens, almost as they love thinking about dinosaurs. They are born scientists. I reflected that every time Brian dropped a cup from a high-chair he learned a lesson in physics.

Early in my writing career I got the idea that people grew old too quickly, falling into social grooves and losing the ability to get up and peer out of those grooves. I could witness these wonders first-hand as I watched Brian and Jocelyn steadily growing from infancy into childhood, soaking in information as they went. And so it became important to me to plead for the maintenance and enjoyment, for as long as possible, of the curiosity we first know as children. It made me sad to reflect that, at the age of about ten, so many of us begin to despise our child heritage and charge away from it at full tilt, running roughshod over that precious, liberating commodity of wonder. Albert Einstein once said it is a miracle that curiosity survives formal education.

Lew James, the fellow journalist I befriended in Bermuda, was a joker with a devilish look about him that was enhanced by the shape of his face and the W of his thick black hairline. The girls loved him, and it had been easy, in Bermuda, to transfer to him the affections of Jan, the woman I had met in Italy and who later tracked me down in Bermuda. We continued to correspond, so I knew he had moved to the Caribbean island of Dominica, a place I would have loved to settle in myself. So imagine my amazement when that face appeared in Albuquerque – Lew James in the flesh, affecting a characteristically manic wide-eyed, big-grin, larger-than-life "hello" at my living room window. It was good to see him, but my way of life had changed so much that I was never quite comfortable with his decision to move in with us, with his girlfriend, for some indeterminate period. Miriam of course had met him and knew his ways, but he simply didn't fit in our new environment.

One Saturday morning at breakfast, the four of us – the two ex-Bermuda couples, Brian, and Jocelyn – were enjoying our toast and scrambled eggs at the big dining table. For some reason Brian and Joss, who had been larking around with their breakfast, left the table and started a wild game, a playtime wrestling match on the carpeted floor, punctuated with wild cries of delight.

"Be quiet!" roared Lew, who was in the middle of a story, "Be quiet, you … you little … baboons!"

He seemed quite pleased with his metaphor, but I wasn't. Lew had been steadily getting on my nerves and I didn't care for the comment. "What did you say?"

He sobered just a little without abandoning the brash persona. "Well, that's what they are. Little baboons, don't you think?"

I didn't appreciate the anthropological argument. I stalked off, had a long think, and about an hour later told Lew that he and his girlfriend would have to find somewhere else to live. That was that. I never heard from him again, and I am sure he felt I had cruelly compromised our friendship. This I regretted, but it had been the right thing to do at the time. Later I realized that human children have a lot in common with other primate children and that the metaphor was justifiable, only it was applied at the wrong time and under the wrong circumstances.

❧

In the late 1960s, I would drive the 600-mile journey to visit my parents in Salt Lake City about twice a year. It was a long way, especially when I was driving alone, but I loved the landscapes with their wind-sculptured sandstone outcroppings. Let me share with you the time when, while returning to Albuquerque, I turned off at the signpost to Arches National Monument, about five miles from Moab, Utah.

Following my nose, I drove to a place in the sand and rocks, parked, and simply walked out into the windless quiet. Past a low ridge of sun-soaked sandstone I came suddenly upon an astonishingly vast landscape. I stood amazed before a strange and magnificent expanse that was knobbed with rock and sparsely studded with the green dots of piñon and juniper, stretching one hundred and eighty degrees and more into an infinity of distance where not even the hint of humanity endured. But for the quiet internal sounds of my heart and breath there was no sound. I was amazingly small and insignificant, and for a moment that ephemeral puff of electricity that is me drifted into all the nameless energies around me and was free.

Then, in this strange and wonderful place, inexplicably and as if being awakened, I heard a wind-chime. The whispering tinkle of the chime might have come from the doorway of some desert spirit, it was so tiny. I looked, and was enchanted. A few yards away, grains of sand were trickling, bouncing, and singing down a small dune, a Lilliputian stream of silicon as bright and delicate as the sound.

139

It was a whisper from the eternal harmony that had visited me nearly ten years earlier, so far away and yet so close, at Juniperhill, in Bermuda. I drank it in for the few seconds that it lasted, and then I found a large flat rock, lay upon its curving shape, embraced its warmth, and thanked the eternal orchestrator, my parents, and my genes, for this moment.

> *Standing on the bare ground,—my head bathed by the blithe air and uplifted into infinite space,—all mean egotism vanishes. I become a transparent eyeball; I am nothing; I see all; the currents of the Universal Being circulate through me; I am part or parcel of God.*
> – Ralph Waldo Emerson, *Nature (1836)*

11. LAUGHTER, SADNESS, SURVIVAL

There were odd moments when the human spirit gave off its finest bouquet,
when it asked for nothing, denied nothing, and was given all.
– Neil Gunn[18]

Nineteen seventy-one was the year of the Big Freeze. On January 7, 1971, an icy finger dipped down from outer space and Albuquerque's temperature fell to minus 17 Fahrenheit (minus 27 Celsius). Before I went to sleep that night I put a small electric stove ring under the old Chevy's block, stuck a heated dipstick inside, and congratulated myself for my brilliant foresight. The next morning the car started immediately and I drove off to work in triumphant mood. But once I got onto the freeway the car turned into a steam engine. Incredibly, the coolant had frozen *inside the radiator*.

I managed to get off the freeway and stopped at a telephone booth. These were the days of telephone dials, and the dial was frozen. For a moment I stood there thinking with mounting panic of the possibility that my ears might freeze and break off, and then stepped onto the roadway and flapped my arms wildly. I must have looked like an insane turkey, trying unsuccessfully to take off. Fortunately a passer-by stopped anyway, said nothing about turkeys, and drove me to a garage where I could get a tow-truck. Actually I wouldn't have minded in the least if he had said that I looked like a turkey; I might not even have noticed.

This was also the winter I borrowed a huge hammer-drill from my Sandia friend and neighbour Tom Zudick and broke into the cinder-block wall of my house to replace a freeze-broken pipe. Typically, I broke into the wrong part of the wall, and replaced a section of undamaged pipe.

We were settled in our own house with a couple of wonderful little children; I was still reasonably young and my job promised me a long and successful career. It wouldn't work out that way. Things were changing at Sandia. By now I had cherry-picked the juiciest technical articles at the lab and most of my remaining information "bank" was associated with classified or sensitive information which

I could not publicize, and opportunities for press coverage dwindled commensurately. Miriam also was having emotional problems that I thought might improve in her home environment, near to her parents and old friends. Result: I resigned; we all moved to England.

Miriam went first, with the children, while I stayed on and sold the house and cars. My parents, always supportive, went to Folkestone to provide backup help.

Rita and Claud were soon feeling harassed with Miriam and the children charging around the premises, so it was fortunate that my mother and dad, before moving to a new home in Chichester, West Sussex, were able to find us furnished accommodation fairly quickly, even before I arrived. It was a charming all-Georgian row house in the oldest part of Folkestone, at No. 28 The Bayle. There was an old church nearby, St. Eanswythe's, and some pre-Georgian houses, so I imagined that at some time a castle must have stood on that high ground, and that the name The Bayle derived from "the bailey," denoting a defunct castle's outer precincts.

◈

I arrived in Folkestone in July 1972. Since I had no job to go to, Mim and I agreed that I should take a shot at freelancing, while keeping eyes and ears open for something that promised a more reliable source of income. The house included a half-cellar of the Georgian type that let in a little light into a small room adjacent to the coal bunker, and an electric lamp dangled from the ceiling. Fine! I thought, just the ticket. I already had a portable typewriter; all I needed was a desk. I went to W.H. Smith's and brought back two flat-packs, each of which contained one two-drawer filing cabinet, made of the kind of cardboard that is used for orange cartons. I put a couple of boards across the assembled cabinets, and presto! there was my desk.

Unfortunately the cellar was rather damp, and the combination of desk-top and typewriter were relatively heavy. After I had finished my first free-lance article I took a look at the desk and realized that something terrible was happening. The cardboard was slowly soaking up moisture from the flagstone floor and the structure was slowly melting. The two boards were decidedly closer to my knees; the cabinet drawers would open only with more force than was wise, and their contents were becoming decidedly soggy.

The imminent collapse of the desk was accompanied by the imminent collapse of the entire freelance scheme. Very soon it became obvious that the venture wouldn't work even if I had access to an oak desk in a snazzy office. I did write something called "Putting Voices in Tubes," about waveguide technology, for the Central Office of Information, and an article on electro-optic ceramics for *New Scientist* was in process. I was also writing an electronics column for the American trade magazine *Electronic Design* and earning a very small amount from the *Euroscience Newsletter*, which I had started in 1970. The income was clearly not enough to support the four of us. Disaster was looming before we had spent a month in The Bayle.

One of the things I am good at complaining about is my lack of helpful contacts in London journalism. England was and is a place where, the better your contacts are, the better your chances for success. I knew hardly any journalistic movers and shakers in those days; if all of them dropped by for a cup of tea, we could have had it quite comfortably in the wardrobe. I did, however, know one media luminary. I had gone to Bracken House to meet David Fishlock, science editor of the *Financial Times*, as the result of my work with Sandia, and the two of us got along famously. We spent a wonderful afternoon with his wife Mary in their Buckinghamshire country cottage; on another occasion he took me for a distant look at the Atomic Weapons Research Establishment (the "Research" part of the name has since been rudely deleted), which, with American collaboration, is the much smaller, British equivalent of the Sandia and Los Alamos labs combined.

That December, with Christmas coming on and the financial situation looking very gloomy indeed, David met an American gentleman by the name of Ray Borland. Ray was in charge of the embryonic publications group at Intercontinental Medical Statistics (IMS), a pharmaceuticals market research company that ran a worldwide system for monitoring prescription drug sales, unique sets of data that were of strategic interest to the international pharmaceuticals industry. Someone decided IMS needed an international health pharmaceuticals publishing group and Ray had come on board to do the job. During some meeting, perhaps over lunch at the Athenaeum Club, of which David was a member, Ray said he needed more staff, and the rest you can guess. David said he just happened to know this science writer who might need a job after leaving Sandia to come back to his native England, and it was not long before Ray was dialling my number. Soon, and with considerable relief, I said goodbye to the cellar and consigned the freelance desk, now a pulpy mess, to the rubbish bin.

David was one of the world's most knowledgeable science writers, and he had a warm, kind personality with a quirky sense of humour. I am proud to say that we would remain friends for decades, sharing adventures in America as well as in England.

The IMS editorial office, located on an original, non-bombed residential side of London's once-elegant Russell Square, was a good place to settle, giving me a sorely needed sense of permanency, a foothold in the big city. The first edition of Borland's handsome, perfect-bound guide to international pharmaceutical markets had just come out, and we were soon planning a weekly typescript newsletter, the *IMS Pharmaceutical Marketletter*, which ultimately made its debut in October 1974. It would last for 35 years, considerably longer than the original IMS organization.

Having an office that looked out from an elegant Georgian town house onto Russell Square, then a rectangle of well-tended grass and plantings overlooked by magnificent plane trees, should have been a proud time in my life. In their royal roles the Russells were the Earls and Dukes of Bedford, who designed important parts of central London in the 17th and 18th centuries, and in a very small way I felt they were my benefactors. From my window the University of London's Senate House was to my left, T. S. Eliot's old Faber & Faber office was to the northwest, and to the northeast, on Southampton Row, towered the late-Victorian Hotel Russell, a strangely attractive French-inspired hulk with statues of queens in the niches above its door and walls decorated with terracotta that was oddly called "thé-au-lait," or "tea with milk." Its great claim to fame is that the dining room is identical to that of the ill-fated *Titanic*. Both were designed by the architect James Fitzroy Doll.

Getting the job at IMS was a godsend. But in retrospect perhaps I should never have come back to England. I was about to embark on one of the darkest times of my life.

I had memorably good times with the family during my short residency in Folkestone, and adventures that included a time when a very large bottle of Seconal (nembutal) narcotic sleeping pills shot through our roof tiles and landed in the attic. An oddly ironic, harbingerish gift from the skies. I never figured out where it came from – worried smugglers in a light plane ferrying the stuff in from France? Another attic adventure occurred when Brian, while exploring with Jocelyn, fell between the rafters and through the ceiling, fortunately straight into bed. These good times were sadly few. Miriam became increasingly and obsessively difficult, refused to seek professional help with or without my taking part, and repeatedly threatened divorce.

Many years later, it occurred to me that one of my favourite memories of home was Christmas at The Bayle, Joss and Brian in their pyjamas exploring excitedly around the twinkling tree, with Miriam smiling close by. Simple reminiscences are often the most precious.

⚜

Mim's outbursts of argument and invective sometimes would last into the early morning. During one of these I found Brian sitting on the stairs, crying to himself. He was only six. I was already demoralized and my heart was broken; in despair I was convinced I was incapable of doing anything to resolve the situation.

On one of these mornings, when I was standing on the crowded Folkestone Central station platform waiting for the 6 a.m. London train, I had one of the most dreadful experiences of my life. As the train came slowly around the curving track from Dover I looked down onto the silvery rails and thought, oh my, how easy it would be, just to let myself fall onto those tracks, a few seconds from now. The engine was grinding closer, a few yards away. The end of my unhappiness was as near as that. It was dangerously seductive, but then it was as though a hand reached from my psyche and held me back. I took a very deep breath, pretended I was just another ordinary sleepy commuter, and when the train stopped I climbed in. The impulse had been momentary, but it scared me very much. If I had followed that impulse, what would have happened to Miriam and the children?

That night I told Miriam I had to move out, muttering the half-true euphemisms that she was too hot for me to handle and that things might be better if I spent the weeknights in London. And so this spinelessly inept coward – me – moved to the big city, staying a couple of nights on the office floor in Russell Square before taking a dreadful flat in a Victorian tenement at the bottom of Theobald's Road. It was four storeys up a concrete outside stairway, private but with no hot water or bath, just a sprinkler head on a hose hanging over something that looked like a child's inflatable swimming pool. There was a broken window that I tried to make wind-proof with a wadded blanket. It was so cold I tried to keep warm in front of the gas fire with an electric blanket around my shoulders, and nearly roasted when its thermostat went berserk while I was sleeping. Another close call. I moved out after some kids literally smashed down the door to get a few coins out of the gas meter.

Sometime in the first half of 1973 – At 1:30 a.m., Miriam rang me at the flat, in a terribly angry mood. And again at 2:15. I was all shook up (funny how flappable I am these days) and tossed and turned. Finally I rang Mim at 4 a.m. to see if I could calm her. Predictably I couldn't. She phoned again this morning at 8:30, and I said I'd call from the office. Before I had chance to do this she phoned my parents and alarmed them to the point that they're going to drive from Chichester to Folkestone to see if they can straighten anything out. When I did call from the office Mim was angry because I had phoned! Often after these outbursts she would call to apologize.

In September 1973 I committed a more deeply cowardly act and ran away to Dallas, where Sue was working on a Trinity University master's degree at Paul Baker's Dallas Theater Center, then located in a marvellous Frank Lloyd Wright building in the Turtle Creek neighbourhood. I can't actually remember leaving Folkestone, but my mother and father were there to say goodbye. "You were practically in a nervous breakdown and never looked back or waved," my mother said. "You went just like that."

At first I couldn't find a job, and to kill the time wrote two bizarre and nondescript three-act plays, *Song of Felix* and *St. George and the Space Princess*. Neither instilled me with enough confidence to send it to an agent. For a short time I was on food stamps, exchanging government scrip for groceries. Then on June 30, 1974 I struck it rich and landed a short-term consultancy with Texas Instruments, where I worked on the company's personnel handbook and wrote a history of their contribution to the development of the hand-held calculator. That year I acted in *Ruddigore* (as Old Adam) and in the Dallas Shakespeare festival (a walk-on part as the Pedant in *Romeo and Juliet,* as unmemorable as my earlier role as the Page to Paris). I also applied unsuccessfully for jobs with Merck Sharp & Dohme (Rahway, N.J.), Alcan (Montreal), and Kaiser Aluminum

(Oakland), which appealed to me because of a remarkable series, "The Dynamics of Change," which had been produced by Don Fabun for the *Kaiser Aluminum News* in the 1960s. Nothing jelled.

I first met Sue in 1970, when she was acting in the Albuquerque Civic Light Opera production of Oliver! She played the role of Old Sally, an ancient pauper who stole a valuable gold locket from the woman who died after giving birth to Oliver, namesake of the Dickens story and Broadway musical. We both donned age makeup, painting dark creases on our faces to appear as Sally and the undertaker, Mr. Sowerberry. With these inducements we did not pay much attention to each other, but when we played the ingénue parts in *She Stoops to Conquer*, mutual attraction was impossible to ignore.

Born in Texas, Sue was the only daughter of a veterinary sciences professor and a retired bookkeeper, and the eldest of four siblings, the other three being boys – Larry, Travis, and Lonnie. Her mother's side of the family were German-speaking people, the Gieseckes, and her father's side was the Gunns, descended from Scots immigrants.

She was a pert young thing, 11 years my junior and of medium height, with naturally curly hair and blue eyes that could be stunning. I was taken by her gentleness, her interest in the arts, her creativity, and her quiet intelligence. She was a fine mother, cook, and housekeeper despite her deep commitment to theatre, where her greatest talents came to the fore. I believe she was attracted to me because of my interest in theatre (which was no doubt weaker than she judged), my unusual history, and the experiences that we would share and talk about for the first time.

It was suffocating hot in Dallas, and to my surprise Sue had been too busy at the theatre center to meet me at the Love Field airport, or even to spend much time with me after that. We shared an apartment on Cole Avenue, which was comfortable enough. But I wept when I saw happy children in neighbourhood playgrounds, and fled the touring Royal Opera performance of *Madama Butterfly* in tears.

Ray Borland came back into my life in September 1974, and unwittingly became the hero of the hour. He phoned me one Sunday morning with an offbeat invitation: "You know, I was in the shower this morning and I was thinking about our plans to expand, and I thought, we need Nigel back here in London." *In the shower?* Never mind that: I immediately accepted. Sue understood my need to return to the children, and we pledged to continue our relationship by mail – a promise that would generate thousands of words of loving prose from both sides.

I had no idea what I would find in Folkestone – there had been practically no communication – and when I did get there I had a terrible shock. Miriam had been committed to a psychiatric hospital and the children were being cared for by a neighbour. I was stunned, and doubly so to think that such a thing could happen without anyone letting me know. *Why didn't even the vicar, whom I knew and trusted, write or telephone me?*

I found Miriam at the Chartham psychiatric hospital. She had just regained consciousness, newly returned from an electroconvulsive therapy (ECT) session. She asked if I was Jesus and a wave of remorse clutched at my gut. Why had I not somehow prevented this terrible turn in her life story?

I got Miriam and the children re-established at the house, and spent weekends with them while spending the rest of my time at a nondescript Paddington flat supervised by an eccentric American woman. The place reeked of an odd assortment of spices that resided in a kitchen that looked like a set for a gothic period drama. I imagined it was last used on the day her last husband walked out in desperation, and that she had kept it that way as a kind of shrine. When I looked for the cobwebs, though, they weren't there.

The landlady slept on a couch to make room enough for three male lodgers, one being a Japanese student who could only get to his bed by way of a long, swaying ladder that wobbled up the deep stairwell to a very small hatch in the ceiling. I visited him once and toured his attic in a crouching position, unable to stand up, then after a cup of tea excused myself and made my way gingerly down the ladder. What on earth would he do, I wondered, if he had a sudden call of nature.

I lived in the largest and most sparsely furnished room in the apartment. It was the best thing about the flat in that it gave me a half-acceptable place for occasional fumbles with lady friends. The shared bath, a great cast-iron affair with ornamental metal birds' feet patterned after a horror-movie monstrosity, commanded the center of our bathroom. It had the flaws of age and careless use on its porcelain surface, so that before each immersion I felt the need to kneel down it in a prayerful attitude it in order to inspect its mysterious marks. This one is permanent. This one can be scratched off. This one moves. After making any necessary improvements I would draw the water and settle in with book in hand and a cup of tea on the stool beside me. It was the nearest thing to heaven that I had in those days.

IMS's publishing arm was now based at Kingsbourne House, high above the Holborn tube station, which in 1977 would reward us with a view of the procession up Kingsway of Queen Elizabeth's Silver Jubilee entourage on its way from Buckingham Palace to St. Paul's.

Mayer Resnick had come over from the States to start the *IMS Pharmaceutical Marketletter*, and, though at the time he seemed a brash young man, we stayed friends and corresponded for decades. Our secretary, also an American, was very smart and proficient but as a good Mormon was anxious to place careers behind her and return to Utah and start a family. I remember asking her replacement, a New Zealander, the best way of distinguishing her accent from the Australian. "Well," she said, "to start with, Australians don't say 'six,' do they?" It took me a few seconds to catch on.

The early male complement also included Alan, a lean and super-nice, super-intelligent young man who possessed a doctorate and served as our technical guru; Patrick, an extremely likeable Irish classical scholar who spoke with impeccable diction; Bryan, a sociable, tousle-haired editor endowed with deep

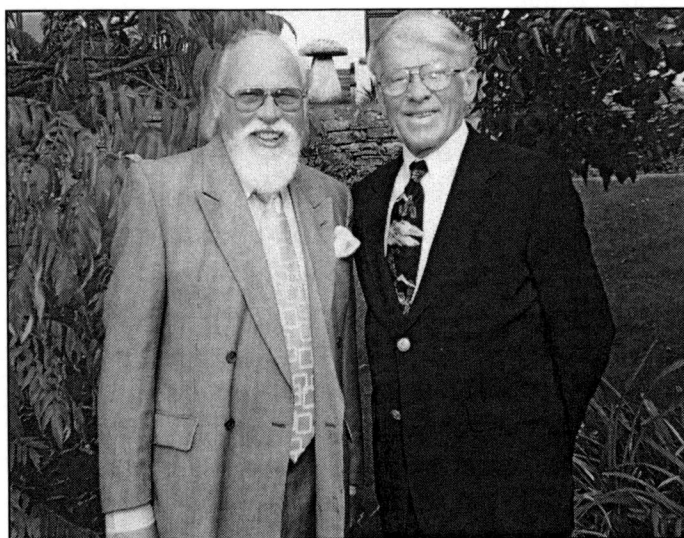

The Jokers. Gerald Bishop (with beard) and I shared uproarious times while we worked at IMS. No one else in the world could soak me so thoroughly in tears of mirth.

and largely unplumbable brainpower who without exception prefaced differences of opinion with the words, "With respect, I would like to point out that …" etc.; and my best friend Gerald, of whom you will hear more later.

Bryan, who boasted a perfect 8 (64) hat size, is the only man I have ever met who had a larger head than I. It was not until I started shopping for hats that I realized that I had an unusually large head, and size 7-7/8 (63) was usually about right; anything smaller and I might get a headache.

Soon after my arrival Dr. Borland had hired an unusually intelligent young man who I heard emitting loud and agonized sounds of torture one morning in the men's room. Thinking he might be suffering some sort of mental breakdown, I mentioned it to Mayer. "Haemorrhoids," he said with clinical certainty, and walked off without further comment.

One morning Dr. Borland called an all-hands staff meeting. After going over the progress of our various projects, he began to criticize Alan quite harshly for transgressions that to me seemed of relatively minor concern. It was as though this outburst of rebuke, by one PhD against another, was the main reason for the meeting. I never quite trusted Ray after that, but thought it inopportune to commiserate with Alan. To my considerable surprise and incredulity, the two soon became fast friends.

⊙≫≫≪⊙

By now Mim knew about the time I had spent with Sue, and had listened to my wretched but true pleas that I had returned to England because the family, including her, was of paramount importance. There were times that I coaxed her into talking over our situation with the family doctor and the Citizen's Advice Bureau, but these consisted of no more than periods of silent fuming, followed by brief but spiteful outbursts directed at the would-be helping hands, and a stormy exit through waiting rooms full of open-mouthed patients.

Stalemate. Depressed but not admitting it, I wrote an imploring letter to Sue, and as a result she stayed with me during the summer break of 1975 in Park Crescent, an elegant arc of John Nash houses very close to Regent's Park, before returning to finish her master's degree work in Dallas. The Park Crescent experience was grand yet bizarre, staying in an IMS colleague's flat, communing with new neighbours who included an eccentric old Iranian exile called Abdi and an assortment of strange and wonderful women who lived in the building. I would turn up some evenings in Abdi's richly decorated flat, drink coffee, eat a few Middle Eastern sweetmeats, and mostly listen.

I had the idea that Abdi had anticipated that trouble would erupt in Iran, and wisely had moved to London while the going was good. And I was right. In just four years revolution would end the rule of the American-supported shah, Mohammad Reza Pahlavi, following unrelenting, year-after-year denunciations from Ayatollah Ruhollah Khomeini, and replace it with a theocracy.

Abdi somehow resented my quiet presence. One evening, after Sue had left for the States, he shouted at me, "Nigel, you're a camel! You *camel!* You sit there and say nothing! Why do you say nothing?" This bothered me only because I thought that through this homely, fat and rich little man's irritation I might be denied these brief soirées, which eased the boredom of sitting alone in my own flat. It would have been clever, if, like Mark Twain, he had asked, "Why do you sit there looking like an envelope without any address on it?" But then if Mark Twain had said this – or even if he had called me a camel – I would have cared, in a way. I had more pressing things on my mind. The tragic leitmotif of Miriam and the children continued, and climaxed in a terrible, wrenching afternoon in Folkestone, with Sue and Miriam sitting with me at the same tiny front-room table. I told them I would try again to restore the family life. It was a dreadful thing for Sue; Mim was rightly confused; it was foolish for me to think I could make amends. When Sue got ready to leave, Miriam gave her a hug. "I love you," she said.

It simply did not work. After that, Mim was just as hard to communicate with, or worse, and I knew the children were suffering emotionally. As was I, caught in a snare that was at least partly of my own making. It was cold comfort that I had something in common with a great author, for Ernest Hemingway knew the anguish of being in love with two women at the same time, and told the world about it in *A Movable Feast*.

Sue returned the following summer, even though I had broken my implicit promises by saying I would return to Miriam and the children. My boarding-house quarters in Earls Court were considerably less than ideal and a far cry from a white knight's castle. Though our room had a tiny balcony that looked out on a pleasant park, the place was cramped and we took our meals with a motley, unintentionally comical group of boarders whose down-at-heel yet pretentious personalities were equalled only by the people who served the meals.

I was delighted, thrilled, and grateful that Sue had come to England and quite ready to put her on a pedestal. But she was understandably disappointed with our lodgings even though they were plainly a temporary abode. And she didn't want, or more likely didn't trust, the pedestal treatment: "Why are you looking at me like that?" she would demand defensively when she caught me admiring her combing her hair, or looking stylish while waiting for the train at High Street Kensington. "Stop staring at me."

A genuinely unpleasant experience emerged from getting mixed up with a couple of men who styled themselves as the artistic brains behind "Theatre 68" and had access to a hall on Carnaby Street, just off Oxford Street. Sue performed there in early August 1975 as Mrs. Hardwicke-Moore in Tennessee Williams' *Lady of Larkspur Lotion* (1975), amid thinly veiled threats that the impresarios would turn her in to "Immigration" if she did not pay them a fee for her association with them – a brutal slap in the face, especially since others were paid to be in the show.

Fortunately, soon after the Carnaby Street episode, Sue found a job with the American Community School, assuring that she would become a legal resident for an indefinite period. Later she worked part-time for the Mountview Theatre School, where among other courses she taught "The Lakeland Poets" to English students. I was particularly proud of her for these achievements. She was, and continued to be, a particularly talented theatre person, on stage, playwriting, directing, teaching, making costumes. But she seemed never to believe in the strength of her talent, and allowed people with much lesser talent, but with courage bordering on arrogance (and social clout), to take advantage of her abilities and her dedication to theatre.

After spending a hot summer at the boarding house we moved to a larger ground-floor flat at Tavistock House, practically under the Westway A40 motorway flyover, close to the Ladbroke Grove tube station. It was close to a tiny park frequented by men whom Sue called "the meths for lunch bunch," because they laced their cider with methylated spirits (denatured alcohol). There were strange and wonderful experiences here, especially during the boisterous Notting Hill Carnival, which is held each year on a U-shaped layout of streets that runs more than twice the length of Ladbroke Grove itself. It could be a dangerous place.

One day the police told Sue that a man had been found stabbed on our doorstep the previous night. The next year, thanks again to one of Sue's connections, we rented a house on Briston Grove in north London. Three years later, on March 19, 1979, we would buy the property from Horace Berry.

Nineteen seventy-six was a busy, dizzy year, clouded with sadnesses in Folkestone (on January 15, Mim was re-admitted briefly to the mental hospital), yet full of promise for the new couple. Sue and I toured the Loire Valley by car in the spring, and then in July flew from Luton to Majorca for a week-long package holiday. In November I travelled to the U.S. for a business visit to Abbott Laboratories in North Chicago, and made a side trip to Albuquerque, where my eyes hurt from the unaccustomed sun. Visiting Abbott got me to Chicago at their expense and was interesting and educative; the side trip to Sandia would prove to be an important investment in my future.

⊚⊗⊗⊚

Sue and I joined the theatre group at the City Lit, on Keeley Street in Bloomsbury, in the late 1970s. There we acted together in *The Tempest, Two Gentlemen of Verona,* and *A Midsummer Night's Dream; and* Sue was assistant director of *The Changeling* in 1976. Sue continued to do well at the American Community School (where she would write her play *Madam Malevola's School for Ghouls*), and soon we had enough money to get a mortgage on the house and buy a car apiece.

When Uncle Ted's sister Em Hewitt died on May 30, 1976, her house at 62 Lane Side, Wilsden, came on the market. I was very interested in acquiring the property, though mostly for sentiment's sake, and talked my parents into buying it complete with contents. The deal was consummated on November 23. Later, when my bank balance increased, I bought the property from my mother and dad.

The divorce from Mim was now in process, a sad and painful, uncontested separation from a mentally ill wife that involved trips to unfriendly, musty offices in Somerset House and the Royal Courts of Justice. The final papers were signed on July 21, 1977.

Sue and I married just a year later, on July 16, 1978. It was an informal affair, and no rings were exchanged (we never used wedding rings and Sue never adopted my surname). My best friend Gerald Bishop was there as best man, but

153

we had to recruit a stranger to "stand up" for Sue. In typical form, Gerry made a joke of the recruitment procedure. After I had raided the waiting room successfully for a likely victim, he insisted that we had to settle for "a bloke wearing a dress." Afterwards we returned to the house, where more people were present, and got pleasantly tipsy on champagne, red wine, and sandwiches. Somehow in all this, we managed to get a set of beautiful photographs to commemorate the wedding.

Gerry and I had a lot in common. We were writers, naturalists, animal lovers; our first wives were even called Miriam. Where I greatly appreciated humour, Gerry not only appreciated it; he also generated it. He was a very funny man, to the extent that our conversations ended up with us both in mirthful tears. He proved to be a staunch friend whose clever and ready wit may have saved my life, or at least my sanity.

One day, and to our surprise, our boss Ray Borland invited Gerry and me to dinner at a nearby Southampton Row hotel restaurant. Ray was not a naturally gregarious man, but may have read somewhere that it was a good management move, and like all journalists of the time Gerry and I could not refuse a free meal. The conversation was considerably less than scintillating, but things looked brighter when we learned that Dr. Borland lived in St. John's Wood, a high-rent neighbourhood, and determined to take that scrap of intelligence as far as we could.

"Wonderful location!" I said. "Right next to Regent's Park, too!"

There was a pause, and, thinking about the park, Gerry ventured, "I suppose you go cycling?"

Dr. Borland beamed. "Oh yes, every morning." We expressed approval, imagining our boss gliding gracefully in sunlight sifting romantically down through the plane trees.

Gerry recalled there had been a few rainy days of late. "Too bad it's been such a bad week for cycling," he said sympathetically, trying to keep the conversation going.

There was a longer pause. Borland looked at us quizzically. "I can use my bicycle any time I want," he said defensively.

Gerry and I were confused. "Anytime?" I asked, thinking of our boss being drenched to the skin, "How is that?"

Borland finally got the idea that we needed help. "Well, it's a stationary bicycle," he said, as if we should have known that all the time. But we were naïve on the subject of indoor activities of this type and had never heard of such a thing.

"Stationary?" I asked absently. The idea sounded absolutely oxymoronic.

"Well yes, of course, bolted to the floor."

If a cartoonist had been recording this exchange from a neighbouring table, he would have drawn a balloon issuing from our two heads at this moment, with an incandescent bulb flashing madly in the middle of it. I tried to make the best of the situation and came up with what I have to admit was a lame suggestion. "Well, I suppose you could put a nice TV in front of it, and run a tape of riding through the woods on a real bicycle?"

The moment had eluded us. Dr. Borland asked for the check and the evening's merrymaking ended rather quickly.

In those days, lunch sometimes consisted of four imperial pints of good honest London bitter ale. These festivities furnished me with some of the most enjoyable social events, completely unplanned and off the cuff, of my life. We would get together at the Queen's Larder and stand outside with our pints, solving the problems of the world while admiring the slim young thing who often would bring her Doberman and sleek black goat to drink at the old pump that rose phallically from the cobbles in front of our York House offices. One time Gerry and I broke away from our deliberations early to walk down New Oxford Street for our first visit to Ann Summers (lingerie, rampant rabbits and "best selling exclusive Sex Toys"). We went together into a one-person peepshow cubicle and staggered out in paroxysms of laughter, whereupon we were asked to leave for "disturbing the more serious clientèle." We retreated quickly to our safe haven at IMS and locked ourselves in our respective offices until we were fit to meet the real world again.

I suppose that one could stretch the point and say that our Queen Square offices contributed to the medical character of the square. A statue of Queen Charlotte sits largely unnoticed at the north of the square, for apparently her husband, King George III, the bane of American colonists, was treated for mental illness at one of the houses there. The Queen's Larder was so named after being used by the queen to store provisions for her ailing husband. Ironically, neurology became the central interest of the square's medical community in modern days. When IMS was quartered there, the Italian Hospital could be seen on one side of us and the Homeopathic Hospital on the other.

We also patronized a pub that was named the Lamb after William Lamb, who improved an existing conduit to bring clean water to the neighbourhood in 1577. And then there was the modern Captain Coram pub, named for a man who in 1739 established a nearby home for foundlings. The home held on for ages, but closed in 1925, by which time the welfare of children had become centered at Great Ormond Street Hospital for Children, founded in 1852 (its patrons included Queen Victoria and Charles Dickens), a stone's throw from our building.

The Nigel and Gerry stories go on interminably – including the time we rescued a lost Swiss girl of Barbie-like proportions from being stranded in a strange city. I put her up for the night (he steadfastly claimed it was for three nights). When Gerry stopped by after she left, he saw that a leg had broken off my bed and was lying accusingly on the parquet, complete with castor. He never let me forget that incident. "Nigel and the three-legged bed" became a staple in his long inventory of anecdotes. Through the years he would drag out stories that even I had forgotten.

A typical Gerry recollection, and this is a direct quote, was, "You may like to recall the time when you offered to impersonate a hot-water-bottle just as a favour to what's-her-name who was a friend of Karen, my chief reporter. Very altruistic, though maybe you were the wrong shape."

Then the story came back to me. We had returned to the girls' house after spending a couple of hours at a West End disco. "We had missed the last bus," I recalled, so we had to stay overnight."

"We *said* we missed the last bus," Gerry corrected me.

"Well, whatever. Do you realize I had to share a bed with *both* of them?"

"Poor old chap," he said unsympathetically.

I remembered clinging to the bed, my posterior hanging perilously over the edge. If bottoms get goose bumps, I'm sure mine was covered with them. I succeeded in getting no sleep, nor anything else, though I had suggested unsuccessfully, in deference to our companion of course, that we try it on the floor. I eventually trudged off miserably in the morning twilight with a painfully cheerful Gerry, who with a bed to himself was as fresh as the proverbial daisy, to catch an early bus.

Gerry soon left IMS and became a public relations specialist with an office a short distance away on Chancery Lane. It was a great location, with the Three Tuns pub across the alley and a Parisian-style *pissoir* a few yards away, on the eastern wall of Lincoln's Inn. Close by on Fetter Lane was another pub, the

Swan, where I met a very special and very attractive barmaid, Valerie, whom Gerry would successfully woo to be his wife.

Those escapades with Gerry were fun and, I suppose, juvenile, but they were harmless. It might not have been so in the case of that sleazy well dressed character from the International Chemical Specialties Association who dropped in at our office to make a business call on Borland. Later, the boss called me into his office and said, "Nigel, there's this guy from the chemical association came by here. We talked for about half a day and that's enough as far as I'm concerned. Would you mind taking him around tonight? Soho maybe. You know Greek?"

Americans are so efficient that they usually omit "street," "road," "avenue," and so on when referring to an address, so, whereas a normal Brit might assume he was being invited to escort a bloke wearing a white skirt and tassely hat, my bilingual talents helped me to respond. I admitted yes, I knew where Greek Street was, not far away in Soho.

Borland was delighted. "Well, he was there a few years ago and he'd like to go back and see it. Like old times, I guess."

Our visitor was called Jim Foulder. We met at the Tottenham Court Road tube station just as it was getting dark.

Foulder had an immaculate haircut, wore an expensive suit and was from the outset what you'd call an interesting type. He said he had worked for the CIA in the Caribbean and Central America, and then he joined the ICSA. I had trouble understanding the connection, but kept my mouth shut.

We found the Tarantella Club at the bottom of Greek Street, not far from the Prince Edward Theatre. It was dimly lighted and laid out like a café. We found a booth and ordered white wine. Soon a young woman approached, said her name was Lisa, and asked if she could join us. She was quiet spoken, and she wore nothing from the sash of her filmy skirt upwards. Of course, we said yes.

This was nothing new to Foulder, but I didn't know it at the time. We talked to Lisa as she took small sips from her soft drink. She looked pretty average apart from her dress, or lack of it. She didn't have tarty makeup or a special hairdo. Foulder had figured it all out and he knew how this scenario would work. I did most of the talking, which was mostly about ordinary things, and then uncharacteristically I asked her if she would like me (not us) to come home with her. It remained a very low-key conversation. "Well, yes," she said reflectively, I could come home with her. She'd like that. But she was concerned about her mother, who was looking after her young son. Her mother might not like it, she said. Wouldn't it be better if we went to the restaurant downstairs, where they had a tremendous chef, and we could talk some more over champagne.

So the wine bar and Lisa had been no more than a shop-window display to attract people to this restaurant, which had so far been invisible, probably charged very high prices and had only one way out, protected by a heavy bouncer.

I wasn't terribly disappointed by Lisa's answer. Foulder pulled at my sleeve and said, "Come on, I know another place."

This man was very, very experienced in navigating the seamy side of London, a point that apparently had not been noticed by the abstemious Dr. Borland. Foulder steered me over to a place the other side of Oxford Circus, where we went down some stairs and came up against a stout black door. He pressed an entry button and gave some kind of a code word. Something buzzed, he pushed open the door, and we walked in like patrons of a speakeasy.

It was an upscale place, nicely decorated, but still it boiled down into a disco fantasy of colour, sound, and human flesh. Here and there Lucite enclosures stuck up above the crowd, each containing a longhaired pole dancer clad (is this the right word?) in a thong. I thought they were all very nice looking and pleasant to watch. I had drunk quite a bit of white wine with Lisa and soon to my surprise found myself dancing. I'm a poor dancer, but this time I thought I was a great dancer.

Foulder got me back to the table, where we watched the performance of a young stripper. She was really very good, I thought in my wine-fuzzed mind. The last time I saw a stripper perform was at a member's birthday party at a gentlemen's club in Salt Lake City. But Foulder was unimpressed. As soon as she finished her act he stood and took out his credit card. On the way out he recognized one of the women and drenched her with a tirade of un-repeatable accusations. When we went to pick up our coats from the check-out girl he muttered something about meeting "the bitch in Berlin."

The next day, Borland asked if I would accompany Foulder for a second night. I wasn't keen on the idea but didn't want to refuse him. This time we went to a club designed rather like a pub, with a large central bar, except that it had a large dance floor. The girls were topless, wearing gauzy shorts and sandals. We found a couple of seats near where the action seemed to be happening. Foulder glanced around. "No grinding here," he growled, and I made a note to look up the word. We watched and drank for a while and I saw one of the girls fend off

Foulder's hands, for which she was rewarded with a raspberry. Then it was my turn. A younger girl made eye contact, deftly moved aside the little cast-iron table that I was using for my beer, and straddled my legs, which, being a gentleman, I closed together to help her with her act. She looked and, importantly, smelled good. She wiggled her bottom close to my private parts for a while, then treated me with a tiny moan, arched back her head, brushed her breasts slowly against my chest and sat straight, silently looking me in the eyes. She stood with her legs apart like an A and I stuck a five-pound note in her waistband. And then she pranced off with, as a touch of visual dessert, a sexy over-the-shoulder grin. All this and not a microsecond of skin-to-skin contact.

A light rain had started, prompting us to put up our umbrellas before we left the bar's entryway. "Did you tip her?" asked Foulder as we stood at the curb looking for a taxi. "Waste of good money," he grunted when I said yes, and spat into the gutter.

We ended the evening at the Tarantella. Lisa was sitting with another customer but there was an empty booth and we took it. This time we were joined by a dark-haired beauty by the name of Ruby. I could see Foulder's neck and shoulders tense just a little, and I'll bet his eyes were dilating too, if I could see them. Ruby was a 3-D centerfold, only she was very much alive. This time Foulder took the conversational lead. Lived in London a long time? How was it, working at the Tarantella? Any kids? What do you do in the daytime? Native Londoner, no kids, worked as a secretary during the day … I listened with a certain amazement as he extracted Ruby's résumé and filed it away in his head. He asked more questions. And then he totally blew me away.

"Hey listen, Ruby. You're a smart girl, shouldn't have to work in a place like this. How'd you like to go to work for me? In America?"

She gave him an incredulous look. "Not much chance of that."

"Why not? You're a free spirit. Think of it. Good pay, a nice apartment in Washington, D.C." He looked at her, waiting for another reply.

She cocked her head on one side. "I like London too much. Wouldn't want to leave my all my friends here. And I have a nice flat here anyway."

"Look, I'll send you a ticket. You'll get it first thing in the morning. How does that sound? We'll pay your way, take care of you and you won't have a worry in the world."

"I can think it over," she said evenly. "It's kind of you to make the offer. But I need time to think of it. And I'm pretty sure the answer will be no."

Foulder acted crestfallen and stood up. He fished a business card out of his pocket and gave it to her. "I think you should change your mind," he said, "and when you do, call me at this number. Collect. Just say it's Ruby and I'll know who it is. We'd sure like to have you on board."

On my way home that night, the novelty of the girlie shows faded and my mind was preoccupied with Jim Foulder. Who was he anyway? He almost certainly had a perfectly respectable job in Washington, and the business card was no doubt real. But what was his *game*? What had he learned in the CIA? How could he interrogate Ruby so smoothly and expertly while she learned practically nothing about him? He offered her a job without saying what kind of job it would be and what responsibilities it would carry. He offered it without running any kind of checks on her. She didn't know his story and he didn't know hers. Was he just trying to pick her up? I thought it was more than that. Perhaps unlike me he had recognized her as a drug addict. After a while I thought he might be dealing in the white slave trade. Perhaps he was a sex trafficker. Probably not. But I was glad to see the back of Jim Foulder. When I got home I took his card from my wallet, tore it into little bits, and dropped them into the rubbish bin.

❦

In a quite different part of my private life, I was sneaking off regularly for treatment at the National Temperance Hospital in Euston, built in 1873 in a style that has been termed "workhouse Victorian Gothic." As you may have guessed it was built in the heyday of the temperance movement to treat alcoholics. But times had changed and I was there not for drunkenness but for dependency on prednisone, which had been prescribed as an anti-asthmatic medication. After years of daily doses of the stuff, my adrenal glands had shrivelled and needed to be rehabilitated so that I could be introduced to inhaled salbutamol (albuterol), which was not yet available in the States. I'm pleased to say that those visits had their desired effect.

The hospital was clean and even cheerful with lots of windows that kept the hallways and waiting areas bright, though I am pretty sure that in those days the needles that they used to take my blood samples were being re-sharpened with questionable expertise before being sterilized and re-used. Today the hospital is a dead, looted relic with boarded-up windows, rotting away after more than two decades of neglect and accessible only on lists of derelict and disused buildings.

Incheba Trade Fair, Bratislava, 1978 – My first trip behind the "Iron Curtain" as an IMS Pharmaceutical Marketletter journalist. We had a smooth flight to Prague on a Russian equivalent of the British VC-10, but missed the connecting flight to Bratislava. After going through the umpteenth security/customs/currency check, we found ourselves in a lumbering Russian airplane of the DC-6 variety, bound for Bratislava with half a dozen passengers standing nonchalantly in the aisle. A fellow writer, Harry, said his fillings were never the same after he made that flight, the vibration was so bad. Once we arrived, the authorities kept close tabs on us. Our interpreters were "debriefed" on our activities at the close of each day, and we heard that the police had been asking for special information on some of the attendees. I scored a good interview with the Eastern Europe chief for Wellcome, who commented that one has to sell to the Comecon countries more and more on the basis of cost-effectiveness. You can do this for pigs or for grain crops but not for humans, he said. A sobering thought. So they were decreasing emphasis on selling human drugs and concentrating on veterinary and agro-chemical sales. Some of my notes I deliberately chose not to write up and pass on to our Telex operator for relay to London. You can guess why.

During these and subsequent years I would regularly visit the children and Miriam in Folkestone, generally every other Sunday. These were surreal: the children were perfectly behaved; Mim was nearly always brimming with a combination of bonhomie, anger and grief. I never forgot one heartbreaking moment at the rickety dinner table in Folkestone, when the air was electric with Miriam's angst, when Jocelyn asked, "Can't we just play happy families"? The precious illusion of normalcy in my relationship with the children occurred only when Brian and Jocelyn were able to stay with Sue and me in London or Yorkshire.

After Aunt Em's house came into my possession, the kids began making regular weekend visits to the cottage with Sue and me. We had joyful Christmas visits there, exploring, making snowmen, having adventures like the time we started walking through deep snow down the beck from the Malt Shovel pub, then, realizing we would never get to Bingley, fighting our way back up the main road. Like the antics with our hamsters Bunbury and Christmas, these were warm and genuine "bonding" experiences, and for me never enough.

12. NEW HOPE FOR A FAMILY LIFE

None of us knows what the next change is going to be, what unexpected opportunity is just around the corner, waiting a few months or a few years to change all the tenor of our lives.
– Kathleen Norris

It gave me a special feeling to own a piece of London, a 1920s row house graced with its own little garden, greenhouse and potting shed. A hydrangea was always blooming in the front garden next door and it was ages before I realized that it was made of Chinese silk.

The house was on a residential street on the brow of Crouch Hill, between Finsbury Park and Crouch End. Before long Sue and I took the kitchen apart and put a cooker where the old fireplace had been, and singlehandedly she made the cabinetwork for a kitchen sink that looked out onto the little garden.

Nearby was the route of an old railway line, an amazing place because it is hidden under the crest of the hill. To get there, we would duck off the asphalt footpath that follows the road, scramble down an embankment and find ourselves in a happily confused state, surrounded by trees and ready to start a delightful country walk in the middle of densely-populated North London. The track, long gone, had been cut as much as 30 feet into the ground so that it could snake under city streets. This meant the houses and traffic were nearly always out of view, and much of the city noise was hidden too, so that we could walk serenely where raspberries and blackberries grew wild, as if in a genuinely natural setting.

We had a number of little adventures at the Crouch Hill house, like the chimney pot falling through the tile roof in a windstorm, the hamster escaping (prompting me fruitlessly to dismantle the fireplace surround and several lengths of skirting boards), the abortive break-in that ended with off-duty policemen chasing the burglars over the back garden walls of the terraced houses, the time that snow completely closed Crouch Hill … But we were always eager to escape on Friday evenings and brave the choking traffic to the M1, northwards to quiet solitude in Yorkshire.

In the 1970s I found enough time to write another book-length manuscript. I had written snatches of diary prose about the human condition, communication, and media, respectively, in the 1960s, and had the notion that I could expand them into something worthy of publication. I heard about an institution called International College and decided that the discipline of producing a related dissertation would help the process, albeit under the auspices of a campus-less school, approved by the California State Department of Education but lacking national accreditation.

The hunch paid off. I was assigned a helpful and knowledgeable mentor who was a lecturer in sociology at Cambridge, finished the 100,000-word study, and received a diploma dated June 30, 1980. From the dissertation was born a book manuscript called *The Bionic Reef* (from a comparison of human society with the reef life I had come to know in Bermuda), which in revision I re-titled *Millennium Three*. The dissertation/book supported the idealism that I felt for the connection of democracy with the print media. It was intended to be a first move in satisfying my imagined life-purpose – helping bring about a course correction in a world that was wrong and getting worse. Or so I thought – perhaps the imagined values of my protected youth were merely receding from those of the real world.

Millennium Three was an attempt at writing a serious if not scholarly book (in earlier days I had avoided the label "intellectual" with the same care as the word "academic"). But I was no Tom Friedman. I sent proposals to a couple of publishers, knowing in myself that the book wouldn't fly. The manuscript stayed in my computer archive, and from time to time I went back to look at it, always to realize that it would be impossible to update and publish because the world and I had changed so much since I first put the words together. And so it had to be.

I had also become intrigued with the concept of progress, which I had not discussed in the book. Note that I had come to believe that progress had a lot to do with improving the mutual understanding, peacefulness, health, and spiritual life of the world's people, and little or nothing to do with social status and material possessions (i.e. fancy cars, big houses, fancy electronic gadgets).

My research resulted in little more than putting together a very large collection of quotations, 99 per cent of which, naturally, supported my own opinions. The rest was, shall we say, less valuable. As Oscar Wilde put it, "Most people are other people. Their thoughts are some one else's opinions, their lives a mimicry, their passions a quotation." Fortunately I realized this before I tried to make a career of being an amateur futurist. Why did I spend my time on such things? Anyway, I considered the Juniperhill experience, back in early 1961, as being the Big Event, the inspiration, the divine influence. It seemed nobody else in the world could have been visited by such a phenomenon. I learned I was mistaken on that count as well.

At first I was inclined to think of the Juniperhill happening as a gift from God, perhaps meant especially for me. But one by one I learned that many others, including the writers Fyodor Dostoevsky, Eugene O'Neill, and Willa Cather, had already written of such things. They, and heaven knows how many others, were in tune with the art historian Bernard Berelson's reminiscence: "It was a morning in early summer. A silver haze shimmered and trembled over the lime trees. The air was laden with their fragrance. The temperature was like a caress. I remember – I need not recall – that I climbed up a tree stump and felt suddenly immersed in Itness. I did not call it by that name. I had no need for words. It and I were one."[19]

I remembered, in response to a sudden subconscious cue, that the Buddha taught that *every sentient being possesses the potential for enlightenment.*

Regardless of my inability to claim any exclusivity in connection with this idea, I greatly valued my experience with Berenson's "itness" – the remarkable occurrence that Dostoevsky considered to be an encounter with "eternal harmony." In fact I valued it enormously while being slightly afraid of it because I was not at all sure that I wanted to end up suspended in this kind of rapture for all time. It might turn out like the frightful sci-fi nightmare in which an astronaut's lifeline to his spaceship is broken and he drifts off helplessly into the oblivion of space. When I was ready to die, it might be okay, but right now, no thanks.

I still wanted to be able to repeat the experience of bonding with what seemed to be an eternal reality, or at least to be suspended in its magic again. But I didn't believe my best purpose was to seek oblivion. I still wanted to *do* something that would contribute to the well-being of humankind, though it was hard to determine just what that something would be.

There's an odd thing about looking back at the usual world from that other, faraway perspective. In fact there are a lot of odd things about it. The one that just caught my attention is that I don't mind casting off some of the irritation about humanity being wrong, or wrong-footed, misdirected. I *know* – not just think or guess – it is hugely important to remember that the world is a marvellously complex planet, including the biosphere and its components and not just our species and its artefacts. Forget problems of politics and economics for a while. The entire *planet* is having a helluva hard time dealing with everything that those billions of naked apes – us – are throwing at it. It struck me that maybe I should be campaigning for a one-child-per-couple policy like the one they introduced in China in 1977; for restrictions on meat production; for extra taxes that would reduce the use of oil; for more investment in renewable and nuclear energy and the electric and hydrogen vehicles that would use it. We use the term "our world" regularly, and it has become just that; yet how disgracefully we care for what we claim to possess.

⚜

In the late 1970s, in my persona as a minor publishing executive, my colleagues and I bought equipment that would allow IMS to modernize its operation and eventually to produce "cold type" pages. Our goal was to produce a million-word reference work almost entirely by computer. This was a leading-edge enterprise for at the time "hot type," made from hot molten metal with machines such as the Linotype, was still the main way of producing high-quality printing. But in this early adventure in desktop publishing, the workhorse was a PDP-11 computer that stored, on a disk I could just about get my arms around, the two-column pages that we had prepared for high-speed offset printing. These were early days, and we used very basic word-processing software. The result was not something that looked like the future *Vanity Fair*, but it was a start.

Without my realizing it, my writing and publishing career was shifting rather dramatically, from the analog age to the digital age. We were part of a sea change that was transforming the entire world of publishing.

In 1980 I bought a gadget that I thought was wonderfully intriguing, a Sinclair ZX80 personal home computer that cost less than £100 and was small enough to put in my briefcase. Incredible! Its capabilities were minuscule by comparison with the similar-sized netbooks that became popular forty years later. But it introduced me to the exciting idea of producing mistake-free manuscripts digitally at home. The infant "word processing" technology that came with it would free me from having to re-type home-produced manuscript pages after obliterating the errors with white paint or skinny strips of sticky paper, then photocopying the result.

⚜

One of my desktop publishing projects at IMS was *Third World Health Insights*, a modestly produced overview of health and nutrition statistics in developing countries. Being an idealistic sort of chap I hoped that the executives who bought IMS products would buy it and be touched by the miserable state of affairs in those benighted countries. Thinking back on it, this was an unrealistic hope.

I wrote and produced the entire book, using information sent by the countries themselves and, liberally, published data from the World Bank and various United Nations agencies. To me the statistics were enlightening and disturbing. For example: "Although 80% of India's population is spread throughout the rural areas, approximately 80% of health facilities are concentrated in urban districts." There were worse statistics. In Nigeria the central government spent the equivalent of $2 per person each year for health care. In Sri Lanka only 20% of the population had access to safe water. In Tanzania the per-capita calorie supply averaged 89 calories, comparable with the *minimum* 100 recommended by the U.N. Food and Agricultural Organization. In Bolivia it was 83 calories, the male life expectancy at birth was 46.5 years, two-thirds of individuals aged under 15 suffered from malnutrition, and half of all nursing mothers were anaemic. In Thailand, though adult literacy was said to be a high 84%, there was only one nursing person per 3,540 individuals.

We had gross national product figures, but these meant very little without data on how the GNP was distributed. In most countries there were a few very rich and a huge number of the very poor, mixed in with the desperately poor who were dying of malnutrition and disease. These realities made GNP a very crude indicator of national standards of living, as it remains today. Even rich countries like the U.S. had a large, and widening, gap between rich and relatively poor.

These figures gave me grim, early indicators of the gross inequities that exist among the loosely knit and often contentious community of nations. Yes, they sprang from all sorts of internal political, social, and environmental problems. But there was a global story here. Poor countries needed more food while rich countries wasted vast amounts of food. And Earth was becoming over-agriculturized, which meant to me that there were simply *too many people*. What could be the answer to this, other than catastrophic deaths through famine? Pandemic plague? Global war with weapons of mass destruction? A natural disaster like a meteor strike or a once-in-a-millennium volcanic eruption? The solutions sounded as bad as the problem, and I felt miserable about having allowed my second book to be titled with the painfully unanswerable question, *How Will We Feed the Hungry Billions?*

The evening-out of inequities between the emerging nations and the more industrially developed nations – if not between their rich and poor residents – probably began in earnest in 2008, when the West's economic crash started to get very serious.

The desktop publishing gambit taught me the basics of writing computer software. I did this crudely, using simple Boolean operators, but with a growing enthusiasm that became so ardent that one night I downed tools and decided not to do any more of it. It was like the time at university that I became so involved in bridge-playing that I gave that up too, lest it become an addiction. It was just too much fun.

For reasons unknown to me, my company then became involved with the International Laboratory Accreditation Conference (ILAC), which had been created to assist the creditable goal of getting the engineering standards of various nations to agree with each other. Our role involved helping set up its international meetings, and, through my efforts, publishing its first directories. I represented IMS at ILAC meetings in Paris, Mexico City, and Tokyo.

In January 1980, the owners of the Georgian house in The Bayle decided they wanted to return home, and so Brian, Jocelyn and Miriam moved to Mim's parents' house at 82 Shorncliffe Road. "The weather is getting bitterly cold," Brian wrote in a letter to his grandma and grandpa Hey. "We had two gas fires on as well as an electric one. It is so cold that Mummy has the flu and Jocelyn, Daddy and I did not stay out for long." While I plugged along in London – business travel provided most of the IMS fun, though nights of insane hilarity with my best friend Gerry Bishop probably did the most to keep up my spirits – Miriam and the family were living a quite different life in Folkestone. At Christmas, 1980, when she was 12, Jocelyn sent me this unedited, mournful lament called "Thoughts of a tinkers child: How I wish I was rich," typed on my old electric typewriter, for her grandmother:

My clothes are tattered,
My shoes are worn.
I somehow wish I aint bin born.
The richest ladys walk down 't street

Wearing lace in the summer,
And fur when it's cold
how I wish I was rich.

They live in big 'ouses,
Well thats what i'm told
And when lyin' in bed
They aint never cold.
But here am I
sleeping out every night,
looking into the sky,
at the stars shining bright

As a matter of fact, Jocelyn did sleep in the cold, in the cavernous unheated conservatory at 82 Shorncliffe Road. "Winter is definitely upon Folkestone, with gales sweeping across the Channel," was a typical winter weather report from her letters. By the time she reached her mid-teens it was apparent that she had a gift for writing. She also had a musical side to her nature. She had started piano lessons with David Leek in the spring of 1980, and this, along with singing in the school choir and ringing bells in St. Eanswythe's church tower (from which her admiring father was once unceremoniously expelled), gave a collective and highly diverse boost to her interest in music. And in 1981 she made her first independent overseas trip, to Chambéry, France, to stay with her friend Céline and family.

My mother and dad were doing well, and enjoying my dad's enviably lengthy and eminently well-deserved retirement, which lasted from 1960 to his death in 1990. They had moved into a comfortable block of modern flats, Lancastrian Grange, near a big archaeological dig in Chichester, and celebrated the move with a trip to Madeira.

⁂

The Wilsden house offered a much-needed escape from the noise and fumes of London. On Friday afternoons we would pack up the Ford Capri and fight our way up Colney Hatch Lane and along the North Circular Road to the M1, and then we were truly on our way. Four weary hours later we would be in the cool clear Pennine air of West Yorkshire, relishing the stars nested in Wilsden's inky sky, and making tea in the little kitchen. That was in summer, for at other times we would sometimes need to stop off at the coal merchant's in Harden, and heave a sack of coal into the boot before continuing up the hill.

Summer or winter, we would visit Honey Pot and see Gordon and Marie Mitchell, who had owned the farm since about 1965, and Uncle Ted, who lived next door in the farm workers' cottage that he occupied in perpetuity as a condition of his sale of the farm to them. After we eased his garden gate open to walk down the flagstone path to his cottage he would see us and we would walk in without knocking, greeting him with a cheery Yorkshire "'Eigh up!" We invariably found Ted in his old mahogany rocker, a cigarette close by, staring into the glowing red fireplace coals, his diabetic whippet Bluey curled up nearby, dreaming of her warm bedtime saucer of milk laced with whisky. I made a few trips to the vet in Bingley to pick up antidiabetic pills for her, and ended up burying her thin little body, wrapped lovingly by Ted in a shroud of sacking, in his garden border.

These visits were generally made merrier with several glasses of Scotch whisky, Grants usually, and sometimes Uncle Ted would totter from the fire to the piano and sing "Danny Boy" in a high, quavering voice, Sue accompanying him at the piano. Sue loved these events, and loved Uncle Ted, whom she recognized accurately as a true Yorkshire "character." In fact these were choice moments for all concerned.

We bought the Wilsden house as a furnished property – and so it was, though we suspected that the easily portable, unbroken items had been taken away after Em was admitted to hospital for the last time. In short, we acquired a large number of chipped and glued-together pots and figurines. But there were a piano, beds, furniture, crockery – all the essentials. Joss, Sue and I redecorated the place and painted most of it in "magnolia" white. I replaced some of the worst wiring, rather gingerly because it was a 240 volt supply and I never forgot exploring a plug with a metallic pin when I was a child at the bakery.

My neighbour and I replaced the roof by shoring up the roof tree (literally a tree stripped of its branches to provide the main load-bearing beam and evening up the roofline with nailed-on planking) and turning the limestone roof tiles so that the less-weathered surfaces would face the elements. In the hallway I attached decorative dado boarding along the bottom of the wall, mostly as a cosmetic touch to cover the unsightly damp-marks and to help me forget that it

Appleby Outing. Sue and Uncle Ted got along famously. Photo was taken at
Appleby Fair, the annual gypsy get-together where Ted could search for and chat
with some of his old Romany friends.

would cost thousands of pounds to get rid of the seepage (someone, maybe Em,
had covered the original flagstone floor with asphalt, but it couldn't seal the
whole house).

⚜

The 1970s were bittersweet years. Wilsden offered the sweet times of enjoying
the house with Sue, Brian, and Jocelyn, and with it many weekends of escape
northward from the bustle of London, summer hikes up the narrow, wooded
valley called Goit Stock to the waterfall, and snowy winters that my elder
children and I will never forget, extrication of errant hamsters from furniture
springs, those old-fashioned sing-songs around Uncle Ted's piano, amazing
gatherings of reminiscing friends, mostly elderly types, in the living room, which
we called "t'ouse," or "the house," in other words the common room, the most
socially significant part of the building.

You may think this odd, but sometimes I would take an empty one-gallon
plastic bottle up to Wilsden so that I could bring back a supply of drinking water
from the kitchen tap. It tasted pure, but it also was tinged with the very slightly
bitter taste of peat, which I loved to taste on my tongue. Then the water

authorities decided the water was too natural and decided to put it through a new treatment plant. Overnight my drink tasted not of the moorlands but of sterile and spiritless chlorine.

At times I managed to liven up trips to Wilsden with my own brand of dour drama. For reasons unknown I hadn't been feeling very well on one particular trip, and about two hours into our homebound journey I thought I needed medical help, right then. Maybe a police cruiser would have some oxygen on board. So I asked Sue to stop at one of the little ramps that are provided for police cars on the M1 motorway. She did, and surprisingly there was a police car in attendance. But the policeman had no oxygen, so this time I was treated to a replay of that time the sheriff escorted me to the hospital in Albuquerque. Only this time we spent the night in hospital in Rugby, a place I knew only for its brand of football.

The sad times were the Sunday visits to Folkestone for those few hours of seeing the children, who were beginning to grow up seventy-five miles away, Miriam doing her heroic best in the kitchen, the leg of lamb Sunday dinners, pretending without hope to be "families," disconsolate walks with the children to the garden center and the harbour, and then my walk, alone, to the dismal, run-down and (for the present day) ridiculously long railway platforms at Folkestone West station, to catch the slow train back to London.

Was Miriam really heroic? The answer: *Yes.*

❦

By 1982 I knew my work at IMS had plateaued, for I had accomplished what I wanted to do and saw no exciting challenges ahead. Sue and I had a circle of friends, enjoyed London, revelled in our escapes to Yorkshire, and I was near the children. But the kids were growing into their teens, either in or heading for secondary school. I was restless, and sensed that Sue was ready to go home.

In the autumn of that year, while I was editing copy in the smoky room with the number 13 painted on its windowless Victorian door, I received a cryptic phone call. At first the voice sounded like a parody, I had been so long removed from Oklahoma and Texas accents. But it was Jim Mitchell, my old boss at Sandia.

"Nigel, I'm getting a promotion. Would you like my job?" Jim asked. It was like a replay of the time when, in that cold Kentish newsroom, I took the perfectly-timed call from Liz Pengelly and returned to a dream job in Bermuda.

171

"Give me five minutes to think it over," I said, and phoned Sue.

I told Sid Seltzer, my IMS boss, that I had been offered a job in America and intended to leave, but he wanted me to go to an ILAC meeting in Tokyo anyway. Perhaps he thought I was kidding him, that my talk of a job in the States was a ploy for a promotion; perhaps he was just being "nice," for indeed he was that sort of a man.

I left for Tokyo on October 13, spent October 14-15 in Hong Kong (sampan sightseeing), was in Tokyo October 15-21 (a capsule-like room in a businessmen's hotel), took a side trip on a bullet train (bed and breakfast in a marvellous traditional Kyoto inn), and returned via Gatwick on October 22. When I arrived at Crouch Hill, movers hired long-distance by Sandia were busy packing a container with our worldly goods. What a shame that there would be so much unused space in that container, I thought, and sped down to the local antique shop to buy a load of extra furniture to ship off to New Mexico.

Perhaps I should have said no to Jim Mitchell. I could have made a career out of IMS and forced our home life, and the house, into the mould that I had pictured years ago when I was at the University of Utah. We could have had children of our own, to share our lives and spend those delightful weekends in Yorkshire with us. Sue would have tried to go along with the idea, but this was not her home. Her home was in New Mexico, or in Texas. It would always be that way.

Deciding to return to Sandia should be ranked as a "thematic conflict" in my life, but did not seem so because my career had truly levelled off and I was keen to return to a place where wonder was part of the job description.

There were many times, later, that I reflected that I should have thought over the Sandia offer more carefully, to give more weight to the positions of Miriam and the children in the equation. I *did* think it over, and believed that moving to Sandia would better financially for my extended family, for my "estate." This was correct, as far as it went. Miriam's mother and dad had died from lung cancer, so that she had the house to herself, the rent from two lodgers, and some spending money from me. The children were 12 and 14 at the time, and fairly mature for their ages, but while Joss was a rock-solid little personality it later became clear that it would have been better if Brian had me around, or at least in London, as he moved through his early teens.

The truth may be that I agonize about it now because I didn't agonize enough about it back then.

"Dad has just left for London in the car," Jocelyn wrote to my mother and dad. "We shall all miss him when he goes back to America but we all also realize that it is the best thing that could happen."

"We are all very excited because Dad is leaving for America, although our happiness for him is mixed with sorrow because understandably we will miss him," wrote Brian.

⚬⚬⚬

We staggered through the doors of Albuquerque's Marriott Hotel on October 31st, Halloween night, greeted by a man appropriately costumed as a Tylenol bottle. It would be six months before the London house finally sold, ironically just before the property market skyrocketed. Another irony was that we didn't need the money, for by the time a new buyer was found we had bought a house in Albuquerque. If only I had accepted our neighbour Steve Brown's offer to rent the Briston Grove house for us!

I began work at Sandia the next day. The *Sandia Lab News* commemorated the fact with a photo of me collapsed, exhausted, at the airport desk of the New Mexico tourism office. After my ten-year private-company "sabbatical," I was again a Sandia science writer, with the additional responsibility of managing the lab's small media relations group. But as a manager I made computerizing the office an early priority too early, by making the change from Selectric typewriters to the soon-outdated DECmate word processor system. It seemed strange that a writer should be taking this initiative in one of America's leading science and technology laboratories, but I kept this observation mostly to myself.

This time around I thought my super-story would probably be something originally called a strained-layer superlattice (SLS), which had caught the interest of a man who was possibly the smartest scientist on Sandia's campus, Gordon Osbourn. IBM had worked on the idea and consigned it to the back shelves of their research program. But Gordon was intrigued. He was a mathematician and knew there was something behind the idea. He soon made the first calculations explaining the unique electrical and optical properties of these structures. They showed that new materials could be made from super-thin sandwiches of semiconductor alloy, each of which will conduct electrical energy in a slightly different way.[20] Each layer of the sandwich was a different kind of semiconductor, which meant that their crystal lattices did not line up evenly. The result was that strain occurred as the crystals were forced into place by natural forces. The built-in strain controlled the capability of the material to produce or detect a predictable wavelength of light.

Fortunately we had many brilliant materials researchers on staff, with advanced equipment that was capable of making strained layer structures like the materials Gordon described on paper. Their work led to revolutionary advances in electronics and optoelectronics. Continued advances resulted in the development of a high-efficiency miniature solid-state laser in the mid-1990s, and the use of built-in strain became essential to the development of light-emitting diodes (LEDs), now used in traffic signals and transportation lighting and a range of other devices that run from chemical sensors to flashlights and solar cells. As I write there is a surge of optimism that strained-layer materials will be successful in the design of high-energy sources of white light, rather than the more common red and green light sources.

This was probably the most difficult (and most significant) science story I had ever written, as I delved into the mathematical esoterica of semiconductor physics, preparing to talk with science-writer specialists who, unlike me, were perfectly familiar with the electronic geometry of the Brouillin zone that was so important to the workings of this new material.

Unfortunately, of all the important basic inventions and discoveries that came out of our lab, none bore anything like the legend "Sandia Inside," for their development into stand-alone devices was soon taken up by private industry.

෴

Less than six months later, Ronald Reagan announced the Strategic Defense Initiative, the Cold War anti-ballistic missile program that was caricatured as a political "Star Wars." Since rejoining Sandia I had made the acquaintance of Gerold Yonas, a super-bright physicist who was overseeing fusion research at the lab. So I bounced into his office the morning after the Reagan speech, brandishing the *Albuquerque Journal* at him and saying something like, "Can you imagine this? They're planning to put an anti-missile umbrella over the entire United States!"

Back in 1983 I didn't know that Yonas and his peers met regularly with their Russian counterparts to talk about fusion physics. Each side was well aware that the other was working on fusion *weapons*, but the discussions were held firmly to the scientific, non-technological, and therefore nonclassified, aspects of fusion as such, in the pure sense. Yonas, who boasted Transylvanian lineage, knew the Russian mind, he had the rare talent of being both outspoken and cautious, and he certainly knew physics and space technology.

I let Yonas know I thought the umbrella idea was ludicrous beyond belief. He didn't argue the point. But then magically he became the program's chief scientist, based in Washington, and in the next few years I shepherded eager reporters like *the New York Times*'s Bill Broad around Sandia as they tried, sometimes successfully, to pry quotable quotes from Yonas, Roger Hagengruber, and others involved in Sandia's SDI effort. I found the whole story interesting and intriguing. But it wasn't until 1999 that I decided to write a book about it.

Jim was still doing after-hours public relations for Maxie Anderson, who was planning his most spectacular enterprise – to circle the globe in a helium balloon. After extensive preparations, and delays until the weather was just right at the launch site, Maxie and his friend and co-pilot Ben Abruzzo lifted off and floated eastward on their epic voyage. Not many days later I answered the phone for Jim and it fell to me to give him an appalling message – Maxie and Ben's balloon envelope had ruptured high over Germany. It was June 27, 1983. Maxie and Ben suffered what I thought must have been a terrible death, though I knew they knew they must have considered the possibility of a catastrophic structural failure many times.

My return to Sandia opened exciting new doors, a boon for the curious man. It gave me the opportunity to re-start my media program, which meant going to New York and Washington once or twice a year, occasional visits to other media centers, the opportunity to meet other writers who worked for the mass media, magazines, and television, and the equally enjoyable challenge of catching up on the science and technology from which I had been isolated for a decade. If I had stayed in London, it would have been more of the same, limited to the pharmaceutical business – *business*, that is, for I never found the opportunity to write about pharmacology, the research side of this huge and powerful enterprise.

With time, Jim and I would assemble a fine group of professional communicators, seeking out people who had prior journalistic experience, in science writing when possible, and who therefore were likely to work successfully with media types. Some of these included:

Iris Aboytes, a native of small-town Hispanic New Mexico who Jim and I hired as a secretary and who as a human-interest specialist became one of or possibly the, best-read writer for the lab newspaper.

Ace Etheridge, a cheerful and sociable Texan I wooed away from the business desk of the local paper, who tried unsuccessfully to be a curmudgeon and succeeded only in becoming a well-liked and productive staffer instead.

Ken Frazier, onetime editor of SCIENCE NEWS, continuing editor of the SKEPTICAL INQUIRER, writer of books and the most talented and sensitive science writer I have known as a personal friend.

Rod Geer, a breezy Los Alamos native who had the enviable patience to take on and conquer some of the most tedious and challenging administrative writing that we were sometimes assigned by the higher-ups.

John German, a super-bright, soccer-playing science writer and editor who eventually left Sandia to become Director of Communications at the Santa Fe Institute.

Will Keener, a witty, dry-humoured specialist writer on geology and energy who became a genuine sci/tech all-rounder and editor of Sandia's quarterly science/technology magazine.

Howard Kercheval, a quiet-spoken, dyed-in-the-wool journalist (and small-craft sailor) who seemed to have an encyclopaedic memory about just about everything that was of consequence to me.

Chris Miller, another staffer whose company I especially enjoyed, endowed with a fine mind and artistic talent, who was a staff writer before becoming media relations manager.

Randy Montoya, a marvellous photographer with a wicked sense of humour, universally liked and unsuccessfully courted by the headquarters folks at Lockheed Martin.

Bill Murphy, editor of the biweekly SANDIA LAB NEWS, whom I considered to be the Mark Twain of our staff, energetic, organized, and a very fine writer.

Larry Perrine, one of the Oklahoma diaspora who fled to New Mexico after the oil bust of the early 1970s and one of the wittiest people I have known, always welcome at the poker table.

Neal Singer, the one true scientist in our bunch and another good personal friend, a genuine PhD who I would usually consult when writing about mathematics or advanced physics.

Sue and I bought the second house we viewed in metropolitan Albuquerque, technically located in the relatively rural village of Los Ranchos de Albuquerque. It was a 20-year-old flat-roofed adobe with a half acre of land on a large tract once owned by Damacio Lucero, sold to me by Sandia retiree Howard Stump and his English wife Nancy.

The container that had been packed on Crouch Hill in October arrived at our new house on February 5, 1983. And it was snowing. This is another film clip that remains filed in my mind. The movers had set up a ramp down from the truck that carried the container, and huge flakes of snow were falling as piano, sideboards, dressing tables, and all manner of boxes were manhandled and slithered to safety. Somewhere there I have a black and white photo of this event. Even though I can't find it, I can see it still. Soon the boxes were unpacked, and because we had planned which piece would go where, the house was quickly furnished, with my grandfather Kershaw's great mahogany bookcase, which had sat for many decades in the front room at Honey Pot, taking pride of place, crammed with books from his days and those of his parents.

The house was far bigger than any other residence we had known, built in modern Pueblo style with brick floors, exposed, rough-finished beams cut from the trunks of pine trees, and curved fireplaces tucked into corners of the living room and den. "Hello, you there?" I would yell from the master bedroom, and from what seemed like a long way away, Sue's voice would answer, "Over here, in the kitchen!" The external walls were built of solid adobe brick – sun-baked clay mud.

The garden was spiked with three tall pine trees, a blue spruce, and three or four junipers, and in the borders were lavender, rosemary, chamisa, and other drought-resistant shrubs. A tall mulberry tree and a cottonwood adorned the west side, and apple, cherry, and wild plum trees graced the north.

Next to the carport was an attractive room with brick floor, heater, and closet that the previous owners called the studio. This became my study, where I edited manuscripts and wrote about whatever had taken my fancy at the moment. I must confess that it was also a sort of monastic retreat, where I could remove myself from the bustle of the household, yet close enough to be summoned for help with an intercom. Writing is a lonely occupation, best done in short spurts when sequestered from the hurly-burly, and this little room was just what I needed.

As for the property itself, we loved it. Nearby a very slim and sinuous strip of "countryside" followed the irrigation ditches, the *acequias* originally dug out by old-time Indians and Spanish colonials. Delicious wild plums, and colonist-planted grapes, grew along its banks, giant cottonwoods with ropy bark towered against the sky, and crayfish were hiding under the underwater rockeries, seeking safety from prowling water rats and raccoons. It was a fitting New Mexico substitute for the walks that we enjoyed along the Crouch Hill railway right-of-way.

When the front room was piled with boxes the doorbell rang and soon Mrs. Black from down the road was chatting merrily in the role of a neighbourhood welcomer while expertly sizing us up. She mystified us, and never returned; not much later she moved away. Next door was our real neighbour, the sandy-haired architectural engineer Jim Puckett, and next to them Stuart Duban and his wife Veronica, a Yorkshirewoman from Harrogate. And so on, around the periphery of our short, unpaved cul-de-sac. Jim was divorced at the time we arrived, but it was not long before noticed a pert, attractive woman in the garden of his house. This proved to be Patti, a veteran of the Albuquerque Public Schools system. Soon they were married, and friendships blossomed between the two adobe households.

While I was proud to be appointed to my new job, I had a couple of fallback plans. One was to start an English-type pub (I had even brought an inn sign with the name "The Old Cock" pictured, in relief, on both sides). The other was to start a tour-guide service for British and European clients. Neither materialized, though I did travel the state looking at places that I thought might be interesting to future clients, studying the history and geography of the place, and spending time with the Indians.

A number of English friends and relatives came to visit soon after our return to America, including, to my delight, Brian and Jocelyn. Joss, who had taken Englishness as part of her persona and seemed at times to regard her New Mexico birth with disbelief, greatly enjoyed the trip and returned with no regrets.

Entertaining visitors was fun, and an easy undertaking. The "big city" of Albuquerque had its own charms, including the old town, dominated by the 1735 Church of San Felipe Neri. There was the Rio Grande, neither large nor deep but grand in its own special way, with mysterious movable islands – actually muddy sandbars – covered with impenetrable willow; and a narrow floodplain wooded with huge cottonwoods, Russian olives, and tamarisks. There was Petroglyph Park, featuring prehistoric hand-inscribed designs in lava rock that had tumbled from the escarpment on the west bank of the Rio Grande. And most magnificent of all, there were the Sandia Mountains, rising 11,000 feet on the eastern edge of the city, said to be given the Spanish name for watermelon because in late autumn the sun will sometimes turn them pink in the last minutes before sunset.

In my first year back in Albuquerque I appeared in two plays directed by my old friend John Gardner – *King Lear* (I had been demoted from an earlier role as the Fool to that of a "walking gentleman") and a collection of Falstaff scenes. They were my last theatrical appearances on stage; John, the Sandia librarian who had blossomed in local theatre during my absence, also began to lose his ardour for the boards and turned his considerable talents to a new interest, video. I gave up acting, but not my love for Shakespeare and the awe I feel for a man who divined the secrets of the human psyche with brilliance that any ordinary human being would find unapproachable, even unimaginable. What inspirational magic moved the pen of a man who illustrated so acutely the inconstant, shifting, ageless, history-making nature of human energies that recur century after century!

I eased into my renewed career with little trauma, the first priority being to re-establish my Q clearance with the Department of Energy. Again, for most of the time, I was a clean-cut young public relations man. I say most of the time, for I had originally taken up pipe smoking while working at Salt Lake City's KUTA, after one of the women at work made a wry comment about what she considered to be my youthful inaccessibility. It was not that this particular woman appealed to me; but she was perfectly capable of doing damage to my young ego whether she intended to or not. What nerve, to decide just like that that I was too young to bed her! Did she know the truth about my virginal state? Thus were born my years as a pipe-smoker, quickly followed by the tweed jacket and beard, none of which had quite the effect that I had hoped for.

Though my sex life had improved long before I arrived at IMS, my smoking became excessive to the point that my office would become so befogged that it was at times hard to identify the people coming through my door. I realized what a nasty pastime it was getting to be, and vowed to give up the pipe when I left for Sandia. One afternoon in Washington's Metro, during one of my infrequent lapses, a man came up to me and said firmly, "Put that thing away, sir. Smoking's not allowed in Metro stations." After that I would very occasionally take it out, even though I didn't much care for it any more. Giving it up was one resolution I really kept, and to be honest it didn't bother me a bit. Especially since virtually no one smoked at Sandia, where only every once in a while – before it became a "non-smoking campus" – did you see a silent figure outside one of the office buildings, taking a lonely cigarette break.

My re-clearance was processed fairly quickly, so that in September, as part of my induction to the new life, I was able to travel to Tonopah, Nevada, to view Sandia's large-scale testing area on the northern edge of Nellis Air Force Base. This required that I fly in a government contractor's DC-9 to a private hangar at Las Vegas's McCarran Field. This was a mysterious start, especially since the inside of the airliner had partly-removed décor that featured a Chinese motif and some partly obliterated Chinese lettering. Then I joined another group of passengers and boarded an old DC-6 for the hop to Tonopah. The route took us over the Nevada Test Site, so we could peer down and see the great dimples caused by the collapse of cavities caused by underground nuclear explosions. One young physicist added drama by throwing up for much of the flight – airsickness. For me it was an adventure, strapped to one of the seats bolted into what was really an air freighter, with the cargo door open and the mountainsides clearly visible to the left and right, and close, when we flew down the last canyon on the way in.

As we drove to the test site building complex I was advised not to look too closely at a long line of hangars not far from the road. Classified Air Force work, someone murmured. (Later the government acknowledged that they housed test-flight versions of Lockheed Martin's F-117A "Nighthawk," the world's first stealth fighter.) Then I had to sign a document that warned against having personal radios, binoculars, or pets, on the range; to "stay away from areas with flashing blue lights (radiation hazards)"; and not to "discuss anything you see or hear on TTR with unauthorized persons. Disclosure of sensitive and/or classified information to unauthorized persons is a violation of U.S. Criminal Code Title 18, punishable by fine and/or imprisonment."

The most out-of-the-ordinary thing I saw at Tonopah was an exercise in which, in the vastness of a huge dry lake, safety personnel with radiation sensors were picking up minute pieces of depleted uranium that had shattered as the result of being blown up with chemical explosives. In this huge landscape the workers looked like foraging ants, inspecting a small plot of ground in a bare and unpopulated region that was the size of Greater London yet one of the most remote places in the United States.

A few months later in Albuquerque, I attended a meeting at which Sandia's executive vice president took a silver ball, about the size of a croquet ball, from an office drawer and passed it around to illustrate a point. It was unnaturally heavy. What was it? Depleted uranium, he replied calmly.

I wondered what would have happened if citizens had been recruited at random to participate in this. Would there have been cries of horror? A mad dash for doors and windows? Frenzied phone calls to doctors and lawyers? But we held our cool. Depleted uranium is considerably less radioactive than even the natural, unrefined uranium found in Earth's crust, and in either form it can be dangerous only if swallowed or inhaled – a distinct impossibility in this case. It can be used as a shield against more dangerous radiation, as a counterbalance on aircraft control surfaces, and to add weight to weapons. Our VP placed his silver ball carefully back in the drawer, locked it, and I knew I was again a true Sandian. Who else on my block had handled depleted uranium?

13. JONATHAN GREETS THE WORLD

We find a delight in the beauty and happiness of children
that makes the heart too big for the body.
— Ralph Waldo Emerson

Brian finished his English secondary-school studies at the age of 16. For several years he had traveled nearly eight miles each way to the site of an old manor with the date 1671 chiselled over one of the doorways. It was a beautiful site for any school, with a far view of the English Channel and modern buildings around the stone structures that conspired to give it, with questionable success, a certain academic gravitas. My first-born was smart and film-star handsome, but alas, he was no scholar, even at this school, whose students had not been selected for high school and thus were branded with the dark sobriquet of early "school leaver."

I knew Brian had the intelligence to do better and convinced him to return to New Mexico, where he could take two more years of classwork and learn more while earning an American high school graduation diploma. Naturally I was delighted when he agreed.

But could Brian legally move back to the States for an indefinite period? I was a naturalized U.S. citizen who legally resided in the U.S. and even had top-secret government clearance. Brian was born in England, had a birth certificate issued by the U.S. Embassy in London, and lived there for less than a month before we all returned to Albuquerque. Now, to make sure that the documentation was complete, I applied to get him a Certificate of Citizenship issued by the U.S. State Department. It seemed logical that he would qualify, since I had been a citizen for decades. But the local *federales*, ardent searchers for illegal immigrants, were on alert and in no hurry to comply.

I filled out and handed in the necessary forms, then one of the immigration officers called me into his office and said flatly, "I'm sorry to tell you this, Mr. Hey, but it looks like you might have a wetback on your hands."

I was shocked and alarmed by this piece of information, and offended by the use of the word *wetback*, a pejorative term for immigrants who enter the U.S. illegally by wading the Rio Grande. My protest was quickly rebuffed: "Mr. Hey, I need to check with some other folks and get back with you tomorrow." Happily the next day the sun shone on our fortunes, and Brian duly received his certificate. And then he obtained a U.S. passport and New Mexico driver's license, which from that time on he never allowed to expire.

◈✿❀

All this time – during most of the first year that Sue and I were back in New Mexico – something wonderful was happening. Sue said it could never have happened until she had returned to the States. She was pregnant. Jonathan was born on November 21, 1983, most appropriately a Thanksgiving baby.

Jonathan arrived with surprising speed. We had been told that first-timers were often 8 to 10 days late in delivery, so I was ready to settle down for a long wait. But a couple of days before her due date Sue's water broke and, at 6:30 the next morning, I phoned the clinic for instructions. The doctor who replied said something like, "It sounds like it might be the real thing," and suggested that I either drive Sue in to the hospital – we had pre-registered the previous week – or bring her to the clinic when it opened at 8:30, which as it turned out, would have been too late. It was much, much different from my two earlier experiences with birth. The trip took 20 minutes. A nurse came down from the maternity wing with a wheelchair and I followed carrying a Lamaze bag, a baby bag, and a dilapidated suitcase filled with Sue's things. NOW I was ready to do my Lamaze stuff. But it was too late for that. Quite obviously there was some sort of race going on between the unknown obstetrician, paged to take over immediately, and the unborn Hey.

The doctor arrived none too soon and I was called into action to apply pressure to Sue's swollen tummy – actually the baby's posterior. Finally, like the films I had seen in the Lamaze class, a vaguely cylindrical object appeared at the bottom of the bed, yellowish white, streaked with blood." Well, said Dr. Pugmire laconically, "you've got a son." Then Jonathan let out his first yell. It may have been a Texas "yee-hah" cheer. I said something to Sue, who was smiling through the sweat, but I don't remember what it was. I do remember there were tears in my eyes. I saw the placenta lying in a silver pan like a liver and was struck with wonder. And then without explanation Pugmire was handing me a surgical instrument. I stared at it and realized it was a pair of scissors. I took it and cut Jonathan's cord, which had now been clamped off, and said "Well lad, now you're on your own."

After a great deal of anguish, physical and mental, a new bundle of hope had entered the world.

Jonathan was and remained a treasure, and I started a diary of his life that would last until 1991. There was something magic about this boy, who at the age of five would tell me, "You can live to be an old, old man, but you can't live to be Infinity," and as I write there still is. Being present at his birth was magic too, and tugged at the near-dormant philosophy inside me, but when I tried to share my marvelling with Sue she reminded me of my slowness in getting to the hospital.

Sue still looked pale and tired when I was given permission to take her and Jonathan home. He would be breast-fed for nine months, and would not have to suffer the indignity of paper-and-plastic diapers, for my Sandia colleagues had kindly arranged home pickup and delivery service for Jonathan's cloth diapers. After he was weaned, Sue would alternate his packaged baby food with meals made in the kitchen blender from fresh fruit and vegetables.

First Portrait. If this were a color photo you would be confronted by two pairs
of dazzling blue eyes, a perfect match. Sue is posing with baby Jonathan under
one of the Alondra Lane apple trees.

We were settled at home, but it was not long before we were planning Jonathan's state visit to his grandparents in Chichester.

Our first visit to England with Jonathan was a continuing delight, with the newcomer the center of attention on this first of many annual visits. He did not, as the baby book predicted, seem shy with his grandparents. He took to them both almost immediately, and it's possible that he understood the words "grandma" and "grandpa" already, because sometimes he looked toward my dad's favourite chair, or the kitchen, even when they were not in the room, when we mentioned their names.

Another easy-but-long plane trip and we were back in Albuquerque, happily greeted by our dog Lass, whom we had consigned to kennel care while we went holidaying. Now she was fully grown, the size of a retriever with the coat of a German Shepherd, a reliable guard dog (my neighbour nicknamed her "Killer") and a great companion for both Jonathan and me.

FLASH!! Jonathan stood up against the rails of his crib on Thursday, August 9, 1984! AND pushed himself up to sitting position twice the next day, Friday, August 10!!

Sept. 29, 1984, Nigel, to parents – Jonathan is hanging on to the rim of his playpen, leering and growling at me. He does growl a lot since Sue started playing a roughhouse "Tiger" game with him.

May 6, 1985 – Jonathan continues to amaze us. His vocabulary is quite large, except that he doesn't SAY the words, at least not as one would expect them to be said. Sometimes he wanders off chuntering to himself. And then there are monosyllable words that seem to stand for longer words. But he understands an awful lot of what he hears, and can follow instructions quite closely. Today Sue said, "Let Snuffles Bear smell the flowers" and he took the white bear (a gift from the Mitchells) over to the bluebells, stuck his nose next to the flowers and went "snuff snuff."

He stages "accidents" to his hand in order to get it kissed. Sue also started the ritual of "Do you want a kiss?" and Jonathan replies with "'iss," which is to say "Yes!"

Brian graduated from Cibola High School with little fanfare. It was satisfying to know that he had successfully finished his American-style "K-12" curriculum with his two years in the United States – though in doing so he lacked the "A levels" of academic accomplishment that are treasured in England. He looked impressive, if a little uncomfortable, in his bright blue robe and cap, and I was proud of him. We talked a little about the future, only a little because it was easily apparent that he was not keen on starting university and that he preferred to start earning some money of his own. Which seemed perfectly reasonable at the time.

July 6, 1985 – Sue has now documented 160 words that Jonathan says, ranging from voof (fruit) to dannu (candy). He understands a lot more than this, but these were from his own personal vocabulary. He is developing fast, and is very active (at times I have to fight against losing patience with him) and terribly curious about everything. A very healthy, intelligent little boy.

Feb. 26, 1986 – Jonathan caught chicken pox (or chicken spots, as he calls it) from Brian in January. However, this cleared up quickly up and he didn't have as bad a case as his half-brother. J. is developing very quickly. Once when Lass was barking he said "Lass is barking at the moon." He crossed another milestone when one night he took off his shirt and put on his coat by himself, which is quite a coup for a 26-months-old kid.

April 11, 1989 – A few nights ago, Jonathan half-woke crying in the night. When I went in, he gave me a big hug, then squeezed his blanket hard, and began to sleep peacefully. The next morning, I asked him if he remembered it, if he had been dreaming. "What did you dream about?" "Foxes. Foxes eating me. And ratacoons biting my toys." He had recently seen a documentary about raccoons, and ratacoons they have become.

One more short item: upon finding a label in a houseplant, he said, "See dat? Plant word. Word means plant." – What a kid!

It was on June 5, 1986, that Lass gave me a body-tackle in the schoolyard and my knee buckled; then on the 15th, at work, I crossed my leg and a main (medial meniscus) ligament in the left knee tucked itself into the joint. That meant surgery to secure the slivers of ligament back into their rightful place. A Texas friend had undergone an identical procedure: "First they punched three holes in my knee," he said, "then they lowered down a flashlight, an eggbeater, and a vacuum cleaner." It turned out to be very much like that.

It was about this time that I also acquired a pulmonologist to help me manage my asthma flare-ups, which, though I usually could control them with daily medication, continued to be bothersome. Asthma had reduced my wind-power, so that it took me five or ten minutes to recover from running 100 yards. With a surprising stroke of insight I also realized that asthma had helped mould my personality. Why had my boss once commented that one of my co-workers sometimes thought my manner was "brusque"? Simple – when you need to save your breath, you compose the thought carefully in your mind, then you express it forcefully in as few words as possible. As I grew into professional life, I am sure that many people mistakenly came to think of me as a placid individual - calm, self-possessed, and inclining to the dull and even indifferent – though I might merely have been conserving energy and oxygen. I believe that, if this were not the case, I would have climbed higher in management even though I worked hard and produced results that even the higher-ups said were impressive.

◦⟨⟩◦

Nineteen eight-seven provided an unusually exciting 12 months, punctuated with trips to England, Hawaii and Mexico as well as within New Mexico and other parts of the United States. In London Joss started college, and in New Mexico Jonathan's development continued well, showing an increasing interest in language and numbers, as well as music. He was a fine lad, tall for his age, lean and lively.

At Folkestone School for Girls, in England 5,000 miles or so to the east, Jocelyn was becoming well prepared for a future academic career. Because she was the only student studying for her A-level tests for excellence in music, she even had a private study room that overlooked the English Channel, a view framed by Scots pines. I was struck by pangs of envy when I heard this, but kept a fatherly silence. She had started playing recorder in about 1983, and bought a treble recorder in 1984. She was singing away in the school choir, and "touring" with them to local venues like Lympne Castle. Later she made an annual event of singing at the Shrewsbury festival in Shropshire. She said goodbye to Folkestone School for Girls in 1986.

187

March 2, 1987 – Tonight Sue was talking to Jonathan about Easter and its Christian meaning when Jonathan suddenly asked "What is God?" Whereupon Sue gave all the easier descriptors of God – omnipresence, omnipotence, loving yet at times wrathful. And Jonathan added – "And shining." Jonathan is a mite disconcerting at times. There was the time he fashioned "a kachina" with his set of blocks, complete with rainbow. It was the shape of a Pueblo kachina doll. And now there is the shining God. I think now of the Indians presenting their sons to their sky father the Sun. Sometime maybe Jonathan will ask me why I didn't do that.

It was a wild year for visitors, crescendoing into a wonderful autumn in which my parents moved back to the States. First Jacqui Brown from across the road on Crouch Hill and her sister visited for three days and four nights, a delight to have around; they soaked up the new experiences and never seemed to tire of doing things, seeing new sights, eating new foods. The next weekend we had David Shukman, then defence correspondent for BBC TV News, staying overnight after a couple of days working at Sandia on an article about verifying the Intermediate-range Nuclear Forces treaty. The Bishops arrived from Gloucestershire at the end of May, and we had a predictably hilarious time, though Gerry and Val became extremely nervous during an aerial tram ride to the top of Sandia Mountain. Being suspended in a cable gondola a mile above the ground didn't suit them, and once they were up there, I couldn't get them anywhere near the edge except to get back into the cable car gondola, the only alternative being to stay up there all night and listen to bears ransacking the rubbish.

In July Jonathan acted in five of the six performances of Sue's play "The Emperor's New Clothes." About this time Sue told Jonathan the tragedy of John F. Kennedy, and how he left two young children behind when he was assassinated. After she finished, Jonathan, moved, asked Sue to "tell it to me backwards so that I can feel happy again."

In August the three of us were off to London, with side trips to Yorkshire (Jimmy Power), Loughton (Nigel and Marion Jackson), Gloucestershire (Gerry and Val), and Hertfordshire (the Browns). In Albuquerque, Brian was playing host to Gerry Bishop's son Simon.

On September 9, 1987, Joss would start her studies at the London College of Furniture, pursuing a program with a long-winded but impressive name, the BTEC (Business and Technology Education Council) National Diploma/Higher

Diploma Course in Musical Instrument Technology. Hurrah! It had been a long process, starting with an interview on February 8, during which she impressed her interviewers and was accepted forthwith.

On our return to New Mexico Jonathan made his academic début at a new Montessori school, more formally organized than the usual "nursery" school, and enrolled for Sue's class for small children at Albuquerque Children's Theater. Our return coincided with the New Mexico State Fair, followed by the international hot air balloon fiesta, with hundreds of participants from all over the world. The balloons then took off fairly close to the house, which as usual drove the neighbourhood dogs absolutely wild. Lass obviously thought we were being attacked by spaceships that had to be driven from the scene. When the balloons eventually sailed away she settled down with a satisfied look, convinced that her ferocious barking had foiled the attack.

Not too long thereafter, Sue announced that a centipede had taken up residence in the bathroom and could I please remove it – it was rather large and had wisely hidden under a towel. It proved to be very lively and quite large at four and a half inches, with 29 pairs of legs. I took it to a more appropriate home in the woodpile. Then, safe in a nest of fresh compost and leaves, an indignant black widow spider imprisoned in a jam jar went to school with Jonathan, where it became a pinup celebrity, with about a dozen photo portraits decorating the schoolroom wall.

Over in West Sussex, my mother and dad were preparing for their second emigration to the United States with, in my mother's words, "mixed feelings." At the beginning of October Joss took the train up to London and down to Chichester – an hour longer than the tortuous road trip – to wish them Godspeed. Both my parents were around 80 years of age now, so this was an amazingly brave enterprise, though I did not appreciate the fact fully at the time. They had to sell a delightful flat with a big garden on the northern outskirts of one of England's truly beautiful medieval towns, arrange for Pickfords to pack and ship the larger items, somehow get rid of the what was left, and say goodbye to the few friends they had made locally. And then they had the long air flight to New Mexico, and to start anew, for the sole reason that they wanted to be near their American family.

My mother and dad moved into a nondescript cinderblock apartment complex near the I-40 freeway, with the big pieces of furniture – they had collected a number of attractive antiques from the Chichester auctions – and the larger boxes stored away with the old Wilsden piano. They had stayed there in the past, during short visits to Albuquerque, but this time they would be house-hunting. They found the perfect place – a two-bedroom townhouse with a tiny but adequate rear patio garden and a small inside atrium that would become my mother's delight. Soon the piano was fitted, just, into a closet space and soon, when she thought no one could hear, my mother was playing her old favourites again.

Mother and Dad kept very busy around their new home, in the garden and the atrium, the latter a miniature jungle covered by a large skylight. My mother was content to be a homebody, even protesting when a Mother's Day outing was suggested. My dad was much more gregarious, again became active in the Masons and Shrine Club, and took an adult education class in Spanish. But Mother was always busy at home, baking, making delicious meals, taking care of the atrium, scrubbing the floor on hands and knees, and coddling their pet tortoise, christened Piedelbaum by my dad. The big festivals of Christmas, Easter, and Thanksgiving, and birthdays, always occasioned a dinner party at their place or at the Alondra Lane house.

It seems in retrospect that after I first launched into married life my parents quietly and unobtrusively followed me around the world, or almost. After I went to London they moved from Salt Lake City to Chichester. And now they were settled in Albuquerque.

Nov. 28, 1987 – The four-day Thanksgiving weekend, with my mother and dad in attendance for the first time in New Mexico, started naturally enough on the last Thursday of November. Early that morning, turkey was cooking under Sue's expert hand while Jonathan and I took the dogs to the river. We saw cranes flying low, southward. Thought they had already left; and a few days earlier we had seen Canada geese. Thought they had left too! The mountain was dusted with white at the top, crows were ranging around, foraging in untidy flying clumps, and flocks of starlings had been resting in the tall cottonwood. Sparrows were hanging around the carport, taking their chances to filch food from the dogs' plates.

Brian's year had been full of stops and starts. In January he was laid off at La Posada hotel; then he did a number of short jobs serving at an idiosyncratic coffee house, making donuts, working in a restaurant kitchen, and helping at a pizza establishment. He was living at our house at the year's start, then moved to a flat with his friend Mary, then moved to another flat with her, then moved into his own flat when he was "born again," and at year's end moved into a sort of dormitory at his new church.

Meanwhile, Jonathan was developing in another spurt, or was it I who had spurts of appreciating him more? One night I was driving to the children's theatre to pick up Sue and thought Jonathan had gone to sleep in the back.

Then I heard a quiet voice in the dark behind me: "Two and three makes five."

"Very good," I said, "now what is five and two?"

"Seven."

"And seven and two?"

"Nine."

Thinking I'd fox him I said, "Well how about seven and three?"

"Ten."

There were short pauses before each answer, and I thought maybe Jonathan was working out the results on his finger abacus. Actually he was working it out in his head, which was even more impressive.

My mother and dad then agreed to take care of the children while Sue and I took a dream vacation to Kauai, the last island to be forced into the Kingdom of Hawaii by King Kamehameha I. And so in the last week of October we left for a week away from "real life," at a Hawaiian hotel perfumed with plumeria, where the coconut palms were being pruned by men shimmying up the trunks with huge machetes slung from their belts. The fronds were huge, and when they crashed down they shook the earth a little.

At Walter Smith's Fern Grotto we admired the lush ferns and tropical undergrowth and a waterfall cascading through the rainforest greenery. No wonder Japanese couples liked to come here for their honeymoons, I thought wistfully. We had approached the spot after a short cruise up the Wailua River from the parking lot on Highway 56, just north of the island's capital, Lihue, and we were entranced.

I thought the trip to Hawaii's "garden island" might help heal our troubled relationship, but it seemed nothing would strengthen the waning bond between us. It would prove the same during our summer trip with Jonathan to England, with a side visit to Sorrento and Capri. By the end of the year we had started counselling sessions with a local psychologist, and I began a daily personal journal as a kind of catharsis.

We had done wonderful things in Kauai, visiting the amazing, rain-soaked high-mountain canyons inland from Waimea, scouting the beaches for sunning and snorkelling, visiting the resorts, and taking lots of photographs of palm trees. Still, when we left I felt defeated.

When we returned to New Mexico on November 17, the leaves from the apple trees and the cottonwood were almost all gone and those that were left were skittering around in the crazy late-autumn dances drummed up by unpredictable winds sneaking around buildings here, zipping around a stand of shrubs over there. Flicker woodpeckers were here for the winter, the last chrysanthemums were gone, and under the woodpile and the evergreen shrubs, snug in their soft humus beds, lizards had begun to sleep the season away.

As usual Jonathan was doing well, and learned the song "Poor Wandering One," with help from mama. He was coming along verbally very well, and had already spelled a few simple words like Duk. He was intrigued with a record we bought in Kauai, and one night he sang the Hawaiian song "Pu'u Elena," complete with improvised hula arm and hand gestures. Again I was proud.

Christmas Day couldn't have been more enjoyable, the more so because Jocelyn had flown over for the holidays. Jonathan woke a little after 4 a.m. to say that Father Christmas had arrived and filled his stocking, then compassionately went back to sleep until a more civilized hour. By 9:15 I had picked up grandma and grandpa and Brian from their respective abodes and Jocelyn had been at the house for almost a week, so we were all together again. There were presents stacked under the Christmas tree and a great orgy of opening them before a fire blazing with piñon pine logs. Brian and Jocelyn took the dogs for a walk and then we had a buffet lunch (smoked turkey with trimmings, followed by traditional marzipan-trimmed Christmas cake from Grandma Hey). Miriam rang from England and had a good talk with Brian and Jocelyn – she was spending Christmas and Boxing Day with friends – and then we had a sleepy afternoon "digesting" while Jonathan played with his new acquisitions. I was a happy man.

At the end of the month Jocelyn, Jonathan and I visited Jemez Pueblo. We knew we were in luck the moment we neared the village center, for we could see people looking down into the plaza from the rooftops. As we approached the plaza a door opened and a little herd of boys came running out, dressed as antelopes. We could hear drums and singing and occasional whoops and then saw the whole band of dancers. There were perhaps four men in war bonnets, the familiar Indian feathered headdress that one sees rarely around New Mexico, and some were holding ceremonial spears. At least thirty were dressed as deer, the headdresses topped with green-painted deer heads carved from cottonwood, personifiers supporting themselves on sticks that represented the forelegs of the deer. Two men in buffalo headdress danced with a woman companion. Solemnly, to the beat of a drum and chorus. The buffaloes were stately most of the time, but now and then they broke out of line as if to butt the deer boys. Two other men were wearing horns from mountain sheep, and many young men and boys were wearing the plumage of eagle and turkey, crouching and hopping in time to the drum, their arms decorated as wings.

I was delighted that Jocelyn was viewing all of this with such depth of interest, an interest that extended to the architecture and the natural landscape that remained absolutely wonderful despite warnings of cloud and possible snow. It was very cold, but the wet weather didn't materialize and we drove home under a cloudless sky full of bright stars, and a dark brown redness on that long, long western horizon, fading into the dark blues of night and the twinkling blackness above. Joss and Jonathan slept most of the way, and then we were in the warmness of the house with Sue's wonderful hot minestrone and hot Swiss cheese-and-ham sandwiches waiting.

As the New Year dawned I could only hope that 1988 would prove as good as 1987. Along with the events and adventures described above we survived a thunderstorm at remote Chaco Canyon and returned there intrepidly the next weekend, when the car broke down and we had to be towed 80 miles across the Navajo and Apache reservations to the nearest garage at Cuba, New Mexico. We had that wonderful long weekend at Sue's dad's hunting trailer near Mancos, in extreme south-western Colorado. We had a gluttonous feast of experiences during our August in England. We returned to the glittering festivities of the New Mexico State Fair and rodeo; then in December I was in Washington at the time of the momentous Reagan-Gorbachev nuclear arms reduction talks. The Cold War was melting fast. Whew!

◌⊗◌

Miriam was now living alone in the big family house in Folkestone, with renters on the two upper floors for occasional company. She wrote to me in March with news of a day out to Canterbury with Jocelyn. "I think she thrives being in London," she wrote. "It is lovely having her home for a while. I suffered from the empty nest syndrome for a while but I'm O.K. now and I want Brian and Joss to be free."

Jocelyn finished her first year at the London College of Furniture, where she was specializing in the construction and renovation of musical instruments, and planned to go for a full, four-year stint. Pity that this will not bring her a bachelor's degree, I thought; but the truth was that it would provide more practical training than, say, a BA in the history of science. She had matured considerably during her months in London, and was able to take a much broader view of things than when she was limited to Folkestone's bucolic style. Sue, I, and Jonathan celebrated the birthdays of all three children in two trips to England – Jonathan's fifth, Jocelyn's 20th, Brian's 22nd.

Joss loved her new academic experience and wrote long and enthusiastic letters. She was in a multinational, mixed-race environment, building a Gregori harpsichord and learning about technical drawing, machine woodworking, math, and "general studies" that included photography and other useful courses. Predictably she had no trouble making a social life, and soon was writing about going to Windsor "to see Roger, a friend of mine, who lives at the castle there. He's doing some kind of post-grad course at the Royal Academy of Music and he's Organ Scholar at St. George's Chapel, Windsor. He's really landed himself a cushy number. He's got a free flat that has little windows that look through the outer wall of the castle, onto the main street, and he's guarded by policemen and soldiers who are awake, standing out there at night. So he doesn't have to lock his door or anything. I know him from the Shrewsbury Flower Show."

At college Jocelyn was surrounded by friendships, music and woodworking. My father relished this kind of setting and, skipping a generation, it was almost as though she was following in his footsteps.

◎❈◎

It had become difficult for me to imagine what it would be like to grow up without a Cold War. Or how my life would have developed without having experienced one. The world had become radically different in the half-century that elapsed between the outbreak of World War II, when I was a small boy, and the fall of the Soviet empire. At the beginning of that period I would go to Saturday movie matinees and watch Flash Gordon zooming around in rocket-ships and zapping bad guys with beams of energy, never even imagining that anything of this sort would be attempted by serious scientists. Those were the times when I tossed in my bed because Britain's first nuclear test, *Hurricane*, was about to be held in Australia. Later, as a fledgling UPI reporter, part-timing my senior year in college, I interviewed Edward Teller in a cloud of doubt, wondering if this small, thick, heavily accented man with the rubbery folded face was a great mind or a monster, or both. Was that a Transylvanian accent? A few years later, standing on Bermuda's North Shore and staring at the weird, vividly red sky to the north, I thought, My God, the Russians must actually have done it. They nuked New York! It turned out to be an aurora, a rare sight so far south. The experiences and impressions went on, cresting, I suppose, when I went to work for Sandia.

None of my children knows much about the Cold War. If, working at my Sandia desk, I heard the news that a Soviet nuclear missile were headed toward the U.S. it would arrive so fast that even if the roads were traffic-free I would not be able to drive home in time to be incinerated along with my wife and family. My family members never felt they had to make such a dreadful calculation, and I pray that they never will.

But the Cold War was part of the real world, and like everyone else I learned to live with it. This part of history is not likely to repeat itself. But something similar could happen again if Russia were to become overly belligerent/defensive, or if some other nuclear power (or group) threatened the West, and thereby the planet, with that degree of devastation.

At some time during this period I was dismayed to discover illustrations of the degree to which politics uses science, including that most terrible of scientific inventions, the nuclear weapon, to further its ends. I was sickened to learn that John F. Kennedy, whom I admired so much during his presidency, actually invented the "missile gap" to strengthen his presidential campaign, and that he launched Project Apollo to outdo the Soviets in international prestige rather than to advance science. And that Ronald Reagan and his cohorts used the "Strategic Defense Initiative," which never approached the sophistication of the space-lasers defence program portrayed in the media, as a ruse to get the Russians off balance – successfully, as it happened – in their campaign against the Evil Empire.

As the two sides increased their nuclear arsenals in 1950-1980, I had come reluctantly to suspect that my life, my family, and in fact all of Western society depended on something called Mutually Assured Destruction, MAD. If the

Russians reduced New York and Washington to piles of radioactive debris, we'd do the same to Moscow and Leningrad, and that was just for starters. *I knew it was possible!* Some people shook their head and said the scenario was unthinkable. But for me it was very thinkable indeed. It had almost happened during the Cuban Missile Crisis of 1963. Many analysts quite rationally suspect that the MAD days will someday return, but the opponent may well be some entity other than Russia.

All this, hanging over us! Yet optimism always seemed to keep us mentally and spiritually afloat. And, when I analyze how this is so, it seems that the font of optimism is to be found in family love.

14. THE RUSSIANS ARE COMING!

In the time of your life, live - so that in that wondrous time you shall not add to the misery and sorrow of the world, but shall smile to the infinite variety and mystery of it.
— William Saroyan

et me level with you. In my business, if you are a frequent international traveler, and/or if you attend meetings frequented by people from countries which might be trolling for sensitive or classified information, there is a fair chance that, sometime, you will get into conversation with a foreign intelligence agent, or even get involved in, or witness, what might be called an international incident.

That may sound melodramatic, but it's true. That's why it's important that people with security clearances are expected to take counter-espionage training and other courses that understandably make a big thing of the importance of keeping your eyes and ears open and, more often than not, your mouth shut. One time I was enjoying a sandwich at an Albuquerque café when a young woman sat down beside me and said hello. My bells started ringing, all sorts of bells, for this was an unusually good-looking lady, even spectacularly good looking, and delightfully dressed. She actually chose to sit next to me, and as I have already made clear, I decidedly do not have the movie-star looks of my elder son.

So I said hello too, and it turned out her name was Ludmila and she was attending a colloquium at the nearby University of New Mexico campus. That's when the second set of bells started ringing. A lovely woman chooses to leave a group of people with common interests, walks several hundred yards to the modest out-of-the-way place where I am munching on my hot pastrami sandwich, and strikes up a conversation in a pronounced and not unpleasant Russian accent. It was an unusual situation; not only that, the experience was unique. The accent muted the bells a little because one would not expect spies to signal their place of origin, but I reported the incident to my counterintelligence friends anyway.

197

I have spoken many times with people from Russia and other "sensitive" countries (i.e. those with declared or suspected nuclear weapons), and declared any detailed conversations to the anti-spook squads, but the meeting with Ludmila was an oddity. Somewhere I have her business card, with her home number penciled in. Hmmm.

Early in March, 1988, I had a brush with the second kind of sticky situation, the international incident. I am still not exactly sure how close it was to being an international incident, but it inflicted some of my friends with a severe, shared attack of anxiety. The story started when, while flying home to Albuquerque, a Sandia colleague happened to sit in the next seat to a tall, well-built, and affable blond man who introduced himself as Stan Odle.

Odle, an independent TV producer from Seattle, had an interesting story to tell. He told our scientist that he had succeeded in getting the Discovery Channel to sponsor a "people-to-people" documentary series, in which the Soviet government was to be a co-sponsor. His technical support team was composed of an American and a Russian.

The series was to be called "Homeland." The basic idea was to promote what Odle called "respect through understanding," which he expected to achieve by producing TV segments on people who had similar professions in the US and USSR. That seemed reasonable enough, but our scientist blinked when Odle said he wanted to talk with American physicists who were involved in the Strategic Defense Initiative, the secretive anti-missile initiative nicknamed "Star Wars." In Albuquerque that could mean Sandia, and so eventually the message got to me.

A lot of people would see Odle's gambit as an overconfident initiative in view of the fact that the Cold War was still in progress, but the TV man said it was all on the up-and-up – he would do similar interviews later with Russian physicists. I was doubtful.

Still, I was curious to learn of Odle's belief that U.S.-Soviet misconceptions and habitual mutual fear could be reduced by giving the people of each country an honest look at each other through the medium of television. So, in the spirit of international relations and a personal lust for adventure, I decided to help.

I believed that the scientist in charge of Sandia high-energy physics research, Pace VanDevender, then out of town, would want to support the enterprise, and started the process of asking permission from Sandia's governmental boss, the U.S. Department of Energy. The bureaucracy was disinclined to give me a prompt reply, however, and Odle was waiting impatiently in the wings. "I'm in a tight spot and I'm not sure what I can do about it," he told me. "Do you think we could arrange an informal interview with Pace VanDevender? At his home maybe?" He figured correctly that staging the interview at a private home, away from government property, would ease the DOE's negative inclinations. As long as no classified information was discussed.

When Pace returned to Albuquerque he said he would sleep on the idea. The next afternoon he told me he'd be glad to see Odle and Co. And then he pulled a big rabbit out of his hat. He had, independently, invited a group of Soviet scientists to his home the following Monday evening, along with some of his own staff, and we were all invited. We would not need to set foot on federal property. It sounded like a coup for the man from Seattle.

Odle and his two crews rolled into the VanDevenders' driveway at about 6:45 Monday evening, frazzled from the frustration of getting lost on the way but cheerfully carrying intact plastic bags of Mexican beer and potato chips. By then many of Pace's colleagues and visitors had arrived and were talking (mostly about the preposterous new idea called cold fusion), the ladies were chatting and doing kitchen things, and the caterer had delivered a smoked salmon and its companion goodies for a cold buffet.

By about 9:30 lights and cameras had sprouted from the VanDevenders' living-room floor, and recording was about to begin. An amazing event unfolded. Gerold Yonas, who does not say such things lightly, told me later that it was quite possibly an historic event. Pace's Russian guests were world-class scientists, prominent attendees at the international meetings on high-energy physics and pulsed power. Their technical papers centered on theory and research while assiduously avoiding mention of the sensitive work that both sides were doing in military applications of their activities. Originally I imagined our Soviet visitors would be accompanied by a KGB representative, but none of this group seemed to fit the bill.

Pace sat at one end of a large overstuffed couch, a comparative youngster still, sitting back against the cushions, slim, open-faced with blue Northern European eyes and thinning blond hair. At the other end was Valentin M. Bystritskii of the Institute of High Current Electronics, part of the Siberian Branch of the USSR Academy of Sciences in Tomsk. Between and around them sat Misha Rudakov of the I.V. Kurchatov Institute of Atomic Energy in Moscow; Odle; Valentin Smirnov, Rudakov's colleague at the Kurchatov Institute; and another of my own acquaintances, the Belizean-American scientist Juan Ramirez. Also present were two more VanDevender scientists, Ray Leeper and Doug Bloomquist.

Odle explained that most of all he wanted to explore the cultures of scientists in the two countries. Neither of us could have guessed how enthusiastically this theme would be grasped by the scientists, especially the Russians. They waded into a discussion of C. P. Snow's "two cultures" concept, which details the separation of science from the rest of society, chatting as though scientists of all nationalities were part of a single brotherhood that had to endure the peculiarities of differing socio-political subcultures. A most extraordinary exchange of views ensued. The Russians proved to be more outspoken than the Americans, who were taken aback by the frankness of their counterparts from what Ronald Reagan had called the Evil Empire. Our guests were remarkably voluble in supporting popular democratic participation in government. "The people must make the choice, and the Parliaments must follow their lead," someone said, in a strong Russian accent. My mouth may have dropped open at this point, for it sounded like anti-Soviet heresy, different from the high-level conversations they (and Yonas) had experienced at the international fusion meetings.

With the cameras recording, the physicists spoke of science as the origin of apocalyptic weapons and agreed reluctantly that the scientist's job is to "do science" and trust in the wisdom of "higher powers" to ensure that the results are properly and morally applied. Smirnov said he was concerned "whose finger can push the button." VanDevender said he could not imagine refusing do research just because it might be applied to weaponry, unless it were some kind of doomsday machine that no other country knew about. Everybody agreed on this point, and the Russians added that more scientists should be elected to the Supreme Soviet. The Russians and Americans concurred that scientists could take the initiative in increasing U.S.-Soviet openness, as a way of easing tensions between the two nations.

One of the Russian scientists told me this was the first time he had participated in such a discussion in the absence of an official observer. We were not in danger of precipitating an international incident, for later I heard that apparently it was no longer even necessary to get prior approval to speak freely – at least not for scientists of this stature. The Russian video director told me that it would have been impossible to undertake the project before the Gorbachev administration and before the Soviet withdrawal from Afghanistan. I realized that

I had witnessed an example of *glasnost*, part of the zealous attempt at reform that would bring the USSR very quickly to an end.

The Soviet and American producers hosted the première of "Homeland" at the National Press Club in Washington on Thursday, September 8, 1988.

The collapse of Soviet communism brought a muted, surprised, awed feeling to the West. In general it was less than a sense of victory. We had lived so long – forty years – with the knowledge that the world could be wracked, even annihilated, by nuclear conflagration, so that we were amazed that this monstrous possibility was quite suddenly gone. Now we wanted to believe that it had melted away and disappeared. Many seemed not to grasp that nuclear arsenals had not been dismantled even in the two former superpowers that were no longer enemies. And few outside the governmental think-tanks stopped to think that other nations might build them, which of course they did, and that tribal anger and despotism was the unfortunate way of humankind. The threat persisted, minus the superpower fist-shaking but very real nonetheless.

We would soon see there were new foes to take the place of the old East-West military standoff, mostly in the Moslem vestiges of the old Ottoman Empire. These political hot-spots, and violence of all kinds everywhere, became staples of the ever-widening hubbub of mass media. And espionage would not shrivel in response to the end of the Cold War. Rather it would mushroom, gradually inserting its covert tendrils into every corner of the West and its real and potential adversaries.

⊙≪≫

In early October I was assigned to a backup team that would help NASA at a launch of the space shuttle *Atlantis*. Its payload was the Project Galileo interplanetary spacecraft, which will go to Jupiter after a roundabout billiards game in which it looped around Venus once and Earth twice before zooming off in the appropriate direction at the right velocity. Galileo's instruments were powered by the heat given off by the radioactive decay of Plutonium-238. And so the Department of Energy (for which Sandia works and whom I was representing) was called in to give special information, when needed, on radioactive power sources.

In the middle of the long wait for safe launch conditions, the Loma Prieta earthquake struck the San Francisco Bay area, smack in the middle of the baseball World Series. The magnitude 6.9 quake lasted for about 15 seconds, resulting in 63 deaths, 3,757 injuries, and as many as 12,000 homeless.

Watching the launch was another awesome experience. Even at the observation point miles away, the rattling roar of the huge rockets ruffled my shirt and trouser-legs with acoustic energy – just like the Apollo F-1 rocket static test years earlier while I was on a Weltech tour to the Rocketdyne test site in California.

It had been a long wait, but I had prepared myself for it. On the spur of the moment, before leaving New Mexico, I decided to bring up to date a book that I had work-titled *Exploring the Outer Planets* and made a digital copy to take with me. Cape Kennedy was a perfect place to talk with planetary exploration people who, like me, might have nothing better to do. I hoped soon to finish the manuscript, send it to a literary agent, and forget about it. That didn't happen. A series of coincidences would combine to give it a far more interesting future.

⚜

Nov. 26, 1989 Just returned from a birthday party for Jonathan. He was 6 on the 21st, so his little friends from nursery school came to Pistol Pete's pizza parlour. Brian had fun and was very helpful watching over the kiddywinks – and eating the leftover pizza. He looked sharp. I had bought him a long-sleeved Royal Engineers pullover at Earls Court and now I see the embroidered crest from it, sewn onto a blazer by grandma. He says something ate the rest of the pullover.

Dec. 22, 1989 – The ritual of trimming the Christmas tree is very special, and so embedded that I think that perhaps an ancient predisposition for its veneration is hidden away somewhere in our genes. But musty history fades into insignificance when compared with living experience. Recollections of bright-faced children tiptoeing to place ornaments on the tree, and of grandparents joining in the joy, are precious to me and my folk. This year I savoured the sight of Jonathan standing still for a silent moment, absorbing the image of the glorious tree, his pinkly perfect cheeks just a little flushed, the lights and ornaments glistening in his eyes. Mama, standing nearby, and grandpa Hey, intent in the wingback chair, were witnesses too. They watched silently as Jonathan and grandma Hey added trim to the green branches, and I assumed ridiculous postures trying to catch the moment on film. How futile these photographic efforts are, these crude reminders of reality, and how imperfect! What is it that we recognize in these occasions, what ancient memories are half remembered? I think that on the face of the child are the hopes and fantasies of us all, incarnate, unassumed, unadorned, and with them the wonder and marvelling that are our keys to all kinds of kingdoms of heaven, scriptural and secular. And we who are scratched and scoured by life look on, envying the child his innocence, lusting backwards in time to days when we believed in Santa Claus, when everything in the world was daisy-fresh and optimism was all we knew. There by the grace of God was I! You don't have to be a Christian to shout hurrah for optimism – the human race would have died out thousands of years ago if it weren't for our belief in the future.

By New Year's Day 1990 Jonathan was reading quite effortlessly, and zooming around on his Christmas BMX bike, complete with skidlid and gauntlets. Like any parent I wondered how he would adjust academically when he began "real" school the following September; and was concerned he would have the challenge he would need. Brian was now 23 and seemed to be doing well at a new job, this time as a clerk at an Albuquerque art-supplies shop; after advising me that he had no desire to go back to Pizza Hut or any other part of the fast-food or catering industry. Jocelyn, 21, in her third year at the London College of Furniture, had with three friends just moved to Rampart Street, a whole neighbourhood scheduled for demolition, from a "legal squat" in Whitechapel.

Brian and Jonathan got along well together from the start (they even shared chicken pox in early 1986). The dogs welcomed the newcomer too, although otherwise we had an unfortunate time trying to get Lass to believe she was a dog and not a small wolf (the vet would only work with her from the other side of a chain-link fence and at one time she bloodied an experienced trainer's hand). Though my neighbour, only half in jest, nicknamed her "Killer," there were times that I thought she was my best friend.

February 10, 1990 – Jonathan is reading well and is busy at the moment writing his Valentine's Day cards. He likes puns and other plays on words, and a few weeks ago read the whole Ladybird children's version of Wizard of Oz. I asked him if he knew what a cyclone was and he said, "Yes, it's like one of those whirlycanes." He talked about a plant that reminded him of having a shot – ivy (I. V.)! He still says charming things like that but is growing fast and soon may be too sophisticated to allow such mistakes. I bought some video games for him to play on this computer, and he is very good at them, better than I, maybe (but not definitely) because I haven't sufficient interest. We bought him a BMX bike for Christmas, and he is getting very proficient on this too, zooming around the house in his crash helmet.

⟳⟱⟲

While working at the office on Tuesday, May 15, 1990, I received one of the most worrisome telephone calls of my life.

Joss phoned today to report that Miriam was going to become a patient at the Chartham psychiatric hospital. Later I wrote her: "I do want you to understand that I am very concerned about what's going on over there and wishing very much that we could be together to talk and plan at this difficult time. I have always had great hopes for you, and great pride that my daughter is doing this or that. But there has been absolutely no time in our lives that we have been together long enough for you to understand and know that this is so. You asked today whether your mother had been on a long "high" before she went into Chartham before. The answer is no, not so far as I can remember. But the pattern of being irrationally stubborn is the same. We went to marriage counsellors and psychologists and Dr. Whitaker together and individually, and got nowhere because she would not take advice or instruction. And finally, after a long succession of those sleepless nights of angry talking mania I could take it no longer. I realised that if we went on like this, I would be a psychiatric nurse-in-residence for the rest of my life – except that even that wouldn't work because I wouldn't be able to cope with it, psychologically. The one thing I don't know, and we will never know, is whether I should have taken you and Brian to London to live with Sue and me.

Mim's latest incarceration at Chartham was a life-changer. From that point onward, her situation was never far from my mind, and I was too far away, and too involved with work and my Albuquerque family to find out for myself exactly what was going on. Later I learned that Joss and Brian took pains to keep the details of these difficulties from me, and that the two of them had taken on the burden of watching out for her. Brian was the hero of this story, since after leaving Albuquerque in 1987 he was living with his mother and was on the spot literally and figuratively. Though my imagination could at times run wild with worry, I was enormously gratified that the children were so willing and able to help, and that at last Mim was receiving modern psychiatric care. On my next visit to London I learned that she had been taken to Chartham against her will. But she did not have to stay forever.

While the troubles in England continued, on and off, Jonathan continued to lighten our lives.

May 12, 1991, to Brian in Folkestone – Jonathan continues to say unusual things. He and Sue were talking about what things are two-dimensional and what things are three-dimensional. Is Daddy three-dimensional? he asked. Yes. Well, what about babies. Don't be silly, can you imagine a two-dimensional baby? What if the mama is a camera? he asked. Wow. Then a couple of weeks ago he just wrote on a piece of paper, "Love is the key." He added two words to it yesterday, making the statement "Love is the key to love." He will be going to a short summer programme at school just before we come to England, and that should be fun, complete with field trips. We talked to his teachers on Friday. We're going to make sure that he gets the most he can out of school, while enjoying it too.

Work at Sandia was regular but demanding. I made it a point to restore and extend the national media outreach program that I had begun successfully with the rolamite and Cerampic campaigns in the late 1960s. The thesis behind the program was that, since the nation's media centers were in the American Northeast and Sandia was stuck in the desert in the isolated desert Southwest, someone had to take the Sandia story *to* them. In other words it was highly unlikely that newspapers would pay their science writers to check out the newsworthiness of telephone tips from faraway Albuquerque.

At first, as in my first Sandia incarnation, the effort consisted of solo trips in which I would set up meetings with science/technology specialists in the Washington and New York media, then spend an hour telling them what Sandia was and the cool things it was doing. By the end of the 1980s I was taking lab spokespersons along with me, of whom the most skilful and knowledgeable performer was C. Paul Robinson, a former Los Alamos National Laboratories physicist-executive who headed the US Delegation to the US/USSR Nuclear

Testing Talks in Geneva from 1988-90, after which he joined Sandia as president. The next year he joined the Strategic Advisory Group for the Commander, US Strategic Command (STRATCOM), so he was very well connected indeed.

In July 2001, Paul and I briefed a host of Washington newsies, including a roomful of *Washington Post* journalists headed by Jackson Diehl and Walter Pincus, and separately John Barry of *Newsweek*, Eliot Marshall of *Science*, and James Kitfield of the *National Journal*. Paul impressed them all, not least because his STRATCOM experience enabled him to talk about defence policy as well as technical innovation, and believed that the nation needed a nuclear stockpile even after the final collapse of the Soviet Union the previous December. "I have always preferred to place the greatest military strength in the hands of those who want peace more than they want power," he said rather grandly. "Thus I believe the U.S. must retain its nuclear strength – for deterring blackmail by the rogues of the world."[21]

Paul was wonderfully relaxed and open in his media interviews – remarkably so, since he had so much classified information in his head – but without showing it was acutely aware of the security sensitivity of what he was saying. He also did not suffer fools gladly. At one time a Department of Energy PR functionary phoned a colleague to protest something Paul had said at one of our meetings with the *Washington Post*. "Why don't you call Paul if it's a problem," my colleague asked mildly. The DOE man didn't act on the suggestion.

Paul resigned effective April 29, 2005, after the Department of Energy rejected a bid by a consortium led by our managing contractor, Lockheed Martin, to operate Los Alamos National Laboratory. The contract was awarded to another consortium, led by the University of California, which had run Los Alamos and Lawrence Livermore since their inceptions. Fortunately for me, Vice President Al Romig enthusiastically accepted the unofficial mantle of Chief Sandia Spokesperson. Al was a nationally renowned materials scientist who had authored about 170 technical publications, was the co-author of three textbooks, and held two patents. I was delighted that such an extremely busy man was so enthusiastic to jump into the media business; we had already worked successfully on two or three papers about nanotechnology and these had been enjoyable partnerships (later I would work with him on global energy and climate change issues.)

Much of the time I treated Robinson and Romig as peers, and they didn't seem to mind in the least. That said, I must admit that there were several

206

occasions when I was rewarded with surprised looks when I was forced into a corner and had to confess that I had earned a B.A. in journalism at the University of Utah. Here I was with an English accent and a passable gift for technical gab, and I didn't even have a science or engineering degree, let alone a wall decorated with diplomas from Oxford, Cambridge, or Imperial College.

Still I was treated with a degree of respect that I may or may not have deserved, when my seniors would have been justified in treating me as an ordinary, generic PR flack. Perhaps this was because, whenever I had the opportunity, I would treat them to my opinions on science, technology, national policy, and the nation's future. After observing the decline of manufacturing in the U.K., and the concurrent shrivelling of its materials and engineering enterprises, I was eager to point out that research in applied science, and in science/technology that had some possibility of being applied in marketable products, was an essential asset in any country which wished to establish and maintain high-end international marketing power. This meant that very smart, very honest people had to pick which research horses to back. It also meant that industrial, academic, and national research laboratories would have to learn how to work together better – and importantly that a flow of extremely well-educated and creative minds would need to be available to do the requisite research and development.

They would listen appreciatively, for I was preaching to the choir. Sandia already had won success in setting up government-industry cooperation in areas ranging from casting to adhesive tape manufacture, working one-on-one with large companies like Boeing, Goodyear and 3M, and had teamed with other national laboratories to devise a new silicon-chip-making process for a private-industry consortium headed by Intel. That time had pretty much gone, obscured by politicians whose technical know-how was at best questionable. But it had to be revived, I protested. The labs had a huge reservoir of creative brainpower and the best-equipped scientific facilities in the world, and they should be doing more to help the country to preserve and expand its place in the international technical community.

My relationship with these men was typical of many that I had with Sandia's technical leaders. There was one time that I was asked by the editor of *IEE Review*, a British publication, if I could get someone at Sandia to write a paper about nanotechnology. I told Al and suggested that I produce the article and put his name on it, since he had by far the greater expertise. He agreed and suggested that a colleague, Terry Michalske, be included as another author. To my surprise, when he saw the article he suggested I include myself as the first-named (principal) author. I agreed to this honour and sent the paper off. I heard nothing from my editor friend for a couple of months, so emailed him for an explanation. It had been published already, so he apologized and sent me three copies. There was the article, splendidly laid out, naming a single author – me.[22] I was highly embarrassed, and confounded when I received an invitation to give a speech at the opening of a nanotechnology center at Cambridge University. "This will make you laugh," I told Romig, and waited nervously for his reply.

"Go ahead," he said without hesitation. "We'll give you all the PowerPoint slides you need. I'll even send someone with you to answer the tough questions."

It was probably fortunate that the Cambridge man did not follow up on his invitation. No doubt he looked me up with an Internet search engine and learned the dreadful truth that I didn't even have a master's degree from a conventionally accredited university. Being a guest speaker on nanotechnology at Cambridge would have been a fine adventure, but this time I was relieved not to take it on.

This is one of the stories I tell when I want to illustrate how fine an experience it was for me to work at Sandia. Computer technology does interesting things with identity, helpful, scary, and peculiar. In my case, after living many years in a place where there are few Nigels and possibly fewer Heys, I learned through the Internet that there existed – in 2011 – at least three other Nigel Heys, one each in the US, Canada, and Australia, meaning that for the first time in my life I had to explain where I live in order to indicate which Nigel Hey I am.

◦❦◦

Sue met Bill and Lucy Hayden soon after our return to New Mexico, and began helping Bill with his Albuquerque Children's Theater. The relationship grew into a fast friendship, and before long Sue was directing plays for Bill, teaching drama classes, and writing original plays for ACT productions. After Bill died of cancer in December 1990, she took over as director. She produced and directed many, many children's plays at ACT, and performed brilliantly as Flo in the Albuquerque Little Theatre production of *Picnic* (1989).

It was my impression that Brian had not fit in very well at Cibola High

School, and I could not help observing that he did not stay with a job for long. I knew that both he and Jocelyn were highly intelligent, but nothing seemed sufficient to get Brian's mind "into gear" as an energetic and creative performer of work that matched his capabilities. I tried to motivate him, bullied him, and did everything I could think of, to get him to conform with "what was expected." But it didn't work. He went from job to job, each time expressing enthusiastic hope for success. He worked at the Boy Scout ranch at Philmont and began classes at the local junior college, but it was as though he would not allow himself to succeed. We briefly went to psychological counselling and soon afterwards, after a 1986 Christmas trip to England, he moved out, riding in the cab of a breakdown truck that was towing away his beautiful-looking, broken-down and useless white Cadillac.

As the truck receded into the distance I walked back into the house, put my elbows down on the desk, and shook my head. To my untutored mind Brian seemed to be haunted by an intrinsic form of depression that he could not acknowledge. He was intelligent, he was friendly, and in general he handled himself well. But, despite brief and infrequent lapses to the contrary, it was as though he simply did not want to prepare himself even for what most would consider a moderately successful life. One time when he was a teenager, I spoke plainly to him about the folly of this outlook, we got into an argument, and he ended up in tears.

When I tried to encourage him to do better in his choice of work, he would invariably answer, as though it were I who was being unreasonable, "But I'm *happy*, dad. I'm happy doing what I am doing." Generally he deflected in-depth conversation. Yet he could easily beat me in chess, and there were times when his mild and overly deferential, noncommittal manner toward me would crack and a brilliant observation would come out.

Brian grew into a quiet, gentle person who had little use for money or other material things. He worked hard and for little compensation, patiently accepting working hours that were difficult for other employees to take on, or which they simply disliked. In other ways he was a puzzle to me, largely because he seemed to have little interest in improving his lot in life. Though his looks alone could have made him a social success, and probably help win him a suitable wife, he almost always chose low achievers or the handicapped as friends. His first teenage girlfriend was a drug addict; in his late thirties he befriended an unrepentant alcoholic who died of cirrhosis of the liver at the age of 40. There were others of whom Brian would speak with compassion, neither condoning nor belittling their problems. When he was about 42, he phoned me and said he would like to settle down with a wife and start a family, but he could not afford to do so. I could think of no good answer, and could have wept.

Like my other children, Brian was an undeniably *good* person, better than I in terms of generosity, charity, and general caring. At this writing he is a certified health care assistant at a hospice for the terminally ill. He genuinely loves his patients, and enjoys listening to the stories of their rich lives. That to me is a picture of genuine goodness. Perhaps it is the same quality of personality that caused him to "adopt" the frail characters who found their way into his social life. Perhaps in the end analysis his is the better way.

At this point I am moved to say something about current events in 1989. It was the most dramatic year in world events since the end of World War II. On June 4 the bloody Tiananmen Square Massacre marked the end of a mass demonstration in central Beijing, and iconic photographs of a single man impeding the progress of a giant Chinese tank appeared in newspapers around the world. The situation in China seemed to improve after that event – certainly in terms of economics, for in early 2011 this authoritarian and once-backward nation would represent the world's second largest economy after the United States. Photos of happy and prosperous Chinese workers began to appear in the media, and we had to pinch ourselves to remember that they represented a very tiny fraction, though an increasingly enlightened one, of that nation's huge population.

Then in August Lech Walesa became the leader of a newly non-communist Poland, and in October the Berlin Wall was breached. In December the Romanians and Czechs threw out the communists, and to our amazement the Soviet Empire fell apart.

We wondered what would happen to the world, now that the Cold War was over. Where would the next threats emerge? There was no Al Qaeda and no Taliban; no nuclear weapons in India, Pakistan, and North Korea. America and Europe would begin a heady, even crazy two decades in which nations and citizens alike would spend far more than they could possibly afford.

Now let me take you back to the isolation of New Mexico, where life was comfortably predictable, even though the demographic statistics were abysmal. I loved living there, yet, considering its figures for education, per-capita income, and the like, I had mused that this state seemed to be America's toehold in the Third World.

Years earlier I had written an article on Reies Lopez Tijerina for *Interplay* magazine, and now I was in the process of gathering information for a book about New Mexico.[22] Partly for this reason I was interested in learning what had happened to this would-be revolutionary who had visions of returning the old Spanish land grants, which cover much of the Western United States, to the heirs of the original settlers. His obsessions had turned him into a troublemaker, and

Vaquero. My mother's painting of an unknown cattleman reminds me very much of a young Reies Tijerina, whom I first met in 1967.

for his pains, while I was away in England, he had served time in a federal penitentiary. One day I tracked him down at the tiny village of Coyote, northwest of Santa Fe.

Tijerina's adobe house had small windows and was very dark inside, making me think that originally it might have been built as a defensible fortress. The living room was roomy and comfortable, dominated by a huge wall of Spanish- and English-language legal books. Reies perched on a worktable beside a north-facing window, half silhouetted against the bright light.

Through the window was a magnificent view of sandstone boulders and pines, but I was diverted from it, captivated by the deeply tanned face under the broad-brimmed hat. It was a strong face, with a broad forehead and bright brown intelligent eyes, the nose aquiline over a well-trimmed moustache, thick steel-gray hair curling under his hat and over his collar. As he spoke, his shoulders, his hands, his entire body, were thrown into the personification of the folklore that was the man himself. It was easy to see how once he enthralled the New Mexico land grant heirs. He was gray now, his face was handsomely lined and he had broadened with age, but he still had the old fire in his guts.

Tijerina quoted a favoured scriptural quotation, from Isaiah 14:31, that "smoke will come from the north, and no one will be alone in his appointed times." Clearly he was imagining an apocalyptic future nuclear war.

"And you see what I mean," Tijerina said, fixing me with a raptorial eye. "The heat will be drawn up, northwards, like so," and a strong forefinger swept away toward North America and northern Europe. "And it is here, Mexico, where we will have to go for help. We should be very good to the Mexicans." Then, in a prophetic burst that sounded straight from Ezekiel: "The skyscraper will scatter on the winds like thistledown, and the genuine America, the America of New Mexico, will start on its course again. This is an interregnum."[23]

A few weeks later, Tijerina's old house, with its library, was burned to the ground by one of his many enemies. Eventually he moved to Durango, Mexico, to live out his years and his memories.

⁂

Back in England, Jocelyn decided to continue at the London College of Furniture for four years instead of two, and finished in 1991 after building two harpsichords from scratch. She lacked a bachelor's degree but passed all her exams successfully – a Higher National Diploma (similar to American junior college qualification), an Ordinary National Diploma in harpsichord making, and City and Guilds certificates in keyboard design and manufacture.

While still at school, she worked for a while in an antique shop that did restoration and reproduction work. She told me with justifiable pride that she was responsible for restoring an 18th century four-poster bed with a gilded canopy and porphyry pillars, gilding the new canopy with bronze powders and repairing and retouching the pillars with matched colours.

Jocelyn worked briefly at Manders', the big pipe organ builders, in 1991, and returned in the summer of 1992. She was involved in several projects with them, demonstrating, in her words, her "ability to work effectively and independently in a male-dominated work environment." Manders had an interesting history. Founded like me in 1936, the company was utterly destroyed by the Blitz, but recovered well, building or refurbishing enormous instruments that included the remarkable 68-stop four manual and pedal organ in the Church of St. Ignatius Loyola, on Manhattan's Upper East Side, and in London the organs at the Royal Albert Hall and St. Paul's Cathedral.

Brian delighted me at the beginning of 1992 with the news that he had started college at Ashford, Kent, while working part-time at the Burlington Hotel in Folkestone. He reported that he found his college work very interesting, and that he would be playing football regularly with some of his classmates. Hurrah!

For a couple of years now, my New Mexico life had been visited by an unusual problem. For reasons unknown – perhaps repeated dehydration – I had several serious bouts of urinary infection, the last of which had hit me with an intractable fever. In 1991, after it became obvious that antibiotics would not help, my urologist sent me to hospital, put me on a bed of ice as a sort of last resort, and when I recovered scheduled an operation to remove tissue from my prostate gland. The diagnosis was benign prostate hyperplasia, patently preferable to the dreaded prostate cancer.

Sue was sceptical of my swift agreement to have the surgery and thought I should try some alternative therapy first, such as herbal remedies. But I was scared and unwilling to put it off. Whether this had anything to do with my decision I do not know, but our relationship seemed to deteriorate more quickly from this time forward.

After the surgery I was put in a semi-private ward for a couple of days, next to a weak and emaciated man who looked very, very old. On my first evening there, the old man's daughter came to talk to him and the curtain separating our two beds was drawn. Then, after glancing briefly into my little cell, a brisk-looking man in a suit joined them and they started to talk. It became quickly obvious that the visitor was a surgeon.

I could just hear what they were saying. The old man had stomach cancer, but surgery had not been sufficient to get rid of the problem. Tests showed that the cancerous growth was re-establishing. The surgeon explained there was not much he could do other than to go in again and cut away the cancer, and hope it stayed away this time. It's a choice, he said. "You and your father will have to decide whether you want to go through with it."

The woman's reply, and a low-volume mumble from the old man, were inaudible. The man in the suit sounded sympathetic enough – he must have had hundreds or even thousands of conversations like this – but quietly persisted. "Do you think you want to go through with it?"

The woman was crying now, but I could hear her defeated reply. "Yes, yes. We must do our best for him."

The surgeon was gone, followed not much later by my room-mate's daughter. The curtain remained closed. Through the thin fabric I heard a deep sigh, more like a groan. For the first time I heard the man's words clearly. "Oh God, why can't they let me die?" he asked the emptiness around him. "Why can't I just die?"

Why not indeed? This little scene from a real-life tragedy stuck in my mind for a long, long time.

15. MARRIAGE SWEET AND SOUR

People say that what we're all seeking is a meaning for life. I don't think
that's what we're really seeking. I think that what we're seeking is an
experience of being alive, so that our life experiences on the purely physical
plane will have resonances within our own innermost being and reality, so
that we actually feel the rapture of being alive.
— Joseph Campbell[24]

It was 1992, the year that Sue directed Kristen Sergel's adaptation of *Winnie the Pooh* for Albuquerque Children's Theater. We were in Bermuda, staying with my old friend Ed Kelly. Ed had been an independent professional photographer while working as chief photographer for the Mid-Ocean News, and my memories of him, his wife Gloria, and his two little boys were bright. The boys were grown men now, and successful, and Gloria had passed away. Ed lived alone on a wooded hill near Flatts, and his only regular company was a white goat called Go-At, which spent most of its time tethered in a cluster of banana trees.

Ed met us at the airport and, after we went through customs, took us to the nearby old town of St. George's. Tourists were everywhere, crowding the shops and photographing the kids and spouses in the tourist board's pillory and stocks. But Ed led us through the throng to a modest fishing boat where his brother sat quietly cleaning fish. We chatted about the old times. I remembered the time I caught that big hogfish while I was out with Ed and the kids in his old Navy-surplus boat, and the afternoon that we got caught in wild seas that had us bobbing in huge peaks and troughs that once, frighteningly, swirled around us in a great bowl, towering over our heads.

Gourmet days, though it seemed Ed was, and remained, just slightly uncomfortable to be seen socializing with a white man. He was now less interested in photography than his ham radio hobby and his sons, one of whom had become the Bermuda distributor for Nike. No more spear-fishing within a mile of shore, he said. And if you went out that far, don't do it because of the sharks. I was crushed, but the disappointment didn't last.

Ed was the only contact left from my time as a Bermuda newspaperman except for Canadian-born Mike Koren, who came visiting with his wife Ronnie to hash over our youthful exploits. I stopped in to see one other Bermuda friend – I like to think it was Bill Zuill from one of those old white Bermuda families, but can't be sure – and he commented on my pale knees. You heard me right. It was always a joke among us, to talk about the pale knees of visitors who wearing Bermuda shorts for the first time – not pale legs, mind you, for the fashion was to wear knee-length socks under one's thigh-covering shorts.

Naturally Sue and Jonathan relished the Bermuda experience, from eating fresh-caught fish to wandering the bazaar of tourist shops at the former Royal Navy base at Ireland Island. One afternoon Sue smuggled, via Jonathan, a bottle of LiLi "Navy Lime" cologne to me, and perhaps if things had not become so tense between us I could have assumed it to be a peace offering. But no, from all other indications it seemed she had simply lost her affection for me, and yet could give me no reason why, nor could I imagine some special reason. I knew most of my faults, none of which had anything to do with violence or meanness.

On a breezy overcast day the three of us visited my old haunts at Elbow Beach – a sentimental journey, for it was here that I first experienced the wonderment of the reefs, years before. I stripped to my bathing trunks and splashed my way out toward my favourite reef. The currents seemed strange, and the water, normally crystalline, was charged with seaweed and other natural debris. When I got out to the reef, I couldn't see a thing for it; I was spooked and hurried back, feeling fortunate to have survived. Then I remembered someone once told me about the swell that comes to the South Shore before a hurricane. The day after we left, on August 15, Hurricane Felix passed by like an omen, 75 miles from the Bermuda coast.

While I was trying hard to maintain equilibrium in our domestic life, my relationship with Sue had worsened. She sometimes reacted defensively, as if she thought I was harbouring some dislike or contempt for her, which was not the case. I was unable to talk the problem out with her, so that soon I was metaphorically walking on eggs, trying to please her without success.

In the spring of 1993, at Sue's insistence, I joined a group therapy class to discuss my marriage problems. To my surprise, after I described and discussed the situation, the group turned on me: "What's in it for you?" "You're twisting yourself into all sorts of psychological shapes, trying to accommodate this woman." "She's trying to get you to start divorce proceedings." I resented these comments when perhaps I should have treated them as well-meaning advice. I told them I was determined to make the marriage work, for the two of us and especially for Jonathan. "There is always some madness in love," Nietzsche said, "But there is also always some reason in madness." The seven or eight members of the group stolidly refused to go along with me.

And so Sue and I now made plans for an autumn family trip to Disneyland. By now I was taking trazodone and diazepam (Valium) to help me sleep. In October I had to confess to the therapy group that Sue and I had made love once in the previous 15 months, which brought strong criticism from one of the female members, again to the effect that I was beating myself up for nothing. In 1994 Sue and I moved our counselling to a psychiatrist, but this didn't help either. Little by little I became extremely disillusioned with the professions of psychology and psychiatry.

I continued to write nonfiction material, this too probably as a healing exercise. I had taken three book proposals with me to the meeting of the American Association for the Advancement of Science in Chicago in February 1992, work-titled *Millennium Three, Education in Disarray,* and *Walking Shadows.* The first was about science, society, education and media; the second about education, science, and media; and the third was a collection of quotations.

None of these ideas came to anything, and I was not surprised. The education book was a relatively short piece of work, an outgrowth of my experiences with Brian's and Jonathan's schooling. I wanted these children, and others, to be able to derive at least as much from life as I. My marriages had been failures. But still I was extremely grateful, above all for being born human, and for three main gifts that sprang from this. I was grateful that I could communicate intelligently with people from all walks of life and, as far as I knew, from all cultures. I was grateful that I had an abundance of curiosity and the belief that I could slake that curiosity and help other people in the process. I was grateful that I had a personal spirituality and that through it I recognized and respected my affinity with the natural world. Sometimes I fear that this last-named must be increasingly rare in society at large. I suspect that the products of information technologies that range from TV natural history documentaries to computer modeling of natural events are coaxing people away from the existential delight of knowing nature in 5-D: by literally being there, and enchanted in the collusion of our full suite of senses.

I credit my parents, and no one else, for endowing me with these gifts in the first dozen or so years of my life. Formal education helped me to expand upon them and to branch out from them. I learned a lot from my peers, in personal life and at work. The person inside me – the Nigel bundle – subtly changed as the years progressed. But the family foundation paved the way for everything I had, including the richness of my own family life, my job, the respect of my colleagues, and the fact that I could exult in the sight of a lilac bush mobbed with butterflies, or the ripe full moon rising over the silent New Mexico desert.

Hence the book-length manuscript *Education in Disarray*, written for a time when so many children have poor home lives. My main observation was to pretty obvious: when children lack a wisely supportive family life, it becomes the awesome and sometimes futile responsibility of school teachers and administrators to compensate as well as they can.

⟨⟨⟩⟩

As you know by now, while I had a strong and abiding love for the sea, I was enchanted by the desert and its ancient peoples, and could find spirituality close to me there. In the final two years of my marriage to Sue I found solace there too, and so in the spring of 1993 I felt that I needed to get back to the desert for a personal pilgrimage, explained my quest to Sue and Jonathan, and headed west, alone with my thoughts.

My journey took me at a fast clip along Interstate 40, first across the Rio Puerco before crossing the Laguna and Ácoma Pueblo lands, and the badlands of frozen lava from Mount Taylor, before reaching the old uranium town of Grants. A cup of coffee, then onward to Gallup and northward to the turnoff named for a trading post called Ya-Ta-Hey, the Navajo welcome greeting. And then I was driving west again, rising across the desert toward the high pine forest – the only part of this long journey that is not desert.

I entered the Hopi Reservation about an hour after leaving Hubbell's Trading Post, a favourite stopover and National Historic Site near Ganado, Arizona. The light was fading fast, a watery sunset under high, twisty clouds. The scatter of habitations at Polacca, under the Hopis' fabled First Mesa, overlooked by the magical village of Walpi, told me I was near my destination. Between the older dressed-stone buildings were government tract houses and prefab "mobile" homes. I crossed Wepo Wash, then followed an end-of-the-earth, twisting road up and over the edge of Second Mesa over a wild moonscape to the left. Finally I pulled into the grounds of the Hopi Cultural Center. The trip meter told me I had driven 263 miles from Albuquerque, and at the same time I was both content and exhausted. I checked in, stumbled to the neat motel room, threw off my clothes, and immediately fell asleep.

The next morning I took the short walk to the edge of Second Mesa and drank in the awe-inspiring view south and west to San Francisco Peaks, though this day was hazy and little more than the white flash of snow was visible on those faraway mountainsides. Behind me, and not far from where I stood, apricot and peach trees were blooming inexplicably, growing from sparse unirrigated ground where later my friends insisted the rainfall is only two or three inches a year.

What I wanted to do most of all on this trip was to visit Walpi. The road to this ancient village seems to corkscrew straight upward into the dark blue sky. Up, up, up, and then I was in a village of flat-topped stone buildings, Tewa. A few more hundred yards, indiscernible to anyone but a local resident, this scattering of desert-coloured habitations became the legendary Walpi.

This was First Mesa, America's Lhasa. Here on the treeless parched rock one has a bird's eye view of a landscape like none other on earth, a vast desert sea of admixed light grays, light browns, light greens. On this day there was no wind, the sky was virtually cloudless, and there was silence with a view of 150 or 200 miles in most directions, that view dominated by far-off mountains and mesas of impressive and sometimes bizarre dimensions, a landscape so strangely huge that one could imagine that God had intended it for some other planet. Up here, one understands why the Hopi believe they have a special spirituality. John DeWitt McKee, a writer and onetime professor of humanities at New Mexico Tech in central New Mexico, might well have been influenced by a trip to Walpi when he wrote these lines:

Man may scratch the past with his frail stick plough. He may fling himself into the future seeking limits to the limitless sky. He may strut upon a stage too vast for any he can make or comprehend. It does not matter. It is the land that holds us here. It is the unrelenting land, this great, fierce, challenging, canyon-gutted, mesa-muscled land, which holds us and which gives us space enough to write a life on – and leaves it to us whether we have courage enough and faith to fill the page.[25]

These days, visitors are required to park a short walk from the narrow neck of rock that leads from the main part of the mesa to the ancient village. Though more houses were stuccoed than the last time I was there, the timeless aspects of the place remained. Ravens wheeled below like spirit messengers as I walked along a wagon-rutted sandstone path that left little room between the precipices that fell from each side. Feathers attached to shrubs were transplanted Shinto-like messages to the spirits, asking for rain. A pack of six silent dogs accompanied me, spending much of their time trotting to different vantage points at the cliff top, standing like little furry statues, scanning the huge landscape below, their paws at the edge of a 300-foot drop. At one point one of their number disappeared behind a rock at the edge, reappearing a few minutes later, bouncing like a goat from rock to rock, hunting a ground squirrel in the boulder-strewn talus far below.

Two husky young men, very darkly tanned, tried to sell me their kachina dolls. The craftsmanship was good and they offered me good prices, but I was more interested in the personifications of the kachinas and the symbolism of the ornamentation, and why they had to use cottonwood *root* instead of any old part of the tree (it's softer and easier to work). When they saw I wasn't a buyer, they told me of the spiritual importance of this special place that they called home, and the hardships of living there. How Navajos and others were copying their kachina dolls and selling inferior products at a fraction of the price – say one-fifth. How the *bahana* whites persisted in calling them savages and how slanders in Marvel Comics, combined with the offensiveness of tourists who persisted in sketching and photographing sacred places, had resulted in dances being closed to the public. How this had strained the tourist trade and choked the sale of kachina dolls and other handicrafts. How the slurrying operation for the open-pit coal mines, up there at Black Mesa in Navajo country, had lowered the water table in their already arid croplands. How fortunate the Rio Grande pueblos were, being able to irrigate from the river, while here the people had to pray, pray, pray to their ancestors for life-giving rain!

❦

Since we moved back to New Mexico, Sue and I had managed to keep our savings account level while maintaining two cars and making annual trips to England. Sue's income from Albuquerque Children's Theater made it possible for her to keep a private, individual bank account from which she bought clothing

Lineup. A happy Miriam unintentionally mugs the camera as Jocelyn and David, newly married, pose in a photo session. That's Brian at the far right.

and other personal gear. The Children's Theater became her great joy in life, giving her artistic fulfillment and the satisfaction of seeing children develop from awkward neophytes into real, though fledgling, actors, as well as the opportunity to associate with others who share her abiding interest in theatre arts.

Sue had earned a solid grounding in theatre long before we met, starting at Texas Lutheran College with the title roles in *Mary of Scotland* in 1966 and Eleanor in *The Lion in Winter* (1968). There seemed nothing she could not do in theatre – directing, playwriting, teaching, acting, sewing costumes, building sets, you name it. She had a beautiful singing voice and played piano, guitar, and recorder. By the time we split up she had about 30 acting credits, had written six or seven plays, including *The Most Marvellous News or Why Don't They Ever Talk About the First Mrs. Phipps?* (performed in Chicago with Eve Arden playing the lead), plus about 15 children's plays, and in 1994 produced *Kickin'*, a Western musical written with a local musician, Jeff Burrows.

What a wonderful record! It is a tragedy that this talent did not attract the recognition it deserved.

❧

The most important happening of 1992 was a Sunday morning phone call from Folkestone, when David Armitage, whom I hardly knew, asked me for his blessing in taking Jocelyn as his wife, followed not long after by a July 16 phone call from Miriam, with the news that David's mother, his only surviving immediate family member, had died. The wedding was scheduled for September 19, 1992, two days before Brian's birthday.

On May 8, 1992, I received what may have been my last written communication from Miriam, though I would see her personally before long. It was composed in her usual very neat handwriting:

Dear Nigel, Thank you very much for your letter and cheque for £200. Joss came down for a few days last week and we had a lovely time. She tried on a few wedding dresses but she hasn't decided on one yet. I spoke to [Vicar] Peter Cole about the marriage and he said the main thing is that they love one another and I really think they do. He also said Joss is a very good daughter. Brian is healthy and happy and he is a great encouragement to me. Dr. W. is cutting down my Stelazine. I now take 2 mgm b.d. I'll soon be drug free. He told me some time ago that I was going to be healed. [Sister] Joan isn't sure whether she will be able to come in Sept., but we are all excited about the wedding. God bless you and your family. Love, Miriam.

My heart fell when I read Mim's closing sentences, so tender in words and meaning. I don't know what I would have done if I knew she had only four years to live.

David was born in North London, but since childhood and after a flirtation with pop music had developed a keen interest in "country" pursuits like folk music and morris dancing. He was a good-natured man with a ruddy complexion and a mop of beautiful black, curly hair. He could have passed as a Turk – especially when he took it in his mind to grow a walrus moustache. He described himself as fat, and he was right. But if that can be counted as a fault, it was the only one I was aware of.

Following, and perhaps during, his days as a morris dancer, David was a founder-member of Blowzabella, a folk band formed in 1978 by students at the Musical Instrument Technology (MIT) Department of the London College of Furniture, a college noted for its instrument-making courses, where David and Jocelyn met. At first David played a melodeon, a type of button accordion (In

America, the name is also given to a type of foot-operated Victorian organ). Then he added bassoon and percussion to his repertoire. He and Joss were both expert folk-dance callers.

Later, the MIT Department became part of London Guildhall University, where David became a senior lecturer in musical instrument technology. In July 2000 he was elected Honorary Editor of the *Fellowship of Makers and Researchers of Historical Instruments Quarterly*. In addition to teaching, he kept busy in the lab, and designed and built recorders under the auspices of the university's Centre for New Musical Instruments (CNMI) at London's Guildhall University, working with his colleague and neighbour Lewis Jones. One student blogger, who hand-made a flute Dave had designed, noted his teacher "has been a professional player and maker of woodwinds, and is a gifted and inspirational teacher. The other students are a mixed bunch, but all sharing my obsession [for the class]."

Guildhall University then was merged into London Metropolitan University and the Sir John Cass Department of Art Media and Design, which offered a bachelors' degree in musical instrument making, possibly the only one in Britain.

David turned out to be a wonderful son-in-law, and later a marvellous father. Miraculously, after a hard day at work (he would generally cycle or walk the mile and a half, which could be accomplished along the Regents Canal towpath), he and Joss would set to work making the children's dinner – always fresh, never out of the can or bottle. Then story time and the nightly bath. Then perhaps Dave would, with relish, make a gourmet dinner for the grownups. He enjoyed the home life. Yes, there were times he would grumble about work, but he realized that his students shared an admiration for their mentor.

May 20 1994, to Mim and Brian. You may have heard from Joss and Dave that Jonathan and I have tickets to come to England this summer. Sue has opted to stay at the "ranch" this time, which means she'll have a chance for a good rest without anyone else to worry about, and with the children's theatre summer break maybe she'll be able to do some writing and planning for the future of the children's theatre itself. Jonathan and I are both very excited to be having our own special trip together. I had lunch with my mother and dad today, celebrating their 63rd wedding anniversary! They are doing quite well – they went to see Jonathan's school production last week – an especially good effort considering they're 86 and 88. Just wait until you see Jonathan! He's about 4 foot 10, slim, and studious-looking in his glasses. We go cycling together often - just short distances with me riding Brian's old bike and him riding a new full-sizer - and he'll be starting music lessons soon, I hope. Piano and/or clarinet. Week before last I was with a CNN television crew on the Hopi Indian reservation in NE Arizona, doing a little news feature on how Sandia employees supplement science teaching for 12-13 year-olds.

My faithful old dog Lass died not long after we returned from England It was a particularly sad event because she had been with me so long, through thick and thin. After she stopped eating I could do nothing but nurse her myself because she would become defensively angry with veterinarians (or with anyone from outside the household for that matter), and sedation would probably have killed her. She didn't seem to be in pain, but simply would not eat as though she somehow knew it was time for her to shuffle off her doggy mortal coil. I spent one Saturday and Sunday feeding her through the side of her muzzle with a liquid dietary supplement meant for human patients. I didn't get much of it down her, if any, but on the Sunday I spent a lot of time just talking to her and bathing her face. Then she just died. Very sad. Even Beauxmont the beagle was sad, and not just *looking* sad, which was his usual thing. We were sitting together the second day afterwards, and he lifted his head up staring at nowhere in particular and barked as if he was calling her. I buried her in a corner of the garden.

⚜

At this point I want to let you in on, well, hardly a secret, not a vice, but a personal failing that you may not recognize simply by reading these pages. When it comes to conversing one-on-one, I know far more about this fine art than I have practiced in life. I could have been a better talker, and a far better listener. St. Peter will probably tell me I got an F+ in Conversation 100. A wandering mind, together with a tendency to let chance remarks switch my mind into lateral thought-channels, compounded the problem. This frustrated me greatly, almost as much as it frustrated my family and friends. In the conduct of one-on-one communication I was a very poor multi-tasker. One time I let show my impatience when Gerry Yonas repeatedly changed the subject of the conversation. His wife smiled understandingly. "Don't worry, he thinks about several things at the same time." If only I had talent like this!

Too often, if I had something to say, it came out in my writing, not my conversation. Once some morsel of "important" information is thoroughly introduced, I can explain it but have trouble spending long periods of conversation about it, for like the stereotype male I want to identify problems or opportunities and, with or without assistance, quickly devise systems to overcome or fulfill them. Not surprisingly the problem hindered my relationships with women. Doubtless another part of this problem was that I had betrayed myself with a misguided vision of femininity, assuming women in general to be the more sensitive, gentler sex. I grew up at an awkward time in the relationship between the sexes, and besides, perhaps I had read too many of those romantic Victorian poems and essays.

❦

I divorced Sue on December 12, 1995, and sadly said goodbye to a greatly gifted sweetheart with natural curls and dazzling blue eyes. We had fallen into a terrible trap, and the counsellors were of no help whatsoever. Each of us was feeling the hurt – in fact an amalgam of remembered and half-forgotten hurts – so much, and dreading the prospect of *more* hurt so much, that we could not step back and talk, and understand what it was all about and what we were in danger of losing. If I had talked more, or talked about the right things – . Such "ifs" will never be washed away, and these retrospective ponderings might as well be forgotten, because even if I had done the impossible and resolved them with a halfway successful personality correction, it would have come to naught.

One of my life goals was gone forever. That Norman Rockwell dream of festive tables attended by a happy gang of mother, father, and children, would never be realized in my lifetime. It seemed not long before Sue returned to Texas, to help her father look after his ranch and care for him as he eased into old age. At this point, Jonathan became lord of the manor at the house she had occupied until then.

I had waited until early November to tell my children in England about the impending divorce, perhaps because I hoped that magically our problems would be resolved. First I phoned Joss with the news, and she passed it on to Miriam and Brian. "I guess you have to be a bit like Edith Piaf and *regrette rien*," she wrote on November 14. "You must look positively to the future and if you must think on the past, think of all the good times you have shared with the people in your life." Again, wise words for her old dad.

225

The divorce marked the most distressing time in my life, as traumatic as my parting from Miriam yet somehow more so because age had overcome those hopes, formulated first in my university days, to fulfill my romantic dream of building an enduring family life.

> *Nature, whose sweet rains fall on just and unjust alike, will have clefts in the rocks where I may hide, and secret valleys in whose silence I may weep undisturbed. She will hang the night with stars so that I may walk abroad in the darkness without stumbling, and send the wind over my footprints so that none may track me to my hurt: she will cleanse me in great waters, and with bitter herbs make me whole.*
> Oscar Wilde, "De Profundis"

At this time Joss and Dave were in the process of moving from their rooms in the rectory at St. George in the East Church, Whitechapel, to one of five derelict row houses on Mare Street in Hackney. A long-term lease on the property, which then belonged to the Crown Estate, was bought with the concurrence of the Spitalfields Trust, a charity dedicated to restoring Georgian houses. Their agreement was that they would restore the old house, built in 1818 (which technically made it Regency, which lasted from George IV's father's death in 1811 to his own in 1820), to a condition resembling the original, using what remained of the original wood and stone and using period colours in the new paintwork. I applauded this as a very good move, especially since both were experienced in working with wood, but may have despaired if I had seen the property when they bought it, with a caved-in roof, rotten floors, and rain-flooded basement. All of this had to be rectified, and much more, from rebuilding the roof to rebuilding the front window, which had previously been destroyed to make a shop front, to installing a frighteningly deep sewer pipe through the back garden.

In case you're wondering, with time and work the investment turned out to be very good indeed.

Joss kept me well informed on the move-in. In mid-November 1995 the house, its basement pumped dry and electric power connected, received its new water pipe and Dave installed the modern water heater, enabling the delights of installing a sink with hot and cold water and a flushing toilet. On the 17th they finished moving in, complete with Felix the cat. "We are really very snug in our dingy Georgian splendour," Joss wrote. "We are holed up in the basement waiting for winter to pass over us. Lewis (Dave's college colleague and their new next-door neighbour) has just supplied us with a bottle of champagne, so I guess that's tonight taken care of, although I'm not sure that Sainsbury's Butcher's Choice sausages are a fitting accompaniment."

⟨∞⟩

The years of 1996-2005 were torn with sadnesses of many kinds. I suspect that most of all the divorce was a brutal slap in the face for Sue; for me it was a tragedy. It saddened me greatly to realize that my household would never ring regularly with the laughter of mother, father, and red-cheeked children clustered around the festive table.

The summer of 1996 brought weather of a premonitory nature; it seemed the elements were hot and humid harbingers of more difficult weather ahead. Alone and thoughtful for much of the time, writing and editing my New Mexico book without really getting anywhere, I took to diarizing and letter-writing.

10 July 1996 – It's monsoon time, humid, the thunder rumbling, and raindrops tapping on the roof. This is absolutely wonderful because last year we had no monsoon whatsoever. Between January 1 1995 and June 1, 1996, we had about six inches of precipitation in total. Last year it was dry enough in Yorkshire to send convoys of water tankers into the Pennines, but here – well, it's already a desert, and to have a drought on top of that is a sobering experience.

Rain is pelting down now and doors are slamming through the house. Thunder everywhere, and the trees are whipping around in the wind. The house is an island in a shallow lake spiked with the tips of grass stalks. Electric power should go off anytime.

11 July 1996 – the newspapers said that Albuquerque had two inches of rain yesterday! And my roof didn't leak! Traffic conditions on the radio noted a fender-

bender on the northbound freeway, a mess of cattle loose on Isleta Boulevard, and a mud bank on Candelaria Road, where water had run down from higher ground.

13 July 1996 – There's a lull in the monsoon, and jimsonweed (Datura stramonium) has sprouted here and there on the Albuquerque pavements, bold mounds of foliage as high as my chest. Their profusion of flowers stand furled like unwanted umbrellas in the daytime sun, and then as the afternoon fades they erupt into white trumpets as big as Easter lilies. While this was once a medicinal plant for asthmatics, when swallowed the alkaloid content can kill a cow.

25 July 1996 – It was hot in the house and humid, 80 degrees at 8:30 this morning. I took off my shirt and stalked around the place, picking at bits from the refrigerator, scanning the newspaper without interest, sipping at a glass of milk. I was ill at ease, depressed, thinking of the old man from San Miguel Pueblo, the one that inspired me to create one of the characters in my new book, work-titled Fire in the Fourth World. What was that he said? Don't write nothing about us, in a voice that was at once accusatory and defeated, because he knew this white man would take no notice.

I went outside and the world changed.

Once I tobogganed into a snow bank and was submerged, finding myself in a magical dimensionless transparency of grey and white shadings. That's the way the clouds were when I ventured out this afternoon, only the air was very warm and they were feathers of gray vapour, crystallizing against a sky that I could not see.

Tiny spots of rain pricked against my skin. A breath of wind, like a woman's soft hand, stroked through the yielding tops of the tamarisk and into the hairs of my chest.

The cicadas were very loud.

The wind and the trees were touching my soul and I let myself melt with them for a while, there in the warm near-dark with lightning beginning to flash to the northeast, and the sun, long descended into the west, reaching back to wash the southern clouds with cinnabar.

I made notes sitting on the cool metal nose of the station wagon. And then I lay down on it, under that sky, inside that tender wind. Dozing. When I roused, Beauxmont Beagle was lapping water somewhere and it was too dark to write though I could see that now the sky was duskily decorated with pale hues of blue and cantaloupe orange. And then I slept, right there under the sky, my ears full of cicada song and the marching beat of the crickets all around. The world had changed. My mind kept returning to that wizened grandfather from the pueblo.

I wanted to share my experiences with my old IMS friend Patrick McGinley, but had misplaced his address. Fortunately an inspiration came to solve the problem. He had become managing director of the *Europa Yearbook* and I guessed correctly that I would find his contact information in the university library. He had asked me if I could find the third volume in a Cormac McCarthy trilogy, but I couldn't find it and told him I was inclined to think it was be a work in progress. I had *The Crossing* by my bedside and was fascinated with it. McCarthy had the knack of putting the reader – *me*, anyway – right there in the picture. I was a participant in a story that was both realistic and ultimately tragic.

I told Patrick that things were all right over here, except that I was alone and Jonathan had been staying with Sue for a short time that seemed like ages. Half-heartedly, rather embarrassed and expecting nothing to come from it anyway, I was advertising for a lady friend.

⊚≪≫

On April 9, 1996, Brian phoned to report that his mother had been at the William Harvey Hospital in Ashford, too ill and disoriented to write checks or give him authority to write them for her. I did what I could, which was and will always be too little. Life went on, savouring happiness, with sadness waiting in the wings. Brian was doing the greatest service a young man can do for his mother, to be at her side as she lay dying. I had been frustrated that Brian was unmotivated to become a peer of those we call successful; but this dissolved to nothing in my admiration for his lonely devotion to his mother as she faded away in the nursing home where she had given him life.

Late that summer Miriam died of motor neurone disease, called Lou Gehrig's Disease or amyotrophic lateral sclerosis (ALS) in the States.

The last time I saw Mim was at Joss and David's wedding, animated as usual,

229

seeming happy and relaxed. As she became terminally ill my children discouraged me from seeing her, and eased me away when she lay in the funeral home. For years she had been a caring single mother, just as in the end Joss and Brian were caring children, with Brian in the forefront of the support team. It gave me no pleasure to be overseas and useless during her last days.

Miriam's funeral service was held on the afternoon of October 15, 1996, at St. Eanswythe's Church in Folkestone. The church was crowded to capacity and, though privately I had cherished the idea of delivering a eulogy, at this occasion I turned out to be a choked-up, speechless mess. Every divorce is a tragedy, the dismal end of hope, struggle, and defeat, but does not bring such a complete loss as this. To see Mim divorced from life compounded that tragedy. In our estrangement we had been true to each other in our peculiar and inadequate ways, forcing ourselves to understand the separateness without bitterness. She was a loving and undemanding soul: as my father said, there wasn't an unkind bone in her body. Despite all the crazy eccentricity she brought joy to the people around her.

My friend Kim Braithwaite told me that his daughter told him many times that he was "just a leaking sack of sentiment." This would have been an apt metaphor for me, that day in Folkestone.

> *Midway on our life's journey, I found myself*
> *In dark woods, the right road lost. To tell*
> *About those woods is hard — so tangled and rough*
> *And savage that thinking of it now, I feel*
> *The old fear stirring…*
> — Dante's Inferno, translated by Robert Pinsky

16. SHALAKO

Out of sheer envy we are obliged to smile at the Indians' naïveté, and to plume
ourselves on our cleverness; for otherwise we would discover how impoverished and
down at the heels we are. Knowledge does not enrich us; it removes us more and
more from the mythic world in which we were once at home by right of birth. [26]
— Carl Jung

It was one-thirty in the morning and all over the village knots of people were walking quietly through the dark, Pueblo people, Navajos, Hispanics, whites. The white man's hubbub was put away and forgotten, and Jonathan and I were navigating a world out of time. Since sunset the Shalakos, messengers of spirits who live with the Council of Gods in the depths of Dawn Lake, had begun to arrive. Now we were searching, almost blindly, for their dancing places.

We picked our way through a world set apart from the ordinary. Western New Mexico's stars were brilliant ice-white, the waning moon a tilted bowl in the sky. Twinkling house lights made the village of Zuni look huge in the darkness, though fifty or more yards of sand and desert weed separated each dwelling-place.

This December night was cloudless and windless and frosty-cold, and we shivered inside our parkas. It was the second night of a sacred and dramatic annual observance in which the Zuni people ask their creators and ancestor-spirits for their blessings and pray that all humanity – not just their tribe, not just Indians – will enjoy peace and good will. Though the event is strange to newcomers, and we would not understand a word of the proceedings, it is a combination of thanksgiving, harvest festival, memorial day, and Christmas, all wrapped into one two-day celebration.

The Shalakos, one for each of Zuni's six ceremonial kivas, are tall bird-like creatures with clacking beaks. The poet Winfield Townley Scott witnessed their coming forty years earlier, and was left awed and apparently uncomfortable. He felt that he was "in the presence of towering, barbaric gods".

"You stand amidst other Anglos at the edge of the village and peer across,

231

barely able to see the gigantic figures as they slowly approach from the hills," Scott wrote. "Eerie cries sound here and there in the sudden dark, and the bitter cold, which worsens all night, sets in …"[27]

Preparations for the festival had been in the making all year long. New houses had been carefully built, complete with a central trench that would allow the dancer in his tall Shalako dress to dance and parade before the clan, family and guests. All are welcome in the Shalako houses – including members of other Indian groups, non-Indians, and the spirits of departed Zuni people – though choice seats are saved for invited guests. The celebration is at the same time serious and joyful, enlivened with a richness of cultural detail that is steeped in the everyday spiritual life of the people, passed on continuously through songs and ritual without recourse to writing.

Wrapped against the cold in layers like onions, Jonathan and I found our first Shalako house and joined a crowd that was squeezing into what appeared to be a kitchen. Scores of people sat under bare light bulbs, shoulder to shoulder, welcoming us as we helped ourselves to chile and bread. The bread, baked in the Moorish-style outdoor ovens, was dry and tasty, the chile a pleasantly piquant mixture that gave needed warmth to our frosted frames.

People were still filing into the kitchen from the outside. Since only a limited number were able to squeeze into the ceremonial room, the house quickly filled and we soon found ourselves under the stars again, making space for newcomers. We sidled along a wall that we thought might be protected from the cold and found a window that gave us a slantwise view of the ceremony. Inside, the walls were sumptuously decorated with hand-woven woollen clothing, belts decorated with hand-worked silver and semiprecious stones, gaily patterned Mexican scarves, blankets printed in bright colours. Among them majestic deers' heads were mounted on the walls, wearing necklaces of turquoise, shell, jet, and red coral as tokens of respect and thankfulness. Directly inside our window a group of singers and drummers chanted long traditional songs that made me think of European sagas.

And then we saw the Shalako who belonged to this house and clan. His beaked face was crowned with a spray of eagle plumes and collared with a thick ruff of raven feathers. Behind his head he wore a kind of topknot of varicoloured feathers, and his horns were hung with pendants of down. His great tapering conical body, fashioned from buckskin stretched around hoops of willow, was decorated with animal skins, dried plants, representations of all things with

232

which the people have been always interdependent. Below this were a white
kirtle and the moccasined legs of the dancer inside, jogging back and forth under
the gliding superstructure, circling, bobbing, bowing. Now and then the great
decorated beak would open and close savagely, and one could clearly hear the
clack-clack from outside the window.

The second house offered even greater variety. Here in clear view were the
young Fire God, a boy in a dark, gold-spotted mask and ruff, and his ceremonial
godfather; and Sayatasha the Long-Horn kachina, who wore a black and white
mask with a single horn projecting from the right side of it; and *Salimobia*
kachinas with green masks and black ruffs. Twice we saw pairs of mudheads
arrive and enter the house – men with grotesque masks of terra-cotta without
any other colouring save a smearing of red mud on naked torsos. The mudheads,
impersonating the oafish offspring of an incestuous coupling at the mythical
beginning of creation, brought chaos to the room. They taunted the Shalako and
teased the participants in general, including the young lad who had been
personifying the Fire God, who was so exhausted that he lay collapsed backward
in his chair against the wall with his mouth open, fast asleep.

It was a few minutes before six when the family and I climbed exhausted

Shalako plume planting. Shalako racers tower high as their plumes are planted
at Zuni in December 1895. Photo: National Park Service.

into our beds at Gallup, 25 miles to the north. Back at Zuni, Long Horn would climb to the roof at dawn to declare the night's celebration complete.

Our alarm clock roused us for a mid-day return, and we dressed and packed hastily before making our way back to Zuni.

In an open field the Shalakos were already racing, in their great unwieldy costumes, to place prayer plumes in six holes before they returned to Listening Spring, the source of Dawn Lake. Legend has it that the Shalakos bring the gods messages and prayers for rain in this way throughout the year.

A little river sparkled across the narrow dirt road that ran between us and the racing ground. After the races the six Shalakos formed lines with their entourages. A short time later, to my delight, two Shalakos came within feet of us, preceded by costumed attendants, flanked by elders, followed by little groups of quietly, gravely singing men. People sprinkled dust-fine corn pollen on the celebrants as they passed, and particularly upon the Shalakos. When the last group had passed, we saw the road gilded with corn, a sacred way.

Shalako was all about journeys, journeys in space and time. Journeys are journeys. You can't separate the physical journey from the metaphysical journey. Even the ancient Irish Catholic priests had this need to travel, and learn, and teach as well. The Australian aborigines, and maybe the Bushmen and some of the North African desert tribes, know the travel-urge instinctively and intimately. But so many modern white-man journeys are done within the confines of the head, with books and television and Web pages. You don't smell them, don't touch them, don't hear or feel them. We short-change ourselves. Or I guess we do, *suspect* we do. Most of our life's experience is a vast series of packaged messages, sequestered in the brain, trapped inside the grey matter, in little zaps of electricity twinkling between the cells of a seemingly quiescent form.

Shalako is part of a tradition that defines the Zuni people, as is towering Mount Taylor to the north; without them and a complex of other ancient conventions, the tribe would cease to be. Years later, Zuni Governor Norman Cooeyate told writer Laura Paskus that he considered his tribe an endangered species: "If any portion of that [tradition] is lost, the knowledge that is gained by us, by our leaders, by our community, is lost now and forever."[28]

Alex Seowtewa knew of this. He had personally shown me the wondrous twin murals that he began to paint in February 1970 at Our Lady of Guadalupe, a mission church originally built three and a half centuries ago, ruined, and rebuilt in 1968 from a shell of adobe brick. In life size, they depict characters from the spirit world, full of colour, full of motion, full of dignified power. The winter kachinas dance across the north wall, the summer and autumn kachinas across the south; I remember staring at them open-mouthed, hearing in my mind's ear the drum and the chanting storytellers. Seowtewa, a marvellously gentle man, articulate, educated, and a world traveller, spoke quietly about what he calls an "ecumenical labour of love," which combined his profound respect for both his native religion and the Roman Catholic Church. Proudly he showed me a magazine article in which his eldest son Ken explained his family's hope that future generations will use the completed mural "as a guide and inspiration for their lives" and "impress upon other people the importance of knowing their heritage – their roots. If they know where they come from, they will know where they are going."[29]

We drove home through sandstone landscapes that were reddened by the setting sun and studded with the dark green of piñon pine and juniper; fluffy chamisa seed heads shone in bright roadside clouds. At seven we arrived at the adobe house on Guadalupe Trail, and I settled down to write. Next to my laptop was the wad of paper that I stuffed into my pocket after an elderly Zuni man pressed it into my hand at the dining table the night before. I unfolded it and read it silently to myself, a prayer for the journey to Dawn Lake:

Do not despise the breath of your fathers
But draw it into your body,
That our roads may reach to where the
Life-giving road of our sun father comes out.
That, clasping one another tight,
Holding one another fast,
We may finish our roads together.
That this may be, I add to your breath now.
To this end:
May my father bless you with life;
May your road reach to Dawn Lake;
May your road be fulfilled.

One morning in the following spring, before taking Jonathan fishing, I bought a "water dog" that was being sold as bait, though we never dreamed of using it for such a purpose. I should explain that the water dog is an immature tiger salamander – like an overgrown newt only not nearly so pretty. In fact it is the most unhandsome four-legged creature I have ever seen. Slugs and earthworms are just ordinary slugs or earthworms; they have few particularly intriguing characteristics. But the water dog doesn't know whether to be a fish or a lizard. Libbleslub's eyes would be beautiful gold-rimmed beads of jet, only they were so small and so widely spaced, lost in a broad polliwog head. Behind this head sprout an amazing peculiarity, soft fringes of gills, three on each side.

So we had a new pet, five inches long and yellow-green like pondweed and saddled with the name Sue had given to a salamander in a story she made up at her dad's trailer in the mountains in Colorado. Soon after we had built him a terrarium in the back patio, our captive escaped. First his gills disappeared, then all of him. I was reminded of Sir Thomas Brown's description of Man, in his *Religio Medici,* as "that great and true Amphibian whose nature is disposed to live… in divided and distinguished worlds." Which gave me pause to think.

Were people great and true amphibians? I reckoned a few people could swim as well as a grown-up salamander, and most of us can walk around a crazy-paved garden path and smell the roses as well. But I doubted that a salamander had much of an intellect. Was Libbleslub capable of falling in love?

My mind wandered off rather erratically on this general theme, for sometime in this period I must have divined certain thoughts about the philosophy of love – or perhaps they had been with me for a long time and no one I dared to share them with had reciprocated. I thought that two people who could share it with words would indeed be a fine thing. But this did not or could not happen, especially in the case of new love, which is such a strange March-hare madness, taking one (or preferably two) into a special part of the cosmos in a way that beggars description, leading almost certainly to the brief bliss of sexual union. *La petite mort.* Perhaps this is even the great goal-paragon of life, or of our entire intellect, this self-destruction and rebirth, the fate and fortune of messiahs and the phoenix brought into being by the closeness of two souls. The philosophers, from the Greek onward, have defined five or six different kinds of love. From my point of view, love most likely comes from the unthought, unnoticed need to produce more of our kind, encouraged by the sharing of similar views of the ideal human relationship, and costumed in the romanticism that only humans can perceive. Is *homo sapiens sapiens* the ultimate amphibian? The last one?

Slowly I was crawling back into the old philosophical playpen. Maybe.

Soon after Libbleslub's disappearance, while my mother was visiting the house, the dogs started a commotion and she said I'd better interrupt my work on the vegetable garden to see what was going on. Right next to the gnarled rosemary bush on the edge of the carport was a snake, cornered by the two dogs. Miraculously, Beauxmont had put aside his beagle's obsession with smell. Now he was the barker, acting the more threatening of the two. Lass was hanging back a bit as though to say "Go on, Beauxmont, you first." Meanwhile their quarry, which was a harmless gopher snake, was wriggling the end of its pointed tail and doing it best to act like a rattlesnake, but silently. "Poor thing," said Grandma, who had been watching from the sidelines.

The snake was hissing furiously, coiled up tensely as though getting ready to strike. The dogs were frantic. So I tied them up and coaxed our visitor into a large laundry detergent tub until it calmed down. Then we released it into the woodpile (where we put the centipedes the previous winter) and untied the dogs. I had never seen such cautious sniffing. There they were, both with their back legs braced ready to jump away, smelling every minute detail of the carport for a visitor that was long gone. At one time there was an unexpected noise, from someone going down the road, and both dogs jumped up in the air at the same time. I was afraid grandma was going to have a stroke, laughing so much. Or me. I thought it would be a good idea if the snake stayed in the garden, but knew the dogs would scare it off.

⚜

My parents, naturally for their age, were failing now, and my dad already had survived a cancer operation when he was living in Salt Lake City. Now the dread disease struck again.

May 12, 1990 – Six weeks ago, my father went into hospital and had surgery for colon cancer. They took about an hour and 40 minutes to cut out the affected section and stitch the loose ends together. He had a bad time with daymares/nightmares for two days after the surgery. There had been a cluster of moths in the corner of the room, next to the ceiling, but only he had been able to see them, and this perplexed him. They call it intensive-care psychosis, or something like that, resulting from the general aesthetic. He was in hospital for a week. Now he has to have his eyes examined by a specialist, since with macular degeneration he cannot see well enough to drive and can read large-print books only with difficulty. My mother is doing a heroic job of nursing Dad (far more heroic than I realized at the time) and having eye surgery herself.

Meanwhile my two sons, in Albuquerque, were following quite different trajectories, naturally enough since there were 16 years' difference in age between them. Jonathan was charging ahead at Ranchitos Elementary School while Brian was experimenting with different ways of making a living.

Sept. 4, 1990 – Jonathan started his first year of elementary school on Monday of last week and is enjoying it greatly. He seems particularly to like school lunches. He said that he wished Jocelyn had been with him at school because they had hamburgers and french fries and chocolate milk and cantaloupe. Now if he'd been offered that menu at home he would probably have eaten the fries and chocolate milk and spurned the rest. He's enjoying it just a wee bit too much and we're having to start early in stressing the importance of doing his in-class assignments! Brian is working part-time as a "salad man" at a restaurant and part-time as fill-in casual labour at the Post Office. I mentioned that he might take the Civil Service or Post Office test so he could get a permanent job in that line, but he doesn't seem keen, which makes me a tad frustrated (again) with him.

The Maranatha Center at the University of New Mexico, a Christian organization, seemed to give Brian some support after he moved out, and following his latest relationship. This sounded like a moderately good thing to me. But when he went to visit England in 1991 he didn't return. I was sad to see him go, but we all realized it was the best thing to do. He had completed those two years of high school, and was happy with that. He had dual nationality so could come back when he wished. But his home was in Kent. He wrote to his grandparents on March 22, happy to be living on Shorncliffe Road again. "Mum's doing a lot better now, and I'm really happy I came."

Soon after Brian left Albuquerque, Jocelyn had written me a wonderfully wise letter:

I'm sorry you were so upset about Brian's leaving. I'm not going to say "It's O.K., my brother has a fine mind," but I will say that he has a mind of his own and you just have to accept it. But you're right; the way he left you does seem to have been callous especially since you have tried so hard. Brian is 20 now. When he came to you he was already 16. Some kids have left home, got a job and even got married by then and it still works out.

Just think, I'm 18 and still not married!

What I am saying is that most children's characters have been formed by about 16 and that their ideas are their own. They should (should I say we?) have also the angry arrogance of youth which can sometimes turn to anarchy under pressure, however slight. I do sympathise with you and I often wonder what sort of luck landed you with two sons – I should say a son and a daughter – in such a short space even with their own joys and sorrows for completely different reasons.

All in all, I'm pleased Brian has left home. Hopefully, now that you are not reminding each other of your respective faults each day, you and he will realise one another's merits.

How blessed I have been by these children!

Not long afterwards I wrote Brian a letter containing what I hoped would be encouraging and motivating words. It was a hard task, and took a long time to write. But how do you write effectively to someone who seldom takes your advice?

Pleased to hear that you are finding life in Folkestone to your liking. You'll be 25 in September and you have your General Certificate of Secondary Education; also, you finished high school in the U.S. and have a diploma to prove it. Regarding school – let's think about education. First you need to really have some passion for the subjects you hope to learn more about. What should you study? I think the best thing you can do is figure out what trade would suit you best, and take courses in that trade, at Dover College or wherever. The main thing is that you should position yourself to earn a decent living at a regular job. That means knowing about the job, either from school training or from learning on-the-job. It also means being able to adapt yourself to the system that exists in the place where you work, and being able to create an on-going constructive relationship with the people where you work. Always work as hard as they do or they will resent you. Always do your job the way the boss wants it done (there will be times when you don't like it but after all he pays you), and then help your mates to do their jobs if and when you have the time.

It might be a good idea to talk to someone at the Job Centre, or a similar place, and get their ideas. That's really the very best advice I can give you. Ask what they suggest and perhaps you can go to school and get some ££ at the same time. The best of all solution would be to have a low-ranked job in the type of business that interests you, and to go to school at the same time with the hope that you get a promotion as your studies continue. Problem is that this would mean making a big change in your life style. You need to make sure that you get enough sleep! Turn off the TV after the 9 o'clock news and go to sleep! Your performance is very much better when you get enough sleep. We've lived together and I know this makes a big difference in you. But for everyone, resting the mind regularly is absolutely essential if we want to be able to study effectively, or if we want to do well at work. Exercise is important too, but I doubt if this is a problem for you.

Writing to Gerold and Valerie Bishop, by contrast, was an easy and enjoyable task, even when the news wasn't one hundred per cent good. I suppose the letter was a catharsis of sorts, writing to this couple whom I cared for so much, far away in their miniature Gloucestershire farm.

Sept. 4, 1991, to Gerry and Val – Jonathan is in his second year of state school and we are in our second year of fretting about it. We feel the teachers are letting him coast while the others try to catch up – instead of giving him individualized attention. We would put him into a private school that we like, though it would cost us £3200 a year (without the extras), but they haven't any room. So the battle goes on. We meet with the headmistress and a counsellor on Monday morning to go over Jonathan's apparent reluctance to go to school... The science editor of The Economist, *Oliver Morton, is visiting at the end of this month, I'm midwifing articles being produced by* Business Week, Time, *and* The Christian Science Monitor, *and the natives are restless around Sandia's rocket range in Hawaii. And so on ...*

As ever, the natural world offered its own kind of purification, calming the wild and unrelenting surges of events that invaded my mind from two continents, all demanding some kind of practical response. But nature is not always kind.

Nov. 27, 1991 – The horizon is crowded with mares' tails. A sulky wind is blowing through a treescape dabbed here and there with orange and umber, and belt lightning is snaking over the West Mesa. The first cranes flew south over the house this morning, and juncos have come down from the mountains to forage outside my window. I came home, and the wind had blown open the front door, sending leaves scampering across the brick floor inside. Cold winter hands are tugging at my father too. I see his shrinking figure on the couch, panting now and then, dentures uneasy on the shrunken jaw, and see his robust earlier self superimposed, the large shadow of manhood behind him now, his ironic smile. Behind my understanding and my philosophy, I weep.

Then came delight in the person of Jocelyn, who flew alone from England to spend Christmas with us. It had been a difficult year, and her presence would heal some of the worries and sadnesses that had accompanied the twelve months of 1991.

Dec. 28, 1991 – Jocelyn and I set out for San Felipe Pueblo shortly after 11 p.m. on Christmas Eve, hoping to attend a traditional Roman Catholic Midnight Mass at the mission church. It was a cold, crisp, dark night. We looked for the torches of stacked wood, correctly called luminarias, that sometimes light the way to the old churches on Christmas Eve, but there were none. It was very dark, and when we left the car there was absolute, eerie silence except for a drumbeat and chanting, faintly, somewhere in a distant kiva. We made our way reverently to the old mission church, which was decorated with coloured lights above the entryway, and joined the others who were walking through the bare-earth churchyard. The doorway beckoned, and the promise of refuge from frigid winter air. I wondered if the Mass would be said in English, Spanish, or Latin. Then without warning there was a rush of sound behind us. We turned to see costumed, painted Indian men crowding through the churchyard gate. Behind them were more, dressed in homespun wool, feathers, and evergreen sprigs. Behind them, still more. There were scores of men, a long line extending into the gloom beyond the soft lights that now glowed around the church. As they came closer we saw they were dressed as warriors, carrying bows and arrows, chanting a song or prayer to the insistent beat of the drum. Later, buffalo and antelope, or at least their human representations, were coming into the churchyard, followed by a chorus of pueblo elders. We squeezed into the church, huddled closely in a great crowd of Indians and a few whites. We couldn't see well, but had a fairly good view of the chorus, toward the back of the church, and could see animal horns appearing and receding as a vigorous dance proceeded in the middle of the church, from which the seats had been removed. At the far end, when I stood on tiptoes, I could see a Christmas crèche had been put up in front of the figure of St. Philip and those of the Virgin Mary and Christ. A padre in white was watching the proceedings impassively.

At one point the congregation broke into laughter at something we couldn't see. The dance continued. The faithful were taking communion. The padre kept his position. More laughter. Then we saw two clowns with mud-coloured be-bobbled skullcaps and face paint. They capered and made jokes in the local language and made the crowd laugh, and then they too took communion and the service was over. Up to now all of this had been quite un-churchlike to our eyes and ears. Then most of the crowd dispersed; the remainder formed a line to go up and pay respects to the baby Jesus, which was swaddled in a thick blanket in the crèche. A young mother suckled a real baby on the step below the pulpit. As if by arrangement, everything rather abruptly turned very casual. The atmosphere became like a church hall somewhere far way from Indian land. Someone said casually that there would be an ordinary Catholic mass in the morning.

⁂

In January 1992, after serving as Sandia's PR division supervisor in charge of media relations continuously for nearly ten years, I was transferred to the President's support office as temporary head of management information. Our president, Al Narath, who had been reminded from Washington that his office had become somewhat ill-informed about national and world events of interest to the Department of Energy and its labs, decided quite rightly that something had to be done about it. I suspected that he had been embarrassed by a call for information from DOE Secretary Watkins' office; maybe the secretary himself. So I was nominated to fix the problem.

My job was to produce a Senior Management Staff Bulletin, produced after combing various information resources for external news of import to Sandia management. Oddly, because it was the only space available, I was given a secure vault, built for the storage of classified information, as an office. It had a lock with a secret combination, and required special training, and documentation, for its use. This vault was no catacomb, but a fourth-floor office with a view that stretched magnificently all the way from Tijeras Canyon in the east to Mount Taylor, ninety miles to the west.

Jim Mitchell had just retired, so the PR office was decimated – neither of us was replaced. Fortunately I was still able to do some national media work, which I enjoyed, "in my spare time," along with promoting advanced manufacturing technology through Sandia and the Iacocca Institute.

In 1992, I circulated a note to the PR staff asking if any would like to try a newfangled but interesting CompuServe service called email. To my surprise I had only two takers. Not long after that, I asked my colleague Larry Perrine to write a feasibility report for the creation of a public website for Sandia. As that project took shape I reflected on my good fortune in being involved so closely in a giant revolution, from the days of Linotypes and flat-bed presses to "cold type" printing, to the transformational electronic media that might eventually crowd out the once-revered fourth-estate world of newspapering, and with it, without doubt, the profession of journalism as I knew it.

17. FINDING DEE

We sometimes encounter people, even perfect strangers, who begin to interest us at first sight, somehow suddenly, all at once, before a word has been spoken.
— Fyodor Dostoevsky

By mid-September 1996, my life seemed to be stitching itself together, while my parents' lives, in poignant counterpoint, were falling apart.

In a letter to Jocelyn I told her that her grandparents were doing all right, considering they were now aged 88 and 89. But this was only relatively true. Though he remained mentally bright my father had become very weak and his sight was failing quickly, and he had to give up driving. His doctor found he had a bleeding ulcer, and with medication he seemed to be getting a little stronger. When he and my mother came over for dinner I had to put his chair close to the TV to watch the Formula 1 racing. Soon a visiting nurse was making regular visits to check his vital signs and blood sugar content. Naturally he was depressed by these inescapable realities of advanced age, and I am sure he knew that he would have to move soon to a nursing home.

Jonathan was still not doing very well academically at Bosque School, though in all other ways he showed promise of becoming an unusually fine young man. His grades were consistently poor, and while his teachers genuinely liked him, they had to report that he had been disruptive and unfocused in class. Sue and I were both confused and perplexed that he *appeared* to be doing homework, and *said* he was doing it, but report cards time after time said that he was chronically behind. After a school meeting in the early spring of 1997, headmaster Gary Gruber, whom I greatly respected as an educator, told me pointedly that some kids "need a swift kick up the backside." I didn't appreciate that comment at the time. The next morning I talked with Jonathan for about ten minutes about his poor performance and his need to start acting like a responsible young man rather than a child who needs to be encouraged and badgered all the time. And so on. I spoke vehemently because I feel passionately about the need for a strong academic preparation for later life, and the need to be a responsible individual, and I raised my voice. Of course I didn't strike him, but this was metaphorically the "kick up the backside" that Gruber was talking about.

When things were not going well during the sad times of the mid-1990s I sought solace touring the back country of New Mexico, alone or with Jonathan for weekends near Grants and Las Vegas, New Mexico. But on Good Friday, 1997, I took off with my friend George, adventuring to the other side of Santa Fe, where the first of tens of thousands of people were crowding into the village of Chimayó and the Church of San Esquípulas.

Pilgrims had been following the roads on foot all week to this small town in the foothills of the snow-capped Sangre de Cristo mountains, a few of them barefoot and carrying huge crosses. I had a chat with George about this custom, and told him I wanted to take him up on his promise to show me the mysterious pit of "holy dirt" that was the focus of the pilgrimage.

We drove through Santa Fe and at Española left the main highway for the high road to Taos, which traces a waving path through a series of atmospheric old towns and hamlets along the hilly western shoulders of the Sangre de Cristo Mountains. After the first mile, the road began to dip into and out of arroyos, across dry fords, and we passed through the leafy Villa Nueva de Santa Cruz de la Cañada. The village, now known simply as Santa Cruz, was established originally in 1695. Its picturesque adobe church, once a center for the flagellant Penitente "Brothers of the Light," is home to some of the oldest native religious art in the state.

We wound our way along country roads into higher ground and on our approach to Chimayó passed artisans' shops where colourful weavings are produced by hand on horizontal looms of ancient design. The sanctuary proved to be a handsome little adobe chapel with twin bell-towers, with a small walled churchyard in front, built by Don Bernardo Abeyta in 1816. It looked out from a mountainous setting on the edge of an arroyo, with a picnic ground that was overlooked by a statue of Christ on the Cross, wearing a real crown of thorns and garlanded with glass rosaries placed there by pilgrims.

A queue snaked out from the roadside, through an adobe entranceway, and disappeared into the rustic church which, George said, was the repository of the Holy Dirt. So we stood in line too, inching forward with other visitors – men in straw western hats, children with pink plumes of spun candy, mothers pushing their pushchairs, and young tattooed men in their muscle shirts. After transiting the small churchyard we walked slowly toward the altar between pews and four large baroque panels of paintings and statuary. Following the increasingly grave procession of men, women, and children, we ducked into a doorway to the left of the altar and through an even smaller doorway that gave entry to the shrine itself.

This was an amazingly simple place, not much more than a very small circular *potito* well in the earthen floor with a sign above: "Please! Only small amounts of Holy Dirt per family." I followed the example of the people who had gone before and knelt beside the bucket-sized depression in the floor, rubbing my hands in the cool, moist, grainy sand and rather awkwardly ad-libbing a small prayer.

We filed out between rough walls lined with dusty crutches and splints, yellowed thank-you notes and artistic expressions of gratitude and devotion. Outside, the brilliant mountain-country sun made our eyes ache.

Near the road the crowd had thickened around a large, shiny car near the entry to the little plaza. Not just a car, it was an immaculate piece of art, a low-rider decorated all over with religious paintings airbrushed in vivid colours. The vehicle likely came from Española, a town famed for these large, low-slung, customized vehicles fitted with special hydraulic pumps and cylinders that allow them (and this can be disconcerting for a visitor who draws up beside one at a traffic light) to hop up and down on their rear wheels. These machines typically have velvety interiors, smoked windows, huge stereos, and steering wheels fashioned from chrome plated chain, maybe with a pair of fluffy dice hanging from the rear-view mirror. They are produced with dedication and devotion by true aficionados. While this is proudly a specialty of talented Hispanic youth, I knew that several middle-aged Anglos were engaged in very much the same avocation, minus the religious paintings.

The sanctuary at Chimayó has a curious and indistinct history, though its lineage traces back to the early days of the *conquistadores* and a shrine in the town of Esquípulas in south-eastern Guatemala, named for a brave and virtuous Indian hero. In the nearby mountains, clay is fashioned into tablets that is blessed by local priests and eaten for the treatment of illness (pointedly discouraged by the Chimayó priests). Interestingly, the locally revered Santo Niño de Atocha also became associated with the healing powers of Esquípulas, perhaps at the incentive of local clerics at the turn of the eighteenth century. "Even the saints are subject to social pressure when they are introduced to a foreign area," commented the anthropologist Stephen F. de Borhegyi. In view of this, he continued, it is not surprising that while local knowledge of Our Lord of Esquípulas eventually became obscure, "the native idea of the healing powers of the earth, in existence long before the advent of the Spaniards, has remained intact in Chimayó."[30]

After leaving the sanctuary precincts, we turned down a rutted alleyway and into an out-of-the-way compound that I later learned was the last intact fortified plaza in the state. All the buildings were joined together, so the plaza could easily be sealed off. Perhaps this happened in 1837, when local residents rebelled against the oppressive Mexican provincial government and assassinated Governor Albino Pérez.

It was a quiet place, overgrown, shaded with trees, parts of the stuccoed buildings cracked so you could see their adobe bricks, melting back to the earth. The only signs of life were a man and his dog, loading something into a pickup truck on the south side of the plaza. He saw us enter from the northeast corner and gestured with a firmness that needed no interpretation: *keep out! go away!*

We drove homeward, downhill and across the arroyos of Chimayó and Santa Cruz, and I remarked what a wonderful corner of the world this was, a bubble of colonial Spanish culture hidden away in the New Mexico mountains, still following the old ways. My friend was not impressed. "At Lourdes you get to drink from pure spring water according to the wishes of St. Bernadette," he said. "Here, all you get to do is rub your hands together in a cupful of dirt that has been dumped in a hole in the ground by a grimy old priest." I preferred not to answer. If pilgrims found the ritual helpful, that seemed fair enough to me.

The old customs are alive almost everywhere in New Mexico, from Mesilla in the south to Mora in the north, spilling over onto the south-eastern edge of Colorado. Old customs, old language traits, old art-forms are jealously guarded in out-of-the-way communities seldom seen by the north-European types who mostly arrived since the 1930s. Matachine dances, originally imported to Spain and then Mexico by Islamic Moors who first moved into the Iberian Peninsula in the eighth century, commemorate Hernán Cortés, who defeated the Aztec empire in the early sixteenth century. The *penitentes*, who also have Spanish roots, kept the Catholic faith vibrant during a time that the established church was not fully represented in New Mexico. Ancient passion plays like Los Pastores and La Posada appear on the calendars of small churches at Christmas. The devout still crawl from the doors to the altars of such churches at Easter, in atonement for their sins. On Good Friday, men still will carry heavy crosses for fifty miles and more, to Chimayó, Tomé, and no doubt other shrines that I have not heard of. And artists still paint religious paintings of the saints, and carve *bulto* statues of those saints from cottonwood root, to prove that Archbishop Lamy did not stamp them out when he arrived in Santa Fe in 1875 and, when the railway arrived three years later, encouraged the replacement of such expressions of devotion with imported oleographs and plaster-of-Paris casts.

Some time later, after I was recovering from an illness, our friend Barbara Dillon sent me a gift of Holy Dirt from Chimayó, wrapped within an attractive primrose-yellow cloth printed with a simple design in chocolate brown. It occurred to me that it was the kind of thing one might wear on one's belt, like a medicine pouch. At first I thought the dirt must be compacted or even made into a clay and baked, since it was round and hard to my touch. When I removed the cloth I saw that the reddish, micacious grains were enclosed within a salt-shaker the shape of a small electric light globe. How original! An accompanying flyer specified that "the Holy dirt is not to be eaten or drunk" but instead one should "rub the holy dirt over the part of your body in need of healing while you invoke the name of Jesus as your Lord and Savior." It must have worked. The illness did not return.

⊛

Back at the ranch, I had adjusted to bachelor life. I was fairly well prepared, having learned the basics of cooking and housekeeping, and had hired a lady named Socorro – appropriately the Spanish word for "help" – to do a morning of laundry and cleaning every other week.

I was busy at work, so there was no time for brooding, but still I felt the need for female company. Most women I knew were married, but still there was a large pool of prospects at Sandia and my pride did not stop me from advertising for companionship. The latter proved to be an interesting and educative experiment that at times saw me lurching perilously between one potential disaster and another.

Mostly I was interested in finding a pleasant woman who shared some of my interests, was not looking for financial aid, and, in the parlance, would be fun to "hang out with." In some respects, my interest in sex was more aesthetic than anatomical. To my mind the "primary" sexual bits and pieces are not visually appealing in either sex, but I did like the perfume, shape, and touch that seems to be the birthright of a healthy woman.

This is not to say that I had no fondness for the looks of women, clothed or otherwise. To the contrary. I could run my eyes over Helen's naked form with a delight that was hardly sexual at all. I was entranced by the counterpoint of her bodily shapes, particularly where the straight line of her tapering rib-cage met the curvature of her hip – visual music! On some Sunday mornings the light would come through the bedroom window just right, so that this special beauty was enhanced by early sunlight, and the fine hairs of her skin glowed like golden satin. Helen, being perfectly accustomed to seeing what she looked like in the raw, unclothed, probably thought I was nutty when she listened to me warbling on about the glories of this visual feast. But for some months, until I realized that perhaps I *was* behaving rather wacky even though I didn't know why, life was made happier by my visual explorations of Helen's lovely body.

Some women (and men) look a lot better in clothes than without, despite the fact that their would-be paramours are so anxious to remove them. Helen looked great with or without. And then there was Clare, a pre-Helen friend who was a writer and PR consultant and definitely a member of the first category. When Clare first snuggled into my bed late one autumn evening, the experience proved entirely different from a morning with Helen. I liked Clare well enough – she was bright and humorous, and good company. But in her case my peculiar preference for small-breasted women kept pushing into the scenario. Clare's breasts were enormous, with the warmth and texture of bread dough just before baking. There were moments that night when I felt like one of the fabled young princes in the Tower of London, in the final moments of their suffocation at the hands of Richard III's minions. And so I was not distressed when I heard her verbal post-mortem, delivered by telephone the next day, ending the affair with the comment that, as a couple, we didn't quite fit.

I have thought of my lack of appreciation for Clare's physique a number of times since then, and self-rebuke follows quickly. My reaction may have in some sense been "normal," but it offends me nevertheless. What peculiarity of modern taste and fashion brought it about?

There were other women, and times when I observed to myself, rather worriedly, that "it would be so easy to fall in love with this person." More often than not my mind would wander off rather erratically on this general theme, realizing that if one is not careful such attachments can morph into a strange narcosis, leading almost inevitably to the bliss of sexual union and then to dependency. Horrors! Or Yes please! Generally I quenched these romantic excursions with the rationale that this sort of mental claptrap is most likely a vestige of the outdated need to increase our kind, costumed in the romanticism that only humans can perceive. Sometimes I believed it.

Thousands of women worked at Sandia, a fair number were single, and a much smaller number were unattached. Soon after I began living alone I remember meeting a young divorcée at the lab's club one Friday night, and there followed a zealous but fortunately brief encounter from which I learned that she was considerably more interested in me than I was in her.

In two and a half decades at Sandia only two women truly broke out into my world of lab-centered planning, writing, meeting and reporting. This was not because I was looking for anyone – they just appeared. There was Marilyn, far better educated and more refined than the girl I had met in the club, who had recently ended a bad marriage. We had met a few times on company business, and two or three of these had led to exchanges of personal conversation. Then one morning by chance I saw her talking with a couple of male colleagues, simply standing in relaxed conversation outside one of the administrative buildings. She was probably thirty yards away, but something about her attracted me, strongly. She waved and went back to talking and I thought *wow*! What on earth caused that reaction in me? Was it the way she was standing, her gestures, the way she looked, the smile when she waved? Surely not. Maybe it was the remembrance of some personal confidence she had shared with me, and the way she had looked at the time, large-eyed and frail. And needful, the most dangerous attraction of all.

The thing about Marilyn was that we could talk easily together, on and on, about everything from cats to sex. Eventually we started meeting for lunch or dinner, pleasant occasions in which conversation was always a great deal more important than the food. I wondered about my physical attraction to her. Nobody had ever affected me that way before.

One night we went to her house for a cup of tea after we had been out for dinner. I talked about our relationship and she said if we ever got married she would make me go crazy, or something else that meant she thought it wouldn't work. I met her three fine children, all of whom had left home by now, and she had Sunday dinner with my parents and me. The friendship continued.

One morning I met her at the entrance of her office building. She was waiting, and from a distance I was captivated by the way the sun was catching this picture of her in my mind's eye. Again something quite mysterious happened and she looked extraordinarily beautiful. Because I was so mystified by the energy of this remarkable mental snapshot, I told her about it. As a scientist she might be able to suggest how it happened. But reasonably enough she could offer no answer.

Much later I decided Marilyn was right: a closer relationship wouldn't have worked. I liked her mind and her looks, and we shared an interest in gardening, travel, wildlife, and domestic animals (though I had difficulty with the cat dander and did not enjoy watching her feed dead chicks to the family's pet snake). She had been badly scarred by her marriage, and from my private viewpoint she was somewhat untidy and, again, she harboured the source of the worst of all my allergies, cats. When I moved to an office farther from hers we drifted apart. I remained mystified by the way she had caught my interest and desire, on those two mornings in New Mexico. Oddly as the years went on, sometimes when walking, or when watching TV or a movie, there were times that I was reminded of her. On all those years we had come close, but we never kissed.

Marilyn was one of only two women I found extremely attractive in all of my years as a Sandia full-timer (numerous others were merely attractive). The other, a tall, striking brunette, married the company president before we even had chance to have lunch together. I consoled myself with the idea that I must have good taste in women.

⬥

The summer of 1997 rolled around, after a period in which I concentrated on Sandia work and did very little socializing. Finally I put an ad in the romance columns, which introduced me to a few available women, the most interesting of whom was a tall Navajo who was educated, well-travelled, and physically striking, but whose cultural background was so different that after a couple of dates I backed off, feeling both defeated and disappointed.

I had been divorced and living alone for a few years when my neighbour Patti Puckett phoned with a suggestion. How would I like to meet a very attractive lady who lived a short distance away and might appreciate meeting someone new? Why not?

I was intrigued by Patti's suggestion and immediately invited Dee for tea.

She was attractive, well-dressed, and seemed to be highly intelligent, and so I was interested. We dated and had some delicious meals at her beautifully kept townhouse, and I learned more great things about this lady. She was a native of the Missouri Ozark Mountains and a recent retiree from Albuquerque Public Schools, where she had taught before joining the administrative staff as a curriculum advisor. She was also thoughtful and rather private, while being at the same time endowed with a high-energy, bubbly personality and an unusually kind and generous attitude toward her fellow beings. She was licensed to practice T'ai Chi Chih and reflexology, loved fluffy animals, and disliked the creepy-crawly kind. One evening on her patio we left all of this behind and shared our ideas and insights on life.

Sharing the insight! The most precious "insight" was something spiritual that I suspected I should keep to myself. I thought that nobody, or almost nobody, shared it and that my impressions were somehow strange. In fact I seldom if ever talked about it, even to Mim or Sue, believing it to be mostly indescribable; thus any influence it might have had on my relationship with others was very, very indirect. In retrospect I am sure my father was similarly inclined. But now my reticence was thrown to the winds, the insight broke out of me, I talked about it, and its sentiments were reciprocated. It was one of those once-a-generation happenings. To think I had found such a person brought me great joy.

Dee's house was always neat and tidy, and she cooked wonderful, healthy meals, introducing me to such delights as orange salad and cooked kale salad, served on her little patio with its rose garden and commanding apple tree. She was also affectionate, and after many emotionally barren years I rejoiced in it.

⟨⟩

By 1999 the idea of writing a book about SDI had become irresistible, and one day, when I had a few minutes to spare at Sandia's Washington office, I called Adm. James Watkins, who had been the Navy member of the Joint Chiefs of Staff in 1982-86, during the early SDI years, and previous to that the Secretary of Energy (1989-93). After a brief conversation, he said it was high time someone wrote "the real story about SDI" in a way that ordinary people could understand. We talked for an hour more and I was convinced. A few months later, I knocked on Edward Teller's door in Stanford and started what would end up as thousands of words of interviews with people in the United States, Russia, and Britain.

Jocelyn was making her own new life over in London. In the winter of 1998-99 the back of the house at Mare Street still was unfinished except for a few square yards of "sunken garden" outside the light well (the basement back window). It was a sad-looking, rubbly picture, for both she and Dave were keen gardeners – Dave had earned a living doing just that, briefly, at the London Zoo, and in early December Joss had started a job as gardener at St. Joseph's Hospice, a few hundred yards away. On January 4, 1999 she wrote an exuberant letter to my mother, thanking her for a Christmas check and saying she would spend it all on plants and seeds. "We have such plans!" She even added a diagram showing their idea for developing their small patch of ground, complete with gravel walk, fountain, trellis, and flowerbeds.

Victorian scene. Jocelyn, always partial to long skirts, readies
herself to run bicycle errands in Hackney.

"I have just been paid money for my new job and am amazed and afeared that they have made a mistake," she added, half-jokingly. "All I do is gardening, you know. At this time of year I'm hard pressed to find things to do, and have been fiddling about with the paths, pulling out tiny blades of grass. I do three short, six-hour days a week, and they have paid me £750 for the month. Hope they don't ask for it back!"

All of this activity was eclipsed by the grand event that closed the year 2000. In London at 2.45 on the morning of December 19, my worn-out but jubilant son-in-law sat down at his computer and tapped out a news bulletin to my mother, Sue, Jonathan, and me: *"It's a boy!"*

It had been a very long delivery, the process starting when Jocelyn's waters, already overdue, broke during a carol singing practice on the night of Sunday, December 17. The labour lasted twenty-six and a half hours, until 9:23 p.m. the next day, December 18. Finally Edward had arrived!

"When he arrived, Jocelyn was almost completely exhausted but still pushing like a Hero Mother of the USSR," Dave wrote. "The cord was completely wrapped about his neck, twice. It looked like a scarf: no wonder he didn't want to come out. Five pairs of doctors' and midwives' hands lurched in unison to rotate him and unwrap the cord. I was sponging Jocelyn's forehead like a pro and we were both in tears at the release of all the tension – plus we were knackered!"

So much for Jocelyn's unfulfilled wish to have her first baby at home. But at last I was a grandfather!

In a few months I had another email from Dave. "Jocelyn and I were thinking of bringing Eddie over to visit the family in the late summer. Would it be convenient to stay with you for the middle two weeks of September, something like the 8th to the 23rd?"

Would it be all right? No, it would be marvellous! Joss and Dave brought Eddie to New Mexico, with friend Andy Willoughby in tow for company and to help with logistics, and I showed off my new grandson with shameless pride.

Apart from my parents and Jonathan, the things that kept me in New Mexico had been the weather, the standard and cost of living, the then-unknown standard of British medical care, and, after retirement, the important source of additional income provided by my consultancy. Dee was added to this list of reasons to stay put soon after we met in early 1997. By 1999 she had become a staunch friend, traveling companion, and overall important person in my life – and she lived in Albuquerque. She was an unusually kind and generous person, trustworthy, and she shared my fondness for animals. Very soon after that first meeting, she and I had several deep conversations, touching often on the spiritual, so that I was elated by the prospect that I had found a soul mate, someone I could trust and perhaps spend the rest of my life with.

My connection with England increased around the time I retired – no more full-time commitments in New Mexico! More time for personal relationships! More time to spend with the family in England! But first I decided to sell the Wilsden house. I made this decision with some regret because of my long and pleasant acquaintance with the place, but followed through with the sale in early 2001. I had renovated its stone roof and installed double glazing, but the house was still draughty and cold and badly needed new wiring, new plumbing, and effective protection against the damp. To make things worse (and irremediable), the front door was not much more than a foot from the paved road, where cars and heavy vehicles would race at speed on the back road from Bradford to Keighley, shaking the foundations and, in the winter, throwing salt against the door. It simply made good sense to sell the house at Lane Side.

The English connection increased in step with the increase of my London family – beginning with Jocelyn and David's marriage, continuing with their residence at 16 Mare Street (officially blessed on March 13, 1999), with Eddie's birth, Brian's proximity, and my determination to buy a nearby flat.

I had fancied myself as an international type in the past, and the dream was coming true. Not many years would pass before I would be spending a quarter of my time based in London.

18. RITES OF PASSAGE

Sometimes the poorest man leaves his children the richest inheritance.
— Ruth E. Renkel

My mother did an indescribably heroic job of caring for my dad in the mid-1990s, single-handedly and without any mention of it. She never let us know about her behind-the scenes work. This meant that, though I should have been sensitive enough to figure it out, I was all but ignorant of the drama that had visited their lives. When I eventually learned of it, and my imagination re-enacted those scenes, I reflected how many countless acts of difficult, selfless kindness and devotion must be playing out continuously throughout the dramas of human life, by all sorts of people, often behind closed doors and shuttered windows, generally unknown by others and unrecognized.

Dad had congestive heart failure now, and eventually, despite my urgings, could not summon the strength even to take little walks around the little group of town-houses where they lived. Finally I took him to a "rehabilitation care" facility, knowing in my heart that he would never see his little home again. I also knew that he and my mother realized that this was a distinct possibility.

I would go to the nursing home and help coax dad through physical therapy, and then the best I could do was wheel him out into the fresh air, which I knew pleased and comforted him though he usually was too weak to say so. One day my Sandia friend Merrie Rockwell came to see him at his nursing home bed. His waxy brown hand came out from under the covers and took hers. "I do want to live," he said. There was a little pause. "You're going to a better place," she replied softly, and it seemed to help.

During this I was also going through my regular routine of working at Sandia and watching over Jonathan's affairs while keeping tabs on my kids in London and Folkestone. I was in Washington, having lunch with Paul Robinson, Sandia's president, when his cell phone rang. Paul exchanged a few words with whoever it was and handed the phone to me. It was the nursing home. My father had died. It was July 25, 1997. I should have been there.

256

I read these words at his memorial, which was fittingly a Masonic service, held at a local Presbyterian church:

This is to celebrate the life of the most wonderful man I ever knew or ever will know.

I am proud that Aaron Hey was my father and indeed is my father, for he still lives within me and I pray that his spirit – what he is – will live on within my children and their children. He and my mother Margery were born to ordinary West Yorkshire families, neither upper class nor lower class, in days when there was no radio, no airplanes, no computers, few telephones and few cars, and before there had been any world wars.

There are not many like him left in this day and age. He had an eighth grade education. His early career was in the textile industry in Yorkshire then in Canada, where my mother-to-be joined him and they were married sixty-six years ago...

When my asthma didn't improve in the south of England he brought us to Utah, and we all studied hard and went before the judge and became American citizens.

By now my father was over forty. He started a new life at the local U.S. Steel plant. He became a fully fledged industrial engineer, and developed computer programs for time studies, and he stayed there until he retired [on April 30, 1970]. And at this point of his life he demonstrated at last that the American dream can still come true...

My father did not accomplish all these wonderful things through domineering ambition. He did them ... through quiet determination and keenly focused intelligence. He had sublime vision – he believed that good things could happen; he believed in people. And there was fun, too. He sang in Eisteddfods, played in Gilbert and Sullivan, directed a choir in the American Fork Presbyterian Church, and sang still more. He loved music.

He was a polite man. A genteel man, self-taught and loved by all those who knew him well. Above all an ethical man. An excellent father not because of the lectures

*he delivered, or the scoldings, or his transliterations of the Bible and the Classics…
My observations of my father's life were lessons enough, for we lived closely
together in my formative years, and I came to believe that my greatest life success
would come in successful emulation of his ways.*

*My mother was always there, supportive, kind, tirelessly helpful as she is today. It
seems neither she nor my father ever told me what to do when I was a child,
though of course they must have done… They willed me to be what I am, and
when I left home for university at age seventeen they did not try to hold on. They
taught me by an endless succession of good examples.*

*Few know that my father was a deeply spiritual man, though he grew up in the
ways of the Chapel at home in Yorkshire. He prayed on his knees beside his bed,
like a child, until after his eightieth birthday. To the end he never approved of my
going to the store or to a movie on the Sabbath. Nor did he condemn those who
did…*

*It is a time for celebration that such a man lived to share his outlook, his personality,
his goodness, with those of us who knew and loved him. I raise my glass to my
father, I celebrate him as he was and as the spirit and memory that he is.*

My mother soldiered on, and I helped and kept her company when I could,
stopping by after work and chatting, and sharing a meal now and then. She was
determined to be tough, and to maintain a parental distance that seemed rather
Victorian, which was both maddening and saddening because I wanted to be
closer to her, especially now that she was alone. I knew she would not have to
work so hard if she would let me help. Eventually she gave in, reluctantly. But
sadly she could not let go of the distant-parent role, even though I had passed
beyond my middle years.

Jonathan and I took my Dad's ashes up to Yorkshire, past Bolton Abbey,
which he loved so much, driving up onto the moorland above the lovely little
village of Appletreewick. It was a sunny, breezy day, and the windswept grass was
dotted into the distance with grazing sheep. We took the car through a break in
the lichened dry-stone wall and into a deserted little parking area. I got out,
clutching the little box with the plastic bag inside that contained all that
remained of my father's mortal self, and a strange thing happened. Impulsively I

untied the bag and ran around the field with it, holding it high like a torch, letting the ashes fly in a great free cloud behind and around me. I skipped and jumped and capered among the tussocks of grass.

There were a few motes of ash in my hair when I got back to the car with the empty bag. I was oddly euphoric, and Jonathan quite understandably was amazed. Perhaps without thinking it I had for those few moments become a dervish, lost with my father in the mystery that we call God.

Soon after that, I discovered a poem that my dad had written. I realized I could have written myself, and in reading it understood the bond that was between us and which will perhaps continue through our family. He had titled it "To the seeker after beauty."

The quest for beauty you pursue
Needs not to call for fields anew.
For beauty fair doth here abound
In sea and air, on humble ground.

Give me the scent of new-mown hay,
The hawthorn clothed in robe of May.
A web star-spangled by the dew,
It's beauty seen by all too few.

The roseate hues of sunset warm,
Which all too oft foretell of storm.
The beauty of a gull in flight,
The fragrant rain of a Summer's night.

The mirror'd lake, the mountains great,
The onward rush of a stream in spate.
The scented beauty of a rosy bower,
Or the simple charm of some lovely flower.

The mountain eagle's upward soar,
Or whirr of grouse on lonely moor.
The winging curlew's plaintive cry,
Or the song of a lark as he spirals high.

The heavy scent of woodland brown,
When Autumn softens Winter's frown.
Or Spring's eternal promise fair,
And sense of Summer in the air.

These woods, these hills, this verdant sod
Where countless searching feet have trod.
My seeking friend, your quest is o'er,
For beauty's here, what want you more?
                    A.H.

I imagined that the poem was a message my father had written to me, perhaps to compensate for the too-quiet, too-reserved relationship that I had shared with both parents. It was an affirmation not of estrangement, but of love. My father was me, and he I. How I wish he were here now, I thought, to talk of such things together! But, except for the memories, the uncompromising door of death had sealed our lives forever apart.

Were it not for my father's absence, and despite the divorce, Christmas 1997 was the kind of holiday one should have. On Christmas Day I had the turkey half-roasted before Sue arrived with my mother and Jonathan, and logs that he had split were burning in the open hearth. They came burdened with presents and food – a pumpkin pie from Jonathan and Sue (he baked it) and mince pies and cranberry dressing from my mother.

December 27, 1997, to the London family – This Christmas was very different because your grandfather was not here. I dreamed last night that he had not died at all, but somehow and for who knows what reason had escaped the nursing home and gone into hiding! My mind has been going a bit metaphysical and someday, who knows, may come to accept the idea of souls and spirits out there, communicating with us. I'm not there yet, but the idea is less bizarre than it has been in the past. I have missed Jonathan since the divorce, but it's been great to have him spending every other week with me. He's almost exactly my height now and wearing hand-me-downs when I can get him out of his beloved favourite rags. I think your grandmother is recovering remarkably well from her loss, but she grieves a lot more than she admits and as you know she is a bit frail and, after all, she too will be 90 next July 6. Sue is doing pretty well, I think, having put together a suite of part-

time theatre-oriented jobs that she likes, and would be physically in good health were it not for intractable dermatitis on her hands and feet. She and Jonathan did a super job of remodelling her house; the two of them put up cabinetwork for the whole kitchen, with kits, and it looks great. In five years' time I expect to retire, for Jonathan will be launched into university life by then. Publishing a successful book could make an earlier retirement possible, but that's a long shot even though my New Mexico book (140,000 words!) is completed and being critiqued by people I know locally. I will enter it in a SouthWest Writers Association contest this spring, and this will bring it to the attention of agents and publishers and we'll see where it goes from there. It could flop, or it could be a lucrative success. The question of where I'll retire recurs. It's still possible I may return to southern England, but this will require a lot of investigation and so many things will happen between now and then. My health, my mother's, Jonathan's university plans, and finances, will be extremely important factors. A woman might come into my life and change things, though there is no way to know when or whether this will happen. I could live more comfortably in America, and I have prospered here, and I am grateful for all of this. But I am at heart English, remarkably so considering the time I've spent over here.

Granddad's favourite job. Reading to Elizabeth (left) and Eddie was a treat for all of us on dark winter evenings.

The great events of life, like loss of a father, or a dear friend or partner, can turn one's thoughts to the philosophical, and in particular to those things which, unlike human existences, change very little and thus provide a kind of consolation. I found this kind of solace not long after my father's death, on my return from work, driving my usual route north and westward, retreating from the mountains, and heading downhill for the narrow Rio Grande floodplain and home. Straight ahead, edged as sharp as a gun sight, was Mount Taylor, in Navajo lore the remains of First Man, his blood turned to cold lava that scattered in cold crusts of nature's slag, southward through the *malpaïs*. For the 180 degrees of my view from north to south was the dominant straight line of what the locals called the west mesa, the edge of the Rio Grande's green strip of civilization and vegetation. Only a thin scattering of towns lay between here and the brown blotch of Los Angeles. To the west-southwest the sun shone as white and as bright as a diamond. This sun was not warm. It was fiercely pristine. It was godlike. It was proudly, arrogantly powerful. It hung there, the power of life and death, and below it the sand and the rocks and the lava and the scrub trees were as insignificant as I.

Above that watercolour mesa landscape of ochres and umbers, mauves and warm gray, clouds sailed across the darkening sky at the unhurried and imperceptible pace of an hour hand. A quintet of dead volcanoes blipped on the ruler-straight horizon like the trace of a heartbeat among the soft cellular murmurings of a living body.

It was always different, that landscape, and always beautiful, in the black and white etchings of winter as well as in the rabbit-brush green of a lush late spring, in the relentless heat of summer as well as in the hatchet-cold ruthlessness of a January night, and on August afternoons when distant storm clouds stroke the western vastness like wet gray paintbrushes.

Out there was Indian country, and part of me envied the Indians for their intimacy with it. And, in the months after the loss of my father, I was sorrowful over the loss of contact with my Indian friends. They were special to me for the reason that, curiously in view of my personal history, I had developed a worldview that matched well with Indian thought. "You can feel it, the atmosphere of it, around the pueblos," wrote D. H. Lawrence. "You will feel the old, old root of human consciousness still reaching down to depths we know nothing of."[31]

There's irony here, for at one time the Indians believed the Europeans would transfigure their lives with beauty. "The Indians thought the white man would awake them," Lawrence wrote, "and instead, the white men scramble asleep in the mountains, and ride on horseback asleep for ever through the desert, and shoot one another, amazed and mad with somnambulism, thinking death will awaken something ..."[32]

By the time I reached home my mind was calmed by what I had seen, and by the thoughts that came from the things I had seen. Humankind spends so much time admiring and ritualizing the inventions of humankind! And yet humankind is such a tiny part of all there is.

19. BACK TO THE BOOKS

[A]lthough each of us gets a different life story – a different part of the puzzle – our tribe needs the wisdom of us all for truth to emerge.
— Tristine Rainer[33]

In the summer of 2000, one of my physicist friends phoned to report that some people from *Nature* magazine in London were visiting New Mexico. Would I like to be part of the reception committee? Silly question, I thought. *Nature* is one of the two most respected science magazines in the entire world. Of *course* I'd join the party!

And so, on the warm evening of June 19, I was happily sitting on the patio of an Albuquerque home, drinking margaritas and swapping stories with the *Nature* people and their Sandia hosts. Philip Campbell, who edited the magazine, was explaining that he became interested in science after his father bought him a telescope, when he was a teenager. There ensued a discussion of science publishing, and at some point, emboldened by tequila, I blurted, "Well, if you know anyone who's looking for a book about the exploration of the outer planets, please let me know because I have a manuscript ready for production."

It was a classic "Funny you should say that" situation. Phil, who was a deceptively ordinary looking chap with extraordinary things constantly happening between his ears, looked at me for a moment and said, "Well, it happens that there IS someone I know …"

Until then I thought such happenings were reserved for the realm of fiction. But no, he was dead serious. Phil invited me to send him an outline and sample chapter so that he could pass it on to a friend. I did that on June 24, and just ten days later heard from Peter Tallack, who was then at Weidenfeld & Nicolson, a top-line London publisher. Ah, the wonders of serendipity – and electronic mail. Soon messages were zipping back and forth across the 5,000 miles that separate Albuquerque and London.

Peter liked my work and asked, almost shyly, "Would you mind including the terrestrial planets?" The earlier book, which now I was fondly starting to call a prequel, had been limited to the five outer planets (I included Pluto) and all but ignored the inner four, hence the rather unusual table of contents. But Peter wanted a book that he would title *Solar System*, for inclusion in a new series of books with titles that started with the words "Mapping the..."

Later, Nic Cheetham, who became my new editor on Peter's departure, would ask me, "Do you mind including the Sun in *Solar System?*"

From such unusual and even bizarre happenings, a book is born. We signed the contract in January 2001.

I did the extra writing, packaged the result together, and sent bits of it hither and yon for comments by the real experts. Two eminent members of the Jet Propulsion Laboratory staff, Ellis Miner and Charley Kohlhase, offered me the lion's share of encouragement and constructive criticism. Miner, science manager of the Cassini mission, then on its way to Saturn, ran a fine tooth comb over my description of the giant planets and critiqued my long glossary. Kohlhase, who was design manager for the same mission, looked over my descriptions of spaceflight engineering. In all, a fairly large supporting cast of scientists from the United States and Britain responded to my networking, and to the cause of celebrating the wonders of planetary exploration.

I emailed the text to London in March, 2001, and settled in for a long wait as it made its way to the top of the queue of manuscripts that were awaiting attention. In the meantime I went back to work on the SDI book and contributed five short essays to another of Peter's projects, a massive, impressively bound production called, simply but majestically, *The Science Book*.

That autumn I set up a consultancy as an incorporated small business, and did some public relations work for a startup nanotechnology company while continuing to work on the two books. Before very long I would be able to boast of having published five books, three out-of-print popular-science potboilers (truly not worth boasting about) from the 1970s, plus *Solar System* and *The Star Wars Enigma,* a history of the Strategic Defense Initiative (SDI). I also was a contributing author for *The Science Book* (Weidenfeld & Nicolson, 2001) and *The McGraw-Hill Homeland Security Handbook* (2005). By now I was a member of the American Association for the Advancement of Science (AAAS) and a life member of the National Association of Science Writers, with additional memberships in the Association of British Science Writers, British Science Association, International Association of Science Writers, and South West Writers.

In 2007 I would be elected a fellow of the AAAS, a relatively rare distinction for a writer.

In 2007 I would be elected a fellow of the AAAS, a relatively rare distinction for a writer.

⧉

It is a peculiarity of certain men that they have a tendency to go wild about cars. Different kinds of men (and some women) go for different kinds of cars – expensive new American cars (one a year if possible), expensive late-model sports cars of the Maserati class; large luxury cars like the big Cadillacs and Mercedes-Benzes and the yummy Jaguar limousine; super-plush mouth-waterers like the Aston Martin and Cobra; Hummers, trucks, and SUVs of different stripes; and special-interest varieties like the Morgan and Lotus. The list goes on. On my little cul-de-sac in New Mexico there are, let's see, ten residences and seven special cars. Our specialty is sports cars – an MG-TF, an old and beautifully restored Porsche, an Austin-Healey Sprite, a Mercedes Benz 380-SL, and my former neighbour across the road had, I believe, the rarest of all – *three* Allards, those macho British-designed machines with powerful American engines that first appeared just after World War II.

Mine was the MG-TF. For years I had wanted to own a Morgan – why, I can't really explain. I suppose I just liked the looks and the exclusivity of this sexy little British car, which was hand-built, *hand-built*, mind you, in Malvern, Worcestershire. You could buy one new for as little as £27,500 (the super-duper ones cost more than four times as much), and I suppose I could have arranged it somehow. But did I really want one that much? As a mechanic I was an embarrassment even to myself, and where could I get it serviced in New Mexico?

Then one afternoon, no more than a quarter mile from where I live, I saw an absolutely delightful little yellow sports car parked by the side of the road, bearing the magic words "For Sale." It spoke to me; it shouted; it even pleaded. It was an MG, last of the "T" line of so-called midgets that had been winning cross-country races in England for decades. What's more, it was an MG-TF, no direct relative to the MG TF that MG-Rover cheekily introduced in 2002 but one of only 9,000 that the original company produced in 1954 and 1955 before moving on to making the MGA model. The TF looked quite a bit like its predecessor, the MG-TD, but its headlights were faired into the bodywork instead of perching on rods each side of the radiator, and the front wings (fenders) were swept back in the style of, well, something that reminded me of a Morgan. No air conditioning, no heater, no radio, no automatic top-raiser. And the engine, I was assured, was strictly 1930s engineering.

But for a few scratches on its instrument panel the car looked immaculate, with left-hand drive and original parts that looked as though they had just come off the assembly line. Even the electrical harness looked pristine. I was easily hooked, in fact I practically forced the man to take my money. As a sort of bonus for giving in to my second-childhood dream I was presented with a photograph album showing the stages in which the car had been restored and an original, suitably oil-spotted owner's guide.

I bought the car, got a vanity plate that read "MG★TF," and took my documents to State Farm to arrange insurance coverage. It was September 22, 1999, and it was with considerable delight when, that evening, I ushered Dee into the passenger seat for a triumphant ride in the cool and dusky evening.

Not quite a month ensued. The collision occurred on the late afternoon of Thursday, October 14, 1999, as Jonathan and I drove home from a tour of Albuquerque's Old Town. It was clear weather, daylight, dry road, and we had pulled up behind a line of vehicles waiting to make a left hand turn. Then Jonathan startled me with a shout, "Look out! We're going to get hit!" I hadn't time to react – what could I do? – and was thrown about in the driver's seat and stunned though I didn't lose consciousness. Jonathan cried out again, "get out Dad, there's gas on us," so I crawled out through the passenger side to get away from any spilled fuel, joined him at the curb, and sat down. There was blood on my shirt from my head hitting the windshield. I looked at the scene of the accident. We had been struck behind by a very large black SUV, which seemed undamaged, and driven into the rear of an old pickup truck. In American parlance we had been well and truly "rear ended"; in English slang we had been "shunted."

Jonathan said the other driver left his car carrying a cell phone; I remember there was no squeal of brakes. I remember the man coming up and saying "I'm sorry, I'm sorry," and offering me a blanket. But I checked myself out before the police motorcyclist and ambulance arrived and decided that I had only suffered broken ribs (painful but unfixable) and a superficial head cut. Jonathan had escaped any injury. We were very, very fortunate. Our condition, I suppose, was a tribute to the solid steel construction of an old car designed on 1930s principles. A couple of men had been killed the previous week, not far away, when their Mazda Miata crashed. There, but for the grace …

There was a reasonably happy ending to this story, though in the cold vernacular of the insurance adjusters, who had never heard of an MG-TF, the car was "totalled," and I won only a minimal adjustment from the driver (a government lawyer) who had hit me. After the hearing, in the hall, he apologized again and the driver of the pickup chimed in, "yes, but you were driving pretty fast, weren't you." It didn't help much.

I foolishly bought my wounded beauty from the State Farm insurance company, even though its title would be stamped "Salvage" (unspeakable insensitivity!) and was fortunate to find replacement original wings (fenders) in Georgia. I brought a radiator grill and spare-wheel mount over from England, sandwiched between wads of clothing that were bound for my washing machine.

Though the mechanic took an unconscionably long time to get the MG running again, the car was eventually back on the road, almost as good as the day I bought her. Well, not really. As Jonathan and I swung off Central Avenue on our way home from the garage, the driver's door inexplicably swung open and I had to hold it shut until we got to the carport at home. When I opened the engine compartment, I found a (functional) mass of nasty black wiring that didn't look at all familiar; I would have to have it replaced. The tonneau cover looked ratty, and so did the carpeting. Then I remembered another MG-TF, a black one, was waiting for repair when I arrived with my banged-up and bruised yellow beauty. It wasn't there when, having run out of patience, I picked up my own car. Hmmm. Did my car's bits somehow migrate to the other TF? Had the whole *engine* been switched over? I'll never know, but the engine compartment in the restorer's photo book looked very different indeed, though the original MG parts remained.

The engine compression rather quickly declined to near zero.

⚬❈⚬

In the autumn of 2001 I began my love affair with cruise travel – a big step up from a nevertheless memorable 1999 trip in which Jonathan and I went to London, then took the Chunnel train to Brussels, continuing on an amazingly slow train to explore the canals of Amsterdam. Then just after the 9/11 terrorist attack in New York I flew to Athens to meet Dee, her cousin Will, and his partner, Jack, for a cruise and land tours of Greece and Turkey. It seemed a perfect way to celebrate the retirement that I would begin on October 8 (Dee had retired from Albuquerque Public Schools the previous year). To spend an afternoon shopping and drinking coffee at the *plaka* in Athens, to walk through Agamemnon's Lion Gate, to wake up at the walled capital of Rhodes, to buy a Turkish carpet, to glide through the straits of the Bosporus, to see the Blue Mosque up close!

And it all happened. There was one word for it: *intoxicating*! Our guide took us to a carpet dealer in the port city of Kuşadasi, near Ephesus, where athletic young men took rolls of carpet from their resting places and magically spun them out into horizontally floating tapestry gems, one after another, until we were confronted by a great pile of hand-crafted beauty. "You like? You like?" Of course we did. And when, as if by invitation, a delicately knotted green carpet, just the colour for my front room, floated into the space before us, I shouted *Stop!* I looked at how it was made. Nine hand-tied knots per square centimetre meant it was okay, but not superb despite, by Western standards, the huge amount of time it took to make. We bartered and then I said I'd take it *if* – and this was an inspiration – we could celebrate the agreement with a glass of raki, the clear white anise-flavoured brandy that I considered superior to the similar Greek ouzo. We did that.

The next morning I learned of disaster, and there was nothing I could do about it.

It was early still and I was resting in an Istanbul hotel room when the telephone rang. I was surprised, pleased, and simultaneously alarmed to hear Jonathan's voice on the other end of the line. Grandma had suffered an accident, but was recovering well. She had fallen through the glass window of her atrium while watering some hanging plants. Amazingly she didn't break any bones, but she suffered a deep slash on her right hand and wrist. At the age of 94, while pumping blood onto the floor among the shards of glass, she managed to push the panic button hanging around her neck, had the presence of mind to actuate the garage door opener, and crawled away into the kitchen to await the arrival of emergency personnel.

So it happened that, at 18, Jonathan became the uncontested hero of the hour, along with Gail Hofstadler, the family friend who arranged for the blood and mess to be cleaned up.

Fortunately we were scheduled to be back in New Mexico in a couple of days and it was a matter of intense relief that I knew my mother was being very well cared for. In fact she was back at home and quite chirpy when we returned.

I marvelled at the microsurgery done on the blood vessels and nerves in her wrist. But she never quite regained the feeling in the index and second fingers of that hand. Neither did Mother paint again, though once in a while I heard her, when she thought I was out of earshot, playing our family's favourite old songs at the piano.

In the middle of February, 2002, I had a shock email from London. What was I doing about the essays we were going to include in *Solar System*? Essays? What essays? It turned out that as well as researching and writing the main text I was responsible for soliciting a dozen or so short articles that would be included as extra spice for my textual soup.

I had been under the mistaken impression that my publisher would round up *all* the essays, and now I had six weeks to recruit my contributors, negotiate alterations to the text where necessary, and get the results to London by April 1, for a possible July launch.

I sent Nic a list of 12 recommended essays and essayists on February 24, and emailed two of my heroes, the eminent Arthur C. Clarke and Freeman Dyson, with whom I had exchanged brief correspondences in the past, asking their approval of essays that I had created by extracting and condensing text from their previously published works. To my delight both agreed to let me publish the material without change. Sir Arthur messaged his approval on April 25. Four days later I heard from Freeman Dyson. "I accept your offer gladly," he wrote, "and I agree with your choice of passages to reprint." Naturally I was delighted, and more than impressed by the graciousness of these two great men. I titled their essays "Humans and Machines, Time and Space" and "Visions of the Future," respectively.

Sir Arthur Clarke, trained as a physicist, was the brightest star in the world of science fiction. I like to think that I knew him for 25 years or so, but that would be misleading. True, he had agreed to let me modify a quotation for one of my early young-adult science books. But I last saw him at the Royal Institution in January, 1982, when we heard Sir Fred Hoyle (incidentally a Bingley man), delivering the Institution's Omni lecture, *Evolution from Space*. This promoted the possibility that space could be very thinly populated with spores which might by chance settle on a planet or moon that was amenable to life – the theory of panspermia. Afterwards Arthur and I walked off together, talking about the lecture as we went down Albemarle Street to look for taxis. We stood on the pavement on Oxford Street and chatted a few minutes more, then went on our separate ways, he to Sri Lanka and I to the United States.

We lost communication until I decided I needed a Clarke essay for *Solar System*, 20 years later. There was a section in his book *Profiles of the Future* that was just right for my book, and I wanted to adapt it for use, with attribution to the original author. Arthur was then wheelchair-bound with the debilitating and painful post-polio syndrome (PPS), and knew he would never return to England. Though I was not optimistic for an answer, on April 22 I edited his text a little and by email asked if I could use it. A cheerful response arrived within 24 hours: "Fine – no problem. In haste – surrounded by TV crews at the moment... Arthur."

With this note he included a set of irreverent sayings – he was notably anti-religious – and invited me to share them with our mutual friend Ken Frazier. One of them read: "Of all the evils that God, in Her inscrutable wisdom, inflicted upon Mankind, Religion is by far the worst."[34]

Maui with Margery. My 92-year-old mother and Dee had a good time together in 2000.when I attended the Maui Writers Conference in Hawaii.

271

"Incidentally," Arthur added puckishly at the end of an email of April 26, 2002, "I sometimes call myself a crypto-Buddhist." So he couldn't have been all that bad.

I heard from him for the last time on January 28, 2006. He was between cataract surgeries, still coping with PPS but busy nevertheless, talking about a film adaptation of *Rendezvous with Rama* with Morgan Freeman and working on his final novel, *The Last Theorem* (co-authored with Frederick Pohl and published by Harper Voyager, 2008). But he still had time to write to me. "Belated good wishes for 2006," he wrote. "I hope to see you here if you route your China travel via Colombo. Sri Lanka is a well-kept secret for discerning travelers." Dee and I were locked into a travel group that was going to China the other way around, across the Pacific via Japan, so it never happened and I lamented the fact. Arthur died in Sri Lanka the following year, on March 18, 2008.

⚬⚬⚬

Solar System carried a publication date of 2002, very soon after the essays had been assembled. We had a complete set of eleven superb essays in hand by the second week of April, including one from the renowned David Morrison of the Astrobiology Institute of NASA's Ames Research Center, who wrote a piece on his specialty, near-earth objects, which I titled "Killer Asteroids." I had completed the final proofreading and last-minute fact-checking, dressing up my website to help market the book, preparing to support a London launch, and eyeing opportunities for a New York introduction. It was and is a gorgeous volume full of beautiful illustrations, printed and bound in Italy: a coffee table book in miniature. Even the cheaper paperback edition was an elegant production.

Try as I might, I could not convince Weidenfeld & Nicolson to give either edition a more interesting title. As I mentioned before, the company had planned to publish a whole series of books with titles that began with the words "Mapping the." The previous book in the series was Rita Carter's *Mapping the Mind*; mine was supposed to be *Mapping the Solar System*. But when the "Mapping the" prefix was thrown into the publishing void by some executive dictum, "Solar System" remained, forever marooned as a mere label, and a very sticky one at that, while I proffered a dozen alternatives, getting nowhere at all.

Writing *Solar System* made me appreciate Planet Earth even more, to marvel that such an unusual planet came to be, and to mull over the wonder that it is

272

peopled with creatures aesthetic enough to appreciate it for its beauty as well as for its bounty. I ruminated again on the position of Earth at just the "right" distance from the Sun for the generation of primitive life, of those first bacteria that eventually evolved into animals and plants that thrive on oxygen and carbon dioxide, of the emergence of mankind, and of people developing the cognitive and imaginative skills that permit them to love (and exploit) their environment to a degree that "passeth all understanding."

After *Solar System* moved from editing to the marketing phase, my brain continued its preoccupation with astronomy and cosmology and, particularly, their significance to humanity. In the spring of 2003, while preparing for a book-signing and radio spot in Cambridge (the English town, not the university), I started putting it together.

In Santa Fe I accepted a complimentary cup of coffee at Borders, part of the now-extinct bookshop chain, and began to think of things I could tell my audience before I sat down to sign books. Certainly I would introduce the idea that people are gradually regaining a sense of affinity with the cosmos – some through liberal forms of religion and philosophy; and some by way of the broader avenues of technology and science. I would explain how popular astronomy, particularly when enlivened with space imagery, was encouraging more people to understand the urgent symbolism of Carl Sagan's "pale blue dot."

People gained two great lessons from the cosmic perspective that the astronauts first gave us in the 1960s. Physically, we may become more committed stewards of our planetary resources – I could see no rational alternative. Psychologically and spiritually, we may now be able to grow our minds so that they reach into the vastness of the universe, where the tiny motes of individual human need and greed are so small that for all intents and purposes they do not exist. It seemed to me that, when this exploration reached full maturity, we might be left, in a Zen sense, in a state of non-being. It might even constitute a non-material state of love. It might be what Teilhard considered his "Omega Point." (More about this subject in the Epilogue.)

I didn't see this objective as fantasy or science fiction; nor did I see it as a sure thing. It was, however, a *possibility*, an *ideal*, and by its nature any journey toward its realization would be transformational. As the Buddha said, "It is better to travel well than to arrive." There can be no road map; in such things people can do little more than hope to place themselves in the path of serendipity. I probably wouldn't have brought this up with the Borders crowd, but this involves freeing and accepting the gifts of mind enjoyed by the protagonists of an old story, *Three Princes of Serendip*, who in Horace Walpole's words were fortunate in "making discoveries, by accidents and sagacity, of things they were not in quest of." We might start, as Sagan urged us to do, by accepting ourselves for what we already are – galactic citizens. We are fashioned from the residue of supernovas. We are energized by the radiance of our home star. We would do well to celebrate those facts.

While I was procrastinating instead of preparing seriously for my talk, a young man in jeans came down an aisle with an oak-stained lectern and stood it up on a raised portion of the floor. Another man put a microphone next to it, and a young woman placed a dozen of my books on a nearby table. They began to deploy a stack of metal folding chairs. A man with acupuncture needles took the front center chair and began to read. He was a tubby young man with a backpack and his face was simply bristling with wires. He was just sitting there, with a book open on his lap, and he was obviously captivated by it.

At this point you may have begun to suspect that I was planning to use the Borders event to cough up the romantic ramblings of my late teens and early twenties, which would have bored my audience to death. Not true, and anyhow there was no one there to notice. Besides, most of that old prattle had disappeared from my worldview, though not quite all of it. I believe that positive mental transformations are *at this moment* taking their place in our individual consciousnesses, though slowly and perhaps too slowly, and that more enlightened thought eventually will become part of the common understanding. By comparison with the incessant, giddy back-and-forth flux of politics and commerce that at once animates and sickens our daily lives, its advance is slow and hard to discern. The transformation is also slowed by the grasping friction of greed. A few, not many, would suggest that "greed is good," even in days of recession and austerity. But the uninhibited desire to acquire unneeded things is a repellent compulsion; by contrast I see the idea of "enlightened self interest," which does not exclude material gain, as both laudable and achievable.

On the more philosophical side, many things are becoming newly possible thanks to the great human gift of wonder. Wonder after all energizes the minds of philosophers, scientists, students, and the religious, and brightens the minds of everyone else. It awakens us to how much we have in common with our planet and the cosmos. It occurs to me that a more universal outlook would also support the conduct of enlightened self-interest.

An important consideration is that my science-writing researches woke me to the fact that wonder is being regenerated and transgenerated all the time, from pondering the possibility of life on other planets to understanding the amazingly profuse and differentiated life of our own planet, to the imitation of nature in nanotechnology. I sensed that, behind the glare of the headlines and the reality of disquiet and bloodshed, a new springtime was beginning for all of humankind. It delighted me to imagine that an increasing number of people were accepting their galactic citizenship. It could grow into something even more exciting than a renaissance, I told myself. It could be a *naissance*, the birth of something new and wonderful inside ourselves, connecting us yet more closely with the stars. Stumbling blocks would remain, from common materialism to rank corruption to the trouble that governments encounter in managing societies that are becoming bafflingly more complex. But we could still smell the flowers of that human springtime.

This is why in my writing career I went so often for the high ground, for science *in general* rather than science as represented by a single disciplinary area; I prefer to think of science as the fruit of human curiosity, wonder, and problem-solving; science as seed-corn for philosophy and awe. From the mind's high ground, free of the distractions of relatively narrow matters, you can see – very clearly and positively – that intentional, planned, personal participation in a balanced global ecology is necessary for human survival. It also seems that, from an anthropocentric, *selfish* viewpoint, setting up a global socioeconomic balance may be just as vital. If such goals sound hopeless, or too risky to take on in the short term, it may be that the point of view you have found is not quite high enough. You may find that moving up another rung in the stepladder to your virtual watchtower is liberating, positive, and perhaps even transformational.

This may sound like an invitation, perhaps even a plea, to take greater interest in ideas or projects that can be observed or accomplished by oneself, without being bound by a rigid need to employ scientific method. This is always a valuable course to consider. Yet the worth of new technical ideas will depend on new fruits of science, linked with the determination to make better, smarter, and more humane use of each innovation, especially in physics and biology. We need *both*, again in balance. Perhaps humankind will come to realize that there is nothing threatening in science, and that indeed science is natural to the human condition (remember my Chapter 11 story about my infant son Brian's physics experiment, dropping a spoon from his high chair?) Science is always curious, always exploring, humble enough to realize that one's conclusions can seldom (or never) be absolutely correct, and always eager to discover a better answer. Science is knowledge and the search for knowledge. It is a fine thing that can go wrong only when used to create and use technologies that cause harm deliberately or through neglect or careless management. *That* is what we have cause to fear.

Forgive me for wittering on about wonder, and imagination, and the good things that can come from them, but these happen to be a cluster of subjects that I am passionate about and I hope you will forgive me for these digressions. Still, as the pioneer Spanish-born filmmaker Luis Buñuel commented, "Somewhere between chance and mystery lies imagination, the only thing that protects our freedom, despite the fact that people keep trying to reduce it or kill it off altogether."

If you think I am flirting with utopianism, take heart. Such thoughts lead me to another curve in the chart of future history, one that comes from a combination of human materialism, tribalism, and population growth, and the terrible Earth-threatening strife that comes with these. It is a terrible irony that people who have the divine capability to sense their place among the stars also have the profane capability to rape and pillage Earth and decimate the complex life-forms that include themselves.

Similar trains of consciousness summon reverberations from my personal life, like the time I suffered the unbearably bleak, vertiginous realization that it would be impossible to drive home if there were news that a nuclear strike was imminent. It was a feeling of profound fear, and I remember it just as I remember where I was when John F. Kennedy was assassinated and the Twin Towers crumbled. I was reminded that the next mass extinction need not be caused by asteroid impact or the eruption of a mega-volcano, or by the emergence of an apocalyptic plague. Weapons of mass destruction can do the job quite effectively. Humankind could face a real-life final battle between hope and utter despair. This time it would not be the David and Goliath story. It would be David versus David, Goliath versus Goliath, bringing the possibility that humans will destroy themselves before they have the chance to emerge into that bright *naissance* of a genuinely liberated species that has lost the need for war. My mind shot forward to a scenario of the death of the last human. Would nature, or the Great Spirit, care? Most likely not. For a moment my old nightmare came back: "I am dead, help me!"

I count myself fortunate that sometimes I can put such thoughts away and remind myself that our species has the choice to change its course and transform itself through the door-opening magic of wonder, in pondering the secrets of the sky and the galaxy of natural marvels that reside at our feet and in ourselves as well as in the unreachable heavens. We spend far too much time in thrall with the diversions of money, politics, illuminated screens, and the noisy madness of self-promoting oratory.

I finished my Borders talk in 35 minutes. It had been a quick tour of the sun and planets with no philosophical content. When I put down my notes the acupuncture man was still there, vibrating. He was my only audience. When I stopped, he stopped reading his book, put it in his backpack, and made his way to the door without looking back. He just needed a warm place to sit and read. The girl minding the books looked and gave me a rueful smile.

❧

While I was wrestling with the birth of *Solar System*, Joss and Dave were grappling with the logistics and the actual arrival of their second-born, Elizabeth, who made her début on February 12, 2003. I reminded myself truthfully that I would not be much use if I was in London, but it didn't do much good.

Jonathan graduated from Bosque School, the private school he had attended throughout his teenage years, in May 2003. As a boy and as a young man, he was very smart, very capable, and very personable. He was senior class president. But in the formal sense he was not a student – despite the best efforts of his teachers and his parents, he affected a strong dislike for "book learning," homework, and other staples of the academic life. He resisted my efforts to help with his homework, and like others of his age seemed downright embarrassed on those infrequent occasions that I left the car and ventured on campus after taking him to school. It was as though he had decided that, if he didn't learn something from experience or conversation (preferably with peers), it wasn't worth learning. I had a streak of that inverted snobbery in myself.

The school administrators would have been justified in denying him the right to graduate on time, but they were lenient. Jonathan picked up his diploma right on schedule.

Jonathan subsequently said he would like to take a year's leave from academic studies, though his friends had continued to various universities, and I agreed. And so he worked as a department store salesman, a bank teller, and short-order cook, mixing these vocational experiments with university-transferable classes at the Central New Mexico Community College, a two-year institution. He worked hard at CNM and was disappointed in those rare times that he didn't earn As. And steadily he began to get better jobs. In 2008, still two semesters short of receiving his diploma, he would become the information-technology manager at a large Albuquerque legal firm that worked with a nationwide network of lawyers.

Jonathan's poor high school performance remained a mystery. Some years later, when I asked him what he thought of the Bosque experience, he said it was great – he had come to know a lot of people and made friends with the teachers too. He admitted he had been immature and won his modicum of academic success by working the system. It was clear that he had learned a lot anyway, just by sitting in class and listening to a number of excellent teachers who I suspected operated, on average, at a higher intellectual level than their peers in state schools. He received his certificate from CNM in 2010.

Jonathan's move to his mother's had left me quite alone in the house, making peace with the reality that this was the first time in nearly 40 years that I had no children for whom I felt continuously responsible. I was concerned about them and eager to stay in touch, but the flight of my youngest and last child left a special vacuum in my life, a whispered signal that another reason for my existence was fading into nothingness. I would remain dogged by the suspicion that I was not a very good parent, though my children and others protested otherwise.

There were still many times that I thought I might sometime return to live in England after my retirement and cope with whatever dreadful things Her Majesty's Taxman would want to inflict on my nest-egg. The debate continued in my mind, year after year. A resolution was waiting in the wings.

20. NOVEMBER IN MOSCOW

I *think science, as a diplomatic tool, is great.*
Secretary of State Condoleezza Rice, 2005[35]

You'll remember that in 1999 I had decided to write a book about the Strategic Defense Initiative, after Adm. James Watkins said it was time someone wrote "the real story" about the project that the media dubbed "Star Wars." I had made some progress with that venture, and in early 2003 thought the book was ready to send to a publisher. But then the project took an unexpected turn.

While surfing the Web I found an article in the journal *Quantum Electronics* in which the Russian physicist Peter Zarubin told the story of Soviet attempts to perfect directed-energy weapons for anti-ballistic missile defence – in the 1960s and 1970s, long before Ronald Reagan announced his SDI vision on nationwide television.[36] Nothing like this had been published before, so I was truly amazed. After I sent Gerold Yonas a copy of the article, he sent me an exuberant email. "The *Quantum Electronics* article describes one of the most secret things ever," he wrote. "We need to talk about this."

Not very long afterwards it was my good fortune to meet another Russian scientist, Evgeny Pavlovich Velikhov. He was meeting at Sandia with a nuclear engineer, Tom Sanders, who arranged for me to sit in, and Al Trivelpiece, retired director of Oak Ridge National Laboratory. Velikhov was no lightweight. Quite the opposite. He was a renowned physicist who was for years a leading insider in the Soviet Union's giant nuclear weapon complex and president of the Kurchatov Institute (now the National Research Center), the long-established analog of the US Department of Energy nuclear arms/energy organization.[37] At the time of our meeting he was an adviser to Mikhail Gorbachev. Anyone who managed to put together a *curriculum vitae* such as his, covering a period that started with the Stalin years, had to be a true survivor.

Velikhov and I chatted talked about my SDI book plans while Tom and Al listened a few yards away, and then this super-smart, witty, and enormously experienced man stood up and took my hand. "You must come to Moscow," he said, "Then you will see how we did all these things in Russia." More than that, he said he would help me arrange the trip and that he would introduce me to all sorts of people relevant to the story.

My mother had recovered well from her wrist injuries, and with help from friends and neighbours I felt she would be fine while I travelled to Moscow. One of Gerry Yonas's friends arranged for a friend of a friend to meet me at the Moscow airport and act as taxi-driver, and I had business cards made with English-language information on the front and Russian on the back. In a drawer I found my dad's old Russian-type *shapka* hat and bought the best audio recorder that I could find in Radio Shack's inventory. I also arranged, via email, to talk separately with Zarubin and Dmitry Mikheyev, a writer-physicist who knew about lasers and Russian politics and had been interned for supporting clandestine meetings in the 1960s; and contacted some Moscow-based science writers whom I thought might be helpful.

I paid a West Coast company to take care of the paperwork for the trip, since I knew it would be a bureaucratic mess if I tried to do it myself. Just the same I was concerned about going to Russia alone, since the mafia held so much power and the crime rate was high. I was told that if I noticed someone from the FSB, the modern KGB, was following me, it might even be a good thing because it would reduce my chances of being mugged. At least this was the assumption.

❦

The British Airways 767 from Heathrow got in early at Domodedovo airport, propelled ahead of schedule with the help of a 95 mph tail wind. I collected my bag, navigated nervously through customs and immigration, and with a surge of relief spied a hand-made sign bearing my name, waving from the hand of a serious-looking man who stood tall and thin above the crowd. It was Alexander Volkov, friend of one of Yonas's Albuquerque friends, and I was delighted to see him. We picked our way across a thin veneer of slushy snow to the parking lot, where his elderly Mitsubishi station wagon was waiting. Alexander spoke some English, but with difficulty. He had spent some time in Mexico, so we agreed to speak Spanglish and it worked.

Alexander easily navigated his way to the wide thoroughfare of Lenininskii Prospekt and we followed a dead-straight route to the Academicheskaya Hotel.

The lobby was small but pleasant enough, and as I signed in I looked up at a bank of clocks – 9.45 p.m. here, 4.45 a.m. in Vladivostok. Nothing about the massiveness of Russia had struck me more boldly than seeing the breadth of these times zones, seven of *nine* that actually exist.

Alexander helped me communicate with the very attractive, very curt female check-in clerk, getting me a small amount of roubles in the process, and disappeared. We would meet again the next day for a quick tour of Moscow.

The hotel room was not luxurious. The sagging bed was narrow, and the table I would use for a desk was scarred and grimed with age. Yet the room seemed clean enough: I decided it was just old and the cheap original furniture had never been replaced. In one corner water had seeped from above – an overflowing bathtub, perhaps. It had separated the wallpaper, revealing a small dirty-white electronic gizmo. It hung there by its wires, one of which had been snipped, and I imagined it was a microphone. I didn't examine it closely, but what else could it have been? A fire detector? Somehow I doubted it.

I turned on the TV – nothing but Russian-language programs – and ventured into the bathroom. The towels were thin as tablecloths. The plastic toilet seat was thin too, and coloured a livid semi-transparent green. The hot and cold water supplies had a mixer with a long spout that could be moved to hang over either the washing bowl or the bathtub.

I placed my computer on the table and stared across it through the window into a dark Moscow night. The window frames were old and shrunken, and strips of yellowing plastic foam were stuck into the cracks to keep out the drafts.

I walked to a nearby corner shop to buy bottled water and, because I heard that Yuri Andropov liked it, a bottle of vodka that was sweetened and flavoured with herbs. The stuff, called Starka, did its job and cheered me up. I accepted the fact that this would be my garret for the next eight days, and resolved that I would enjoy the experience.

Next morning I pulled my short black leather jacket over my black shirt and undershirt, my black denims and comfortable old shoes, and waited for Alexander. He arrived at 10 precisely, huffing and puffing and apologizing for being late. He wore a sensible peaked Russian cap, short jacket and red wool scarf, over a business suit with dress shirt and tie. We got into his station wagon, there was a clank as he detached the anti-theft mechanism from his clutch pedal, and we were off.

The windshield wipers clattered back and forth, coated with half-frozen slush, and now and then the fan assembly screeched like a reluctant banshee. My new friend concentrated hard on his defensive driving, speaking haltingly as if speaking English were a considerable effort, warming up a bit when we slipped into Spanish. He brightened when I mentioned that he might sometime visit Albuquerque.

As I walked up the little hill to Red Square after touring the museums, the elements reminded me of certain cold days in London, and Albuquerque, when I had come up against climatic experiences I would prefer to escape. But then the cold, or the wind, subsided a bit, and we were staring at Russia's Eternal Flame, watching as soldiers performed the Changing of the Guard. When we arrived one immobile soldier was standing at attention at each side of the flame. Then, a hundred and fifty meters or so distant, two more appeared, met a third who served as escort, and slow-marched toward the flame in a militaristic ballet, bringing each leg straight and level with the ground as they marched, their left arms swinging around in a Romanesque salute against the chest, rifles on the right. There was silence but for the clockwork cadence of stylized marching.

And then we walked around the square, taking pictures of the Church of St. Basil the Blessed, with its brightly whorled domes, walking through the lavish indoor mall that is the ultra-high-end reincarnation of GUM, the State Universal Store. And then we were off again, out from Alexander III's 1893 centerpiece into the icy chill.

After a day of sightseeing Alexander delivered me back to the hotel, where I made more notes in my journal and thought about money. Where would I get some roubles?

The girls at the reception desk were well acquainted with the slot-machine gambling shop and remembered the little exchange-rate sign bolted to its wall. It was not the rush hour, and there were only a couple of customers, impoverished-looking locals who were hopelessly pulling levers on a row of one-armed bandits. A man in a black Armani suit appeared and pointed me to a corner where there was a bullet-proof glass window with a half-moon opening at the bottom. It was a bleak-looking prison of a place. You knew someone was there behind the scratched window because a bare bulb was glowing inside. A shadow appeared behind the security screen, a shoebox of a drawer slid outward towards me, and I pushed the dollars in. The drawer disappeared and I could just see a pair of grimy hands, carefully inspecting the notes. Paper money dropped into the box with the clink of a couple of coins, and then with a rusty scraping creak the grubby box reappeared, filled with Russian notes. I stuffed them into my pocket and left, trying to look inconspicuous.

This evening I bought a litre and a half of water, a roll, and a pre-packaged salad (peas, tiny cubes of potato, mayonnaise, minute scraps of ham) at the little *magazin* at the corner, went up to my room, ate the salad, and had a palliative slug of Starka. Good stuff, that Starka; it washed the taste of the salad from my tongue. I called my science-writer contacts to tell them I had arrived, and fell asleep thinking about my visit with the Kurchatov people tomorrow. There had been suggestions that Velikhov might be able to arrange a meeting with the USSR's last leader, Mikhail Gorbachev, which would be a coup, but in view of the first meeting he arranged I was a little sceptical.

Grey skies greeted me again the next morning. But Yuri Schors, whom the Academy had assigned to act as my official guide, would arrive at mid-day, after which Peter Zarubin would come visiting. Things were looking up. And for a change I had a couple of hours to spare. I looked out of the window and made notes as I tried to determine just where I was.

It reminds me of a grim early 20th century landscape, this view from the ninth floor. More snow has fallen during the night, not much but enough to crust the dome of the nearby church like icing on a Christmas pudding. But mostly it is a citiscape of white and gray, the darker grays being in the sky and the other grays on closer inspection being the terra-cotta red and muted greens of building walls. Then there is the concrete greyness of half-completed high-rise buildings where, from one tiny spot, comes the intermittent heliograph spark of a welding torch. The wind has come up now, I hear it against my window, blowing sleet, and drifting it over rooftops where pigeons are gamely trying to court, and making the tall pine sway, over there near the tramcar sheds. The sheds take up a large part of my view in the middle distance, though apartment blocks are visible behind. Eight or nine roofs cover them, undulating gently over a distance of maybe four hundred meters, joined to make a single building. The building has dozens of tall narrow side-by-side doors painted in slightly bolder shades of yellow and green, and every once in a while one of them opens and a tram comes sparking its way along the overhead line, crawls in like a strange mechanical insect, and the door closes quickly behind. But this morning a red-jacketed driver had to jump from his tram with shovel in hand, and scrape the ice from the rails before he could take cover from the day.

Early in the afternoon Schors arrived with his son Alex (not my guide Alexander), who would provide transportation and was more comfortable with English. Though the father was not a young man he walked at an unusually fast pace without seeming to do so. Alex attributed this to his father's Army career, and laughed when I asked if he ran Kurchatov's military division, as suggested by his business card.

We were driven to the Russian Academy of Sciences headquarters, an attractively designed modern building, and took the elevator to the top floor. Here Velikhov held court once a week; otherwise he worked at the Kurchatov Institute. His secretary told us he was busy. He wanted me first to meet a colleague who was waiting in the next room, and then Peter Zarubin.

To my surprise my first visitor was a technology business development specialist, Sergey Karabashev, director of the International Foundation of Technology and Investment. I was taken aback, for he knew nothing about lasers or strategic defence. Fortunately I would next be meeting Peter Zarubin, the man Gerry Yonas nicknamed "Mr. SDIsky." We had spoken by telephone and exchanged emails, so I knew Zarubin was a knowledgeable man, fluent in English and willing to talk about his career. I also knew his father had been the KGB's Washington chief during World War II, during the time of the Soviet spy Klaus Fuchs, and that his half-sister had translated for Stalin at Potsdam and elsewhere. He would no doubt be a trim, manicured bureaucrat in a thousand-dollar suit.

I was due for a surprise. Zarubin was a short, stocky, owlish man in glasses and a baseball cap. He had been waiting somewhere in the building and appeared immediately when Karabashev left. I felt a sense of rescue. He was a little dynamo, an agile 72-year-old with a penetrating staccato tenor voice. "You may wonder why I speak so good English," he said. "That is because I come from top intelligence family." I wondered if he meant his remark to be a *double entendre*.

We had chance to talk for about ten minutes before Velikhov's secretary arrived and told us her boss was free. I followed her into the main office, but not before making a date to meet with Zarubin the next day, hopefully on our way to see Oleg Krokhin, an eminent physicist and head of the Lebedev Institute.

Evgeny Pavlovich sat behind his desk in a floppy beige cashmere sweater, tieless and fiddling with his Apple laptop. Electronic beeps, dings, and musical excerpts were coming from his computers and an assemblage of telephones, and continued during our tape-recorded conversation. While we talked he was

Visiting the Famous. Visiting with high-energy laser pioneer Oleg Krokhin at the Lebedev Institute, Moscow. Lebedev's historic instruments are displayed in the cabinet behind us.

multi-tasking in a big way, answering my questions with perfect lucidity despite the distraction of the bells and whistles.

What he said was interesting and before I knew it (in a mere 30 or 35 minutes) his assistant buzzed him to announce his next appointment. I didn't actually say, "Migod, I've come half way around the world for this?" but I did remind him that I had a lot of questions that only he could answer. Also, I growled to myself, he had invited me and his preparations were nil. The meeting with Gorbachev, which I believed had been arranged by Velikhov, had also disappeared into nothingness.

"Meet me at five o'clock on Thursday and we'll have four hours to talk," Evgeny said jovially, as if he had read my thoughts. His secretary muttered Maybe, *mozhet vit*, and this was not encouraging.

The next morning the weather had turned warmer and from my window I could see rivulets of dirty water running from under banks of soggy piled snow. A man was trying to clean the windows of his car with a bottle of mineral water.

Peter arrived on time, with news that Krokhin had sent a white Volga to pick us up. We hurried downstairs, stood on the curb, and waited. And waited. Fifteen minutes later we were ready to give up.

November 25, 2003 – Without warning Peter Zarubin's thickset, compact little form shot off down the middle of Shabolovka Ulitsa and through the gray Moscow slush. My yells from the curb were pointless. Peter ran erratically down the middle of the narrow street, dodged between a few cars, and disappeared. Then back he came, clumping resignedly back up the street. He caught my eye, spread his hands shoulder-high, and shrugged dismally. We had missed the car from Lebedev, which meant we were late for the meeting with Krokhin, who was near the top of my list of people who could help me unravel the story of the Soviet Union's version of America's future SDI. Amazingly, Krokhin came up with the idea of using nuclear-powered lasers to destroy American ballistic missiles in the early 1960s, and Peter watched over its chemically pumped successor for more than a decade before it was shelved. This was after his colleagues had created the world's most powerful pulsed laser, and five years before Ronald Reagan confronted the American nation with his famous "Star Wars" speech.

Finally Peter and I crossed Leninskii Prospekt and looked for a ride. Trams and trolleybuses run along this wide boulevard, but we were in a hurry and looking for a minibus, an unmarked van that will hold ten or twelve people at a time. A clot of people squeezed their way into the first that arrived, but we were soon clambering aboard a second van, bundled together with a cheerful mixture of shabby old men, modish young women, shoppers, and businesspersons.

⚬⚬⚬

The Lebedev Institute is housed in an elegant Greek-influenced building, with a semicircular drive flanked by thick pines. It is named for the physicist Peter Nikolaevich Lebedev, who in 1900 produced experimental evidence that electromagnetic radiation possesses momentum, explained five years later in Einstein's special theory of relativity. Lebedev used fascinating little instruments, like toy electroscopes, to show that light will actually push the blades of something that looks like a tiny windmill inside a light bulb. And here was the real thing, Lebedev's invention, in a modest glass-fronted cabinet, being shown proudly to me by the current tenant of the great man's study. As a boy I had been fascinated by electroscopes, and I was fascinated again.

Krokhin was, as Yonas had described him, "suave and debonair." The physical contrast between my two hosts was remarkable – the chunky Zarubin, whom

286

you'd almost surely miss in a crowd, and the tall, slim, handsome, silver-haired Krokhin. Yet it was apparent that they were fast friends.

We talked about the Soviet design for a high-energy nuclear x-ray laser in the early 1960s and its conversion to chemical power, and of the testy relationship between the institute's Nikolai Basov and Alexandr Prokhorov, who shared the 1964 Nobel Prize in Physics with the American Charles Townes. Tea came with sugar wafers and good chocolate biscuits. Then came the Armenian cognac, Churchill's favourite, with which we toasted the book project in a single swallow. We had tea, and then we had cognac again. Afterwards, Peter took pictures of Krokhin and me together, and we sped away, this time in a chauffeured car that was going in the right direction.

Next day the weather was still mild and nearly all the snow had disappeared from the rooftops. I breakfasted and went over my notes, preparing for a long interview with Velikhov. Handsome and clean-cut, Alex drove me expertly through miles of end-of-the-day traffic to the Kurchatov Institute's International House. We hung up our coats and waited on comfortable leather sofas in a large foyer with a marble staircase. Evgeny arrived and the two of us walked into a cavernous adjoining conference room. We sat under massive crystal candelabras at a black table that could have seated fifty or more. Someone had laid out mineral water and glasses and cups, saucers, sugar and milk. A woman brought us tea and coffee and disappeared.

Evgeny looked tired and yellow and didn't want to waste time with preliminary chat. But to my delighted surprise I was able to record nearly an hour and a half of tape from the world's most knowledgeable man on high-tech Soviet nuclear arms and fusion technology. His information was nontechnical and contained no surprises, and much of it was not useful for my book. But I needed confirmation on many points and now I had it from the expert.

After Alex dropped me off I went back to the room, put aside my briefcase, and took off my coat. Then I felt it was time for a celebration and made my way to the buffet for a goodnight snack.

Vodka was produced in a flash, but when I asked for caviar the barmaid screwed up her face in confusion. *Caviar? Skolka Kaviar?* I had assumed the word was Russian, but from her expression the assumption was undeniably wrong. Determined to make my point, I started drawing pictures of what caviar should look like. The cluster of round objects didn't help, so then I drew a new picture which I thought was a fair enough representation of a fish producing eggs. The waitress gave me a wary look. Fortunately the English-speaking bartender arrived in the nick of time, before she called security, and found me the caviar. Turned out the Russian word for caviar is *ikrá*. "Caviar" is French.

My red caviar came with bread and butter and a garnish of parsley. It was tasty but somehow strange, certainly not sturgeon and probably not salmon roe but maybe the synthetic gelatine and casein concoction that comes from, or used to come from, Murmansk. I shuddered and ordered more vodka.

Next morning I woke remembering the sound of shots in the night, for the second time since my arrival. When I mentioned this to Peter he creased his forehead, said "Bad guys," and shrugged reassuringly as if to say, "Nothing to do with us."

⚏

It would be a quiet day, so I called Tanya Pitchugina, a TV writer with whom I had exchanged emails after learning of her existence through the International Science Writers' Association. I asked if she were free that evening, and to my delight she was.

She would be waiting for me at the Tratyakovskaya Metro station at 4 p.m. She was, she said, slim and dark-haired, one meter 70 centimetres tall. She would be wearing a blue jacket, carrying a copy of John Dixon Carr's mystery masterpiece *The Hollow Man*. Her directions, given carefully with a soft Russian accent, sounded like words from a spy movie.

She arrived at Tratyakovskaya five minutes early, shortish black hair, olive skin, handsome dark eyes, dark slacks under her jacket and pointy shoes. We introduced ourselves, then Tanya pulled her knit hat over her ears and we walked up the concrete stairs to street level. We walked around the block until we came back where we started, then dived into a Hokey-Pokey, a restaurant decorated light-heartedly in rustic Russian style and one of a chain apparently named for the old dance tune. I had strawberry-flavoured Klukovksa vodka and mushroom fricassee, Tanya a large chunk of Black Forest gateau and a latte.

"Do you want sparkles?" Tanya asked when I tried to order some mineral water. The question first confused, then amused me. But no, I said, no carbonation, no gas, *ne gaz*. All I wanted to do was drown out the taste of the Klukovksa.

So what next? There must be something neat to do on a Friday night. Well, she asked, would I like to go to a theatre, even to see some *balyet*? Definitely. So we returned to the Metro and came up at the Teatralnaya station. And there was the Bolshoi, the real thing, one of the world's earliest and most famous opera houses, majestic and glowing white in the glare of lights.

It was getting late now, but Tanya said we might be able to get tickets from a kiosk for one of the theatres in the neighbourhood. There were many kiosks, lined up on the pavement like glass-paned outhouses, but I had no idea what specialties they were selling – cigarettes, vodka, condoms, or tickets to *Boris Godunov*.

Tanya talked to a few of the vendors but without luck. I probably scowled at this point, but then I noticed a few helpful-looking men hanging around the bank of kiosks. Scalpers! I'd know them anywhere.

"See if any of those men have tickets for *Giselle*," I suggested eagerly.

Tanya negotiated with one of the scalpers, and then turned back to me with a sad face. "They're so expensive," she said.

"How much?"

"Twenty dollars each."

This was the best no-brainer I'd heard for ages, so I grabbed for my wallet. "Then get them!"

I was elated and from the look on her face I'd say Tanya was, too. We walked up that great stairway to the theatre doors, under the 19th century facade with its hammer and sickle, and soon were drinking martinis (no vodka here!), waiting for the curtain bell.

Forty dollars had bought us a box so close to the stage that I was afraid I might accidentally drop something on the horn section. In fact we were right next to the brocaded curtains, looking out at the fast-filling five tiers, the huge crystal chandelier, the big VIP box under (again) the Soviet insignia. A mere half dozen people were sitting there, and Tanya craned her neck to see if she could recognize them.

The performance was superb. I had seen the Bolshoi's *Eugene Onegin* at Lincoln Center and been disappointed. But this was perfectly beautiful, beautifully perfect. All those difficult adagios, the concert of the six pas-des-quatres, all on stage at once, the tours de force, then the lovely graceful développés … I doubt I will see a more transporting stage performance. After the ballet came to its tragic end, the audience shouted bravos, flowers arrived, and everyone clapped, Russian-style, in unison.

I liked Tanya. She was patient with the language problem, sophisticated, good company. We had lagers and an enjoyable cafeteria meal, then she saw me to a

Metro station, we touched cheeks, and she was gone, leaving me trying to puzzle out the Cyrillic metro map again. Oh God, where was I, where was I going, how would I get home to the hotel? I did OK.

In the morning I got my gear together and, wearing my disguise as a Russian pensioner (*shapka*, old leather coat and jeans), ignored the turnstiles and grabbed a metro train to Red Square and the Kremlin, which I had toured too quickly during my visit with Alexander. On this dreary Saturday, wedding parties were straggling into the great open space of Red Square to have their pictures taken. A young gray-coated soldier lounged in front of Lenin's rectilinear tomb of brown and terracotta stone. He seemed to be supporting himself on his rifle as though it were a crutch. A trio of uniformed army officers strolled up grandly from the direction of the Kremlin, and one of them broke away to speak to the soldier. He straightened with a slightly offended look, and then resumed his slouch as the officers passed out of view, walking toward the river. He's done that before, I thought. An expert drinker-napper.

Lenin's tomb, surrounded by a rectangle of blue spruce, was closed to visitors. "Kremlin wall is world's most famous cemetery," I heard a passing guide tell his charges, referring to the vertically-arranged interments behind the tomb. "Every year tomb is closed for a few months for renewing Lenin's body."

At Archangelskii Cathedral I sat down to rest my feet for a few minutes but was distracted by a wonderful sound. It was ethereal, unaccompanied religious song, reminding me of Gregorian chant but more beautiful. Somehow through some magic spirituality of their own, those old Russian religious composers were able to communicate with the deep spirituality of people, and there were choristers who could convey their meaning perfectly. They shared a gift that was imbued with the special pain, longing and sadness that seem always to have coloured the Russian soul.

I thought how marvellous it was and yet how strange that this church should have such a wonderful electronic sound system – but no, three men and two women were standing in front of a great carved gilded door, and this exquisiteness was coming from them. Awed, I stayed to listen, and then bought their compact disk, which was identified with the name "*Anima*" – Soul.

I took a Sunday morning walk to a deserted Gorky Park, which despite its cheerful signs made me think of a spooky old abandoned movie set. Around me were small icy mounds of old snow, with black tips like tiny melted cathedrals or browned meringue. To my left, bizarrely, English-language rock music pounded eerily from a deserted octopus-type fair ride named "Break Dance," its cars immobile against a much-faded, painted backdrop of scantily dressed female dancers. When I stopped my note-taking to look at it, the music stopped, too. There was the plosive cough of pneumatics, somewhere behind the frozen two-dimensional dancing girls, and another, *kissshh*, and mysteriously one of the cars made a spastic half-spin, then another, and then all was silent again.

Where was everyone? What did they know that I didn't know? At the park gate a man was buying a pony ride for his little girl.

Soon after lunch I met Alexander at the hotel for my farewell ride to the airport. He looked wan – his 40-day "winter Lent" fast would last until the Russian Orthodox Christmas on January 7. As a devout Orthodox Russian he could eat no red meat or dairy products, and so unlike many others in Russia he wouldn't celebrate twice and have Christmas Dinner on the 25th as well. I gave him my sympathy and, though it probably didn't help, told him I had bought a St. Nicholas icon to put on my mantel at the Orthodox Christmas.

After Alex delivered me to the airport I found a place to put down my gear and enjoy a coffee while I waited for my call to the gate. Domodedovo airport was newer and less-known in those days, and exciting because it had flights to Baku (capital of Azerbaijan), and other exotic places on Utair, Adria Airways, Air Malta, Krasnoyarsk Airways, Ural Airways, Siberia Airways ...

I slumped into the seat of an Aeroflot plane bound for London and slept. When I woke I could see lights down below, twinkles of different colours against the black. And then we could see the roads and motorways. The clusters of light faded away briefly then came back as we passed over patches of light cloud. Closer to Heathrow the lights disappeared altogether, obscured by cloud, the wheels dropped, and we were in England, rolling along shiny runways to Terminal 4. After a few days of mental decompression with my Mare Street family I'd be back at the airport again, this time on my way to Albuquerque. Thanks to my telephone charge card and the luxury of email, I knew all was well on the home front, but nothing would beat being there.

⚜

The Moscow research trip yielded tens of thousands of words – no one had cared that I was audiotaping everything – and added colour to my growing manuscript. Nothing dramatically new or spectacular came out of the conversations with Zarubin, Velikhov, Krokhin, or another interviewee, the physicist and *gulag* survivor Dmitry Mikheyev – though all contributed to the background story and Zarubin gave me a treasury of useful information in subsequent emails. They believed that the SDI program was real and not a hoax, while at the same time they believed it was impossible to complete. On the other hand, the prospect of an SDI eventually emerging from the land of the Manhattan Project and Project Apollo, improbable as it was, was powerful enough to cause a great deal of worry to a Soviet leadership that was naturally suspicious and not scientifically astute. After all, if it worked, it would topple the USSR's superpower status, and with it "nuclear parity," which rested on the possibility of mutually assured destruction (MAD) and the maintenance of the Soviets' nonstop, conveyor-belt ICBM factories.

I wasn't disturbed by security issues during the Moscow trip, nor did I notice any security people watching me. The tall, serious-looking man that several times I had seen standing alone in the lobby, who looked like a character-actor spy from "The Third Man," was a candidate, though I never saw him outside the hotel. And then there was the outstandingly gorgeous Russian woman in the red fox *shapka* who struck up an animated conversation with me at the rebuilt super-church, then disappeared when she realized I was accompanied by a Russian man.

The Soviet dimension, with the material I had gathered in Moscow, was duly woven into my book manuscript; and *The Star Wars Enigma: Behind the Scenes of the Cold War Race for Missile Defense* was published by Potomac Books the first week of September 2006.[38]

It wasn't a technical book, though this had been my original plan. Most of it was about the genesis, development, and outcomes of the original SDI concept. It naturally included some information on science and technology, but mostly it illustrated how political systems use science, and the cachet of science, to advance strategic political goals. While Ronald Reagan was briefed on exotic space defence many times, the technical details were hardly more relevant to his SDI vision than the sci-fi film fantasies he appeared in as a movie actor. The Strategic Defense Initiative was more than this. I took special note of Reagan's line from his book *An American Life:* "SDI wasn't conceived by scientists."[39]

Naturally I loved the reviews. Jim Asker, executive editor at McGraw-Hill, called *The Star Wars Enigma* "the definitive history of U.S. efforts in missile defence." Robert C. McFarlane, Reagan's national security advisor, called it "the most rigorous scholarship yet to appear on this climactic period of history."

A number of people came forward to offer me useful new information *after* the book was published. Among these was O'Dean Judd of Los Alamos National Laboratory, who was chief scientist of the Strategic Defense Initiative Organization (SDIO) from 1987 to 1990. His predecessor in that position, Gerold Yonas, had contributed mightily to the story. Judd said he loved the book, though he disagreed strongly with a number of points, including Yonas's pivotal suggestion, backed up by suggestions from Robert McFarlane that SDI was something of a hoax. "If I had thought for a minute that SDI was a psychological operation, I would not have agreed to the Chief Scientist job," he told me. In fact, McFarlane called it a "sting."

We won't talk about the sales success of the book. Let it be said only that it was just as successful as *Solar System*, though it was less attractive and far, far richer in previously unpublished information. But it contained nothing about Gorky Park on a winter's day, of songs in the Kremlin, ballet at the Bolshoi, or the difficulty of ordering caviar in Moscow.

21. MOTHER GOES HOME

What is life? It is the flash of a firefly in the night. It is the breath of a buffalo in the wintertime. It is the little shadow which runs across the grass and loses itself in the sunset.
– Crow Foot, Blackfeet Tribe (1890)

I was immensely proud of my mother. She lived bravely alone in her own house until she was 95, firmly determined to hang on to her independence. After the atrium accident she was still managing to cook her meals, do the laundry, and tidy up, with two or three hours of contracted help coming in three times a week. I would usually stop by on my way from work, and on weekends she would often come over for dinner, at which Dee usually officiated, and sometimes we would go over to Dee's place. Mother got along tremendously with Dee and when Jonathan was at the house it was a special treat for us to be together.

Help or no help, she pushed herself as hard as she could. It was her way, and had been so since her childhood in Bingley. One day I found her on her knees, washing the floor, and I knew this couldn't go on forever.

The moment came when I had to gather my senses and control my emotions enough that I could have that crucial talk with a woman I had known for so many decades, who had cared for my father and me so faithfully through the years without a word of complaint, and had always "been there" for me even when I didn't ask for it. She realized, sensibly but of course very sadly, that it was a big place for one increasingly frail old lady to take care of.

Dee and I considered the possibility that Mother might move to my house, which was an attractive enough idea and I thought that I could get a better bed for her and perhaps engage a local Buddhist caregivers' organization for supplemental daily help. But the floors were all brick and potentially dangerous for someone who was becoming more susceptible to falls, and the doors were too narrow to accommodate the wheelchair that she might need before long. We found a residence that was bright and modern and could have been an upscale apartment house, except that access to a restaurant with good, varied food was included in the rent (we sampled the menu), the residents were mostly elderly single women, and each apartment was provided with a help button. It was expensive, but I knew we could make it.

Mother got along well at her new residence and made a couple of good friends, but had now developed atrial fibrillation, which meant we had to consult regularly with a cardiologist and her general practitioner, as well as the psychiatrist we had acquired after she overdosed on iodine from kelp supplements. Though she refused to admit it, she soon had difficulty walking from her room to the dining room, she had become very deaf indeed, and her old hearing aid seemed not to work any more.

May 1, 2005 – Dee rang me from Mother's flat, said Mother was ill and it would be a good thing to come over. I did and she was indeed in a bad way. Since it was Saturday noon, her GP was unavailable, so I rang her psychiatrist, David Ewing, and he kindly offered to come. He found that her pulse was, incredibly, down to 27. Apparently too much heart medication. I summoned an ambulance and the medics attached an external pacemaker, which is a frightening but lifesaving apparatus that applies large voltages to the entire chest. They took her the short distance to St. Joseph's Hospital and there followed a terrible afternoon in the intensive care unit, keeping her heart going with electrical shocks that made her whole body jump on the table as if animated by invisible marionette strings. Dee looked on as Mother and I were repeatedly asked, "Do you want to go on living? Does she want to go on living?" We both said yes. Through some terrible miscommunication between doctors, she had taken two different medications instead of just the one. But to our relieved surprise she recovered rather quickly and after a few days in the heart hospital was soon moved to a rehabilitation center. In a couple of weeks Dee and I moved her back to her little flat, and I went on a business trip to Washington with Pace VanDevender. Amazingly, he and I both had emergency phone calls while we were there, reporting that our mothers were again back in hospital.

This time my mother had pneumonia and a urinary infection. She got over that, but the assisted-living people said they couldn't take care of her properly. Eventually, after a couple of false starts, we moved her to private sheltered care in nearby Corrales. This had been a fast-paced cascade of events. It was hard to believe that only a couple of months earlier she had scampered up the concrete steps to Dee's apartment without assistance. "I'm tough," she would say, "I'm from Yorkshire." She needed to be. But I suspect she was still in shock from losing my dad. A couple of times she looked at me sadly and, without mentioning him, would say, "Oh, I wish I could cry. If only I could cry." It broke my heart, I couldn't find my way into her mood, and I didn't know what to say or do.

Mother's latest residence was a comfortable place in a beautiful setting, but the owner had a difficult personality and I could not put up with her surly reluctance to deal with medical professionals and her dark insinuations that in truth I would like my mother to die. So we moved yet again, to another sheltered care home, Andrew House.

September 10, 2005 – Yesterday afternoon, shortly after 5, I had a call from Andrew House, reporting that my mother had refused food at dinnertime and fallen asleep at the table. I went to see her, and there was Mother, sat straight at the table, eyes closed, food, and a couple of pills in front of her. I phoned Zia Hospice, and it was not long before Jane Brown arrived and started taking vital signs, blood sugar, etc. While she was there I called Dr. Ewing, who was still at his office, and told him what was going on. He was shocked when he heard she was taking two Prozac a day and said no, she was supposed to take two a week along with amitryptilline for sleep. The hospice nurse, Jane, arrived and reported that Mother had a temperature of 101 that probably meant an infection. I got ready to go and get aspirins and antibiotics, but Jane again came to the rescue and picked them up for us.

This morning I was dopey after too few hours' sleep, but got to Andrew House at about 8:30 to find the fever was gone and my mother had been to breakfast though she hadn't eaten much. She was back in bed and dozing.

At midday there was a call from Lana, the owner/manager. Did I know what happened to my mother's teeth? Well, no, I didn't know they were missing. Fortunately I had an extra set of her lower teeth, so I took them over. Mother was back in bed. We talked a little but it was hard for her to stay awake.

My mother liked the new place, and the other residents loved her, but gradually she was being taken down by congestive heart failure. When things got really bad she decided she was going to die. She made it quite clear that she wanted to die, and stopped eating. I tried tempting her with her favourite foods, but to no avail. When that spoon approached her face, she clamped her mouth determinedly shut, and there was nothing I could do.

One afternoon while I was keeping Mother company and trying to coax her to eat, with very little response even though she was sitting up on a living room couch, she suddenly said, "I want to go upstairs now, I want to go upstairs." It was a single-story building but I knew what she meant. Bedrooms were always upstairs in the old English houses I knew. And people, if lucky, died in bed.

Somehow I carried her to her room – fortunately it was on the ground floor and not very far away. I made her comfortable and kissed her goodnight as she might have done when I was a sick child in Heysham. "Everybody loves you," I said. She knew I meant it and she smiled. And then she drifted off to sleep. At about 3 o'clock the next morning a hospice nurse phoned me to say she had passed away. She died peacefully, at the end of a long life. Sometimes I think she could have clung on a little longer if it were not for her acute deafness and her isolation from the stimulus of conversation. But, as she would have said, she couldn't be bothered with it any more.

I included these words in her memorial service eulogy:

My mother, Margery Kershaw Hey, died in her sleep early on the morning of September 19, 2005, aged 97, after a long life in which she enriched and entertained the lives of many. On our last afternoon together we shared some sweet remembrances about the old days, and she told me she was ready to go...

In life she was a delightful lady and the greatest source of inspiration to my own life. She nursed me through a long childhood illness and with my father ignited my interests in reading, writing, music, and the natural world. When they came to the States, they gave up their business, and their proximity to relatives and friends, entirely to give me a chance of better health in a warmer climate.

And so I grew up thinking of our family – my mother and father and I – as a kind of web that held us together, and it seemed that we knew what each of us was thinking and there was no need for protracted discussion or argument, and perhaps I was right, not just merely naïve, because it seemed to work. This tiny family was, we assumed, part of a greater web that included all humanity and perhaps stretched out into the stars. My mother and father are gone, but as Jack Lemmon once said, death ends a life, not a relationship.

⟨❦⟩

My mother's death was the second great loss of my year.

One evening late in the month of July, Carletta Garcia had phoned to tell me that Myron, her husband and my friend, was ill with cancer of the pancreas. I had not heard from her for a long time and the news was a shock. We agreed that I would go over to Ácoma that Saturday afternoon and visit with him. I was too late. Their son Zack phoned with the news that Myron had died in the night. The only good news was that Skip, their friend and Carletta's adopted brother, had visited the previous afternoon and he and Myron had played guitar songs together.

Just recently I had told Dee that I felt badly because my Indian friendships seemed to have melted away; now this seemed a sad confirmation of the fact. Myron had offered to show me the special place where his kinsmen placed *paho* prayer sticks in communion with the spirit world. I felt deeply honoured, but had promised to return early to Albuquerque. Foolishly I had missed the opportunity. I was reminded of the time in 1982 when, for a similarly flimsy reason, I had declined a friend's invitation to introduce me to a Buddhist temple on an island near Tokyo.

The funeral was held at beautiful little St. Ann's church in Acomita, a small Pueblo mission style building, finished in 1940, that features beautifully carved inside beams and a nave that curves inward at the pulpit like the prow of a boat.[40]

Myron's body, swaddled in a colourful Pendleton blanket, arrived in the back of a pickup with eight pallbearers, four on each side of the truck bed. Behind them a procession of cars and pickups snaked back eastward toward the main road.

I sat between two ladies I didn't know, who had almost surely come from Ácoma or Laguna, and felt their kindly gentility. Then the priest arrived. This was one of his customary duties, and he would not remember whose funerals he attended. His sermon, delivered in a croaky voice, had little or nothing to do with Myron and a lot to do with ingesting flesh and blood – as wafers and wine. Then, unnecessarily, he explained that he was not talking about cannibalism: this was something we all abhorred, wasn't it? I was astonished and wondered why, if he wanted to go on about the sacrament, he did not explain the Christian symbolism of transubstantiation. He must have known that archaeologists had been arguing for decades about indications of cannibalism at ancient Pueblo settlements.

The little memorized speech left me offended and saddened, feeling empty.

After the service I got into the car and joined the cortège – no limousines here, no plumed horses, just a line of modest cars and pickup trucks. We drove west and south through the desert to the pueblo burial ground. Two miles of vehicles drove through a metal gateway with a tiny cross on it, and found places to park in the grassless dirt amid the sage and chamisa and rabbit brush. A backhoe had dug a very deep hole in the sand. We waited; ladies fanned themselves and shaded their eyes against the unrelenting sun. The Catholic priest came in his robes and stood next to the medicine man, who was wearing plain working man's clothes with a headband and a medicine pouch on his belt. The priest said something to the medicine man, who answered with a chuckle, dissonant to me in that place.

The scene was overlooked by Mount Taylor, towering to the north. The sky was deep blue with small white clouds high in the stratosphere. Carletta sat in a folding metal chair near the grave, with her son Zack towering over her, holding her shoulders. The day of burial was also her wedding anniversary and she was racked with grief. The priest said a prayer and abruptly left. The medicine man said some things in the tribal language. Someone put a long ladder down into the grave and six men eased Myron's blanketed body, on its bright yellow plastic-coated bier, to its final resting place. Gifts were handed down to be buried with my friend.

I bent down and took a gift of sand from the ground and it was warm in my hand. We lined up to throw our handfuls down onto the still shape, and then men began quickly to shovel more earth into the grave. After it was done the medicine man, carrying a painted pot of water, said prayers to the north, south, east and west. Then he tossed the pot on a rough stone that had been placed on the grave. It shattered and the water soaked into the dirt. Everyone was very quiet, in this very quiet hugeness of desert.

Women came forward and covered the grave with flowers. Carletta's cries grew calmer and both boys were with her now, with her old aunt Virgie at her side. The crowd was so large, it was hard to see them now except for Myron's Zachary, the gentle giant. I followed Carletta's car back to their house, away from this place of solemn oblong mounds.

A little shrine for Myron had been set up in the living room. A painting of the Virgin of Guadalupe, some of the tall. bottled Mexican religious candles you can buy at the local supermarkets, a few flowers, some tiny gifts of food.

Driving home, I wondered what the Pueblo people think of death, and it occurred to me that a lost life had to be very much like the water that spilled from the decorated jug and soaked into the earth on Myron's grave.

I know very little of American Indian spirituality, one reason being that its adherents have not described it in writing, but from my association with the Pueblo peoples I suspect that it is particularly close to Taoism, a polytheistic set of religions that honour their ancestors and place special importance on mankind's union with nature.

Life went on, powered unceasingly by the things that went before.

⚜

Sadness naturally lingered with me after my mother's death, particularly when I thought with ineradicable futility of the things I had forgotten to ask her, or forgotten to tell her. It was the same with my father. Yet now they were free of earthly worries, sorrows, and pain, and with Dee's help and the comfort of my children and grandchildren I gradually re-emerged into what I considered a normal life.

A good part of the emergence had to do with getting seriously active in new things, and above all with travel. When I retired my name had magically been transferred to the mailing list of a local Albuquerque travel agency. Normally I deeply resent it when such things occur. This happened when, without my permission, I was listed in one of the proliferation of "yellow pages" directories and phoned by well-meaning people who needed the advice of a literary agent. But this time I was pleased. The company offered dozens of tours to destinations all over the world, the prices were reasonable, and, because all the flights originated locally, they included costs of transportation.

And travel we did. Hold onto your hat, for the rest of this chapter is a rollercoaster of experiences from my diaries in Costa Rica, French Polynesia, China – and New Mexico.

First I was intrigued by an ad for a trip to Costa Rica and Dee agreed to join me. I was impressed by a place that put so much emphasis – officially – on ecology. And so in November 2006 Dee and I embarked on our "eco-tourism" visit to the Pacific coast of that small country, on a ship that carried only 65 passengers. Most of our fellow tourists were our age or older, but marvellously game all the same. What a trip! The monkeys and macaws were great, and the majesty of the rainforest, but it was also remarkable – and admirable – to see an overweight lady with a crutch, gamely climbing a jungle path that consisted mostly of mud and rocks.

In 2006 we decided to keep on traveling, first to China on May 14-28. Orgies of skyscraper-building in Beijing and Shanghai, with some interesting, creative architectural construction in downtown areas, to complement the stolidly repetitious rows of high-rise apartment blocks in the suburbs. Old buildings were being torn down either to build modern structures or to make way for the rapidly rising Three Gorges Dam reservoir (the concrete for the dam was poured the day we were at the site). Few of the millions dislocated could afford the rents.

Communist rule was hard for the casual visitor to discern in the metropolises except for reminders like the huge Mao portrait on his mausoleum on Tiananmen Square. The semblance of Western cities was evident in the high-rise big-city buildings, hotels, restaurants, traffic jams, and people on the move. And the great gap between the poor and the well-off.

Our tour group members were treated like princes and princesses and we stayed at the best hotels. But we were left virtually no free time, and the idea of wandering around by ourselves hardly had a chance to come up.

It's impossible to describe this remarkable trip satisfactorily because so much was happening, on practically a nonstop basis. I had never (truly) taken so many photographs and videos. I was amazed to learn, once I had transcribed them, that my notes were 7,500 words. That's my *notes*, which is to say, just the facts, ma'am. If I filled them out into readable form, I imagine they would be four times as long. And if I added extra research, well, I'd have another book.

Sorry to say, we didn't get a chance to ride the Maglev train to the Shanghai airport on our way back. I heard that Angela Merkel did, that very same day. I just gritted my teeth as the thing whizzed above our motor coach and steeled myself for the 30-hour trip back to New Mexico.

In September I made a pilgrimage back to Paguate, the little village where I first met Myron's wife, Carletta, and their children Zachary and Spencer. Technically it was the feast of Saint Elizabeth, but the main reason for the celebration was to have a day of ancient Indian dancing, which would attract many old friends from widely scattered, far-off reservations in New Mexico and Arizona. It was a warm, satisfying time, though all were sorely missing Myron's benign and cheerful presence.

And then we were off again, on a trip that bore very little resemblance to the visits to China and the Indian Country. Next stop Tahiti!

Dee and I left for San Francisco one October morning, eagerly anticipating a nonstop flight to Papeete and the first day of our ten-day cruise in French Polynesia. I rationalized that the Tahitian capital is closer than London (by about 200 miles) and that I should undertake such things while I'm still fit enough to enjoy them.

It was almost dark when we arrived at our destination. Buses picked us up at the airport and sped us to the ship and the welcome comfort of our bunks. Early the next morning we left for a leisurely 2,100-mile round trip to the Marquesas Islands and back. The weather was perfect and the sea generally calm, though at Hiva Oa, in the Marquesas, we could not land because of the swell; in fact the tender/lifeboat was unable to come alongside after a short visit to shore and had to follow the ship into calmer waters before being winched aboard.

The geography of French Polynesia takes a bit of getting used to. The land area is small, about a third that of Connecticut, which is one of the smaller United States. It's not just an island colony like Guadeloupe or Martinique, but 118 islands grouped into five coral archipelagos spread out halfway between Australia and South America and on the other side of the Equator from Hawaii, with which its people are ethnically related. It was hard for me to believe that French Polynesia is considerably less than half the size of Hawaii, landwise, and has a tiny fraction of Hawaii's population. On the other hand, when you include the amount of sea that separates the islands, the colony is huge, considerably bigger than Hawaii. It seemed to take the ship ages to get from Papeete to the Marquesas – I had no idea it was a thousand miles away.

French Polynesia is a calmer, much less commercialized, francophone version of Hawaii, and I loved it. It is likely to remain my favourite holiday destination. No – I take that back. I would like to live there.

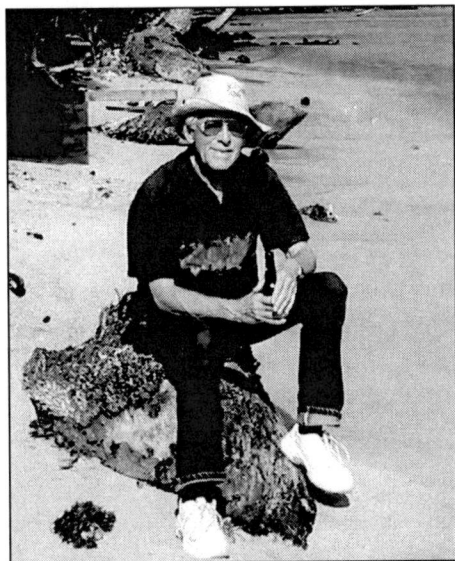

Happy man. Nothing but happiness and wonderment was on my mind as I
perched on this weedy rock during our visit to the Marquesas Islands.

Over breakfast on the morning of January 14, 2007, I asked Dee again to
marry me, and she agreed. Later when she left she hugged and kissed me, and
said "I love you." It was the second time in our relationship that she said the
magical three words first, rather than in response to me. After she left I thought
this must be significant, and that perhaps I had been able to persuade her of my
deep and long-felt desire for a trusting, open, and affectionate relationship.
Marriage!

22. GOING INTERNATIONAL

*I feel no need for any other faith than my faith in other human beings. Like
Confucius of old, I am so absorbed in the wonder of earth and the life upon it
that I cannot think of heaven and the angels. I have enough for this life. If
there is no other life, then this one has been enough to make it worth being
born, myself a human being.*
– Pearl S. Buck, This I Believe (1951)

In 2007 I scratched together just enough money to buy a 70-year lease on
a "pied-à-terre" or "boutique" flat close to Jocelyn and family, in Hackney,
part of London's East End. It was my birthday present to myself, but an
investment for my personal estate rather than a future permanent residence. It
would be a source of rental revenue and a place to stay between tenancies.

For years I had been looking for a flat in this area, with limited success
because I did not know the ropes. One year I found an attractive corner third-
floor flat very close to Joss, Dave, and the kids. It was a Saturday afternoon. At 1
p.m. I asked for a few scraps of extra information on the property, but by 5
someone else had snapped it up. Of course I kept on looking. There seemed to
be a hole in my memory where thoughts of home should reside. To balance this
deficiency it seemed I would need more than one place where I could live
and/or can be near to people I know and love.

The flat was part of the Victoria Park Estate, a short walk from the
western entrance to the 200-acre park for which the estate was named, which
had been handsomely laid out by architect James Pennethorne in the 1840s.
The flat was part of a well-designed, attractive building project built and
owned by the Crown Estate. These relatively new buildings extended west
from Gore Road, near the north-western corner of the park, where, as in
other parts of Hackney, there was severe aerial bombing during World War II.
The bombed-out area, including Christ Church, was bulldozed in 1966-7.
Christchurch Square and St. Agnes and Pennethorne Closes then were built
on the church grounds and the west end of Gore Road; all three had been

named by 1979. Today the property, with additional street names, extends to the Regents Canal.

Yes, my landlady was the Queen, at least prior to the estate's sale to the giant Peabody organization in 2011.

It was what Americans might call a furnished efficiency apartment, with a bedroom, bathroom, and combined kitchen and living room. It was also expensive, especially since the housing boom had not yet collapsed, with a market value that approximated that of the three-bedroom custom-designed house that was my American home. If I had found the refugee's $150,000 hoard of gold coins that was dug up in Hackney that summer, that wouldn't have paid for it. But it was well-built and comfortable and had a garden larger than the inside floor plan, and a picnic table on the strip of concrete outside our back door. Dee, bless her heart, approved. Though the bedroom was small enough, and the bed large enough, that we had to approach the pillows crabwise between mattress and walls, I was encouraged by the fact that the couple next door had done wonders with a flat of approximately the same size.

To the south, Mare Street became Cambridge Heath Road when it crossed the canal and stretched southward a mile and a half to Whitechapel Road, where Asian traders tended a long white line of tented stalls through the day. To the north it led to the borough's retail and government center, Hackney Central, mostly a mixture of unappealing shops, commercial buildings, and apartment tower blocks that had been built on the proliferation of World War II "bomb sites."

Perhaps I am being overly critical. St. Augustine's Tower, the remnant of a 16th Century church, stands over the Narrow-way, near to the Hackney Central "Overground" train station, and where strings of red buses congregate to take passengers to points all over London. Hackney has a good library and museum, next to the town hall, which in turn is a neighbour to the Hackney Empire, a restored 1901 music hall that has featured such luminaries as W.C. Fields and Charlie Chaplin. There is one historical treasure, Sutton House, built by one of Henry VIII's courtiers in 1535, now managed by the National Trust close to a number of handsome, privately restored Georgian residences.

Hackney people come from all over the world and from all ethnic and racial groups. My personal impression was that the Bangladeshi community was large and well-mannered, the Turks ran corner shops and cafés, the Vietnamese kept to themselves but had good restaurants and beauty parlours, the blacks were mostly neighbourly residents from decades past, the whites included an unusually large complement of artists and media specialists. Intermarriage and general socializing between blacks and whites seemed more acceptable than elsewhere in Britain and was generally considered unremarkable.

There were occasional incidents of serious crime and a fair complement of hooligans, certainly enough to provide a focus for the riots of 2011. The ruffians were generally invisible during the weekdays, including Saturdays, when the enjoyable, upscale Broadway Market was in full swing. But at the end of the day they would appear in pairs or little groups, talking loudly with cans of cheap lager in hand, and you'd be tempted to move to the other side of the road. I was delighted in 2008 when drinking on public transportation, which until then was not an uncommon sight, was finally banned.

When you have a chatting relationship with the neighbours and get to know the streets, Hackney is just fine, and can be downright enjoyable.

I was not returning to the England of my childhood, or the England where I laboured at the Victorian carrels of the *Kentish Express*, or the England that presented my career with a diversion into pharmaceuticals publishing. This was a quite different place. Demographically London had changed radically, due to the arrival of people from the old British Empire and most recently from France and the eastern European members of the European Union. Money-wise it was in a mess, shown most vividly in September 2007 when customers lined up daily to withdraw their savings from Britain's fifth-largest mortgage lender, Northern Rock. It also *looked* different, and the only way you could pretend to escape from its differentness was to hide in an old pub, examples of which were harder to find each day, and reminisce with the natives about the (sometimes) good old days.

The city was now spiked with metal and glass pinnacles that towered toward low scudding clouds, competing for attention with St. Paul's, Westminster Abbey, and the Nazi-shattered, finely reconstructed legal society hub called simply the Middle Temple. Christopher Wren's mid-1670s memorial to the end of the great Fire of London, known simply as "The Monument," has long been reduced to matchstick scale, surrounded by skyscraper monsters that would never appear in Paris. That said, the development along the north side of Bishopsgate, the British Library, and the splendidly revitalized St. Pancras station, hotel, and shops got my thumbs–up sign for excellence in the architecture of the day. These were the big projects. You could also see lots of living talent in newly revived stations, old wholesale markets, and other smaller projects, some of which fit in remarkably well, niched between historic buildings that had survived the bombings of World War II.

The new London was peppered with examples of millennial architecture planned during the impulsive 1980s, when it was decided to convert the worn-out Isle of Dogs into the huge new office and residential development that includes Canary Wharf, the heady 1990s, and the early years of the new millennium. To me these were, well, interesting, but so many seemed to be products of overreaching architectural peer groups working for moguls who were, I would say, somewhat deficient in the arena of aesthetics.

Would my new flat be a stepping stone to permanent residence in England? After I mentioned this daydream to my accountant in England, a note of forewarning and muted distress attached itself even to the matter-of-fact wording of his emailed reply. Something Dreadful would happen if I attempted to do such a thing. Tax and immigration laws would keep me from staying in the U.K. for more than 90 days in any one year unless I were ready to take on an extra tax burden. Probably for compassionate reasons he restrained himself from going into further detail. I composed myself by recalling one particular winter night walking in the West End, when the cold rain, driving horizontally into my face, was joined by fingers of cold that insinuated themselves between the buttons of my trench coat, through my business suit and into my ribs and spine. I resolved to spend two months at the flat, if possible in the warmer months of each year, plus another month as long as there were room for me at my daughter's house on Mare Street. At other times the flat would be leased with the help of a local agency.

The year 2008 was so rich in experience that I had to go back to my old calendars to work out what happened, and when. The first half of the year was dominated by writing – mostly science articles for my pals at Sandia Labs – and the second half by travel. January we spent a few days in Las Vegas with the theatrical/home-sales duo Henry Avery and Dehron Foster, my first tenants at the condo I had bought next door to Dee's place, half-way up the dry, eroded river-bank that separates Albuquerque's valley from its gently sloping Northeast Heights. February was highlighted by a trip to the AAAS meeting with Dee in Boston. I was awarded my Fellow of the AAAS certificate and rosette, which I wore with pride for the rest of the meeting. I already felt my life goal to achieve career excellence had been achieved over decades of work. This was the confirmation, affirmed by my peers.

⚜

It was early in the year, mid-February, when I looked out of my New Mexico bedroom window one morning and to my great surprise saw a jungle fowl hen walk out from underneath the pyrocanthus hedge at the corner of the patio. Jungle fowl run native in tropical climes, but thanks to Virginia Feather they were running wild in our patch, too.

Virginia Feather was our local chicken lady, all eighty pounds of her. She had a surname to go with the sobriquet, and what she didn't know about chickens wasn't worth knowing. She was good company, a remarkable, tiny retired lady who had been a teacher, learned the writer's art, and nursed her mother mostly at home until she passed the century mark. Importantly, Virginia had a collection of jungle fowl and Guinea fowl, so we suspected rightly that this slim little animated clump of dark brown feathers had wandered from her garden to ours. But I wasn't ready for what happened next.

As I watched, a line of 13 fluffy little chicks followed their mother into the garden. Thirteen! Over the following months we would watch the little ones grow into scrawny pullets as the mother gradually increased their time in the open and taught most to fly, clumsily, to the top of the wall and into the boughs of the apple tree. This "school" was remarkably effective and we marvelled at it. But Virginia warned us that the neighbourhood was a dangerous place for such creatures, and she was right. Within a year most of the youngsters disappeared, to provide dinners to the hawks, raccoons, coyotes, and other "critters" that roam about our neighbourhood.

⚜

I flew off to England on March 19th and dossed down with Joss, Dave, and the kids. As usual my brain performed the mysterious magic of flipping a few neural switches and putting my built-in Albuquerque reference information on the back shelves while similar information for London was briskly dusted off and brought to the front. Almost immediately I knew which side of the road to drive on, which radio frequency was tuned to Radio 4, which buses and tube trains went where, and probably how to speak English without an easily definable American accent. (While I have never admitted this publicly, on a couple of occasions I caught myself driving on the wrong side of parking lots in America. Please don't tell anyone.)

School holidays provided the opportunity for everyone to decamp for Suffolk, where we spent four chilly days at a house owned by one of Dave's colleagues. The house, situated on a winding country road bordered richly with daffodils, had two bedrooms on the upper story and another in the loft. From the outside it had the look of a storybook country cottage, and inside it had the untidy, comfy, perfumed atmosphere of a home whose occupants had gone for a walk and would be back in a few minutes. Dishes were stacked in the draining board, books left higgledy-piggledy in the living room, shoes left at the door to stop tracking in the mud. The children went running joyfully in the lush garden and we started to unpack. Soon David was on his knees before the shrine-like fireplace, blowing life into a pile of reluctant kindling.

Chef David. My multi-talented son-in-law David Armitage cooks up another superlative meal at Christmas, 2005.

That evening, and the next, I carried the one electric heater from my garret in the loft to the sitting room and back repeatedly, just to keep us warm. When the sun came out on our first vacation day no one but I felt the stubborn chill, and I kept my mouth shut. The children gambolled on the beach at Southwold in defiance of the cold as though it were a midsummer day, and Eddie cheerfully allowed himself to be buried in the sand by his energetic sister. Good times, taking me back to the days when Joss and Brian were the same age. The morning we left, while I was making the bed, I learned that an electric blanket was fitted neatly to the mattress.

In April there was a welcome climatic shock to the system when Dee and I spent a two-week break at the Big Island of Hawaii, at a condo owned by her cousin Will and his partner Jack. It was our second visit to Kona. The year before we had learned about the local farmers' market with its delicious, softball-sized avocados and small sweet bananas. Sea-turtles were still nibbling at the rocks a few yards from the lanai. We knew where to buy fresh fish from the morning's catches. The vog (volcanic smog) was worse than the previous year, but did not interfere with our fun – one great outing was a day trip to the north-western corner of the island, home of the huge Parker Ranch, one of the largest cattle ranches in the United States.

As soon as we arrived in Hawaii I wanted to go snorkelling. "Ah, then you must go to Kahalu'u Beach Park," I was told by the tour specialist in the lobby. So I piled my equipment in the back of the car and took off. It was only five miles to the south, along Ali'i Drive, so I didn't have much to lose.

I had no trouble finding the beach, which is next to the big Outrigger hotel, but getting into the water – backwards, while wearing flippers – was an ordeal. To begin with, the water was too shallow. I could ease myself in, carefully, and truly there were tiny, colourful fish everywhere; but I realized that if I moved more than a few yards I was in immediate danger of scraping my keel on the rocky bottom.

So again I asked the tourist advisor for help. "You need to go to Hononaunau," he said. "It's a fairly long drive but you'll never forget it." He should have told me it was right next to the well-known "Place of Refuge" National Historical Park, which I could easily pronounce. The third time I tried, I found the spot. It's a large sheet of lava next to a bay where spinner dolphins play, and to the north you can just make out the monument of Captain Cook, near where he met his maker on Kealakekua Bay during a major misunderstanding with the natives. One of the best Big Island snorkelling and SCUBA spots is in the deep water next to the Cook monument – on our first trip to Kona we went there by boat since it is all but inaccessible on foot.

Hononaunau was very tricky. The place was busy with people carrying diving equipment of all kinds, including plastic dolphin-tail prostheses that they could wriggle into, and signs stuck out from the lava rock, asking people not to disturb the dolphins. The people were all heading for one small spot, to a smooth shelf about four feet wide, cut into the lava at the water's edge. This little ledge was the easiest way in or out of the sea. I put on my gear and slid in, not thinking of how I would get back. I was immediately immersed in a clear, deep and wondrous paradise of tropical fish – including scores of yellow tang, which were once so numerous that this part of Hawaii was nicknamed the Gold Coast.

My enjoyment of the adventure was hampered by my confusion about how I would get back on dry land. There were no steps, handholds, floating docks, or ropes with which I could return to terra firma. So I watched the Hawaiians, who seemed to be part fish anyway, and who were hauling two-tank SCUBA equipment out of the water as thought it were made of balsa. Probably without even thinking of it, they were letting the waves lift them up onto their lava-rock perches, backwards. I tried it, and to my relief it worked.

We are used to thinking about Hawaii as a volcanic chain of islands, and can become entranced by the stories of Péle, the volcano goddess, and her fights with her sister Na-maka-o-kaha'i, whose husband she had seduced. These superhuman volcano problems are attributed to the volcanic eruptions that rumble on throughout the Hawaiian year.

The one truly scary adventure in this Polynesian holiday happened during a swimming-with-dolphins event that had been set up by a man who had bought the best-equipped inflatable boat I could ever imagine, new, at an auction organized by the Department of Homeland Security. Our skipper equipped us with masks, snorkels, and flippers, but after half an hour of sailing directly west into the Pacific I was taken aback when he urged us into the sea, saying nonchalantly, "The depth here is about 600 feet and you won't be able to see the bottom. When you look up you may notice that I have taken the boat away, to look for dolphins, but don't worry, I'll know where you are and I'll be back."

The captain's mate, a lovely Japanese girl, free-dived into the depths, graceful as a dolphin herself, and disappeared from view. As for me, I spent quite a bit of time coming up and looking around for the blasted boat as I paddled around, alone in the Pacific and out of sight of the land, looking down into the green abyss and wondering, where are those flippin' dolphins and why don't they call them porpoises like everyone else? I had a brief love-hate relationship with a revoltingly bright orange, six-foot length of spaghetti foam that the skipper had thrown me in case I needed added buoyancy. Then a few dolphins did show up, a quiet group of adults and youngsters 40 or 50 feet below and just visible through the pale green water.

Of course the inflatable speedboat did show up, or you wouldn't be reading this.

The next month Dee and I were back on the mainland, on a 12-day, 2,500-mile motoring trip/tour across Texas and Oklahoma to the beautiful Ozark Mountains, amazingly green after a very wet spring, with grass so high it was tickling the tummies of some very happy cows. We spent two nights in Branson, enjoying raucous hillbilly entertainment in a no-drinking, no-smoking nightclub. When I asked for the bar, the burly attendant said with reproving firmness, "This is a family restaurant, suh." We said hello to Dee's old family house in Plato, from the car, then left for Bennett Spring and Kansas City to enjoy a family wedding and visit some of her other relatives. Plato is no more than a hamlet, with a population of fewer than one hundred. But in 2010 it had the distinction of being the center of U.S. population – if everyone in the United States weighed the same and the country was a huge perfectly flat map, that map would balance on a tiny spot that is 2.7 miles east of Plato, Missouri. Disprove that!

For a while I worried how someone could actually sit down and figure out details like this, and why, but then I realized that probably such details are spat out by a computer at the U.S. Department of the Census, with no trouble at all.

⚜

June came too soon, and it was time to go to Washington and New York for two and a half days of media visits starring Sandia's Al Romig. Somehow I had put together short articles on 24 "talking points" about individual Sandia innovations, to support a dozen or so meetings with science writers at media that included *Science, Nature, The New York Times,* and *Scientific American.*

But something was beginning to bother me. First I could see the writing on the wall that would end my consultancy. Separately I was concerned for the once-great empire of American journalism. In the face of the financial crash that had begun in 2008, choking off the flow of advertising revenues, and the bootless effort to survive the onslaught of the electronic new media, newspapers, magazines, and even television were being twisted through a hapless sequence of managerial experiments. Its controllers were trying this, trying that, to win back the favour of readers and advertisers while their expert, specialist, better-paid reporters, including many U.S. science writers, were forced to search for jobs elsewhere.

I styled myself a science writer, and such I was, for the reasons that science and technology intrigued me, aroused my curiosity, and provided an income. Originally I wanted to think of science as a branch of philosophy and technology as the crafting of tools, but saw with resigned regret the insistent pull of technology on its gentler sibling. Science writing was a worthy vocation, encompassing so much of human endeavour, from cosmology to physics, chemistry, biology, engineering, medicine, computer technology, nanoscience, climatology, genetics, *ad infinitum*. And science touched upon all parts of modern life; it portended the extension of human capabilities and promised relief from suffering; it also portended death, destruction, cataclysm, the vanishing of species, including our own, from the planet.

Science writing fit well into my vision of the often-forgotten Fourth Estate principle. People should know about science, I reasoned, and understand at least the pros and cons of science and technology, so that they could express their opinions to their leaders and, when they thought it necessary, demand support or rejection of given scientific ventures.

In the world inside my head I saw science writing, more accurately science *journalism*, as unquestionably a benefit to humankind, akin to the investigative journalism that seeks out and exposes malfeasance, but with the advantage that it often describes human pursuits that are enlightening and even fun. I could see the erosion of both in the growth of an Internet that was able to blanket the world with information of all kinds, sometimes spreading untruths in powerful, seductive, and destructive rhetoric. I could see the strangulation of media, particularly newspapers, which generally produced truthful, balanced, information that would inform a democratic populace and which, when they had a bias, could advertise that fact with pride on their editorial pages.

The first decade of the 21st century would see the number of newspaper jobs fall by 50 per cent. This was depressing to me. The ideals of journalism that meant so much in my early professional years were withering, and with them a vital part of the nation's ability to inform its democratic electorate. I was concerned most for the future of investigative reporters, who are prime targets when costs must be cut because they generally command a higher salary, and their close cousins in science writing. I was delighted when the non-profit investigative news organization ProPublica arrived, promptly shared a Pulitzer Prize with the *New York Times Magazine*, and had its reports distributed regularly by Associated Press. And I was happy when Bill Moyers' televised investigative journalism returned to public television.[41] The ideals of the Fourth Estate were still alive, but in my mind needed a stronger revival yet. Just how this could happen, especially within the Internet, was a big and at the time a possibly unanswerable question.

⊙❈⊚

By contrast with my own story, Jonathan's career life was just beginning. He had been working at an Albuquerque bank, on his way to winning good benefits, help with college costs, and the first rung in the management ladder. But in October of 2005, during Sunday dinner, he announced that he had resigned. Why? "They wanted me to arrange loans for people who couldn't afford it," he explained, "and I didn't like it. It's not right." That was all I wanted to know, and my heart swelled in appreciation of 22-year-old Jonathan, the youngest of my three wonderful children. He then worked for a while doing data entry and database management at the Center for Adolescent Research and later landed a job at Bill Gordon & Associates, a prominent locally-based law firm. Within two years he would be the firm's Director of Information Technology, responsible for electronic communication among 100 full- and part-time employees located throughout the United States, at a time that the nation was enduring the early part of the financial crisis that emerged full-fledged in 2008.

⊙❈⊚

Dee and I spent August and September of that year at the London flat. The garden, with its seclusion of shrubbery and the big sliding glass door, made an extra room where we indulged in many gourmet meals on the sunny picnic table. A cheerful, friendly English robin (smaller and bolder than the American species) visited us there, and later a playful young tabby cat. In those times, before

314

my grandchildren started riding bicycles, a treat was hearing them ring the doorbell so we could walk together across Victoria Park to their school.

Weekends also tended to be special because on Saturday mornings we would enjoy the pricey hubbub of Broadway Market or, less frequently, walk to Brick Lane market or the Columbia Road flower market. At other times Dave would surprise us by announcing we would go on a road trip, whether to the Highgate or Essex woods or a property run by the National Trust or English Heritage. There would be a flurry of sandwich making and fruit packing supervised by Dave while Jocelyn detached the children from the TV so they could dress for the trip. Then we'd squeeze into the family's bright red Escort, already bristling with bulging supermarket bags, cameras, and water bottles, and head for the open road. Usually we'd fit, but as the children grew one or two of the team would travel by public transport, with Dave providing shuttle service at our destination.

Our most exciting summer venture was the Towersey Village Festival, held annually in a huge Oxfordshire field. Dee and I took the train while Dave drove with Joss and the children, Brian and his friend Sally following in a big red van crammed with camping gear. We settled into a zippered pouch in one of Dave's tents for four nights of music and dancing, of every kind that could be called "folk." At first I had my doubts about "tenting it" while having a good chance of having to walk two hundred yards across an unlighted, boggy field to the loo. But I wouldn't have missed it for the world.

The next month Dee and I motored to Morecambe, to see and photograph my childhood haunts before descending on my cousin Jimmy Power in Harecroft. Over 80 years old now but acting much younger and cracking jokes like a pro, Jimmy was a great host, taking us to two small but top-rate jazz gigs at which he was a lead player, then to an amazing Yorkshire-accented country-western night in nearby Harden. We went on side trips nearly every day – to the Lake District (a jaunt on Lake Windermere), York, Shipley for a welcome rainy-day look around Titus Salt's huge mill (now housing shops and a good restaurant), and Keighley for a visit to the mostly 17th century East Riddlesden Hall. And we saw Marie Mitchell, now the *grande dame* of the Honey Pot Farm I had known for so many decades.

Back in London, in the kitchen of Joss and Dave's house, I presented Dee with an engagement ring, part of a modest wedding-ring set that she fancied when we visited an antique shop at Salt's Mill.

Our two months in England gave us the delight of many hours with my grandchildren, and to share the magic of their growing-up years. Elizabeth had quickly excelled in interpersonal skills, though she too went through the stage sometimes called the "terrible twos." There was an inexplicable period in which she avoided me like the plague, but which ended as if it had never happened, and we became great friends again. There was a thoughtful mind under that mop of curly blond hair. She excelled in her schoolwork, as she did in the manipulation of her elders, and I was sure she would grow up to be a company director.

While I was in America, which was most of the time, Joss and Dave would encourage both children to write letters – generally notes of appreciation for this or that – for the old folks back in New Mexico. These were always a delight, often written and illustrated with crayons and in Eddie's case featuring highly imaginative, painstakingly drawn pictures of robots.

The children generally had their dinner at 5:15, followed by homework, unstructured play, story time, and bed. The living room shelves were lined with children's books, with the exception of a small section reserved for soft toys, and from them, every night without fail, two or three small books would be selected for reading. In her reading, Elizabeth caught up quickly with Eddie, whose comprehension seemed not quite to be in sync with his ability to vocalize the words. Both could memorize the stories, so that they sometimes seemed better readers than was actually the case, and Eddie, with his mind racing ahead, was expert in grasping the meaning of a sentence, then inserting his own words, different from the author's, when the context seemed to make sense.

Raising Eddie was difficult, in some ways a career job for Joss and Dave, who served as his unflagging advocates and mentors throughout his school years. Diagnosed early with Asperger's Syndrome, a mild version of autism, Eddie had difficulty communicating with adults and schoolmates, consistently lagged behind in language skills, and had trouble with short-term memory and understanding the cause-and-effect relationships that govern human activity. After spending some time with him I realized that this husky, cheerful lad was also very smart, and, although he detested the (rare) experience of losing, he was extremely good at playing chess. Otherwise he was happy when he was on the move, whether capering about the house, running wildly in the park, or splashing in the icy North Sea. When this wasn't possible he would resort to computer games or long sessions of assembling and re-assembling Lego components. Still, he was naturally gregarious: Joss recalls that in his early years he took a seat beside a stranger in a bus and extended his hand: "Hello, I'm Eddie Armitage. What's your name?"

In his pre-school and early primary school years I had difficulty understanding Eddie's speech, though Joss and Dave, being better accustomed to it, seemed to have little trouble. Then one day I got the idea that he was trying to speak at the same rate that he was thinking – that is, pretty fast – with rather indistinct diction. When I explained that some people had trouble keeping up with him because they didn't think as fast as him, he slowed down. For me it made a big difference.

In September Dee and I went on a short side-trip to Valencia, half-way down Spain's Mediterranean coast. We ogled the great bull ring, which reminded me of the Coliseum, walked the black marble pavements of the city square, sampled various local versions of paella (none better than Dee's), foiled a purse-snatcher, were peed on by a local dog when we ignored his begging, then took a look at the huge *Ciudad de Artes y Ciencias*, where the architecture alone proved worthy of the trip, all by itself. We had just enough time to tour the huge biopark, devoted almost exclusively to water creatures, and to enjoy a world-class dolphin show.

We had many memories to take back with us to New Mexico – including the most unusual pleasure of being able to celebrate both Brian's and Jocelyn's birthdays in the same year. The whole gang met at a pub-type restaurant in Hackney for Joss's; then a month later, on a gorgeous afternoon in Folkestone, we celebrated Brian's birthday at the appropriately named Grand Hotel. We'd be back in New Mexico in time for Jonathan's birthday.

We didn't stay still for long. Soon we were on our way to California and Stanford University, near Palo Alto, for the annual meeting of the Council for the Advancement of Science Writing, now grown from a smallish gathering of friends to a large annual convocation matched only by the press room contingent at the annual meeting of the American Association for the Advancement of Science. It was a pleasure to attend these two meetings every year and to see science writers I hadn't seen for a year or more. Though I got around a lot, I didn't spend much time in so-called media centers like New York, London, and Washington. This meant I was something of an outsider when I joined in conversation with people who worked and lived in close proximity, but the friendship was priceless and I reveled in it.

While flying home from California I snapped photos of the rugged landscape east of the Sierra Nevada and reflected how – though people were forever asking me where I would eventually "settle down" – I loved living in the West. One of the great things about Albuquerque is that you are amid thousands of square miles that have hardly been scratched by human intervention. It is so very different from England, where 95 percent of the landscape has been refashioned by man. From the air much of it looks like a cluster of conurbations, separated by the legally required "green belts" where new buildings have been all but prohibited since the mid-1900s. I appreciated the country's winding roads and its natural hilliness and haziness, which do so much to increase the impression of distance.

Take a look at Albuquerque's place on the map – there is hardly anything between it and Los Angeles, 670 miles away, but for the old railway town of Flagstaff. That's the distance from London to the northern tip of Scotland! The sight of those magnificent hills, mesas, buttes, and mountains, spreading as far as you can see from an airliner 35,000 feet above the ground, is no less than inspiring. It brings a kind of serenity into your head. If every minute or so you spot a dirt road or a pipeline route, it hardly matters because it is less than a hairline artefact, insignificant as the trail of an insect in the dust. A divided highway is no more than twin black threads against the sand. Then appears the farming – first the great green tiddlywinks of mechanized water-sprinklers, then the agricultural squares irrigated from open, well-fed channels, and then the towns. And a great hazy chaotically coloured green, brown, and gray blotch, as far as the eye can see. Civilization.

England was a place at least as dear and yet so different that it might belong to another planet. I think of lush summer foliage; the facades of old buildings that had been gutted and modernized inside; clouds moving a few feet above the high-rises; the softening quality of filtered sunlight; nourishing rain; the pervasive sense of history; people of many origins, faces mapped with untold histories; walls that if living would have known a myriad tragedies and triumphs; winter magnolias; and my own little flat, the unpretentious hideaway near the magnificent park and the Regents Canal. Most of all my small family – Jocelyn and David, with their two marvellous children, living just a few hundred yards from the flat; Brian 75 miles to the south, working at the hospice in Hythe in the same building where he was born and his mother died; and memories. Watching the children in their Christmas plays; plunging hell for leather in Yorkshire through the thick Hewenden undergrowth with Brian and Jonathan; taking the entire family to the moors above Bolton Abbey to cast my mother's ashes into the sheep-cropped turf, in my dreams to blend with those of my father.

23. A RESTLESS YEAR

All truly wise thoughts have been thought already, thousands of times; but to make them truly ours, we must think them over again honestly, until they take firm root in our personal experience.
– Goethe

It had been another juggernaut year in 2008, as though I were trying to out-do the road-warrior days of my full-time years at Sandia. But ever since Dee and I returned from England that summer I had missed my children and grandchildren. I fought against the idea of spending part of the Christmas holiday with them, as I had done two years earlier, and then gave up the battle and asked Joss and Dave if I could have my old bed back for a while.

I arrived at the end of November with one white shirt and one tie packed in with the rest of my baggage. Mixed in with family life, I spent a day with Al Romig at the Royal Academy of Engineering and another at the Rutherford Appleton Laboratory, and a pleasantly beery evening out with other members of the Association of British Science Writers. Eddie celebrated his eighth birthday in fine style; the entire English family plus Brian's friend Sally saw the uproariously Anglocentric pantomime "Mother Goose" at the Hackney Empire, we saw two school Christmas plays, and then I was back at Heathrow waiting for my plane.

Though I had been away in America for barely two months, I saw subtle changes in the children. They were moving quickly toward "mature" girlhood and boyhood, serious school-kids. Elizabeth had almost lost her baby fat (Eddie already had) and seemed to have abandoned her attention-getting naughtiness. She was writing "books" and "stories," and taking real interest in school activities. Dolls were not quite so important, but she still liked to dress up in fairy-tale costumes. Eddie was quieter too. He said he was enjoying school more, seemed to be learning to control his hard-to-understand floods of rapid speech, and perhaps was not quite so narrowly focused on Lego and computer games. Both were benefiting from a couple of important household innovations – strict limitation of screen time (TV/computer) and the institution of a point system (redeemable in cash!) for good behaviour and general helpfulness.

I returned to Albuquerque to find that Dee had almost finished painting a second room of the house. She had just received somber news, the death of her sister Deana's husband, Dale Fulks. And so on New Year's Eve it was her time to travel, to spend important time with her sister in Kansas City. Another brother-in-law whom I particularly liked, Henrietta's husband Charlie Morton, had been stricken with a blood disease, was scheduled for radiation therapy. The prognosis did not sound good then, and he too would pass away, in May, 2009.

❧

I began to feel the effect of the recession on my retirement nest-egg (mostly stocks and bonds) in the New Year. Their value declined by about a third, then to 40 per cent after the recession stiffened in late 2008, and I was more fortunate than many. I was reminded often of the Third World economic/health research I did at IMS, and my realization then that at some time there would have to be a levelling-out of international resources. Maybe this was the way it would start. I thought many people would be well advised to plant their vegetable gardens and allotments in the coming years.

❧

The world economic slump, and the increasing year-by-year possibility that my Sandia contract would cease to exist, encouraged me to look around for additional writing work elsewhere, perhaps in the ever-popular branches of health, medicine and biology. These were not my usual fare but they interested me nevertheless. For example I was intrigued that no one has figured out how, as an organism forms, the atoms and molecules that make up cells "know" how to organize themselves into the intricately arranged structures that become reef animals, trees, or people.

So, propelled by the prospect of finding new sources of wonder as well as income, I contacted the Albuquerque-based MIND Institute. MIND's success depended largely on the application of functional magnetic resonance imaging (fMRI) technology for studies of neuroscience, and was dedicated to "improving the diagnosis of mental illness and brain disorder; and helping people in the

321

future by finding methods of prevention, better treatments and, ultimately, cures." Part of its work involved touring New Mexico prisons with state-of-the-art fMRI equipment loaded in a semi-trailer tractor, recording brain scans of prisoners who received a small reward for their participation, something like coffee and a doughnut.

I first learned about MRI in the 1960s, when early versions were used by Sandia for materials science studies. When it became a medical diagnostic technique, I had an MRI brain scan after being shaken up in a car crash. When *functional* MRI made it possible to image activity in different parts of the brain at the same time, I wanted to know more. Though my writing experience was mostly in the physical sciences I got to know the people at MIND and to prove my mettle set up a teleconference with a contact at *Science News*. In the process I learned about blood flow in and around the amygdale, which create a "fear center" in the brain. Apparently if these little organs do not function in a more or less normal manner, the individual might have a predisposition to addictive or even psychopathological behaviour. Fascinating! At an AAAS meeting three years later, a speaker from the University of Pennsylvania announced that: "Psychopathic individuals show reduced amygdala functioning when processing moral dilemmas, suggesting dysfunction to the neural circuitry underlying moral decision-making."[42] Other studies indicate that many parts of the brain are involved in controlling the degree of benevolent empathy that is employed by individuals in conducting their lives, and which is a vital part of the attitudes that contribute to moral decision-making.[43] Did Hitler and Stalin possess these organs? What about Idi Amin? Caligula?

The MIND people looked very important and impressive. They wore expensive suits and ties and brought identical computers that they set up carefully on the shiny new executive conference table. They listened politely to my pitch but said little. Nevertheless they wrote a nice contract for me, and for a while it looked as though I might be embarking on an exciting new science-writing specialty. But my MIND contact had a surprise in store for me. Before I could do a microsecond of contract work she told me there was no money to support it. My brief dash into neurology writing came to an abrupt and unambiguous stop.

To my surprise I was soon writing again about the biological sciences, this time at the invitation of the Santa Fe Institute, a collection of very smart people who spend their time thinking about, studying, and trying to unscramble difficult questions – on the evolution of languages, perhaps, or the deadly, crafty habits of the HIV virus, something so primitive that learned people were arguing over whether or not it was a living entity.

In the foothills of the Sangre de Cristo Mountains I found a hive of diverse, interesting, and engaging individuals who share a common interest in complex systems, mathematics, and game theory. They were based in a picturesque, sprawling complex with a layer-cake series of floors, each not much more than a meter and a half above the other, with stairways that follow the contours of the hillside. There are many windows, many places to stop and talk or discuss the day's seminar, and sliding glass doors open onto patios where one can talk with one's colleagues or simply sip a coffee and think while looking off into the scrubby forest of piñon pine and juniper. In the library there was to my surprise a workspace for Sam Shephard, and another for Cormac McCarthy, each overlooking, as from an airliner seat, the vastness that slopes down to the Rio Grande from the Sangre de Cristo Mountains.

Costa Rica. Naturalist Rudy Zamora and I pose aboard ship before disembarking from a wild week of exploring the coasts and rainforests of this Central American ecotourism centre.

My editor was very helpful, in fact more helpful than most, in providing me with background information. I was however stumped for a while by his suggestion that I include thoughts from the following unedited excerpt from a verbatim transcript of one of his technical colleagues' conversation with a TV interviewer:

> *Most people don't understand that evolution is a kind of an interesting combination of both the random and the sort of determined, or the precise, so it's sort of built on this random process of mutation and how that is always generating novelty, but that novelty, through a process that's very kind of deterministic can produce these very, you know, interesting fits between organisms and their environments, so it's, there's things, despite looking designed or sort of fit for a particular function, they're really built on this kind of random foundation, so it's sort of a non-intuitive process, but that's how it works.*

I also had problems with my editor's statement that, "Darwin's is seen today, I believe, as an adolescent, naïve version of evolutionary theory." But not to worry. The business of being a successful flack hinges largely on one's ability to make correct assumptions about what an information source really means, and to "write around" other dodgy statements. I did this, to an extent that made me more nervous and twitchy writing this piece than I had with any that I could remember.

During my day's visit to the institute I sat on an outside patio and talked about evolution and genomics with an extremely bright and personable young man called Jeremy Van Cleve. Listening to his enthusiastic story, and trying at the same time to understand his unfamiliar lexicon was, to put it lightly, a challenge. The truth was that I had intermittent flashes of panic as I suspected that I would never, *ever* be able to decipher the story of how genomics could teach people about the workings of evolution. I chafed about this a bit more, talked to some more people who were at least as erudite, did some Internet research, and then wrote the article, knowing that at least half a dozen people would have chance to tear it apart before it went to print.

Fifteen hundred bucks in the old man's chest.

In the fall of 2008, Barack Obama and his Democratic party swept to power in the U.S. general election. In his victory speech, in Chicago, the nation's first African-American president promised: "The road ahead will be long, our climb will be steep. We may not get there in one year, or even in one term – but America, I have never been more hopeful than I am tonight that we will get there." I was happy, but despaired when I thought of the colossal challenges that faced this new man in the White House. Voting? I voted for the person when I thought I knew enough to have a decent opinion, otherwise I generally voted Democrat.

Perhaps Barack Obama would be different, I thought, but it was not long before he too was snared in the tentacles of a two-party wrestling match that would embarrass the United States in the eyes of the world.

The orchestrations of government are so complex that a conspiracy theory might be based on the proposition that they are dreamed up to baffle the public and drive their attention away from unsavoury realities. By my mid-teens I had realized that most Americans and British including myself were almost completely confused about the way government works, and that realizing their ignorance feeds their rage against whomever is in power. To most it was amazing and confusing that modern governments could even work, though by 2012 we were wondering whether this had become a false assumption. "Throw the bums out!" While some younger Brits appeared to be becoming more politically active, their seniors had an annoying and almost bovine way of saying, with a wan smile, "I don't know how it is; we always seem to muddle through." In the United States, citizens watched in wonderment every year as national budgets remained unadopted until the next fiscal year began, to the point that it seemed all the various levels of government would have to close their doors. But then it seemed there were always "continuing resolutions" to keep things going. Following the economic crises that in the late 1990s began to ooze from the profligacy of so many rich countries, the character of national wealth, in terms of Gross Domestic Product and/or debt and/or per-capita income, was really too mind-boggling to contemplate. Meanwhile, the gap between rich and poor continued to widen.

Obviously politics was never quite my thing, though I am made somewhat uncomfortable to admit the fact. I feel overcome by the complexity and clumsiness of democratic government, am sometimes embarrassed that I don't consider myself knowledgeable enough to put up a banner or rally around an election campaign, and yet I know no better way of governing nations. The devil is in the details of how the governing is done — by humans whose natural fallibilities are grossly magnified by illusions of power and righteousness, and who so often infect each other with not-quite-right notions of rightness, wrongness, and risk.

I worry about the kind of world that my children and grandchildren will inherit. If only there were some way of predetermining, among political hopefuls, their resistance to corruption, their intelligence, their leadership ability, and the durability of their commitment to fair-mindedness, openness, and impartiality! The need for such virtues would become even more urgent as the economic woes of the new century crescendoed, as the euro fell into deep trouble, and as people began to agonize over the decline of capitalism. We would even be discussing such heresies as the redefinition of democracy, and indeed by the end of 2011, after many years of neglectful economic management, both Italy and Greece would be led by men who were appointed and not elected. As the nature of Western democracy changes, it follows that there will be qualitative changes in each of the varieties of civilization to which people of democratic countries have become accustomed. However the current situation evolves, it is extremely unlikely that the West will regain an economic state where life carries on "as usual."

⸙

I met the New Year alone, since Dee was in Kansas City with Deana, and Jonathan quite naturally was celebrating with friends. It was 2009 now, and in June I would celebrate my 73rd birthday. I had lots of time to think.

If there's any vanity in you, better get rid of it before you're 65 — earlier if possible. On New Year's morning I looked in the mirror and saw the same old moonscape of a face — it had changed too slowly for me to notice — with a mop of gray hair that needed cutting. Still not bad for my age, I thought, and my physical exams of the past year had been encouraging, I was going to the gym three times a week and sweating it out in the garden. I was living the good life on two continents. On the other hand my skin was losing or had lost its elasticity, age spots (*yukh!*) were proliferating and expanding, and the remorseless tug of gravity was distorting my tissues, an unforgiving, merciless attack of time in which I became reacquainted with the terms *dermis* and *epidermis* while pondering why they seemed to be increasingly losing touch with each other, a situation that

Brian said was made worse by my use of prednisone over the years. A slight brush against a toothpick-sized stub of dry mint opened a triangular gash on my arm that measured an inch on each side. It looked dreadful even though it was painless, meaning that I needed to wear a bandage for cosmetic reasons alone. So there was a new personal-care rule now as well as the ones that curbed my intake of sugars, starches and salt – Thou shalt not do garden work without a long-sleeved shirt and gauntlet-style gloves! Then there was the annoying muscular discomfort glorified as fasciitis or myalgia – in my next annual physical I could imagine myself saying, "Doctor, why is it I can't stand up unaided from a squatting position these days?"

I hate to tell you youngsters this, but these are common examples of what we all must go through after passing a certain magic age. After all, people are living to be much older – older than they should, as the American opponents of universal medical care may privately think. Another, naggingly troublesome part of my personal aging process was the mental baggage that had increased unforgivingly for all those decades. This included most of the things I had learned and experienced (driving cars, learning about nanoscience), sadness and regret, happiness, irretrievable moments of delight, pleasant and not-so-pleasant anticipations for the future. Nearly all of it was tucked away in my unconscious along with instructions on how to use and react to the waking-hours tsunami of sensory stimuli. It kept company with all the software that kept this information tidily catalogued, along with that relatively small selection of interacting algorithms which could be brought to the forefront, automatically and unaware of the expenditure of the least amount of effort, in the seemingly simple process of conscious thought.

And there in the baggage were the memories of people lost to death and circumstance, the famous mixed in with relatively anonymous friends and relatives. These were people whose legends had ended, fading away in the thickening ischemic dead-ends of my brain, and I was irrationally disturbed by this. When the world lost Alexander Solzhenitsyn, Harold Pinter, John Mortimer, and John Updike, I felt personally diminished by their deaths though I had never met them. It seemed to me that good and great writers were returning to earth in unfairly large numbers, castaway leaves from a great tree, and I wondered whether we were going through the fall of something great, not of civilization perhaps but of one of the great humanizing markers of civilization. I wrestled with the possibility that there may be too few people who will or can take up the legacy of these people, that these bits of text will be frittered into Tweets, emails, text messages, and 500-word blogs; that these minuscule firings will be lost, forgotten, and ultimately rendered meaningless among the uncountable, constantly firing neurons that are keys to the totality of shared human consciousness.

I wonder how many fine brains have been somehow diminished by the post-1945 advances in microsystems, computer sciences, and information technology, which have made ever-increasing niches in fields ranging from children's toys to medicine and national security. How many Shakespeares have been drawn into the amoebic arms of the World Wide Web? Question: Will the Internet eventually bring an end to the evolution of humankind and condemn us to a timeless recirculation of hackneyed ideas? Will we settle into a mindless imitation of progress that consists of repeated mistakes and short-lived solutions, astride a spinning top that consumes energy and goes nowhere? Will the instant calling-to-arms made possible by social networks unzip the authority – maybe the whole *meaning* – of law and order? Will law and order itself become a hybrid of techno-cops and watchful electronic sensors?

This winter, in a month's time, I had written three technical articles and a commissioned book chapter by using information derived almost completely from the Internet, my computer archive, and a few brief phone calls – no eye-to-eye contact was necessary. How different this was from the time when, as a reporter for the *Kentish Express*, I walked down country lanes to search out a local parson who was preparing a service to lay at rest a graveyard ghost. How intellectually sterile in its hands-off technique! What was being done to the capacity for creative thought that I had believed so precious in my formative years? And for that matter how sobering it was to think that my whole life's story, complete with the manuscripts of four books, research documentation for those books, and a library of photographs, resided on a tiny piece of silicon, a "memory stick" for my computer!

⚜

Perhaps not unnaturally, as I communed with myself at this opening of a New Year, my thoughts moved to the inevitable effects of aging that would descend on Dee and me in the next few years, and the likelihood that one of us would end up looking after the other. Was this a reason not to marry, since she or I would be eligible for state-administered Medicaid assistance only after both of us were completely broke? Probably. We'd have to ask for expert advice on this. But the onset of increased deterioration with age was on the doorstep and quite naturally had already begun. Would my mind steadily descend into an unsure night of unsure thought? Would those thoughts end up as part-recalled and incongruous fragments within a brain left limp and porridgey by the overburden of experience? A dismal thought indeed. I could not imagine just how my aging would proceed, or how we would cope, only that it would happen.

Some of my mental baggage fell open during an assault on the daunting amount of stuff that had been accumulating in my little studio building since early 1983. Sorting a boxful of old mail was torture because most of the letters were from my dead parents and the two women I loved and left. I loved Mim but was constitutionally too weak to cope with her mental illness even though, as Brian would remind me, she truly loved me in spite of it all. I loved Sue and she me – scores of long letters! – and inexplicably and implacably she fell out of love with me. I could never fall completely out of love with either. But now thank goodness I had Dee beside me, and had learned too much to let her down.

How is it that human beings are so adept in hurting each other? How is it that I was drawn into this trap after decades of suspecting that God is love, yet not being convinced by the idea enough to sit back long enough to understand Mim's problems, or Sue's, and to work through them? Perhaps I loved people in too abstract a way, perhaps my thoughts and writings went on too much about humanity in its entirety, lingering too briefly on individual people. And then perhaps there's nothing wrong with me at all.

> *I'm multi-tracking right now, composing this paragraph while scanning old prints to my computer. They go back a long way, but mostly to the early 1980s, when my youngest lived his first years. It's wrenching to see those happy hopeful pictures, but I think the experience is helping dispel the sadness. It is strange, how one covets the memories and wants to live good times all over again, and is unhappy and even resentful not to be able to do so – instead of rejoicing to have had such joyful experiences in the first place.*

My cleaning-out exercise, in these first few days of 2009, was cathartic, and Mim's and Sue's letters found their way to the rubbish bin after years of surviving silverfish, cockroaches and mice in that stuffy airless little room. Mim's short, desperate attempts to communicate were the most heartbreaking, and I would not need to see them again. I had not really wept since the final years with Sue, but on this day I did. I had diarized Jonathan's glorious first eight years in fair detail, and I needed to review them for the new journal, but even this process had become a tortuous affair that, irrationally, I wanted to avoid. For a while it was as though the divorce from Sue had erased, nullified, or somehow soiled those wonderful times when they could do nothing of the sort.

A couple of weeks later I half-reluctantly took the green wheelie bin to the curb, with its sad collection of letters, to be picked up by the big truck with the unthinking and untroubled, roaring robotic arms.

⚬⚬⚬

I wondered for a while whether my New Year's resolution should have been to return permanently to England, where I can be near my two children, my grandchildren, and my fine son-in-law. They would like that, and I know I could be helpful. I thought Dee would go, and maybe Jonathan too. I could sell up again in New Mex, turn everything over to the auctioneers. I reckoned that with the proceeds from the house I could sell the London flat and probably get a three-bedroom row house in the same housing complex.

And yet … Houses, buildings, what traps of possession and pride! Surges of escapism engulfed me – I wanted to rid myself of the cult of possessing and belonging, wipe my hands of it though it were something that soiled and restricted my being. I would sell up completely, become a gypsy, spend my savings exploring the country and the world. What was it that Thoreau said? – "Most of the luxuries and many of the so-called comforts of life are not only not indispensable, but positive hindrances to the elevation of mankind."

Fortunately I had plenty to divert my thoughts – the possibly crazy, possibly smart idea of extending the lease on my London flat by 90 years; the sensible idea of finishing painting the study and front bedroom; and a profitable assignment to write an 800-word article on energy policy/strategy, rewritten from the transcript of a talk given by Al Romig.

I resolved to write, get good exercise, and eat healthy. Getting back to writing my own stuff (not just Sandia's) seemed the right thing to do. I determined to try fiction again, and ordered a book on the subject, James Wood's *How Fiction Works* (Farrar, Straus & Giroux, 2008), which had been recommended by Fiametta Rocco of *The Economist*.

The next morning I woke about two hours too early, with an asthmatic episode that I could not explain (for the *n*th time, after studying the condition all my life), *what did I do to bring this on, so I can avoid it next time?*). But I felt better in my mind. The remorse of the previous day had washed away, and I had become more positive – after all, was I the only person responsible for those disasters in my life? There was still the gladness of sunlight to rejoice in, the warm breeze fingering through the answering trees, and, as I lay looking into the cornflower-blue sky, afternoon light stroking the wide landscapes with the soft shadows of gathering cloud. This vision was followed gently by the unsought memory of a warm Maying-time afternoon in the lush hedgerows above Heysham, smelling at the pinkish hawthorn blossoms, chewing on the young, tender green shoots as young children do, many years ago. I was healed.

A month or two later I nearly fell from my chair after reading an email from Ray Farress, a neighbour in the Victoria Park Estate, where Dee and I had our London flat. We were being invited to buy leases for (wait for it) 999 years. No, that's not a typographical error. I, and more than a dozen other tenants, had the opportunity to keep our little pieces of property for one year short of a millennium, by the Queen's pleasure. Who wouldn't be gobsmacked by that? If I had gone back in time instead of forward, which seemed almost as feasible a proposition, we'd all still be waiting for the Plantagenet King John and the Magna Carta. And the deal would cost *less* than my then-current plan to add 90 years to my existing lease.

I reeled around a bit, thinking about this. Would my flat still exist 999 years hence? Surely it was impossible. Would London still exist, for that matter? And what about the rest of the world? My mind was boggled for the rest of the day and part of the next. And then I signed up.

⚬⚬⚬

Sometimes you have to do something slightly mad to break through the mental doldrums of a waning winter. So, on April 10, we decided to have an adventure for no other reason than it was Good Friday.

Dee, I, and two friends rode the new, full-sized Railrunner train from Albuquerque to Santa Fe – about an hour and ten minutes for a trip of say 60 miles, approximately the same time it would take me to drive up and find a parking space, cheaper, and a lot more relaxing. We glided through five Indian reservations – Sandia Pueblo, Santa Ana Pueblo, San Felipe Pueblo, Santo Domingo Pueblo, and Cochiti Pueblo – and then followed arroyos through the high escarpment called La Bajada on brand-new track, for the gentle descent into Santa Fe. For most of the way we ran between the lanes of Interstate 25, then onto the old Santa Fe freight right-of-way that goes into the town center and a terminus that long ago sent narrow-gauge trains northward into the Rocky Mountains. Jack and I sipped coffees at Starbucks while the "girls" successfully reconnoitred the dress shops.

We walked toward the station, and in the precincts of a church we admired a sculpture of the Virgin of Guadalupe, Catholic patroness of Latin America, enclosed in a statuary brilliance that resembled a partly opened ear of sweet corn. Pressing on our way around the property, we were surprised to see a number of wooden crosses – a few piled against the low inside wall, two planted upright in the churchyard. We were mildly startled when a beautiful bearded youth in a white loincloth appeared, walked up to one of the crosses, jumped up onto a wooden peg, and looking outward put his arms through wire loops on the cross-arms. *What was this?* Half a minute later a second youth who could have been his twin ran out from a passageway and mounted the other cross. Two crosses with live, Jesus-like trophies! Ah, I remembered, this is what the Penitentes still do, up there in the mountain villages.

We walked on, incredulously into a crowd of Roman gladiators, right there in Santa Fe. A third young man was carrying a truly huge cross, helped by another youth. The actor-soldiers were laughing and jeering, threatening his bare sides with leather lashes. Scores of people followed as the procession progressed to the standing crosses. I would have stayed there gawking, but church marshals arrived and held the traffic and waved us on. We weren't meant to be there. Street theatre, but more than that, the serious spectacle of a medieval morality play, created and enacted in 21st century America.

Good Friday is so special in New Mexico! I have talked with Penitente leaders, walked with penitents up the Golgotha of Tomé Hill, south of Albuquerque (wires hanging from the crosses there, too), and visited the great Lourdes of New Mexico, El Santuario de Chimayó! Where else in this most modern of modern nations could such things happen?

24. REFUSING TO QUIT

The happiness of life is made up of minute fractions—the little soon-forgotten charities of
a kiss, a smile, a kind look, a heartfelt compliment in the disguise of a playful raillery,
and the countless other infinitesimals of pleasurable thought and genial feeling.
— Samuel Taylor Coleridge

You will have realized by now that Dee and I had been talking about marriage on and off for at least eight years. We had traveled to faraway places together, agreed on the important things, and got along well in just about everything. Over the years my enthusiasm for marriage increased, and her dogged commitment to the bachelor life very slowly wavered. Finally, in the late spring of 2009, she said yes, *definitely.*

We agreed that we would exchange vows on September 9, 2009 – the ninth day of the ninth month of the ninth year of the century – at 9 a.m. I had no peculiar numerological reason for suggesting this though I realize that certain mathematical and mystically inclined people may observe that well, 9 divided by 3 is 3 and the bride and groom are celebrating (more properly observing) their third weddings. Nonsense of course. If anyone really came up with this theory they haven't said anything about it, which would be a very wise decision on their part. A couple of people suggested, rather rudely, I thought, that the date 9-9-09 would be easy to remember as I slipped into the twilight of elderliness. But no, the choice of timing was nothing more than a whim.

Dee, who belongs to a local Unitarian Universalist church, asked her minister, Christine Robertson, to officiate. We were delighted when Christine agreed, myself included because I had attended some of her services and liked them well enough that I muttered to myself, *if I ever decided to join a church, this would be the one for me.* More important than anything else, our appreciation of the church and its minister, our decision to ask her to be the wedding celebrant (is that the right word?), and the order of the service itself were also affirmations of the "soul-mate" concept which, though I realize this is an overused and even trite expression, embraced the depth of the love that I believed Dee and I would share.

333

Christine took her duties very seriously, and was meticulous in their execution, which surprised neither of us. The three of us arranged to have a serious discussion about marriage, including such vital qualities as compatibility, empathy and understanding, and, as a study guide were even supplied with a questionnaire about our attitudes and expectations.

⚜

And then, at the end of June, I flew to England to see my London family. This may sound abrupt and shameful, for by rights I should have been pacing back and forth, wearing a hole in the Turkish rug, sipping increasingly expensive brands of whisky and generally driving myself daft over the fateful question, *Will the wedding go right?* After all, my Internet-assisted conscience reminded me, this *would* be a time of momentous significance or consequences, decisively important.

Dee had taken a short trip earlier that month, and an excellent international science writers' meeting was planned in London for the week of June 30, so maybe I shouldn't have felt guilty but I did anyway. Blame it on the distance factor, and the fact that I was away for four weeks as compared with Dee's one. Time makes the heart grow fonder, that sort of thing. But, once I had returned to New Mexico, my schedule would allow me only about six weeks to prepare for the wedding. I reminded myself that since Dee and I had lost our parents, I was father of the bride by default. What was I doing about it?

You might already have concluded that I left my betrothed behind while I was celebrating an inexcusably extended stag night in jolly old England. I, on the other hand, could have offered the honest riposte that the most exciting event was getting swine flu and being taken by Joss to see a host of medically masked nurses and doctors at Homerton Hospital. The infection was a real oinker, since my temperature zoomed up to an unacceptable level of 104 or 40, depending on which side of the Atlantic you're on, early on a Sunday morning. The clinic was closed, which meant that Joss had to drive me to Homerton Hospital to see a doctor. This was an impressive procedure, since England was geared up for a super-epidemic and everyone was wearing surgical masks. But, perhaps with the help of anti-virus tablets, the fever soon abated and my more or less normal self returned, leavened with those sharp but mercifully short spasms of guilt.

Dee and I corresponded daily, and every few days she would give me a subtle reminder that the Day was Near. Did I want to add (or delete) any names from the invitation list? I would look over all the names, which were pretty evenly distributed between my friends and Dee's, and reply yes, they were fine. Others could be invited, but we wanted a smallish, relatively intimate affair. Did I like this layout for the invitation design? Absolutely. It was undoubtedly better than anything I would devise. Did I like the idea of having champagne punch with the reception hors d'oeuvres? Did I think the catering cost estimate was reasonable? Absolutely!

While all these preparations were being made with great care and judgment, I realized that Dee was charging ahead and getting things done while it seemed I was doing nothing but playing with the grandchildren and going to jazz gigs with my second cousin Jimmy Power in Yorkshire. I would be left with nothing to do but ordering the flowers and helping set out the chairs. It wasn't fair. Couldn't Dee have waited just a bit longer so that I could help with the things she was doing so well without me?

⚜

Finally, on July 26, I found myself back again at the Albuquerque International Sunport, worn out from the long sleepless trip from London but full of joy to see my fiancée waiting to meet me at the gate. In a few moments she was in my arms, which meant I was home and suddenly content.

We met with Christine Robinson the morning of August 13, compared our questionnaire notes, and mulled over the decision. Well, actually there wasn't much mulling at all. None, as a matter of fact. We, or at least I, thought there might be questions about my desire to include some American Indian content in the wedding service. That was just fine with Dee, and Christine acted as though she did this sort of thing all the time.

When Deana Fulks, Dee's elder sister and maid of honour, arrived on August 19 it was even more obvious that things were getting serious, so I arranged to have my teeth polished, booked a haircut, had my best clothes dry-cleaned, and had an intensive talk with the florist. Brian, my best man, arrived on Sept. 5, and the two of us started thinking about wedding decorations. We thought we might have some sort of backdrop, to help our guests to focus on the ceremony, along with some ribbony, garlandy and good-natured sillinesses. Balloons, streamers. But not much else. So we consulted the Internet.

The message that struck me first was this: "It's very important that you decide on an overall theme to your wedding before you actually spend any money on decorations." Omigod, we didn't *have* a theme. Would everyone expect us to have a theme? What was a theme anyway, in the context of a marriage? And what would an appropriate one be? "Third time lucky"? Dee and I had never discussed this. Maybe we should have hired a wedding planner. The website didn't give us a list of possible themes, but it did offer to sell us reusable (reusable?) place markers and scores of other small items, of which I liked the set of pillar candles the best.

I scrolled down the message on my screen and for a few seconds was riveted by another statement: "Although our wedding day is all about you, you should keep your guests in mind. They can really make or break the emotional state of your wedding ..." I thanked my lucky stars that we had invited no one who was likely to break the emotional state of our wedding. On second thought, it was just was well I had planned the event for 9 a.m. and not 9 p.m. because somehow the rules of propriety are much easier to manage in the morning than the evening, when booze tends to flow more freely, even when the average age of one's congregation is probably around 60.

Jonathan and I drifted over to the mall and visited the party shop. Did we want a large, brightly coloured picture to put on our honeymoon car, showing us careening down the road, trailing tin cans, beside the announcement in giddy lettering, "We've tied the knot." Not really. Finally we bought some artificial flowers to decorate the wedding arch that Dee had found for us, and a few knick-knacks, then drove home, feeling more than a little inept because our hunting and foraging had yielded so little.

Meanwhile, totally behind the scenes, good neighbours were working to make sure that this would be the best wedding ever. Originally I wanted to have the wedding ceremony take place in our front garden, but ended up next door in Jim and Patty Puckett's front yard. Dee pointed out sensibly that our garden is mostly a combination of gravel landscaping and grass. This xeriscaping arrangement, dotted with trees and shrubs, left little in the way of sight-lines for our guests unless we were to plonk most of them in the fake stream beds and bumpy baby berms that lay on each side of the curving front lawn. Jim and Patty, on the other hand, had a big front lawn, perfect for our needs, and guests could get there via a break in the fence that divided our properties.

We had a wedding walk-through with Christine on the 8th, marvelling at her proficiency in organizing little details that we had thought about but not quite nailed down in terms of "when" and "where." She was very, very good, very professional, offering practical advice as well as managing the ritual. As mentioned, my elder son Brian would be best man, and younger son Jonathan would be vase-handler (cradling the traditional two-necked water jug used in Pueblo Indian marriages) and stand-in emcee in case I lost my composure in the melée. I asked Jim Mitchell, who hired me (twice) to work for Sandia, and my witty friend Larry Perrine to give us a few post-ceremonial remarks.

After the walk-through Brian and I went to work making arrows of cardboard and tinfoil, so that guests would not get lost after we sent them off down our garden path to that opening in the fence that I had not surrounded with a gauzy pink heart.

The day before the wedding I caught Four and Piedelbaum (the origins of our tortoises' names are complicated and must be explained elsewhere) *in flagrante delicto*, almost as if they were offering us a vaguely uncouth but well-intentioned reptilian good-luck pre-wedding gesture. How do tortoises do it? In New Mexico, tail to tail, in a very odd position indeed with Four upside down and looking absolutely ridiculous and Piedelbaum the right side up but gazing off in the other direction. Dee and Deana inspected the tryst with incredulous interest while Four lay looking exhausted with his head and neck hanging limply over his carapace, almost touching the ground, and his eyes closed. Piedelbaum, sensing the lack of privacy, started to drag him into the iris bed but gave up when she encountered the concrete blocks. About ten minutes later I checked on them again and Four was still absolutely helpless and immobile. I approached them, wondering if he had died from the exertion, but he heard me coming. He opened one leathery eyelid, exposing an angry red eye, and so I retreated. A couple of hours afterwards I saw him having a rest and gave him some banana. I think he forgave me.

❦

The next morning Jonathan and I were up early, leaving Deana to help the bride prepare herself while we put the arrows in place and decorated the arch with white silk bougainvillea and Virginia creeper plucked fresh from the fence. We waited for the caterer to bring tables, chairs and the edible goodies, and then disappeared to spruce ourselves up and change into our wedding attire. From this point, and probably earlier as well, Jim Puckett was watching over the preparations, keeping an eye on the placement of tables and chairs, and in all acting as a superb front-garden *maitre d'*. Patty was helping and socializing. She had contributed the best gift possible years ago – introducing me to Dee.

The setting was sumptuous (this time I feel entirely justified in using the word), with the big cottonwood tree spread over the Pucketts' lush lawn and a row of fruit-laden apple trees. The food table was well stocked with sweets and savouries, and the punchbowl was brimming with orange juice and champagne. The dining tables were decked with chrysanthemums that Dee and Deana had decorated with translucent pink/violet film and white bows. Balloons rose from the gateway to our house, which was brilliant with violet clouds of volunteer wild asters, and sunflowers trimmed the front wall with gold. One red yucca was still blooming, sending up, like fireworks, bright red fronds.

As if giving us their home for half a day were not enough, the Pucketts had arranged to give us music as a wedding present, in the form of guitarist John Martinez, who knew exactly what tunes would be appropriate, and where to insert them in the program. He also had a microphone – something that the father of the bride should have remembered – and with fervent thanks I borrowed it for the ceremony.

My worries and misgivings, and in fact everything else in my mind, disappeared when Dee arrived. She looked splendid, and quite lovely wearing her pearls in a pink ankle-length dress and carrying a nosegay of pink roses and gerbera, while I wore dress slacks and a pinstripe black velveteen jacket over a cream-coloured silk shirt with a tie that matched her colours. Our hair colour matched too, remarkably exact shades of grey, as can be readily discerned in the photos from our court photographers, Joseph Laval and Ed Cardona, who were good friends with special talent. Deana (her hair matched, too) wore a lightweight pearl-gray full-length chiffon skirt and matching top. Brian was solemnly impressive in a dark suit with a wing collar and bowtie for his shirt; and Jonathan, who could have worn anything and been an instant hit, wore a light gray suit.

There were no mishaps, though one photo would show Brian's eyes fixed on Dee's wedding ring as he realized with unspoken alarm that I'm having a hard time getting it over her finger. His anxiety was justified, but we continued nevertheless as Dee easily adjusted the ring. We anticipated problems with the double-spouted wedding vase, which Dee and I each drank from to symbolize our unity with a universal spiritual and physical source, but all went well.

Another New Mexico touch to the wedding was the inclusion of an Apache benediction that I have always loved:

Now you will feel no rain, for each of you will be shelter to the other.
Now you will feel no cold, for each of you will be warmth to the other
Now there is no loneliness for you, for each of you will be companion to the other
Now you are two persons, but there is one life before you
Go now to your dwelling place, to enter into the days of your togetherness
And may your days be good and long upon this earth.

At last! Dee and I pose for a photo memorial of our wedding in our
neighbours' garden on September 9, 1999.

At mid-afternoon Dee and I escaped to a splendid old-fashioned bed and breakfast at Los Poblanos, a large estate that specialized in growing lavender and organic produce, a few miles from the house. The manager knew we were newlyweds and gave us prize accommodation, a spotless 1920s vintage room decorated with Mexican folk ceramics collected by the designer Alexander Girard, with a front window that looked out onto a half acre of autumnal lotus.

⚜

The next day we picked up Brian and Deana and left for Missouri, spending the first night in Amarillo, Texas, remembered from my boyhood trip West, in 1949, as the "Helium Capital of the World." At that time a monument representing a helium atom sprouted from a patch of grass next to the road, and we spent the night at a Motel 8, but both apparently had surrendered to progress. The second night, after traveling the length of Oklahoma, we were happily in the town of Ozark, Missouri, having dinner with Deana's daughter and son-in-law at Lambert's Café, another no-beer, family-friendly establishment and "the only home of throwed rolls." Fulfilling this promise provided great entertainment, and fortunately the mashed potatoes and catfish were not delivered to our tables by the same method.

We spent a couple of nights and a day at Bennett Spring, a very large natural spring in lush Ozark woodlands north of Lebanon, Missouri. Dee and her sisters kept a large and well-appointed mobile home there, with two double bedrooms, roomy living room, kitchen, and enough equipment for year-round residency. When we pulled onto the grass in front of the place, turned off the engine, and got out, the night was full of the sound of insects and tree frogs. Brian was enchanted.

In St. Louis we walked around the city center, visited the famous Eero Saarinen Arch, and the next morning said goodbye to Brian as he boarded a hotel van to go to the airport and his flight home to England. Soon Dee's cousin Will and his partner Jack joined us and we were off on the highway rollercoaster again, first to Dee and Will's high school class reunion (they were the same age), then the next day to the Williams family reunion. After some badly needed down-time back at Bennett Spring, we drove north to Kansas City, stopping off to visit four generations of Williams women – Deana, her daughter, granddaughter, and great-granddaughter – before moving on for a night with

340

Honeymoon Time. In Edfu, en route to Abu Simbel, Dee and I are dwarfed by a
massive depiction of Horus, falcon-headed prince of ancient Egyptian deities.

another sister, Henrietta, who was now a widow of four months. I was being called "Uncle Nigel," for the first time in my life, which seemed very odd, and also I had never before witnessed middle-aged people calling *anyone* "uncle." But I liked it anyway.

Finally we were on our way home, driving across all of Kansas and slantwise through corners of Oklahoma and Texas before stopping for coffee in Tucumcari, New Mexico.

I had met a very large number of Dee's relatives. I liked them and they seemed to approve of me, but it was good to be back in the Land of Enchantment. The house on Alondra Lane was my dream house, like it or not, and I would make it so for Dee. There would be no children to frolic around us, no baby faces to wipe of tears, no young minds and bodies to marvel at as they grew from infants to striplings to teenagers to young people who would swell our hearts until they burst with pride. But there was Jonathan, whose mother was still caring for her aging father in Texas, and he visited often, a blessing to us both. We had no children, no dog, no cat, but there were finches and hummingbirds, and tortoises.

You'd think we had done enough traveling for a while. But we spent only a few weeks in Albuquerque before departing for our two-month visit to England, which included a 12-day tour of Egypt while a gang of eastern Europeans attended to redecoration and "upgrades" of the flat.

I had hopes of having a second wedding reception in London, so that Joss, Dave, and the kids could join in and perhaps some of my old friends and theirs could participate as well. I even had picked a place in Victoria Park to have it. But it was too much to take on, and we had loads of fun anyway. Predictably we had great times with the family, cruising Regents Canal, visiting Constable's gently beautiful homeland in Suffolk, reading stories at bedtime.

The domestic routine at the Georgian house in Mare Street had changed. David had decided to take an early retirement package so that he could complete refurbishing the house, a project that had come to an abrupt stop with Eddie's arrival ten years earlier. I approved the retirement plan. Dave's college was hard-hit by the recession, and it followed that his department, which specialized in the esoteric art of making musical instruments, was at risk more than the more utilitarian departments. Dave thought that if he didn't take a retirement package voluntarily, early in the game, he would have to leave anyway at some later date, without the package. It turned out he was right.

⌘

Our excursion to Egypt, one year previous to the revolution of early 2011, was the most amazing, most wondrous overseas trip I have ever made. After a few hours' sleep in Cairo we were up very early for the road trip to Alexandria, to visit the museum and view the sites of the fabled library and lighthouse. Then onward past the luxury apartment blocks of West Alex to El Alamein, and hours of driving across inhospitable rock-strewn desert to Siwa, a dusty, atmospheric oasis town (think of donkey-drawn taxis and flamingos in a lake at sunset) founded by Bedouin not far from the Libyan border. Two nights there, in a room where we could pick dates from the tree on our way to breakfast, and then by boat from Luxor to Aswan, and by coach to Abu Simbel, in Nubian country not very far from the Sudan border. It was the kind of pace I thrive on, and I revelled in experiencing new places, new views of life, new foods.

While on the road we were accompanied (i.e. protected) by burly guards who sat on the front seats with machine guns on their laps. By contrast I was impressed by the demeanour of a dusty, turbaned, middle-aged man who caught up with us in the dark passage of a tomb in the Valley of the Kings and interposed himself, uninvited, as our guide. When we finished our tour he indicated he would appreciate some *baksheesh*, but I had nothing to offer but large-denomination paper money. So I offered him an inexpensive LED flashlight that I had bought in London. He inspected it, visibly impressed, then looked into my face. "Change?" he asked. Finding simple, thoroughly genuine honesty among poor people never fails to touch me.

Each of these historic places, and many others, revealed astonishing treasuries of historical and cultural information that left us open-mouthed time and time again. To see beautifully executed friezes from as far back as 2500 BC – in colour! – was an enormously humbling experience. By the end of the trip Dee was able to translate the stories behind some of the friezes, and we were both beginning to recognize the different deities, kings, and queens. I was very favourably impressed to learn that the ibis-headed deity Thoth represented both writing and wisdom. How appropriate to pair the two! I bought a beautiful statue of him to grace my desk in New Mexico, hoping it would prove to be my personal muse.

343

We were privileged indeed to have the opportunity, and the energy, to undertake this tour, which was physically fairly demanding even though the members of our 14-member group were mostly around our age and some older.

Some observers said that the Egyptian revolution of 2011 was the most significant geopolitical event since the breakup of the Soviet empire. I was inclined to agree, but had to think also of the poor state of democracy in post-USSR Russia, for which mirror images might well form in North Africa and the Middle East. The Arab Spring, supercharged with the aid of new social media, was a significant but shaky benchmark of the new century, encouraging, in its way, the anti-austerity, even anti-capitalist demonstrations that flared throughout the West, and the admirably courageous anti-establishment protests that confronted the Russian government at the end of the year.

⁊⊗⊙

Just before Christmas we were back at our second home in London, doing family things, enjoying some theatre and exploring in and around the city. After seeing brilliant performances by Patrick Stewart and Ian McKelven in *Waiting for Godot* in July, I felt extremely privileged to see *War Horse* and then *Inherit the Wind* with Kevin Spacey (and later the pantomime *Aladdin* with Clive Row at the Hackney Empire) in December. I thought that sitting in the choir stalls for a 17th-century version of evensong at St. Paul's Cathedral was extraordinarily special. As it was, in a completely different way, to see my grandchildren performing in the primary-school Christmas pageants.

Though it may be hard to believe, there were quiet times in all this rushing about, and happenings that made one think. This happened the second week of December, after Dee had returned to New Mexico early to take advantage of an airline fare deal. I had just finished a bowling outing to Surrey Quays with Dave, his friend Emanuel Mitchell, and their children. Manny and I were making our way together through the big car park while Dave watched the kids. I was to leave for America on the 19th, and my companion listened intently as I talked about my other life in New Mexico.

Mannie is tall, dark-skinned, good-looking and athletic, the son of immigrants from St. Lucia. Though habitually talkative, he let me ramble on. When I paused he looked at me and asked a puzzling question. I was at a loss to answer. "What was that?" I asked, not believing what I heard. Manny replied as if the question

344

was not at all out of the ordinary. "I said, how far do you live from nowhere?"

At first I thought he was thinking of a place. But where is nowhere? My mind turned a few cartwheels, then something clicked "Aha!" and I turned back to him. "About thirty-five minutes, I'd say."

Thirty-five minutes was about the time it would take me to drive from the Albuquerque house through the city of Rio Rancho and to the edge of the Rio Puerco valley. This was a very quiet place. In the mind of an urban dweller, it might be "nowhere," for there were no motor vehicles, no housing, nothing to signal human activity. There were crows, rabbits, coyotes, lizards, snakes, and insects around, but in strictly human terms it was indeed "nowhere," and if you shouted loud into the canyon or threw a rock into its depths, no one would know.

I explained, and Mannie was delighted. Now we both knew what he was thinking of. Peace. Non-threatening, quiet, natural surroundings where the whole of one's self can let go and enjoy the experience of simply being.

Albuquerque, January 10, 2010 – Dusk, driving westward and down into the darkening valley of the Rio Grande, struck by the sight of ancient volcanoes in near-silhouette, a dozen miles across the valley, lighted only by a palette of earth colours against a turquoise sky and a few silky strands of pinkish cloud. I hold the wonder close, watching without thought until the colours melt away. Then I thank something far beyond my ken for this moment, and for the gift of knowing its wonder. The joy of natural beauty is not new to me. But this particular view, descending into the valley with the mountains at my back, is my favourite, the most precious. It seems only to happen at special times, when the light is just right, a few minutes after I turn westward from the freeway. It prompts me to reach for my camera, but I know this would be foolishness, for no camera could catch the visual magic. Rumi said, "No metaphor can say this, but I can't help pointing to the beauty."[44] The experience stayed with me until I reached home. When I settled into my patio chair I realized that my set of mind was such that I could begin a game I play with myself, almost an actualized dream of flying that was controlled and accessible at my whim. When I transport myself into a leaf, dancing on the top of that elm tree, and move with it in the wind, or when I melt into that sun-warmed, rain-washed, water-rounded chunk of granite, something wonderful happens. The ego disappears! and suddenly in this wedding with natural things there is no separation in life or death. I wonder whether some people will encounter something similar only to have it fly away frightened before they are fully aware of it, and do not commit it to reasoned thought. Could something inside us dismiss it automatically, as being foreign to the culture of which we are part? Is it something that comes with age? No, for I have known brotherhood with my non-human companions since my early years. There is no way I can explain it, except to say that it is a wonderful thing.

⁂

For years I flattered myself in imagining that I was unusual, and highly fortunate, that I could be enraptured by the quite spellbinding knowledge (obvious, really, when you think about it) of being united in all ways with the universe. Such experiences generally come upon me without invitation or human involvement, and so they seem very special indeed. But then so many have thought themselves blessed by God, or visited by a religious miracle.

As you well know, for a long time I wanted somehow to help people to experience the event that visited me first at Juniperhill. This was part of my college-days notion that I had some sort of duty to help ease society onto a better path, which sounded foolishly pompous fifty years on. Now I realized that the metaphysical avenue of "understanding beyond understanding" is available to just about everyone. Perhaps you never recognize it; perhaps it opens up to you only once or twice in a lifetime; most likely it's always with you, winking through the clouds of the mental and emotional storminess that seem to be part of the human heritage. Perhaps it masquerades as union with Brahma, the Holy Spirit, the golden staircase to heaven, or the gift of being able to communicate with God. I suspect all of these are of a sameness.

In other words I had realized that this occurrence is by no means peculiar to my own life's chain of events. It had to do with solitude, and/or meditation, except that in my experience one could not plan the occasion with any precision – it happened, or seemed to happen, with neither warning nor invitation. In Dostoevsky's book *Demons* it occurred just before an epileptic seizure; he called it awareness of *"the presence of the eternal harmony."*

The awareness, which she called rapture and "the strongest pleasure known to me," would come upon Virginia Woolf in company with the *aha!* moment of bringing a piece of writing to the point of perfection. In her unpublished autobiography, she observed that a certain pattern is hidden behind the activity of all human life and that "we – I mean all human beings – are connected with this; that the whole world is a work of art; that we are parts of the work of art." Great artists rise gloriously from this pattern, but "we are the words; we are the music; we are the thing itself."[45]

Woolf found her pathway to enlightenment through her art; others will by nature find other avenues, for those pathways are all around us. I believe that in all people of normal intelligence there is a secret place, a sanctuary within the personality. It is a lotus-like source of enlightenment in which and with which we may overcome the trials of journeying through life. This occurs through the realization that we are small and transient phenomena in a system that is immeasurably greater than ourselves. Sometimes this source of illumination is undiscovered, unexploited, perhaps unneeded; but it is there. Tranquility induces its own gentle ecstasy; when it is achieved we have no need to contrive special means of avoidance and distraction.

Everyone shares a quite beautiful connection with the universe; it delights me to think that an increasing number of people may be discovering this fact. If true this is an extremely encouraging sign. By its nature the discovery of *connection* strengthens the bond between people, and between us and the natural world. This trend, though very subtle, would complement the unveiling of a freshly cosmic perspective when people saw photographic images of Earth from space for the first time, and Carl Sagan's philosophical musings upon the humbling image of that pale blue dot.

Let me put this in another way. Early in my life I was visited by the idea that human beings may inherit certain cognitive codes – tools for the classically human reasoning that all of us carry as part of our subconscious. Such codes, in what I knew could be my own fictional fantasy, might include keys to a universal source of enlightenment. Some everyday basics of psychology offer modest support to the idea that cognitive codes could act as communicative arms of what neoplatonists call *soul*. All creatures are programmed with the complex neural instruction book that helps them use and interpret the sensory clues that, to many degrees of complexity and specialization, are built-in elements of life. Our own infants are born with instructions on the simple acts of sucking and crying in response to simple stimuli; they begin to crawl, then to balance and stand; they interpret expressions and sounds as communication. Why should not human beings also carry in their genes, waiting to emerge, the inclination to recognize certain clues to the reason for their existence? Such clues might have been sensed by Dostoevsky and the other "seers of the light" mentioned earlier.

I am under no illusion that finding some sort of "enlightened awareness" can make an ordinary person into a spiritual superman; to the contrary, I believe it is a personal and even private state of mind. I am reminded of David Ewing's comments when one afternoon he pulled his office chair close to my mother and looked her firmly in the eye. He was about 55, she 94 or 95. "Margery," he said softly, "do you realize that in this world, in this great universe, you are nothing? That I am nothing, and nobody is, really? When we are gone, everything will continue as if we were still here and everything will be fine?" I felt slightly shocked when I heard this bleak, true statement, but when my mother hesitated, expressionless, he went on: "Well, do you understand all of that?" Finally she smiled and nodded and said yes, she did. David did not say that his "everything" is an all-encompassing pattern, like Woolf's, but then perhaps it is.

It was Einstein who wrote, "The true value of a human being is determined primarily by how he has attained liberation from the self."[46]

25. BRAIN FEVER

If I had a world of my own, everything would be nonsense. Nothing would be what it is, because everything would be what it isn't. And contrary wise, what is, it wouldn't be. And what it wouldn't be, it would. You see?
— Lewis Carroll, *Alice in Wonderland*

"Don't you think you'd rather live in England?"

After she moved in with me, Dee came up with this question more frequently as she got to know how much I enjoyed our overseas trips, as the grandchildren grew and became more fun, as we both celebrated new birthdays, and as our concern increased about being infected by re-circulated aircraft air. In three successive years I contracted swine flu, double pneumonia and – you guessed it, brain fever.

The idea of lugging heavy suitcases while exhausted from travel grew even less pleasant as we grew older, especially after U.S. airlines stopped using Gatwick, which was more convenient for us than Heathrow. Dave would often pick us up, but the 22-mile drive through the tangled streets of London was arduous and I didn't like to ask him. It was said you can pay $75 and get a private taxi to take you to Hackney, but I'm sceptical about that price. But otherwise it's necessary to lug your bags out of the airport and carry them around the London transport system, where most underground stations lack elevators and some require you to negotiate a series of stairways when changing stations.

The official London Transport website says that, to get from Heathrow to our flat, you have to walk, take the train, walk again to the Underground, change to a second Underground line, then catch a bus, then finally walk to the flat. In an hour and twenty minutes. I'm sure it could be done in this time, but not by me lugging a large suitcase, computer bag, and backpack. There was a time not long ago when I very slightly resented people who offered to help me carry my stuff up the Underground stairs, but not any more.

And so Dee would join me in my double life, shuttling between New Mexico and England for as long as we could and until the fates determined

349

something new. As it was, the fates *did* have their collective eyes on us, and would zap us with near-catastrophic force less than a year into our marriage. More on this later.

Moving in together in New Mexico had its problems, particularly for Dee, who had to change her name and move her things. It took well over a year to get her name and address sorted out with social-security and other government offices, banks and credit unions, and a host of outfits that sent her bills, publications, etc. The task of deciding which furniture and other bulky items, and which of her admirable collection of clothing and shoes, was a problem of similar magnitude, though it didn't last so long (someone was in a hurry to rent her condo) and it was distressing to send familiar and treasured items to charity stores and consignment shops. We compromised by renting a storage unit.

Our relationship strengthened even more after the marriage, though each of us had lived through many habit-forming decades. For example, each day Dee read *all* the incoming mail. Whereas my habit was to empty the mailbox and stand by the recycling bin, throwing away many items without opening them, she would carefully go through the contents, making shopping notes and clipping occasional items that might be of use to us and our friends. How civilized!

If you are still with me, you have read my ponderings over what happiness is: whether our species has a chance of improving itself (or even surviving), and so on. What I am about to say may mildly surprise you. You may suspect that I have a perpetual burr under my saddle. Not so. Wherever I was, in England or America or while traveling elsewhere, I had access to a strong and readily accessible sense of fulfillment. This was provided by my family of thoroughly *good* people, by the richness of many friendships, by the wonder that had grown so great within me through observation, thought, and travel, and by my good fortune in having a career that I thoroughly enjoyed. That career seemed to be at an end now, with the arrival at Sandia of a PR administrator who, while he seemed affable enough, remained attached in his heart to an outdated form of severely top-down management, and was surprisingly uninterested in my specialty, which focused on telling the world about the laboratories' technical innovations.

During his short tenure Sandia's media and employee relations department lost all but two of its experienced media relations staff, who were replaced with people who were talented but naturally unfamiliar with both the national science writing fraternity and the workings of this large R&D lab. When the newcomer left, the entire information group, which included TV specialists, printers, technical writers, and other communications specialists, was left with no leader. The manager of the media group had transferred and not been replaced. And there had been a behind-the-scenes declaration that my contract must not be renewed: it seemed the short-time director had decided I was "against him" because I had the temerity to suggest new strategies.

I suppose I could have brought myself to dislike this individual, but his actions were too baffling to provide me with anything more than a deep curiosity, which was never rewarded, to figure out how that personality functioned. Memories of these and certain unrelated questions would plague me and stick with me as I searched for solutions despite the nonsense of hanging onto the annoyance of a problem for years after it is dead and gone. Why did my second marriage really break up? How did what's-her-name get the idea that I was being sexually suggestive and take her fantasy to a supervisor who then told me I would never get a promotion? Why did he discourage me from taking the matter to the company ombudsman? How, later in this story, could a clearly unsuitable man be hired as head of a large institution's widespread communications organization?

These frustrations occurred over a period of years, small blips in a Sandia career that I loved and fit me perfectly. I would miss the joy of working with all those creative Sandia people, and with the scores of equally brilliant people I had come to know in the national media, and I would miss the income. I was extremely fortunate not to be chained to this relationship by a hungry ego, by material *want*, or by obsession with a need for continuity.

⊙≫≫

June 21, 2010 – I left the modern world for a few hours today and visited Piñon Street, a place in the desert that is unknown to Google Maps and, as far as I know, to any GPS navigation system yet available. I had the urge to enjoy the great quietness of the desert and to visit Maria Jojola and her family. Maria is a Pueblo Indian, which is to say she belongs to one of the small tribes that mostly live in villages on the Rio Grande and its tributaries. They are eddies in the flow of modern life, near-forgotten by choice. Mostly they are pagan universalists, their lives governed by a rustic belief in an immanent great spirit that binds their existence with the cosmos. Some philosophers call their beliefs "panentheistic" suggesting a kinship with Hinduism, the European neoplatonists, and American transcendentalists like Emerson and Thoreau. Maria is a large and handsome woman, and her two sons are huge, with long, thick, glossy hair. When I call myself an English Indian Maria laughs merrily, and when I say I married a paleface she literally shakes with mirth. All three are highly intelligent and artistic, and they are believers. I returned home feeling both refreshed and reflective. I remembered walking into the Isleta Pueblo plaza in 1966 and finding a ceremonial dance in progress, just a few old men in ragged clothes, going through a mumbling near-forgotten ritual in the dust. A quarter century later the feast days were great celebrations with hundreds of brightly costumed, painted dancers dancing in the plazas – old people, middle-aged people, and children right down to pre-schoolers, watched intently by hundreds of lookers-on. It was a good thing and it gave the lookers-on a good feeling, and I relished the experience, especially the sight of those little children, keeping the tradition alive.

June 22, 2010 – Wow! I'll be 74 tomorrow! And I still have all my faculties and can walk around like any normal person! And I am still able to laugh and cry and to love. At the moment I'm experiencing a touch of the wet-eye syndrome, having received a card from Jonathan, printed with the words, "Dad, by your example I know the value of hard work, loyalty, and what it means to be family. You're a good man and a wonderful father. I'm thankful every single day that you're my dad." And then, in clear, careful handwriting, he had written, "Dad, Thanks for being there to show me so many wonderful things about life and the universe. I love you! Jonathan." Who wouldn't be choked up by such words!

⚜

Preparations for the 2010 London trip went swimmingly, and after cleaning up the flat we settled in for an "English holiday" in which we would ignore the temptation to make side trips to Tuscany, Venice, or Spain, and never even cross the Channel. Jonathan would follow on August 19, with plans to go with Brian to music festivals in Barcelona and Hackney, then to the Notting Hill Carnival, returning to Albuquerque on September 1.

Dee, Dave, Eddie and I spent a few delightful days in Norfolk, but then things began to move off kilter. On August 7, after we showed a couple of

Albuquerque visitors around Broadway Market and the park, I mentally checked my flight systems and decided I wasn't feeling too good. It wasn't asthma; it didn't seem centered in any particular place; it wasn't anything I was familiar with; and it didn't seem very serious. But something was nagging at me, somewhere.

The next morning I was groggy and listless, not particularly interested in anything at all. I felt as though I had wakened from a long, deep sleep into a mental fog from which I had no desire to emerge. My daughter Jocelyn came over for a conference with Dee. I passed out and gained consciousness just in time to realize that I was in an ambulance, being unloaded at the Royal London Hospital, Whitechapel. Then I remember being on a gurney, on an Alice-in-Wonderland trip past a medications trolley that was labelled "Royal Suite" with a thick marking pencil, to a hall that was being guarded by police with machine guns. And then I passed out again. (Later I learned that my bizarre recollections of that gurney ride were not imaginary. One explanation was that a patient had been brought in after being shot several times by a hit man and the police didn't want his attacker to finish the job.)

A fair amount of the next two weeks was a feverish blur. I was incoherent, uncoordinated, and, though I knew perfectly well what it was, couldn't produce the word "spoon" when the thing was brandished in my face. "You were not misbehaved," Dee reported later. "You were just pulling your tubes out and things like that. But you were very courteous once you managed to slide out of bed. You always insisted, 'Excuse me, excuse me,' when you tried unsuccessfully to push your way past the nurses to the bathroom."

I would think up things I wanted to tell Dee, but those words wouldn't come, either. I knew exactly what I wanted to say and when she came I tried to capture the actual words. Strangely the words would start to form visually, then fade away when, as in a dream, I snatched for them. I was a comic-book character in a world with balloons drawn in for my speech, but the balloons were blank. It was dysphasia. Did stroke victims experience this kind of thing? Or people in comas? My goodness, I thought, maybe this is what it is to lose one's mind! I was more bemused than frightened by the idea, no doubt because I couldn't believe it was true.

Poor Dee. She was genuinely afraid she would be widowed before we had been married a year. She was nearly right, though in the first week I was not aware of this or much else either. I remember her spoon-feeding me, and

353

coaching me on who I was, where I was, what day it was, and so on. There was no specific remedy or cure for what I had, which the doctors could only name as "lymphocytic meningoencephalitis," provenance unknown. A virus had settled in the membrane that seals my brain from my skull, and was determined to make a home there. Though the film *Contagion* had not yet appeared, the early diagnoses of the diseases were identical.

Each day the neurologists would visit my bed, perhaps four of them, and the ritual would begin. "What is your name?" "How old are you?" "Do you know where you are?" On one of these occasions I saw something happening in my peripheral vision and was amazed to see my hands waving about at the height of my temples. When this "myoclonic" spasm recurred the next day, the head neurologist said with some amazement, "Look, he's flapping again."

My bed was in a sparkling clean, modern semi-private ward, next to a large window, and the shooting victim was gone. The window offered a fine view of the world, except that the view kept changing. I knew I was facing north. Looking down, I could sometimes see Whitechapel Road, which would be correct, while at other times I saw Gibson Boulevard in Albuquerque, New Mexico. Or I would find myself staring out at a nonexistent train platform. Twice at night the window looked out onto a life-sized diorama that suggested a scene from the last days of the doomed King Charles I, similar to the images I fancied, crazily, that I could see etched in the high-tech ceiling lights.

The nursing staff took note of all this, and I did my best to entertain them. Without exception they were a wonderful mix of people from Zimbabwe, Zambia, Nigeria, Sierra Leone, Congo, and other exotic places (including two nurses from Russia and Buddhist nurses from Ireland and Nepal). I would miss them. After daydreams about organizing parties for their children, after planning a roast-chicken picnic together in Victoria Park, after dreaming up a song about drinking fictional jacaranda tea under big blue-flowered trees in the parks of Bulawayo, how could I help it?

After a series of hallucinatory experiences, realistic daydreams, and imaginary adventures conjured up by my discoordinated gray matter, and after suffering an unbearably itchy rash brought on by a penicillin allergy, my condition began to improve. Slowly my neurons started to link up with each other, like jigsaw pieces self-assembling into a poorly defined but improving picture. It amazes me how much we are helped along by secret talents within the mysterious lump of grey matter between our ears! It joins up the dots so brilliantly – if you have the right subconscious backup, just a few dots of language, sensing, and memory can be transformed into a Mona Lisa of newly reconstructed knowledge.

There was one last hallucination, one that for a change I remembered well. The face, *that* face, appeared behind the plate glass window and turned into a skull and appealed to me, *"Ich bin tot! Helfen Sie mir!"* I was struck at first with dismay, then I calmed and when my mind returned to the hospital bed it seemed I understood it completely and quiet returned to me. My visitor spoke not for Germany but for all foreigners as well as all of humankind. All ordinary people, in fact all life, need compassion, and deserve compassion. Will *we* survive? Perhaps that message had stayed with me all through my life, and perhaps I had tried too little to propagate it among my fellow mortals.

Elsewhere in this book I mentioned that some kinds of illness may cause people to become in some way "spiritually altered." However, though some of my hallucinations were pretty vivid, I should point out that this encounter with meningoencephalitis didn't fit the pattern. And my absent-mindedness and my short spells of being at a loss for words result from being lost in thought rather than from lingering dysphasia. Honest.

About a week into my sojourn at the Royal London, my consultant neurologist Dr Salek-Haddadi and his staff started saying encouraging things, and he began appearing less frequently and with a smaller retinue. He allowed me out of my berth, first to a bedside chair (where I was originally deposited with a hoist), then with a Zimmer-frame walker, then the next day with no support at all. It may be that one of the antibiotics, or the anti-virus medicine, had taken effect, but no one knew for sure and I'm a little sceptical about it myself. The doctors were completely frank about this – "all we know is, you seem to be getting better, and that's the main thing."

Finally the speech therapists and physiotherapists arrived, meaning that I would soon be discharged. And then one evening one of the nursing staff came in and briskly asked, "Why are you still here? You're supposed to be going home." In a couple of hours I was presented with a sheaf of papers and a load of pills, and David picked Dee and me up at the hospital entrance. At no time in my 16 days of care at the Royal London had there been any mention of cost or payment: very fortunately I had lived and worked long enough in the U.K. to become entitled to National Health Service benefits.

Dee made me comfortable at the flat and arranged a garden party with Jonathan, Brian, and my London family. I had no new medications to take, just instructions to exercise, have another EEG and see the doctor again. The follow-up appointment, with a likeable neurologist called Richard Sylvester, told me that, like the host of earlier tests, the remaining two had proven negative and that I was fit to fly back to America. He was adamant that I should take a medical note in my carry-on that said that I had suffered "probable" viral meningoencephalitis after being admitted with "an acute history of confusion, fever and focal neurology including left-sided hemiparesis and dysphasia."

It would be foolish to pretend that I emerged unscathed. At first my thought processes were much slower than usual, I walked more slowly, and I tired more easily though Dee and I would soon be walking about a mile each day, with the cooperation of summer weather.

Safe at the flat I would sit at my tiny computer next to the big sliding patio door, composing email messages to my friends, but was greatly disturbed by the fact that, try as I may, I had great trouble getting my fingers to hit the proper keys. I wrote a few messages using the middle finger of my right hand, making sense but very slowly. This experience made me think that maybe my writing days were over, and that certainly I would need to give up my writing career and the remains of my little private consultancy. To me it was a picture of a very dismal future indeed.

And then something marvellous happened. I carefully walked the few hundred yards to Jocelyn and Dave's house and asked to use their computer. Magic happened. When I began to use that full-sized keyboard it was though I had been liberated from a kind of muteness – I could touch-type again! That half-hour on Dave and Joss's computer filled me with good cheer. Nigel lives!

❦

I always assumed, without questioning, that I had a happy and fulfilling middle-class life, asthma or no asthma. Looking back over the years I still feel that way. Yes, I experienced various near-death experiences and some difficult times with people I loved. I was bruised financially by the stock market and the rise and rupture of the housing bubble. But there is nothing unusual about this. There were always many, many good things to be thankful for, including and beyond the blessings of nourishment, warmth, and a roof over my head. Marriage problems were eased by positive desk and garden work, illness by a good book (and by the armoury of medications that is never far away), boredom by eating out or seeing a movie with friends or family (or enjoying an evening with the "boys"), writer's block by skipping the problematic section and tackling the next until I was ready to return. As always I had the wonder of the natural world to soothe me, and my feeling of connection with phenomena that ranged from the Milky Way to the tiny creatures wandering about my garden.

I was never rich, but seldom in debt, thanks to the examples of parental parsimony, to that relatively austere wartime bringing-up, thrift, simple tastes, and wives who shared these views though they were different to me and each other in many ways.

In married life what I wanted most of all was a warm, solid family circle. Most likely in my case this was an unachievable Norman Rockwell fantasy, a counter-desire being that I always wanted to have "roots *and* wings." And let's face it, even if I had solved my early marital problems the full-blown scenario couldn't have become real without money to employ a small army of housekeepers, butlers, nannies, chauffeurs, etc., to support the stately-home, Pickwickian life that for a while was being coddled by my romantic imagination.

From the foregoing you will have noticed that no country house appeared. Still, divorces notwithstanding, I daresay that under the circumstances I took

Teatime. At the time we went to press, this was the best-available group photo of my children Brian, Jocelyn and Jonathan, with me at the far right. We were all together again when I was convalescing in 2010; we were also ten years older.

good care of my families, one of my main ambitions being to prepare the children to have happy lives that did not depend upon (or avoid) the possession of a large bank account. As they got older I learned not to get in the way of their need for independence, but made sure I was able to provide protective and supportive care, if needed, as they grew into adulthood.

With their mothers' and teachers' guidance as well as mine, all three children grew into fine adults. My two elder children took jobs in the British health-care sector (as well as caring for their ailing mother), and as his first major job my youngest became the information technology manager for a New Mexico legal firm. They worked for modest salaries for undeniably good causes, but never expressed a need for money, and never asked me for money although sometimes they would receive some anyway. They had made it. They had become people of good character and I was chest-thumpingly proud of them all.

In one sense the happiest times of my life came from seeing my children and grandchildren for the first time, and then following their successful journeys into adulthood. Happiness also came from savouring the experience of new cultures and new friends; completing a certain piece of prose and realizing that it is perfectly right for its purpose; and discovering exciting books, music, and paintings with a joy that I had not known before. But the greatest happiness is to love, to be loved, and to know without question that one is loved. To these I suppose in honesty I should add the brief March-hare madness that comes with a newly found love.

The star quality that I see in television advisors on personal success and self-realization has eluded me, which occasionally I regret, and I never worked on becoming the sort of fellow that women pant for. I confess I have never hung up the phone saying, "Damn, another woman. Why don't they leave me alone?" As a social being I see myself more in the image that Woody Allen cast for himself than the Tom Cruise image that you read about in the celeb magazines. For some reason such things never bothered me much. I was still the Juniperhill chrysalis, ready to emerge and fly.

The life goals that came out of my college years had stuck with me, and but for one exception – my wish to have a continuous, solid family life – I managed to make them happen. I was driven by three other main interests – my career as a writer, my spiritual pursuits, and the determination to succeed in spite of whatever obstacles turn up. The last-named consisted mostly of living a normal life while hiding the fact that my lungs were working at a little less than half of normal. Most of the time this was not a big problem because I had a desk job, medications improved greatly after 1970, and I was very much accustomed to living with asthma. I became a reasonably successful writer. As bonuses, by seizing some completely selfish opportunities I satisfied (almost) my lust for adventure and spent an enjoyable decade and a half as an amateur actor.

Since you have read this far, and I thank you for your patience, you will not have been able to avoid my notes on spirituality and religion – here you have my permission to decide how successful I was in expressing myself. It won't be easy. I remember my confusion that special morning when I was walking back from my swim off Bermuda's North Shore, close to Black Watch Pass. I could take you to the exact spot where that little blond-haired American boy came up from behind, confronted me and asked urgently, "Are you God?" I remember how bewildered and unsure I was in my reply that day. I am no longer unsure of the answer, but the *reply* escapes me because I am absolutely confident that I cannot reduce it to words. As for the bewilderment, I recognize it now as a bolt of pure wonder, perhaps even a harbinger of the wonderment that came upon me a short time later at Juniperhill.

As I write I am still living in New Mexico. And London. Enjoying the company of my small family. It's likely to stay that way for the time being. The Dalai Lama noted that, "From the very core of our being, we simply desire contentment." Finally I had arrived.

EPILOGUE

One great question underlies our experience, whether we think about it or not: what is the purpose of life? ... From the moment of birth every human being wants happiness and does not want suffering. Neither social conditioning nor education nor ideology affects this. From the very core of our being, we simply desire contentment... Therefore, it is important to discover what will bring about the greatest degree of happiness.
— Tenzin Gyatso, fourteenth Dalai Lama[47]

One evening in January, 2007, I was stretched on the sofa watching a remarkable PBS *Nature* production about the interdependence of wasps and the sycamore fig, "The Queen of Trees," when my mind went wandering. First the program made me think how much living creatures depend on the death of others, then I did another little mental glissade and right there on the couch, with the TV merrily going on about wasps and figs, I began to think again of the flimsy epiphanies of my early life in Utah and Bermuda, when my mind first settled on the built-in natural-ness and *importance* of death. How strange it is, I thought, this habit of avoiding thoughts of death. Yet we celebrate when life is completed! — not because someone has died but because they have lived. And so we should. Humanity is after all the planet's most blessed and most capable tribe; the life of the poorest, hungriest and least educated person is deserving of at least a few hurrahs.

So why be so edgy about death in the first place? It is one of the two great natural events of each individual existence, and will happen no matter what. And yet we create all sorts of escapes from the death-fear — recreational drugs, food-fetishism, the mad drive for wealth and material possessions, the mindless fascination with strife and violence, any number of vices, commercialized and otherwise. These are the things we need to shake off, if we have the strength to do it. Why? Because they are "bad"? Not exactly. It's because they get in our way.

As I jumped from the couch and rushed for my pencil and notepad, I was struck again by the realization of how much time we spend on things that get in the way of thoughtfulness. (I was tempted to say "simple thoughtfulness" because we play around with the word thoughtful so much and in such a thought*less*

360

way.) If you ask me, thoughtfulness, and wonderment, are the greatest gifts that nature has given our kind.

Albert Schweitzer claimed that "the spirit of the age is filled with the disdain for thinking." I would not go so far as to say that. Yet it is a dreadful irony that, because we want to blot out things that we don't want to think about, including death, we work very hard to avoid being thoughtful. Examples of those institutionalized time-spinners flashed again into my mind. I thought how little, if anything at all, they have to do with the special, *positive* abilities that set humankind apart from the rest of the living world, and which some of us suspect provide special links with the divine. The time-spinners are *negative* human capabilities. They are mind-deadeners that help us to deal with the death-fear that was cultivated, and pardon my heresy, to keep people in the power of religious groups. Think of the irony here.

Fear of death – and the related unwillingness to look history in the eye – increase and keep alive many things that degrade and endanger western society and the compassionate Judeo-Christian institutions that created it. "To fear death is nothing other than to think oneself wise when one is not, for it is to think one knows what one does not know," said Socrates. "No one knows whether death may not even turn out to be the greatest blessings of human beings. And yet people fear it as if they knew for certain it is the greatest evil."

❧

There are many kinds of happiness. As I write I am very happy after sitting outside our New Mexico house, enjoying a light breakfast with my wife. I just stretched out my legs and enjoyed the morning while we chatted. The air was cool after days of very hot weather, the sun was shining and the breeze was soft, and a cicada was buzzing away in the cottonwood tree. That is one kind of happiness. Another kind is when you finish a project and are satisfied that it is well done (and hopefully when others agree with you). Another is the kind that lies deep inside you, takes no effort at all, and lasts forever.

And then there is the quality of satisfaction with one's life. You may be surprised that, after writing my first five books and many articles about science and technology, none of these efforts quite satisfied me. I wondered what kind of writing project *would* satisfy me, if any, and a message tunnelled up from the murky depths of my mind.

When I was a kid, the old-fashioned view of science was still taken as gospel. It held that people learn about nature from personal observation as well as from information gathered by others. This idea, and not some 21st century stand-in, is still an honoured resident in my mind. I believe in the appreciation of nature for *what we can see and hear and smell and touch, and taste*, experiencing it fully as a self-generated super-entity that is beautiful in all respects. Personal fulfillment – happiness – isn't going to come from studying the fine-grained physical details of one slice of nature and leaving it at that. My scientific friends call this reductionism, and it can be a pernicious thing. No, the fulfilment variety of happiness comes by totally accepting the fact that we are part of the infinitely larger cosmos and by knowing the reality of this truth throughout one's heart and mind. Getting there may have a lot to do with the serendipity I mentioned in Chapter 20. To borrow a saying from the Swiss-French poet Jean-Petit Senn, "Happiness is where we find it, but rarely where we seek it."

And as for truth? Anthony Lane of the *New Yorker* commented that "Truths are misty and multiple, like ghosts. Believe in them all you like, but you can't pin them down."[48] I'm happy with that description.

Once upon a time I thought that writing about science and technology would bring me happiness. This was natural because my career had put me at the dead center of applied science, which presented a rich resource of wonderment. So I wrote and published books and articles that run from cosmology to nanoscience and space technology, to illustrations of how science is used by politicians to achieve geopolitical goals.

After some of the things I've said you may be surprised to know that I *believe* in science; and that some of my friends are world-class scientists. But some years ago I realized that, narrowly defined, science would give me very little in terms of personal self-fulfilment. Not only that, but if blinkered, reductionist science were taken too far, its products could breed catastrophes beyond our imagination.

Please don't think that I have ignored or set aside the life goals I listed at the beginning of this book – maintaining a stable family environment, practicing the art and craft of writing, discovering a personal spiritual path, and staying healthy in mind and body. You already know, maybe even more than you wanted, what happened with three of those goals. What I need to do now is to wrap up my ideas on the fourth, which is far and away more difficult to explain. Many have said it is impossible. But let me try. In a couple of sentences here's what I learned about the spiritual path. When we get our heads around the truth of our unity with the universe, it seems our minds break away from the confines of flesh and blood, so that we can lose ourselves for a time in the awareness of the magnitude of the beauty that is "out there" instead of the fragments that are "in here." To lose ourselves is just that – to lose our *selves*, to let go of our desires to be respected or even recognized as individuals. We become great, or, more aptly, we rise beyond greatness as we surrender to the awareness of how small we are.

After the previous few paragraphs you may think this chap is dotty: he should be put away somewhere safe. How, for example, can our minds possibly break away from the confines of flesh and blood? True, the mind is resident in the physical brain. Yet the conscious mind may at times have knowing access to aspects of the subconscious; even to a metaphysical realm that is somehow outside oneself. A tenuous metaphysical linkage has been described by many eminent and knowledgeable people. Because it is near impossible to describe, and because it is so far from what we usually talk about, we tend to keep such confessions to ourselves.

If you have stayed with me to this point, perhaps you will see how one can come to suspect that we are all in, and part of, a special "other" reality even when we don't talk about it and *even when we do not know it ourselves*. It seems to be here in the midst of us, always present, without time, without place, always shifting as we move into and out of different states of mood and mind. We swim in a cosmic sea in which all things are unified; and yet we choose to value, too rigidly, the separateness of such concepts as mind and body, nature and nurture.

I realize this will be familiar ground to many readers. But I hope there are some novices out there. Some people surely will recognize for the first time the wisdom in Henry Miller's observation that, "We have been educated to such a fine – or dull – point that we are incapable of enjoying something new, something different, until we are first told what it's all about."[49]

One of the themes of this book has been to celebrate the good things that we can experience without using any of our usual set of senses. I love the way

363

Fyodor Dostoevsky put it in *Demons*: "There are moments, and it is only a matter of a few seconds, when you feel the presence of the eternal harmony ... A terrible thing is the frightful clearness with which it manifests itself and the rapture with which it fills you ... During these five seconds I live a whole human existence, and for that I would give my whole life and not think that I was paying too dearly."[50]

These are passionate words from a marvellous writer. When I first read them I thought them over very carefully. Eternal harmony felt for a few seconds, yet worth a whole lifetime of experience? Hold on, wait a minute now, I thought, was Dostoevsky believable, or was he, confidentially now, a bit of an eccentric, even a nutter? I wouldn't be surprised if people talk like this after taking happy-making drugs. But then Dostoevsky wrote these thoughts down, published them, and became recognized as one of the world's greatest writers. Besides, Dostoevsky was describing what I experienced in Bermuda, during the innocent afternoon walk through the gray Juniperhill cedars described in Chapter 7.

It is not difficult to flirt with the impression of losing our selves, at times attempting to grab hold of it pointlessly and even tragically by using drugs. It is best that we lose ourselves after putting ourselves in serendipity's path: when we simply let the majesty of nature overcome us during a solitary walk in the woods, by the sea, or in the desert, or when deep meditation has freed us of the common ailment that I heard someone call "inflammation of the mind." Whatever its origin, it is best when this experience of ultimate freedom comes upon us unexpectedly. At such times it is most brilliantly convincing because it appears to come from nowhere and everywhere at the same time, and we never intended it to happen in the first place. To me it is the divine gift above all divine gifts, inspiring a sense of elemental trust. Dostoevsky says it is both frightening and joyful. Willa Cather and Eugene O'Neill were among others who described similar experiences in words, successfully, and there can be no doubt that they refer to the same thing. And yet to have partaken of this gift can bring a quiet loneliness because it is so unusual to our experience, so delicate, and so hard to discuss with friends.[51] I say this, and yet the same feelings reach to me from the writings of Wordsworth, Melville, Ibn Rushd, John Muir, and so many others, from the Buddha to the American songwriter Jimmy Webb, in his lyrics for the popular song "Highwayman."[52]

This sense of universal connectedness may go together with religious notions of soul and afterlife. Or it could be a short, brilliant, insightful daydream that will someday be explained by neurologists, as part of the amazing *physical* bundle of mental capabilities that make up a human being.

Why does it matter? It offers the gift of a special perspective, a view of the world from a place in the mind where the machinations of society mean little or, more likely, nothing. Because, for the moment or the lifetime that this state of consciousness remains with us, it causes avarice, envy, jealousy, and other frailties of the human condition, simply to melt away. And then truly death, in Dylan Thomas's words, has no dominion.

There are times when I think this type of experience may be the most precious thing available to the human mind. I am reminded of the writings of the philosopher and writer Olaf Stapledon, who in 1930 published *Last and First Men*, introducing something he called the cult of evanescence. Freeman Dyson explained that: "The essence of it is a profound sense of the nobility and beauty of short-lived creatures, a beauty made the more intense by the fact of their evanescence. The cult is made up of joy and grief inextricably mingled. In Stapledon's vision of the future, the cult of evanescence keeps mankind in balance and in contact with the natural world. It holds in check our tendency to unify and homogenize and obliterate nature's diversity with our technology. It holds in check our tendency to unify and homogenize ourselves. It keeps us forever humble before the universe's prodigality."[53]

We are of course Stapledon's short-lived creatures, but we struggle mightily in our attempts to achieve nobility and beauty and the positive sense of empathy that underpins them. Our salvation, and our claim to greatness as a species, lies first in our ability to take in the fact that such things exist and hold great value, not least as counterbalances to ego-driven desire.

In these paragraphs I'm examining some of the most remarkable products, feats perhaps, of mind and imagination. Suppose they – the things that I dare to call "good" – are part of human evolution, pathways to the development of an organism in which specifically human traits, especially the benevolent and humane, acquire more dominance than they have now? Perhaps we are evolving in tune with the ideas of the palaeontologist and priest Pierre Teilhard de Chardin, author of *Le Phénomène Humain*. The book was written in 1933 but not published until after Teilhard's death.[54]

I find it mind-boggling that, in a time before efficient radio transmission, computers and high-speed telephone links, before the term *globalization* was invented, Teilhard imagined that a worldwide increase in communication and trade would cause humanity to evolve into a collective identity. This would represent what today we call a "community of minds" that represents our shared culture. He looked to the evolution of an earth-circling "thinking layer," the noosphere, a cut-down, humanized slice from Plotinus's cosmic, neoplatonist One. It would allow everyone to be "present" at the same time, in every corner of the world. From that point the priest's ideas seem as outlandish as the rest of his book must have been in 1933, for the noosphere is a genuine collective consciousness that binds together humanity's emotions as well as its thoughts. With this degree of togetherness going for it, he says, humanity would be "planetized" in an ideal state identified by a science-fiction name, Point Omega.

On the other hand it is vital that we believe that some similar ideas really do matter and must be acknowledged without waiting for Point Omega or for Stapledon's fairytale climax, in which individuals develop a shared consciousness in another eon. Certain moral truths exist and are essential to civilization now, though they are often extraordinarily difficult to pin down. Perhaps they will never be defined; perhaps they are not even inventions of humankind. But in my mind they are closely associated with good things and good actions – for example the recognition and appreciation of beauty, gratitude for knowing the experience of being human, compassion and benevolence for other people, love of nature. No one knows exactly what these qualities are; arguments over this question will and should last forever. The search for moral truths matters because it is part of our human heritage to find, embrace, and propagate good qualities and perhaps to smother the bad, however we choose to define them.

◦◈◦

Ralph Waldo Emerson and Henry David Thoreau were the great luminaries of what came to be known as American transcendentalism. Each wrote enthusiastically about related subjects, and perhaps the core of Thoreau's understanding can be found in these words from "The Over-Soul," which appeared in 1841, in the first series of his *Essays*:

> ... *that great nature in which we rest ... that Unity, that Over-Soul, within which every man's particular being is contained and made one with all other... .*

We live in succession, in division, in parts, in particles. Meantime within man is the soul of the whole; the wise silence; the universal beauty, to which every part and particle is equally related; the eternal One.

American transcendentalism never *really* became an "ism"; as a movement it probably lasted 25 years or so and there was not much left of it by the end of the 19th century, except for the writings of Emerson and Thoreau. An offshoot of Unitarianism, it had even less patience with traditional Christian ritualism than the Unitarians. And, at a time when the industrial revolution was transforming the United States, it favoured intuition over science.

No doubt there are some who would again like to "spread the word" propagated by the American Transcendentalists, though useful and *precise* words are so damnably evasive. But the idea refuses to die. Julian Huxley ended his 1957 book *New Bottles for Old Wine* with the assurance that: "The human species can, if it wishes, transcend itself – not just sporadically, an individual here in one way, an individual there in another way, but in its entirety, as humanity. We need a name for this new belief. Perhaps *transhumanism* will serve: man remaining man, but transcending himself, by realizing new possibilities of and for his human nature."[55]

That is very likely enough about this subject, which I tend to go on and on about because I am forever trying to nail a glob of gelatine dessert to the wall. Funny how so many of the most interesting things seem to have this quality.

⟋⟍⟋⟍

Please forgive me if at times I have teetered on the edge of promoting utopia, a perfect existence which by definition is nonsense, a fictional never-never land. That is not my intent. Still I think, and I earnestly hope that you will agree, that people do need to change their ways. We can't afford to wait for little green men to arrive on Earth and save the world. The reality is that, after dreadful wars, after Stalin, Hitler, and other political madmen, people still ignore the lessons of history and persist in being badly behaved to their fellow mortals.

Why is it that Christians, with their reverence of the Golden Rule and Ten Commandments, who pin the beautiful invocations of *Desiderata* on their walls, can be so cruel to others and to each other? Why is it that Christians and Jews and Moslems, all spiritual children of Abraham, become so obsessed by doctrinal differences that are truly not worth dying for? My only answer is that the differences, however small, are seized upon by demagogues and others among the power-hungry, inflated with clever deceptions, and transformed into ugly tools of hatred that keep them in power. Too often, by the time the tool is sharpened the deceivers have hardened themselves into true believers and their contorted creeds made real by the arts of rhetoric, fear mongering, and sloganeering. At times it seems that, once initiated into the ways of a powerful élite – politics comes to mind – the most idealistic, caring person can become such an individual.

Still, humanity is a hardy breed. We saw how populations survived the Black Death, and how so many learned to adopt more prudent lifestyles during wartime, during the Great Depression, and following the worldwide economic upheavals of this century's first decades. We know that populations can adjust to great catastrophes – war, natural disasters, even genocide. But what quality of life will be enjoyed or endured by our descendants? The most powerful teacher, capable at last of fortifying our civilizations with the awesome knowledge that will preserve our species and the planet alike, may prove to be climate change. Worst-case scenarios picture a grim schoolmaster, armed with dismal promises to drown islands and low-lying cities in brine, to cause terrible havoc in the supply of fresh water and food, to create new opportunities for the spread of disastrous fires, to create frightful new reasons for people to war against each other. On the other hand, a global epidemic may reach us first, with its own apocalyptic lessons. Or nuclear war, bursting from some new quarter.

The good news is that if our species survives, and manages to hold on to something that can be called civilization, there is a good chance that it will find itself in a more just and more humane society – because we will have no choice. There's also the chance, and I'm crossing all my available fingers and toes at this point, that by then we will have learned that it is the right way to be.

It took me a shamefully long time to realize that Charles Darwin, champion of competition and villain of many religionists, saw a divine hand, and a "plan by which this universe seems governed by the Creator,"[56] at work in writing the story of evolution. Consider these lines from his *Beagle* diary:

Among the scenes which are deeply impressed on my mind, none exceed in sublimity the primeval forests, undefaced by the hand of man, whether those of Brazil, where the powers of life are predominant, or those of Tierra del Fuego, where death & decay prevail. Both are temples filled with the varied productions of the God of Nature: — No one can stand unmoved in these solitudes, without feeling that there is more in man than the mere breath of his body.[57]

Darwin goes much farther, referring to the evolution of mankind, or "the production of the higher animals," as "the most exalted object which we are capable of conceiving."[58] Further, moral qualities evolve in humankind among individuals with strong social instincts to "take pleasure in one another's company, warn one another of danger, defend and aid one another in many ways." He wrote: "It is not improbable that after long practice virtuous tendencies may be inherited,"[59] leaving the question open while saving himself from suggestion that he might agree with Lamarck's evolutionary theory. But he doubtless believed that morality is a product of social instincts that we share with few if any other species. Personally I would *like* to believe that most people favour individuals "with virtuous tendencies" as mates, though this is a long-outdated idea easily confused with eugenics, and integrity is by no means joined at the hip with high intelligence.

Teilhard was wrong after all. We may not be born bad, but we don't inherit goodness, either, and certainly not good manners. We have to be taught these by parents, carers, and peers, and teachers must then make the best of the children that are presented to them. That is not to say that we must forsake Julian Huxley's idea of transhumanism, even if Teilhard's moral evolution is nothing more than a pleasant myth.

"I am pretty sure religion will remain a major interest of the human race and new forms will arise and new prophets will attract a new generation of devotees in the endless search for meaning and goodness," wrote the polymath economist and philosopher Kenneth Boulding in 1978. "What the content of these new sects will be one cannot, of course predict. Perhaps, however, we can detect one possible trend — the movement from threats into exchange and on into integrative systems… The religions of fear of hell and of trading on the hope of heaven may give way to religions of grace and love."[60]

In these days perhaps the world needs people like Akbar the Great, the descendant of Genghis Khan who conquered much of 16th century India. Akbar was a great warrior and a fervent Moslem who became more moderate in the multicultural milieu of his new lands and created a program that promoted mutual understanding among all faiths. It worked, for a while.

This is part of my life story. I suspect that at some time in their lives just about all people become intrigued with questions about the nature of God, the source and nature of goodness, the purpose for their existence as intelligent and thoughtful beings, and other subjects that are equally hard to understand. You may come to the conclusion that I believe the spiritual experiences of my Bermuda days led me to The Answer to All Things. Not so, though these and similar experiences remained precious throughout my life, and at times seemed to provide windows into an elevated level of existence. They take the edge off our everyday lives and lighten our view of the world by subtly supporting so-called soft qualities like compassion, empathy, and the desire to strive with others toward a better future. Indeed our wise and well-intentioned relationships with others, especially our families, along with proper management of our material lives, contribute the essential parts of the puzzle of "right" existence.

I suspect our role in life is simply to be, and to care compassionately for our planet and our kind. In doing this, we should call upon the physical *and* the metaphysical, the reductionist *and* the intuitive, the empirical *and* the theoretical. For their part, metaphysical and spiritual thought can provide personal outlines for scenarios that do not need to be proved (or even be provable) but serve as platforms where new theory may sometimes be built. We need to use them in working out what we think is the proper use of the physical world, whether our tools and resources are humans, human artefacts, nature, or the products of nature.

I am positive that neither science nor metaphysics will ever provide answers for everything for everyone, which is as it should be. Society needs diverse points of view so long as they do not support the myth of final answers. When they're wanted, answers to ancient questions on the meaning and proper conduct of life – answers that are pleasing to our predispositions – can and will be provided to us ready-made, for example by religionists, philosophers, and politicians, sometimes in radically different ways. But they are not for me.

Even when it's impossible to find satisfactory answers, the process of personally looking for them can be just as important as finding them. It may be vastly *more* important. I also believe that whenever possible it is extremely important to share our experiences in the search – and our opinions – with other folk, including those who outrank us in one way or another. The bottom line is that, unless people keep on searching for the meaning and proper conduct of life, then our quest for peace among humankind, and balance in the natural world, will come to nothing.

～※～

You will have noticed that in this book I have included extra detail in some of the more colourful, dynamic parts of my life story. These times of fun and adventure parallel my domestic life and writing career. Dig deeper and you will find something else. This is my quest, through the gift of wonderment, to find continuing, positive patterns in the life story *of all humanity*.

In the quiet times of my story, not always recorded here, I found lines of wisdom and reason that began with Buddha, Plato and Aristotle – perhaps even earlier – and continue through the Abrahamic scholars of the dark ages, the middle ages, the Enlightenment and the 19th century, to the free thinkers of the present day. Slowly, because I am not a scholar in such things, I saw parts of the story emerging delightfully like bubbles from a glass of champagne, all the way to

Eddie and Elizabeth. My first two grandchildren enjoy the snowstorm that applied a generous coating of white on London in early 2012.

the writings of Charles Darwin and the American transcendentalists to Olaf Stapledon, Teilhard de Chardin, even the writers of country-western lyrics. These lines of logic from humankind's greatest thinkers may waver, but they point in one general direction. It is unquestionably upward, toward a positive future.

At the Santa Fe Institute I learned about Harvard's Martin A. Nowak, an expert on evolution and game theory, and was convinced easily that a hitherto unappreciated factor is required for evolutionary success of the human species – *cooperation*, which he called the constructive side of evolution. I also read about Richard Dawkins' *memes*, which he envisions as the behaviouristic, non-heritable analogues of genes. These could parallel and complement classical evolutionary theory and in a broad sense support Nowak's premise.

I already knew about the transcendent man described by Ray Kurzweil in his book *The Singularity is Near*.[61] This blueprint for future human existence is based on the idea that human-machine symbionts – entities co-existing in a mutually beneficial relationship – could cause human society to become a "technological singularity." If all went according to Kurzweil's scenario, this would be enabled by progress in nanotechnology, robotics, and genetics. This is a slight deviation from the previous pattern. Kurzweil quite naturally makes his singularity technological because he lives in a technological era replete with tools that were unavailable to the likes of Teilhard and Stapledon.

I prefer to visualise a different future in which our species acquires an experiential wisdom by strengthening its sense of personal union with other creatures and the cosmos itself. This can occur not by learning a fixed technique for acquiring wisdom but rather by easing one's internal *perceptiveness* into a state, which exists apart from time and space, in which some degree of cosmic awareness may become accessible. I can assure you that it does exist. I believe that here lies the way to making cooperative transcendentalists of us all. Perhaps I prefer this avenue to Kurzweil's for the same reasons that I like natural history. It is a personal connection between human and non-human that requires not a gram of special technology to bring it to reality. When you have it, it is yours alone, a personal treasure discovered from your own spiritual dance with wonderment.

Years ago I read and revelled in Robert Heinlein's *Stranger in a Strange Land* and learned a remarkable new word that has no synonym and can be found in most of today's dictionaries: the verb *to grok*. Heinlein described it as to understand so thoroughly that the observer becomes a part of the observed – to merge, blend, intermarry, lose identity in group experience. Do you grok what I wrote in the last paragraph? If you do, then we agree on the most important point of this book.

I proposed in Chapter 25 that the greatest happiness is to love, to be loved, and to know without question that one is loved. That is true. There is also another happiness that hardly needs a verb. It is a love that one experiences entirely with ease, with contentment and without fear. I have found this, can revisit it, and know it for what it is. It brings an unspoken freedom, and with it a belief in the essential goodness of human beings. Why? Because if we can experience it, so can others. With that shared understanding we can confidently anticipate a positive future for humankind. That is why I remain a happy man and, as I see it, death has no dominion.

THE END

APPENDIX: FAMILY HISTORIES

In a time that genealogy has become surprisingly popular, some readers will be wondering who, exactly, *were* the Hey and Kershaw families? When I asked for detail on this subject, most people, including my parents, seemed either unable or unwilling to say. Years later, on a trip to York in 1995, I happened by one of those computerized family-name-lookup services and suffered a bout of curiosity. I ventured in and learned that the surname Hey is of English origin associated particularly with Yorkshire and Lancashire. It is one of many surnames which take their name from a natural or man-made feature where the original bearers once lived or held land. Clues from the old languages once spoken in England indicate that the name was given to people who lived in an area enclosed with hedging or forest. Alternatively, they may have come from a family of tall (high/hey) people.

In Albuquerque I was excited to meet one person with my surname, after seeing it on his lapel name badge. "Ah, so you're a High too," he said, as though that, and not a name that rhymed with "weigh," were the proper pronunciation.

The Hays spell their name differently and treat my linguistic argument as mostly rubbish, counting the Heys as one of many septs (subdivisions) of the large Clan Hay. Their version of the name's origin is distinctly pre-Norman. A favoured story dates to the late 970s. It explains how my ancestors' name was given to a Scots farmer and his two sons who successfully led a counterattack against invading Danes in the Battle of Longcarty, terrifying them with fearsome shouts of "A Hay, A Hay!" The battle was the subject of John Lane's epic poem of that name (1834) and now the site of the village of Luncarty, just north of Perth between the A9 road and the River Tay. According to *The Montgomery Manuscripts*, King Kenneth III, whom some say did not come to the throne until 997, came up with the name because it was "the word of encouragement, which the farmer and his sons often cried out aloud" when they stopped to parley. Hay was created thane of Erroll and received an armorial bearing consisting of three escutcheons, gules, the supporters' countrymen, armed with yokes and bows: the crest a falcon with spread wings. The motto, dispiriting to me, is *Serva Jugum*. "Keep the Yoke." Or, alternatively, "A Hay, A Hay, A Hay!"

The Hays of Erroll continued in possession of their ancestral lands from the date of the original grant in 980 until 1650. The title Lord Hay, a subsidiary of the Earlship of Erroll, was created in 1449. Merlin Sereld Victor Gilbert Hay, 24th Earl of Erroll (b. 1948) is a baronet of some distinction, and an Admiral of the Navy of the (landlocked) Great State of Nebraska.

The greatest concentration of *Heys* is in West Yorkshire, mostly in Keighley and Bradford (which has an "old" Hey Road – possibly a corruption of High Road – and a New Hey Road). It seems there was a Richard Heye living in Bingley, just outside Bradford, at the close of the 16th century, for parish records note the baptism of his four children soon afterwards, and then the burial of his daughter Isabel on December 5, 1677. Two hundred and fifty years later, my own mother and dad were Bingley folk too, living in this rather typical West Yorkshire mill town of stolid stone built houses with stone flagged roofs.

My mother Margery was born in Bingley on July 6, 1908, on the upper floor of Kershaw's fruit and vegetable shop, where the whole family was living at the time of the 1911 census. I have a precious photograph, more than a century old, which shows Kershaw's tall greengrocery shop jutting into the metalled Hill Street crossroads like the prow of a ship. The name "KERSHAWS" was clearly visible even at night, for a gas streetlight, its ladder-arms sticking out as if to signal "stop," was planted right outside the display window. My mother liked to show me the upper-floor window, at the rear of the building. She was born in this room, close to the time the photo was taken. At the time her twin sisters Annis and Elsie, 16 years her senior, were plying the streets with my grandfather's horse and cart, selling groceries stocked from the shop. This site is now buried under rubble left from the clearance of old neighbourhoods in the 1980s and 1990s.

That side of my family tree starts with Er Kershaw and Hannah Greenwood, born in 1811 and 1813, respectively. Their grandson Fred, my grandfather, was born at School Green, Thornton, on April 22, 1866. (The name Kershaw comes from Kirkshaw, a Viking-inspired place-name meaning church-grove.)

Er and Hannah's son John, my great-grandfather, was born at Chattell Farm in Thornton on March 10, 1836. He met Selina, a daughter of Joseph and Hannah Ingham of Thornton, and they married on June 11, 1859. Like me a century later, John spent part of his life in England, part in the United States, so much so that the births of each of their ten children all but alternated between the two countries. John died in Philadelphia on October 6, 1906. Two of his siblings, Susannah and Alice, also migrated to Pennsylvania, and another, Abraham, died in Ogden, Utah.[62]

My mother's younger sister Maria Doris, known by her middle name, died of a brain tumour during the war, leaving a son, Michael Lee, who was two years younger than I. She was only 29. An elder brother, Louis, immigrated to New Zealand in the late 1930s with his wife Ruth (Cissie) Verity and their son Chris. Twin sisters, Annis and Elsie, were born in 1892, and settled in Wilsden. The earliest-born sibling, Ada, died in 1891 at the age of four, perhaps of influenza.

My mother would talk of great-grandfather Bartle, who headed the Wilsden young men's club, so respected that the lads would quickly stub their cigarettes when they saw him coming. He had cornered what we now call a niche market.

Edwardian threesome. My father, Aaron Hey, stands between my grandfather Harry and my grandmother Clarissa.

He would get yeast from a Bingley brewery, in the form of seven-pound (half-stone) sacks, and walk up the three hilly miles to Wilsden to sell it to the bakeries. Apparently he was so tight with his money that he refused to get water from the spring that lay midway down Wilsden main street, much craved by his wife, because he had to pay for it. My mother called such people *nipkerns*. I imagined the word originally applied to miscreants who would snip off the edges of gold coins for the metal, but could find no learned reference to it.

On the Hey side, the earliest genealogical records we have are for Aaron Hey (born May 1750) and Hannah Aspin (born 1755). They were married in Keighley on May 8, 1771.

My father's first name goes as far back in the Hey family tree as I can go, to my 4th great-grandfather. He and his wife Mary Sharp had a son, Edwin, in about 1823. Aaron Hey (my great-grandfather) was born to Edwin, then a weaver, and Ann Wilson in 1846. My 4th great-grandfather's son Aaron was born in 1791, also in Keighley, and apparently joined the milling trade. He married Hannah Aspin in 1771, and the two of them produced a family of nine children. In 1880 they became the parents of Harry Hey, destined to become a textile-business entrepreneur who married Clarissa Binns in about 1905. (While there are plenty of Aarons in this story alone, I am told that 14 Harry Heys were born in the West Riding between 1875 and 1885!).

My dad's lone sibling, Walter, fascinated me when I was a child because (a) he had an unusual speech impediment that meant that his wife Lucy (Craven) often had to interpret for him; and (b) he had a most unusual occupation, that of a spline-grinder, which involved cutting high-precision spiral grooves into metal shafts. He won an award for his work, convincing me that he must be the world's finest spline-grinder.

Walter and Lucy lived in a neat little row house near the town cricket field, with a long, meticulously kept garden that led down to the River Aire. In their forties they produced their only child, Judith, who married a Scot and settled in the western outskirts of Glasgow. The Aire is usually a calm and majestic river, but one week it went wild and swept the lovely garden away, planing it into a flattened sea of mud, and her flowers ended up with her neighbours' plantings in aggregations of jetsam beached all the way to Leeds and beyond. The fire brigade had to rescue Lucy, now widowed and alone, from her swamped home. I think she never recovered. She moved to Scotland to be near Judith, slipped into gentle senility, and there she died.

Another insight, albeit on the shady side: my father's uncle made nettle beer and dandelion and burdock drinks, and sold off-colour postcards, in a shop at the bottom of Albert Road in Morecambe.

Though there are a lot of Heys in Halifax, Keighley and Bradford, their connection with me is murky. My dad would laugh when I asked about our ancestry and reply, "I don't recommend you dig too deeply," "don't go there," or some such remark. Perhaps he was thinking of Job Hey [1771-1813], a Luddite who was executed for stealing firearms in Halifax. If not the noose, Job escaped the ghastly Halifax Gibbet, an early axe-head guillotine that dispatched miscreants until the mid-1600s. Or Samuel Hey, who in 1834 was fined two shillings for selling his wife at Halifax market. (This practice was not so dreadful as it might seem because the cost of a divorce was so expensive in those days; and more often than not, a potential new husband was in the wings. Until the law was changed in 1857, divorce could be obtained only by Act of Parliament.)

John Edwards Hey leaped to the rescue of the family reputation as a partner in the engineering firm of Hill & Hey (one of the gang who stole the guns a generation earlier was a Hill), supplying ventilators to the Royal Family, and was rather obviously not one of the Luddite cause. A Hey was mayor of Halifax in the early 1920s, the time when Joseph Hey & Co. Ltd. was the name of a flourishing brewery.

It was a family of mixed interests indeed. For years I treasured a little advertising card for Hey's Victory Ale, and once felt a gentle twinge of something like pride when I saw a beautifully etched hotel window advertising "our" beer – which Uncle Ted said tasted like something that ran off the top of a haystack after a rainstorm – on the door of a Keighley hotel.

Bingley has changed considerably since World War II, and my grandfather's shop on Hill Street, where my mother was born, succumbed to bulldozers long ago, though the ancient White Horse pub, Myrtle Park, the adjacent Victorian swimming baths, and many of the old high street retail buildings remain, though the businesses within them have greatly changed. The A650 motorway bypassed Bingley in about 2004, doing away with the terrible tooth-rattling tumult of lorries and smaller traffic that thundered all day through a narrow, one-lane-each-way high street that was built in 1903. While it brought relative quiet, the advent of the A650 reduced the town to an even more shrivelled version of what it had been before. All that was left of any pretence to greatness was the Bradford and Bingley, originally a building society and more recently a bank, headquartered in a grotesque modern building (subsequently razed to make room for a supermarket), not far from the park. The business itself was toppled when its mortgage operation – mainstay of the organization and the postwar town – was nationalized in the credit crisis of 2008. Its savings business was sold off to the Spanish bank Santander.

By now I imagine the reader's thirst for information on my family and its provenance is more than slaked, and I will bring this final narrative to a close. I realize that few in fact will persevere to this point. But some will, and it follows that their interest in the subject is deep enough that they deserve the gift of these extra pages.

ACKNOWLEDGEMENTS

After writing this biography I found it extremely difficult to determine whom to thank most for their help and encouragement. Countless people contribute to one's life story, and the older one gets, the more there are. My mother first encouraged me to be a writer, and then by serendipity I found my way into journalism, science writing, and the social and professional surroundings that fit me just right. I can thank providence, and luck, for that, as well as my fellow wordsmiths Ed Lewis, Liz Pengelly, and Jim Mitchell, each of whom did me the great compliment of hiring me twice.

With specific regard to this book, I owe the most to my wife Dee, for her editing expertise and mild criticism, and for her patience in sharing a home with an individual who spends so much time hunched mutely over a computer keyboard. Suggestions were offered (and accepted) by Iris Aboytes, David and Jocelyn Armitage, Sam Baty, Kim Braithwaite, Marty and Lois Fleck, John German, Howard Kercheval, Dennis Meredith, Norman Ritchie, Linda Swindle, and Rob Treichler. Tristine Rainer's *Your Life as Story*, published by Tarcher/Putnam, 1998, provided very useful guidance. People at Matador helped too, as they dealt with a man who spent his life in journalism and publishing, had five books behind him, and yet was ignorant of the peculiarities of preparing a sixth for "printing on demand."

I may owe most of all to my children Brian, Jocelyn, and Jonathan, for simply being there, supporting the project, and being generally deserving of an explanation of how and why they inherited a father like me.

Notes

1   See http://www.aaaai.org/conditions-and-treatments/asthma.aspx, accessed July 23, 2012

2   *Koran: 2:62 and 5:69*

3   *Holy Bible*, Deuteronomy 5.17

4   *Koran*: Sura 5:32

5   Peter Anthony Bertocci, *Introduction to the Philosophy of Religion*, p. 9. New York: Prentice-Hall, 1951

6   Thomas Robert Malthus, *An essay on the principle of population.* Chapter 1, p. 13. (Oxford World's Classics reprint.)

7   Dmitry Mikheyev, interview with the author, November 26, 2003.

8   See http://www.mormonwiki.com/Celestial,_Terrestrial,_and_Telestial_Kingdoms (accessed March 9, 2011)

9   http://www.mormonwiki.com/Kolob (accessed March 9, 2011)

10   Richard Jefferies, *The Story of My Heart.* London: Longmans, Green, 1883

11   Daniel M. Ogilvie, *Fantasies of Flight.* New York: Oxford University Press, 2004, pp 99-100

12   See http://en.wikipedia.org/wiki/Vernal_Utah

13   Patt Morrison, "Stewart Brand: Earth man." *Los Angeles Times,* April 3, 2010. www.latimes.com/news/opinion/commentary/la-oe-morrison3-2010apr03,0,4871739.column, accessed July 12, 2012

14   Paul G. Zolbrod, *Diné bahane': The Navajo Creation Story.* Albuquerque: University of New Mexico Press, 1984

15   Quoted by Tony Hillerman in "The Very Heart of Our Country," *New Mexico Magazine,* March/April 1973, p. 7

16   H. J. Muller, "Life." *Science,* January 7, 1955, pp. 1-9

17   Martin A Nowak with Roger Highfield, "SuperCooperators: Altruism, Evolution, and Why We Need Each Other to Succeed." New York; Free Press, 2011

18   Neil Gunn, *The Well at the World's End.* London: Faber & Faber, 1951

19   Bernard Berelson, *Sketch for a Self-Portrait.* New York: Pantheon Books, 1949. O'Neill's reference is from the fourth act of *Long Day's Journey Into Night*, in a soliloquy at sea by the character Edmund. For the Willa Cather reference, see her introduction to *My Antonia (London: Virago, 1980).*

20   See Gordon Osbourn's "Material Properties of Semiconductor Strained-Layer Superlattices," presented at the 1983 MRS Meeting. http://journals.cambridge.org/action/displayAbstract;jsessionid=339929E5AD29AB86A2E 5CFF3B397BF08.journals?fromPage=online&aid=8134129, accessed July 23, 2012

21   See text at http://www.nukewatch.org/media/more_media/08-00-02/08-19-02/robinson.html (accessed March 2, 2012)

22 Nigel Hey, "Nano Revolution," *IEE Review*, April 2003

23 Nigel Hey, "Reies Lopez Tijerina: A Study in 'Brown Power.'" *Interplay*, March 1968

24 Joseph Campbell, *The Power of Myth*. (with Bill Moyers) New York: Doubleday, 1988

25 John DeWitt McKee, "*Two Legs to Stand On*" (1955), reprinted by Tony Hillerman from the *New Mexico Quarterly 27*, No. 3 (Autumn 1957) by permission of the author

26 Carl G. Jung, reprinted by Hillerman from Jung's *Memories, Dreams, Reflections*, recorded and edited by Aniela Jaffe and translated by Richard and Clara Winston. Copyright 1963 by Random House, Inc.

27 Winfield Townley Scott (1910-68), Reprinted by Hillerman (1986) from *Exiles and Fabrications*, copyright 1957 by Winfield Townley Scott, printed by permission of Doubleday & Company, Inc.

28 Laura Paskus, "By Any Name." *New Mexico Magazine*, August 2009, pp 52-55

29 Ken Seowtewa, "Adding a Breath to Zuni Life." *Native Peoples*, Winter 1992. Photographs by Suzanne Page

30 Stephen F. de Borhegyi, *El Santuario de Chimayo*. Santa Fe: The Spanish Colonial Arts Society Inc., 1956

31 D. H. Lawrence, "New Mexico," *Survey Graphic*, May 1, 1931

32 D.H. Lawrence, "The Sacred Fire" (poem), c. 1922

33 Tristine Rainer, *Your Life as Story*. New York: Putnam, 1997, p. 36

34 A transliteration from Daniel Defoe: "Of all the plagues with which mankind are cursed, Ecclesiastic tyranny's the worst."

35 Audrey T. Leath, "Secretary of State Rice on Scientific Openness, ITER." *FYI: The AIP Bulleting of Science Policy News*, No. 26: March 1, 2005 (http://www.aip.org/fyi/2005/026.html), accessed July 23, 2012

36 Zarubin, P.V., "Academician Basov, High-Power Lasers and the Antimissile Defence Problem," *Quantum Electronics* 32:12, (December 2002)

37 http://www.kiae.ru/e/engl.html, accessed May 25 2011

38 Nigel Hey, *The Star War Enigma: Behind the scenes in the Cold War race for strategic defense*. Potomac Books, 2006

39 Ronald Reagan, *An American Life*. New York: Simon and Schuster, 1990, p. 547

40 The church is run by Franciscan friars who report to the wide-ranging Roman Catholic Diocese of Gallup. This diocese includes nearly 60 missions on or near Native American Pueblo, Navajo, and Apache reservations in New Mexico and Arizona.

41 Similar organizations have established in other regions. For example in Britain the University of London hosts the like-minded Bureau of Investigative Journalism.

42 Adrian Raine, "Neurocriminology: The Brain Basis to Crime," paper presented at AAAS annual meeting, February 21, 2011

43 Simon Baron-Cohen, *Zero Degrees of Empathy*. Penguin Books, 2011

44 Coleman Barks, tr., *The Essential Rumi*. New York: HarperOne, an imprint of HarperCollins, 1995.

45 "A Sketch of the Past" was written in 1939-40 and eventually published posthumously in *Moments of Being* (1976)

46 Einstein Archive 60-492, 1932; published in *Mein Weltbild*

47 Tenzin Gyatso, "Compassion and the Individual,"
http://www.dalailama.com/messages/compassion. Accessed May 6, 2011

48 Anthony Lane, "I Spy," *The New Yorker,* December 12, 2011, pp 84+

49 See chapter "With Edgar Varèse in the Gobi Desert," in Miller's *The Air-Conditioned Nightmare.* New York: New Directions, 1945

50 Quoted by Oliver Sacks in "Speed," *The New Yorker,* August 23, 2004. Note the different translation at http://www.librarything.com/work/7576788, accessed July 23, 2012

51 See references in introduction to Willa Cather's *My Antonia* and in the fourth act of O'Neill's *Long Day's Journey Into Night.*

52 Here I was inspired by the song recorded by Johnnie Cash, Waylon Jennings, Willie Nelson and Kris Kristofferson. There are several versions of lyrics for this song, though each retains the same general theme.

53 Freeman Dyson, *Disturbing the Universe.* New York: Harper & Row, 1979

54 Pierre Teilhard de Chardin, *The Phenomenon of Man* (1959), Harper Perennial 1976

55 *New Bottles for New Wine,* London: Chatto & Windus, 1957, pp. 13-17

56 Francis Darwin, ed. 1909. *The foundations of The origin of species. Two essays written in 1842 and 1844.* Cambridge: Cambridge University Press, p. 87

57 R. D. Keynes, R. D. ed. 2001. *Charles Darwin's Beagle diary.* Cambridge: Cambridge University Press, p. 444

58 Charles Darwin, Origins, 490.

59 Charles Darwin, *The Descent of Man and Selection in Relation to Sex.* Gutenberg Project Etext #300, August 2000 (http://www.gutenberg.org/cache/epub/2300/pg2300.html, accessed July 23, 2012

60 Kenneth E. Boulding, *Ecodynamics.* Beverly Hills: Sage Publications, 1978, 338

61 Ray Kurzweil, *The Singularity is Near,* Viking, 1990.